The **DICTIONARY** of **SPORTS**

CAPTIONS
Page 1: GOLF: Splashing out of the bunker;
Page 3: ATHLETICS: Dip finish
Page 4: (top) BASKETBALL: Steal; (below) BASEBALL: Home run;
Page 5: (top) WRESTLING: Getting to grips;
(below) SWIMMING: Breast stroke.

THIS IS A CARLTON BOOK

This edition published in 1999

10 9 8 7 6 5 4 3 2 1

A CIP catalogue record for this book is available from the British Library

ISBN 1 85868 800 0

Project editor: Martin Corteel
Picture research: Lorna Ainger
Production: Sarah Schuman
Designed by Brian Flynn

Printed in Italy

The publishers would like to thank the following sources
for their kind permission to reproduce the pictures in this book:

Action-Plus/Steve Bardens, Peter Tarry
Allsport UK Ltd./Jack Atley, Al Bello, Markus Boesch, Shaun Botterill, Simon Bruty, A.C. Calvel, David
Cannon, Phil Cole, Michael Cooper, Jonathan Daniel, Tony Duffy, John Gigichi, Didier Givois, Elsa Hasch,
Tom Hevezi, Mike Hewitt, Jed Jacobsohn, Vincent Laforet, Alex Livesey, Andy Lyons, Adrian Murrell,
Jon Nicolson, Doug Pensinger, Mike Powell, Craig Prentis, Gary M. Prior, Ben Radford, Dave Rawcliffe,
Dave Rogers, Billy Stickland, Oli Tennent, Mark Thompson, Anton Want, Todd Warshaw
Gordon Lennox
Sporting Pictures (UK) Ltd.
Tony Stone Images/Martin Rogers

Every effort has been made to acknowledge correctly and contact the source and/copyright holder of
each picture, and Carlton Books Limited apologises for any unintentional errors or omissions which will
be corrected in future editions of this book.

The DICTIONARY of SPORTS

The complete guide for TV viewers, spectators and players

GENERAL EDITOR: **GERRY COX**

CARLTON

Contents

Introduction

Sport is no longer a matter of simply playing games. It is a multi-billion dollar business, has a global economy of its own and is a way of life for people all over the world. It can also be an international language, a force for peace or a political weapon.

People have died in the name of sport, wars have started and stopped because of it, and countless millions have been uplifted and inspired by it. In short, sport is something that touches all our lives to a lesser or greater degree. Not only is it played in every country on Earth, but sport takes place on frozen Arctic wasteland, in the skies, and even by astronauts on the Moon!

Any attempt to compile the ultimate dictionary of sport is an ambitious project, not least because of the sheer breadth and diversity of sports. Some are genuinely global – there cannot be a country in the world where small boys and increasingly girls do not start kicking a small ball around as soon as they are able to walk. Others are more localized, although the growth of televised sport and the migration of nationalities have taken different sports into new countries. While some have declined in popularity towards the end of the twentieth century, others have grown and prospered. Many sports have changed beyond all recognition through the ages, others have stayed essentially the same for hundreds of years.

New sports are springing up all the time. Just after completion of the main text of the book, the authors were contacted by the World Wakeboard Association about the new sport of wakeboarding, which is water-skiing's equivalent to snowboarding, with such colourful terms as "Butter Slide", "Hoochie Glide" and "Roast Beef". Hopefully we will be able to cover this and any other new sports which come to our notice when we revise and update the book.

We would like to stress that this is not a definitive guide to the rules of each sport, or an encyclopaedia of sporting personalities or places – constraints of time and space make that impossible in a single volume. What we have attempted to do here is to give a basic guide to the terms and idioms used in as many sports as possible, so that a newcomer to Jai alai, for example, should be able to understand what it is all about.

We accept that the ever-changing rules of certain sports mean that some descriptions may well be out of date already, and there may be other points which can be debated, and we welcome any correspondence on possible improvements.

We would not expect readers to sit down with this book and read it from cover to cover, just as you would not read any dictionary from A to Z. Instead we hope it will be a rich source of information and inspiration, a fount of sporting knowledge to dip into whenever required.

Happy reading.

GERRY COX

June 1999

1 StadiumTeam Sports

This section includes those sports that are played either in stadiums or in large outdoor areas, usually because they are played by teams consisting of at least 10 players per side and require large pitches. They are often some of the most popular spectator sports, attracting as many as 100,000 people.

Stadium Architecture

Arch A curved structure used as support for a roof, or as an entrance to a building.

Beam A horizontal supporting piece of a building's structure.

Brace A strengthening piece of wood or iron used as a support in a building.

Coliseum Was the largest Roman amphitheatre ever built when it opened in Rome in AD80, accommodating 87,000 spectators.

Column A slender, upright pillar that is used as a supporting or ornamental feature of a building.

Concrete Cement mixed with pebbles or crushed stone, sand and water. Used in most stadium construction.

Dome A rounded vault forming a roof.

Foundations The base of a structure, often below ground level, carrying the weight of the building.

Granite A very hard rock which is grey to pink in colour.

Louisiana Superdome Opened in 1975, it is the world's largest indoor stadium and holds 78,000 spectators. The doomed roof covers an area of four hectares. The actual dome measures 673ftin diameter and rises to a central height of 270ft

Obelisk A tall, four-sided stone pillar that tapers towards its pyramid-shaped top.

Pavilion An ornamental building that is used for entertainment.

Pylon A tall structure that is used to give support for floodlights.

Strahov This Czech stadium is the largest in the world with a capacity of 240,000.

Strut An iron or wooden support bar.

Truss A framework of bars or beams used to support a roof.

Twin Towers The nickname given to England's most famous stadium based in Wembley as it has two towers that can be seen for miles around.

American Football

American Football is a field sport played by two teams fielding 11 players each. The team that manages to score the most points by running the ball over the opposing team's goal line or by kicking it between and over the goal posts is declared the winner.

AFC The American Football Conference. The AFC is divided into three divisions: East, Central and West.

American Bowl As a part of its commitment to developing the game on a world scale, the NFL agreed to play at least one (now three) games outside America. These games are known as American Bowls.

Audible A play change at the line of scrimmage. The quarterback changes the play using a spoken code.

Backfield The area behind the line of scrimmage, where the fullbacks and halfbacks line up and the quarterback passes from. Also the collective term for running backs and fullbacks.

Back judge Operates the same side of the field as the line judge. His duties are to monitor any action between the closest receiver and his defender. He makes decisions about catches, fumbles, etc.

Ball Consisting of an inflated rubber bladder, it is made of leather, pebble grained and natural tan in color.

Ball control The ability of a team to keep possession of the ball for long periods of time.

Bench The area where the coach and substitutes sit during the game.

Blindside The area outside the quarterback's vision – usually the area a defense will target in an attempt to sack the quarterback.

Blitz Defensive tactic in which players (other than linemen) are assigned specifically to attack the quarterback.

Block A block is the act of legally stopping a defender from getting to the player in possession of the ball. There are two types: the pass block – usually offensive linemen stopping players from sacking the quarterback, and giving time to find a receiver; and run blocking – aggressive, as opposed to obstructive.

Bomb A long pass completion. Often used either at the very beginning of a game, or when behind at the end of a game.

Bootleg A trick play. The quarterback fakes a hand-off (pass to running back), and then runs around either end.

Bump-and-run A pass defense tactic. The defender bumps the receiver, then covers him downfield.

Center Starts each play by passing the ball backward between his legs (snaps).

Chain crew A six-man crew who assist the officials. They measure whether a first down has been achieved.

Chuck A push or shove on an opponent who is in front of a defender.

Clipping An illegal block, involving hitting an opponent from the rear. Legal on the line of scrimmage.

Coach An instructor who is responsible for a specific area of the game.

Coin flip All games are preceded by a coin toss – with the captain of the away team making the call while the coin is in the air. The winner has two options: either to take the kickoff, or to choose which end they wish to defend first.

Completion A pass that is successfully caught by an eligible receiver.

Cornerback A defensive back whose job is to defend against the pass. They will be assigned either to guard a specific man, or an area of the field.

Cutback Sudden change in direction by a ball carrier, usually against the flow of the play.

Dead ball When the play is whistled dead.

Defense The team that is not in possession of the football is known as the defense.

Defensive back Any player on the defence who is situated behind both the linemen and linebackers, cornerbacks and safeties.

Defensive end Concentrates on pressuring the quarterback or getting into the backfield and tackling the ball carrier.

Defensive line The area occupied by the defensive linemen – defensive tackles, nose tackle and defensive ends.

Defensive tackle The positions in the middle of a four-man defensive line. Their responsibilities are mainly focused on stopping the run and tying up the offensive line to create opportunities for others to pressure the quarterback into a mistake.

Delay of game A penalty called when the offense fails to start the play before the play clock expires. The offense is penalized by five yards, and no play can take place.

Double coverage Coverage system in which two players are assigned to guard one player (i.e. the most dangerous receiver).

Double foul A foul by both teams on the same play.

Double teaming Two offensive players blocking one defender.

Down A player is down when any part of his body other than his hands, arms or feet touches the ground, during or after contact with a defensive player.

Downs The system by which possession is determined. The offense has four attempts (or downs) in which to make 10yd (or more), and if they do so they keep possession.

Draft Before each season a draft takes place in which teams can sign players who have just completed their college careers.

Draw A run play, where the quarterback fakes a pass before handing off to the running back, who goes into the gap left by the defensive linemen.

Drive An offensive series of more than four plays is termed a drive.

Drop The movement of the quarterback, as he "drops" back to pass the football field. This action earns him more time as he is farther away from the defensive pressure.

Drop-kick An alternative to the place-kick method, seldom used on field-goal and extra-point attempts.

Encroachment A penalty for which the offending team is penalized 5yd.

End around A variation of the reverse in which a receiver or tight end is the ball carrier.

Endline The line at the back of an end zone where the goalposts are situated.

End zone The 10yd area at each end of the field where touchdowns are scored.

Extra point A kick taken after a touchdown that is worth one point. Also known as a PAT (point after touchdown) conversion.

Face mask Mask worn on the front of the helmet to protect a player's face.

Fair catch On a kickoff or punt return, the kick returner may signal a fair catch; this offers him a chance to catch the kick unhindered, and the ball is ruled down where it is caught.

False start A penalty given should any lineman move before the snap, after assuming a three-point stance. The offending team is penalized 5yd.

Field The area of play, 100yd long, with a 10yd end zone at both ends of the playing surface. There are field numbers at 10yd intervals pointing to the nearest goal line (except, obviously, at the 50yd line).

Field goal A score worth three points. A field goal may be taken at any time and can either be a place kick or drop kick. To score, the ball must go between the two goalposts and over the crossbar.

Field judge Stands 25yd downfield. Concentrates on the tight-end actions and keeps an eye on the time on the play clock.

Field position The position from which an offensive series begins.

First-and-goal A team reaches a first down within 10yd of their opponent's end zone. They cannot get another first down without reaching the endzone (goalline).

Flag When any of the officials sees what they interpret as a penalty, they throw a yellow flag on to the field.

Flanker The wide receiver on the tight end's side of the field. They line up a yard behind the line of scrimmage.

First down The starting point of an offensive series. On first down, the offensive team has four plays to gain 10 yards. If the offensive team games the 10 yards, it returns to the first down and has another four plays to gain 10 yards. This repeats until the offense scores, turns the ball over to the defense (through a fumble or interception) or punts.

Flat The area of the field behind the line of scrimmage and between the sideline and the offensive line.

Flea-flicker A trick play where the quarterback tosses the ball to a back, who fakes a run, then tosses the ball back to the quarterback for a surprise pass.

Flooding To flood an area is to send more offensive players into an area than there are defensive players.

Fly pattern A long pass pattern in which the receiver runs flat-out down the sideline.

Force A defensive tactic whereby the defenders try to force the ball carrier into an area where they have defensive cover (e.g. the middle of the field).

Formation The way in which the players are positioned, prior to the snap.

Forward pass Ball thrown from behind the offensive line of scrimmage by an offensive player, usually the quarterback. Once an offensive player crosses to the defensive side of the line of scrimmage, forward passes are illegal. Only one forward pass is allowed per offensive play.

Forward progress The progress of the ballcarrier towards the opposition's goalline.

Four-three defense The defensive formation of four defensive linemen and three linebackers.

Free agent A player who can be signed by any team.

Free safety A position in the defensive backfield. The free safety is not responsible for any specific player, but is a safety valve to prevent plays going for big yardage.

Freekick A kickoff after a safety or fair catch.

Fullback The most powerful member of the backfield whose main job is to block on running plays and to protect the quarterback on pass plays.

Fumble The act of losing the football after establishing possession. Once the ball has been lost by the ball carrier, anyone is free to recover it.

Gadget play A play designed to trick the defense.

Game plan Before each game, a team's coaches will design a set of plays and tactics on offense and defense specifically for that particular game.

Gang tackle A tackle on the ball carrier involving more than one player.

Gap Defense system where there are players in every gap betwen the offensive linesmen.

Goal line The line that starts the end zone. In effect, the zero yard line.

Goalposts Y-shaped posts placed at the end of the end zone and bright yellow in color. Each of the two upright posts is 30ft in height, and the horizontal crossbar is 10ft above the ground.

Guard Offensive linesman whose job is to protect the quarterback.

Hail Mary Long pass to the end zone, where multiple wide receivers converge to increase the possibility of catch the pass. Often used at the very end of a game.

Half Two halves, each consisting of two 15-minute quarters, make up a game.

Halfback Lines up behind and to one side of the quarterback, in the backfield. The halfback is generally the quickest member of the backfield and the featured running back.

Halftime A 15-minutes interval that separates the two halves of the match.

Hall of Fame Great players are enshrined into the Pro Football Hall of Fame in Canton, Ohio.

Hand-off The pass from the quarterback to a running back where the back takes the ball out of the quarterback's hands.

Hashmarks Marks one yard apart, 703/4ft from each sideline, which are used to mark the spot where the next play will start.

Head linesman Works in partnership with the line judge on the opposite flank. He assists ruling on forward passes and monitors forward progress.

Helmet Each player must wear a protective helmet when on the field.

Holder Holds the ball for the kicker on field goals and extra points.

Hole A space into which a ballcarrier may run.

Huddle Before each game the teams go into separate huddles to choose the play they wish to use.

I-formation Offensive formation in which two backs line up directly behind the quarterback.

Ineligible receiver The center, tackles and guards are ineligible to make a reception with the exception of the tackle – if he notifies the referee prior to the play.

Intentional grounding A penalty called against the passer should he throw the ball to the ground deliberately to avoid being tackled for a loss (sacked).

Interception A pass that is caught by a defensive player. An interception results in a change of possession.

Interference A penalty against either an offensive receiver or defensive coverage player, should they bump each other while a pass is in the air.

Interior linemen General term for a nose tackle or a defensive tackle.

Kicker The player responsible for all ground kicks – field goals, extra points and kickoffs.

Kickoff First play of the game, when one team kicks the ball off a tee on its 35yd line toward the opposition's goal.

Kick returner After a kickoff, the opposition may return the ball back upfield by running with it.

Lateral When one player tosses the ball to another, usually on offense. Unlike forward passes, a lateral must be thrown away from the direction in which the player is trying to advance the ball. Laterals can take place anywhere on the field, not just behind the line of scrimmage.

Line judge Duties are similar to those

of the head linesman, but he lines up on the left-hand side of the field.

Line of scrimmage Is an imaginary line that exists once the ball has been placed on the field for offensive play. The imaginary line runs through the center of the ball and on either side across the width of the field. Players from both teams are not allowed to cross this line until the ball is snapped by the center.

Linebacker In a typical defense there are three or four linebackers, as they occupy the positions behind the defensive line.

Live ball While play is in progress the ball is live.

Man-for-man A pass defense where each defensive back is assigned a particular player to defend against.

Man in motion Before each play, the offense is allowed to have one player run parallel to the line of scrimmage in an attempt to confuse the defense.

Midfield strip The strip across the 50yd line.

Mouth guard Most players wear a mouth guard when playing. Made of plastic, it is molded around the players' teeth and placed in the mouth to minimize the risk of injury.

Muff A failed attempt to catch a kickoff or punt.

Neutral zone The space (the length of the ball) between the two lines (offensive and defensive).

NFC The National Football Conference. Like the AFC, the NFC is divided into three divisions of five teams: East, Central and West.

NFL The National Football League is the overall governing body of American Football, as well as being the league itself.

No-huddle offense The system, usually when behind with little time left, in which the offense saves time by calling plays at the line of scrimmage.

Nose tackle When defense uses three defensive linemen. The man in the middle of the line is known as the nose tackle, because he lines up nose-to-nose with the center.

Offensive line The area occupied by the offensive linemen – the center, guards and tackle – and known as the offensive line.

Onside kick A kickoff that travels the minimum distance of 10yd (the defense can touch before, the offense cannot) so that the offense has a chance of recovering the ball.

Out of bounds A player is out of bounds if he steps over the side line.

Overtime All games tied at the end of regulation time are decided in overtime. The first team to score wins the game. Regular season games use one 15-minute period, and if there is still no winner the game is a tie.

Pass pattern Describes the route a receiver runs on his way to catch a pass.

Pitchout A long toss, usually from a quarterback to a halfback/fullback.

Play All plays are started when the ball is snapped and ends when the player with possession is downed (or a score occurs).

Play clock Independent from the game clock, the play clock measures the 45 seconds in which the offensive team decides on the play and any personnel changes can be made.

Playoffs When the regular season games (each team plays 16) have been completed, each conference stages a series of playoff games, culminating in the Super Bowl for the NFL Championship.

Pocket Area between the two guards that applies on pass plays. From this area the quarterback may not intentionally throw the ball to the ground.

Power sweep A running play around either end of the offensive line where both guards pull to block.

QUARTERBACK: The glamor position in American football, he often decides what offensive plays to run

Punt A kick used by the offensive team to relinquish possession of the ball if it has not gained the yardage needed for a first down. A good punt travels a long distance in the air and gives the kicking team a to chance tackle the punt returner before he gains much yardage. Punts nearly always take place on the fourth down.

Punter The player who makes punts for his team.

Punt returner The play whereby the receiving team runs the ball upfield, following a punt.

Quarterback Leader of the offense who lines up behind the center. The quarterback is the first player to touch the ball after the snap.

Quarterback rating A statistical measure of a quarterback's passing ability. The system uses statistics from four categories: percentage completion, percentage interceptions, percentage touchdowns and yards per throw.

Quick kick A surprise punt, designed to give the receiving team bad field position. The quarterback lines up in the shotgun and drops back just before the snap, then punts before the defense can get to him.

Read The ability of a player to predict what other players will do.

Red zone The area inside the opposition's 20yd line from which the offense is expected to score.

Referee Has the final say over penalty calls and has overall control of the game. Stands 10–12yd behind the line of scrimmage in the backfield.

Reverse A trick offensive play where a ball carrier runs toward one side of the field to draw the defense in that direction, then laterals the ball to a speedier offensive player.

Ribbon Attached to the top of each goalpost so that the kicker may read the direction of the wind.

Rookie A first-year professional player.

Rotation Shifting the zones of pass coverage (left or right).

Running back A term used for a back (full or half) whose main responsibility is to run with the ball.

Sack A tackle on the quarterback behind the line of scrimmage.

Safety The general term for either a strong or free safety. It is also a score worth two points. Occurs when the defense downs the player in possessionof the ball in his own end zone.

Screen A short pass to a back to either side of the field.

Shotgun Offensive formation, where the quarterback lines up three or four yards behind the center to allow him more time to pass and to make a sack less probable.

Side judge Works on the right-hand side of the field with the head linesman. His duties are to watch the receiver and ensure nothing illegal happens.

Sideline The out-of-bounds line down each side of the playing field. Also refers to the out-of-bounds area beyond the playing field where the coaches and substitutes watch the action.

Situation substitution A substitution where a player with a required specific skill is brought in for a specific situation.

Slant Any play in which a receiver goes left or right as opposed to straight ahead.

Snap The term given to the action that starts all plays.

Snap count The signal on which the ball is to be snapped.

Special teams Offensive and defensive squads that play in specific situations, like kickoffs and punts, are referred to as special teams.

Spike The quarterback throws the ball straight to the ground instantly after a snap.

Split end This position is similar to a tight end, except that he stands a few yards from the offensive line.

Strong safety Defensive back who lines up opposite the side of the offense that has the most players (the strong side) and is responsible for picking up the tight end on a passing route.

Super Bowl The championship final game for teams in the NFL. Always played at the end of January, the game is played at various locations throughout the US.

Tackle To stop a ball carrier and force him to the ground.

Tee A small rubber implement used to prop the ball up on kickoffs.

T-formation Offensive formation

SNAP: The starting point for all plays in American football, with the quarterback calling the shots

where two backs line up behind, and on either side of the quarterback.

Three-four defense The defensive formation where three defensive linemen and four linebackers are employed.

Tight end Utility offensive player who lines up on either side of the offensive line. On running plays, a tight end would be expected to block, while on passing plays they are a potential receiver.

Time-out A stoppage in play at a time chosen by either team. Each team is allowed three time-outs per half.

Toss An underarm throw in any direction.

Touchback Should a player receiving a kickoff or punt in his own end zone, catch the ball then he may go down and play will resume with his team in possession on the 20yd line.

Touchdown A score worth six points. To score a touchdown, a player must break the opposition's goal line with possession of the ball. The ball does not have to touch the ground.

Turnover The term used for any change of possession other than after a score, or after a punt.

Two-point conversion Like an extra point, a two-point conversion is taken after a touchdown from the 2yd line. The difference is that the ball must be passed or run into the end zone.

Umpire Positioned five yards behind the defensive line. Responsible for ensuring the legality of equipment, and blocks in particular.

Wide receiver Offensive position. They occupy positions away from the offensive line – wide, near the flanks, and make runs in an attempt to catch (receive) the ball.

Wild card The term given to a non-division winner that qualifies for the playoffs.

Zone coverage The defensive system where each defensive back is assigned an area to defend as opposed to a man to guard.

Canadian Football

Similar to American football but played on a larger field. There are 12 players on each team, and the object of the game is to score the most points by gaining a touchdown, a convert, a field goal or a rouge.

....

Backfield motion Describes the movements of the backfield players, who are allowed to move in any direction during a snap.

Back judge Responsible for players of both teams who are not in possession of the ball behind the scrimmage line.

Ball The exterior is made of leather, which encases an inflated rubber bladder. The length of the ball measures 11–11.25in. The circumference along the long dimension measures between 27 and 28.5in, and the shorter circumference is between 20 and 21in. The ball weighs 14–15oz.

Convert Occurs after a touchdown when the scoring team is allowed to try to add points by a scrimmage among the hash marks on or outside the opposing team's 5yd line. A field goal is worth one point and a touchdown is worth two points.

Dead line Is one of the outer lines of the field. Once the ball goes over this line it is deemed out of play.

Down Three downs are given to the offense to make 10yd.

Downsman Indicates the forward point of gain and loss after each play.

Drop kick A player drops the ball to the ground and kicks it toward the goal area in an attempt to put the ball between the goalposts and over the crossbar to score three points for his side.

Duration The entire game lasts for 60 minutes, split into four quarters. The half-time interval takes place between the second and third quarters, and lasts for 14 minutes.

Field The length of the field is 110yd with a width of 65yd. The space between the goal lines is divided by 5yd lines that are parallel. These lines are intersected by short lines that are 24yd from the sidelines; their official name is hash lines. The boundary lines are outside the field of play.

Field goal Occurs without the ball touching the ground once it has been kicked via either a drop kick or a place kick. The ball must go over the crossbar, and the kick is worth three points.

Forward pass Occurs during a down. Only one pass is allowed. It is taken from behind the scrimmage line toward the opposing team's dead line. The pass is considered illegal if the ball touches the ground, goalposts, crossbar or any other object.

Foul A foul is deemed to have been committed if a player holds an opposing player who does not have possession of the ball; tackles an opponent from behind when they are not in possession of the ball; hits, kicks, trips or elbows a player; grabs a player's face guard; holds hands or locks arms in a scrimmage; or is unfairly rough and abusive toward anyone.

Handoff pass The action of the ball being handed to another player rather than being thrown. Occurs behind the scrimmage line. There is no limitation to the number of handoff passes allowed during play.

Head linesman Has a supervisory role in charge of the linesman. Also logs the downs, keeps a record of the substitutions and controls the scrimmage line and sideline.

Interference Occurs when a player impedes or charges an opposing player in order to get to the ball, or obstructs a player from getting to the player in possession of the ball.

Kickoff The fellow team members of the player who is taking the kick-off must be behind the ball, and the opposing team must be at least 10yd away. Once the ball has been kicked, it must travel at least 10yd toward the opposing team's goal line or the kick will be judged to be illegal. The ball cannot be kicked out of play.

Kit Players' jerseys must be numbered on the front and back as well as on both upper arms. Players wear a helmet, face mask, chest and shoulder padding, rib and kidney padding, thigh, shin and below-the-belt padding, trousers and lightweight boots.

Line judge Checks the substitutions, scrimmage line and sideline.

Offside Occurs when a player crosses the scrimmage line when the ball is not being played. Also applies to a player who has possession when the last person to touch the ball was a team member who was positioned behind him – except when the rules of onside, hand-off and forward pass apply. A player becomes back onside when the ball comes into contact with an opposing player or when a team member carries the ball past him.

Offside pass A player can be caught offside if he is in front of the ball when a teammate plays it to him. The offside pass is penalized by a scrimmage, taken from where the pass was made.

Onside (or lateral) pass Occurs when the ball is propelled toward a player's own dead line through being thrown, handed or knocked. The final resting place of the ball determines whether the pass was onside or offside.

Out of bounds If the ball or the player in possession of the ball comes into contact with the sidelines in front or beyond the goal or the dead line, the ball is deemed to be out of bounds.

Penalties Can be awarded as the loss of a down, a player, yards or the ball. There are 5, 10, 15 and 25yd penalties.

Rouge, or single point Always played in the opposing team's goal area. The ball becomes dead if the opposition gains control or if the ball crosses the boundary lines.

Safety touch Occurs when a team plays the ball into their own goal area and the ball then becomes dead in the team's possession, or if the ball touches the dead line or the sideline in the goal area. Worth two points.

Screening The term given to interference, but without any physical contact.

Scrimmage An imaginary line positioned parallel to the goal line. It is marked by the forward point of the ball when placed on the ground and the defensive line marked 1yd beyond it.

Snap The term given to the action that starts all plays, when the centre while facing the opposing goal "snaps" the ball back between his legs in one constant motion. He is not allowed to touch the ball again until it has been handled by another player. The other players on the field are not allowed to move once they have positioned themselves until the ball has been snapped.

Tackling Describes the action of an opposing player grabbing the player in possession in order to try to take the ball from him.

Team Each team has 12 players.

Three yardsmen Control the sidelines and assist in measurements.

Touchdown Occurs when a player in possession of the ball manages to enter the opposing team's goal area and touches their goalline. A touchdown is worth six points.

Australian Rules Football

Australian Rules Football is played on a large oval pitch between two teams, each consisting of 18 players. The aim of the game is to gain as many points as possible, either by scoring a goal between the center posts or by scoring a behind. The ball can be kicked and handballed by both teams as they try to attack their opponent's goal. The team with the most points wins the game.

54yd line An arc drawn on the field 54yd from each goal.

Baaaaallll A raucous cry when a player is tackled in possession of the ball. An abbreviation of "holding the ball". If the free is given it is invariably followed by the cry of "Yeah".

Backmen The six defenders in a team's defense.

Ball The oval-shaped ball is made of leather. A standard ball weighs 16–17oz, and has a short circumference of 22in and a long circumference of 29in.

Ball up The field umpire throws or bounces the ball up to restart the game after a stalemated pack.

Behind Worth one point and scored when: the ball is kicked or carried over the goal line by a defender; the ball hits a goalpost; the ball crosses the behind line without hitting the behind post.

Bench Where the interchange players sit. When a player is substituted he is said to be benched.

Bouncing A player can run with the ball, but he must bounce the ball or touch it on the ground once every 11yd.

Boundary line This marks the perimeter of the playing field. The ball must be completely over the line for it to be ruled out of play.

Boundary umpire Two of these officials patrol either side of the pitch, judging when the ball is out of play.

Brownlow Medal The highest individual award, given to the player judged the best and fairest by umpires on a weekly voting system.

Bump A player uses his hip and shoulder to knock an opponent out of position. This is deemed legal if it occurs within 6yd of the ball.

Center bounce Made by the field umpire in the center circle at the start of each quarter, and after a goal is scored.

Center circle The area in the middle of the pitch, from where the center bounce is taken.

Center square A 49yd square in the center of the field. Only four players from each side are allowed in this area for a center bounce.

Checking A player with the ball can be tackled on the hip, chest, shoulder, arms or open hands. A player without the ball can be pushed in the chest or side, as long as the ball is within 6yd.

Drop punt The most common type of kick in Australian Rules, in which the ball turns end over end in flight.

Field umpires The three officials in charge of the game, each controlling about a third of the ground.

Flag The team that wins the title is said to "win the flag", since they are awarded a flag.

Followers Three players in the side who follow the ball all over the pitch. They are known as the ruck, rover and ruck-rover.

Footpass The method of passing the ball to another player by kicking it.

Free kick Awarded to the nearest opponent of a player who is alleged to have committed an offense.

Full back The deepest defender in the team who stands the full forward. Usually takes the kick-outs after the oppositions scores a behind.

Full forward The key forward in a team who plays closest to the goal. A good fullforward can score more than 100 goals a season and sometimes more than 10 in a game.

Goal Scored when an attacker kicks the ball over the goal line without it touching another player. The ball has to be directed between the goalposts. Six points are awarded for a goal.

Goal line The line drawn between the goalposts, which are 7yd apart.

Goal square The area directly in front of the goalposts. It is 10yd long and 7yd wide. The ball is kicked off from this square after a behind has been scored.

Goal umpire Two officials, one in each goal. They judge the scoring of goals and behinds and wave two flags to signal a goal and one for a behind.

Handball The method by which a player passes the ball with a clinched fist, while holding it stationary with the other hand.

Holding the ball When a player is tackled and deemed by the umpire not to have made a reasonable attempt to kick or handball the ball away, a free kick is awarded against him.

Interchange area The zone through which interchange players must pass to enter the playing field.

Interchange players These are a team's substitutes. At any point in the game, they may be interchanged with one of the participating players.

Mark When a player catches a kicked ball in the air, the ball having traveled at least 11yd and not having touched another player, he is then allowed an unhindered kick from anywhere behind where he caught the ball.

Out of bounds The ball goes outside the boundary line. The boundary umpire then throws the ball back into play over his head for a contest between the ruckmen.

Pitch The pitch is oval-shaped, usually between 120yd and 148yd wide and 148–202yd long.

Play-on The umpire allows the game to continue, despite appeals that a free kick should be awarded. Also refers to when a player chooses to keep playing rather than stop to receive his free kick because he feels he has an advantage.

Pockets The areas on the field that are close to the behind posts.

Quarter The game is made up of four separate quarters, each of 25 minutes' playing time. Teams change ends after each quarter.

Ruckmen Usually the tallest players in the team who contest the ball-ups and centre bounces by trying to palm or punch the ball to team-mates.

Runner Carries messages from the coach to the players during a game.

Shepherding A player may use his body to block an opponent from the ball or from a teammate in possession, as long as he is within 6yd of the ball.

Siren Sounded to signal the start and the end of each quarter.

Suspension The field umpire can report a player for an offense to the controlling body. This, in turn, can suspend them from further matches.

Throw-in The ball crosses over the boundary line. The boundary umpire will then throw the ball over his head toward the center of the field. The ball must travel between 11yd and 16yd at a minimum height of 11yd.

Torpedo punt Otherwise known as a screw punt, this is a kick that spirals the ball through the air.

Gaelic Football

Gaelic Football is contested between two teams of 15 players who attempt to score points by getting the ball between their opponent's goalposts. Players can kick, catch and fist the ball. The team with the highest number of points wins the game.

49yd free kick When a defender plays the ball over the end line, the attacking side is awarded a free kick which is taken on the 49yd line, opposite where the ball crossed the line.

Attacker Player whose role is to score as many goals as possible against the defendants.

Ball The ball is round, with a circumference of 27–29in, and weighs 11–15oz.

Crossbar A pole connecting the two goalposts horizontally, 8ft above the ground

Defendants Players whose role is to stop the attacking side from scoring goals.

Duration The game lasts for 70 minutes, with a brief interval halfway through.

End line The line that indicates the end of the playing area. If a team puts the ball out of play, the referee awards possession to the opposition.

Fist Punching the ball away with the hand clenched.

Foul The referee awards a foul if he feels a player has made an infringement against a member of the opposing team.

Four steps Players are not allowed to hold the ball for more than four steps at a time when carrying the ball.

Free kick Awarded for any kind of infringement by a player against an opposing player. The referee will award the free kick from the spot at which the incident took place.

Goal A goal is scored when the ball is struck between the goalposts and under the crossbar. This will score three points.

Goal umpires There are four of these officials for each game. Each stands outside a goalpost to determine whether a goal has been scored or not.

Goalkeeper Member of the team who stands between the goalposts and tries to stop the attacking team from putting the ball past him and scoring a goal.

Goalposts There are two of these at each end of the field. They are normally 16ft high and are connected by the crossbar halfway up. Players aim to strike the ball between the posts in order to score points for their team.

Halftime The brief rest period that comes exactly halfway through the game. Teams also change ends during this period.

Hop Playing the ball by bouncing it with one or both hands.

Kicker A player who strikes the ball down the field with his foot.

Kick out This takes place after a goal has just been scored. All opponents must stand outside the 22yd line, while the defending team must be outside the 14yd line. The ball is then kicked out from within the parallelogram.

Linesman Two of these officials help with each game. One stands on each side of the playing surface and each covers one half of the playing field. They determine when the ball goes out of play and which side should be awarded a sideline kick.

Parallelogram An area directly in

front of the goal that measures 15 × 5yd. No points are scored if an attacking player enters this area without the ball.

Penalty kick Awarded to the attacking side, if a defender commits a foul inside the parallelogram. The kicker then has an opportunity to score a goal against the goalkeeper from the centre of the 14yd line.

Pitch The pitch size varies between a

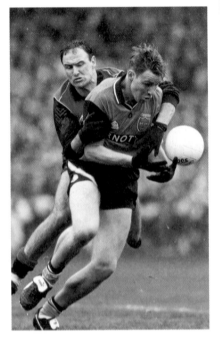

TACKLING: A player can shoulder-charge an opponent in a bid to regain possesion of the ball

minimum of 142yd × 88yd and a maximum of 159yd × 98yd.

Point A point is scored if the ball goes between the goalposts and over the crossbar.

Side kick Awarded to the opposition when a player plays the ball over the sideline. The ball is placed where the ball crossed the line, and is kicked back into play.

Sideline Runs down the length of the pitch to indicate the playing area. Once the ball crosses this line, the linesman will award a side kick.

Sideline kick When the ball runs over the sideline, the opposition is awarded a sidekick. The kicker then strikes the ball back into play.

Substitutes Players who do not start the game, but are allowed to enter the game at any time are known as subsitutes. They are allowed to come on to the pitch only during a stoppage. Each team has three substitutes.

Tackling A player is allowed to shoulder charge an opponent who is in possession of the ball. The ball can also be knocked from a player's hand, if it is held in an unprotected position.

Team Consists of 15 players plus three substitutes.

Tipping The act of bouncing the ball on the hand, which is not permitted in a game of Gaelic Football.

Speedball

Speedball is played between two teams of 11 players who, by carrying the ball downfield, attempt to score a field goal or a drop kick between the two goalposts. Players are permitted to catch, kick and throw the ball. There is a slight variation between the men's and women's versions of the game, but the scoring system remains the same.

Aerial ball The ball is kicked up into the air. When a player catches an aerial ball, they are not then allowed to run with it.

Ball An official soccer ball is used, with a circumference of 27–28in and weighing between 14 and 19oz.

Crossbar The bar connecting the two goalposts. For a field goal to be scored, the ball must pass over the bar.

Dribble The method of bouncing the ball on the ground while running with it. The ball must be bounced in one continuous motion of the hand.

Drop kick A player kicks the ball forward, after it has bounced once.

End kick Scored by an attacking player kicking the ball from within the end zone over the end line outside the goal.

End line This marks the end of the playing surface. Once the ball crosses the line, the ball is dead and the timekeeper stops the clock for the quarter.

End zone The area directly in front of goal. Players can score touchdowns and an end kick within this zone.

Extra time If the scores are level at the end of the game, an extra period of five minutes is played.

Field goal Scored when the ball is kicked over the end lines between the goalposts and under the crossbar.

Foul An infringement against an opposing player. The referee will award a free kick to the opposition at the point at which the foul took place.

Free kick Awarded to the opposing team after a foul has been committed against one of their players. The kicker takes the free kick from where the foul took place, and can punt, drop- or place kick the ball toward the opposing goal.

Goal There are a number of ways in which a team can score points, ranging from a field goal to an end kick.

Goalline The line from which a penalty kick is taken. If a receiver runs over this line and catches the ball before he reaches the end line, then he scores a touchdown.

Goalpost There are two goalposts at each end of the field. For a team to score any point, the ball must pass between the two posts.

Ground ball The ball is rolling or bouncing across the ground, or may even be stationary. It can be converted into an aerial ball with the feet, but must not be handled.

Interval At the end of each quarter, there is a period when each side is allowed to take a short break. After the first and third quarters, this lasts two minutes. After the second quarter, it lasts 15 minutes.

Linesman Two of these officials stand on opposite sides of the pitch, and in different halves. They blow their whistle when the ball has gone out of play, or if they have seen a foul committed.

Middle line The halfway line of the pitch.

Overhead dribble A player throws

the ball into the air, continues running and catches the ball before it hits the ground.

Penalty The referee awards a penalty if he feels that a player on the attacking side has been fouled within the end zone, either by a technical or personal foul.

Penalty area See "End zone".

Penalty kick Once a penalty has been awarded by the referee, one of the attacking team places the ball on the penalty-kick mark and attempts to score a goal past one of the defenders, who will stand on the end line until the ball has been kicked.

Penalty-kick mark The spot on the center of the goal line from where the penalty is taken.

Pitch A full-size pitch measures 120yd long by 53yd wide.

Place kick This takes place at the beginning of each half and after a team has scored in the game. It takes place from the center of the kicking team's restraining line, and the ball must reach the opposing team's restraining line, unless it has been touched by another player. Each team must be behind their own respective restraining line.

Punt A player drops the ball and kicks it before it touches the ground.

Quarter The game is split into four separate quarters, each lasting 10 minutes.

Restraining line The line the players have to stand behind when a place kick is taken. No player is allowed to run over it until the kick has been taken.

Safety A defender plays the ball over the end line without scoring. The attacking team automatically picks up possession of the ball.

Substitutes These are players who do not start the game, but can join play once the ball is dead to permanently take the place of one of the participating players. Each team is allowed five substitutes. Players who are substituted cannot return to the game.

Suspension A player can be ordered from the field by the referee if they have behaved with unsportsmanlike conduct. If a player commits five personal fouls in a game, then they are automatically suspended.

Tackling A player can attempt to guard the opposing player who has the ball, and then try to win the ball back from them. However, they are not allowed to make any physical contact with them.

Team Each team consists of 11 players.

Time-out This is the process of a team deliberately stopping the clock to allow them to review their tactics or have a rest. Each side is allowed five time-outs in a game – not exceeding two minutes' duration.

Tip off The referee or linesman throws the ball up between two opponents, who stand opposite each other in a bid to regain possession of the ball.

Touchback An attacking player puts the ball over the sideline in the end zone without scoring; the defense puts the ball back into play.

Touchdown Made by a player who receives a forward pass when in the opposition end zone. They must be completely within the end zone and not be touching any boundary lines for a touchdown to be awarded.

Soccer

Soccer is played between two teams of 11 players. The aim of the game is to put the ball into the opponent's goal by kicking or heading it. A game lasts for 90 minutes, divided into two halves of 45 minutes each, although some competitions allow for an extra 30 minutes if scores are level at full-time. The team that has scored the most goals wins the match.

4-4-2 A team formation consisting of four defenders, four midfielders and two attackers.

4-3-3 A team formation consisting of four defenders, three midfielders and three attackers.

5-3-2 The traditional team formation consisting of five defenders, three midfielders and two attackers.

Advantage The referee will signal for play to continue and call, "Play-on", despite appeals from the players for a free kick to be given. This is because he feels that the team in possession already has the advantage of a passing or goalscoring opportunity.

Anchor man A player who operates just in front of the defense, playing as a defensive midfielder.

Assistant referee Formerly known as a linesman, there is an assistant referee on each touch-line who is expected to keep level with play in order to advise the referee on throw-ins, fouls and offsides.

Backheel Skillful technique used to trick opponents, when a player kicks the ball backwards with his heel toward a teammate.

Ball The inflated leather or plastic-coated sphere used in all games. At the start of the game the ball must weigh between 14 and 16oz and should be inflated to a pressure of 0.6–1.1atm at sea level. The circumference of the ball must be between 27 and 28in.

Banana kick A shot that swerves laterally, achieved by striking the ball with the outside of the shoe.

Bosman ruling A ruling by the European Court in 1995, obtained by Belgian soccer player Jean Marc Bosman, that a player is entitled to leave his club when his contract expires, and move to another club within the European Union on a free transfer.

Byline The line at each end of the pitch (the shortest sides), including goal line.

Cap Every time a player makes an appearance for his national side, he is awarded a symbolic cap.

Captain A nominated player from each team who is responsible for motivating his players during the game. At the start of the game, he tosses a coin with the opposing captain to determine who will take the kick off, and which half they will start in.

Caution See "Yellow card".

Center circle A circle with a 10yd radius in the center of the pitch, radiating from the center-spot.

Center-half A player who plays in the heart of a team's defense often to deal with aerial passes to attacking forwards.

Center spot The mark in the middle of the center circle from which the game kicks off.

Chip A move in which a player attempts to deceive the opposing goalkeeper by knocking the ball over his head into the goal with a delicate, looping kick.

Corner When the defending team puts the ball over the byline, the attacking team is awarded a corner kick, which is taken from the quarter circle by the corner flag. It is taken from the same side of the goal on which the ball went out of play.

Corner flag A post marking each corner of the pitch, not less than 5ft high and topped with a colored flag.

Crossbar A horizontal bar connecting the top of the two goalposts; it should be 8ft from the ground.

Curling ball A player can make a ball swerve in the air – for example, around a defensive wall during a free kick just outside the opposing penalty area – by striking it with the inside or outside of the foot, as opposed to the instep. A ball struck with the outside of the right foot makes it curve to the right, while one struck with the inside of the right foot makes it curve to the left.

Defense A player who normally operates nearer to his own goal, rather than in the opposing half, with the main intention of stopping the opposition from scoring.

Defensive wall A line of two or more players who try to position themselves in such a way that they block the route to goal, when the attacking side is taking a free kick near to the penalty area. Must be 10yd from the ball.

Direct free kick Awarded against a player who has deliberately held or tripped an opponent, or committed any other offense that is not in accordance with rules of the game. The team taking the free kick is allowed to take a direct shot at goal, without having to pass the ball to another player.

Dragback A skillful move in which the ball is rolled back with the sole of the foot to fool the opposing player.

Dribble A move in which a player runs with the ball at his feet past one or more defenders, usually in a twisting run.

Dugout The [usually covered] bench at the side of the pitch on which a team's manager, coaching staff and substitutes sit during a game. There is normally a separate dugout for each team.

Dummy A tactic used by a player to trick an opponent, by pretending to pass the ball but actually keeping possession– sometimes dodging in one direction but taking the ball in another.

Duration A soccer game consists of two separate halves of 45 minutes each, for a total of 90 minutes.

European Championships An internatinal competition held every four years between the best teams in Europe. The competition begins on a group basis with matches played over an 18-month period; the top teams then progress to the finals, which are held over a three-week period. Holland and Belgium jointly stage the 2000 finals.

Extra-time The time added at the end of a match in certain competitions when the scores are even, usually comprising two periods of 15 minutes. If the scores are still even at the end of this period, a penalty shoot-out normally decides the result.

FA Cup Run under the auspices of the Football Association, this is the second most important trophy in English football after the Premier League Championship. With non-League clubs able to qualify, part of the competition's appeal is the potential for minnows of the lower leagues to pull off major shocks against clubs in the Premier or Nationwide leagues. The winner of each season's FA Cup gains a place in the following season's European club competition, the UEFA Cup.

FIFA Fédération Internationale de Football Association, the governing body of world soccer, founded in 1908 and still in charge of the game.

Flat back four A defensive formation in which a team's four main defenders generally play in line across the pitch.

Flick Light touch by an outfield player, with head or foot, that diverts the ball to a teammate. With a goalkeeper, any sudden movement of the hand that deflects away a shot or header bound for goal.

Floodlights Powerful lights – either mounted high up on pylons or on the top of the stadium stands, to avoid glare at pitch level – which direct artificial light on to the pitch when a game is played in poor lighting conditions or at night.

Football Association The governing body of English football formed in 1863, which drew up the first formal rules of the game.

Football League The original league, set up in England in 1888, and now comprising the three divisions of professional football below the Premier League, made up of 72 teams.

Formation The shape of each side's outfield lineup at kickoff; the most popular formation is 4-4-2 four defenders, four midfielders and two in attack.

Foul An illegal tackle by a player on an opponent resulting in a free kick, or in a penalty kick if the foul was adjudged to have been committed in the penalty area.

Foul throw When a throw-in is taken incorrectly or from a place other than where the ball crossed the touch-line.

Free kick A kick awarded to a team resulting from an offense committed by the opposition; to be taken from where the offense occurred.

Free transfer The term used when a player moves to another club without any money changing hands. This often happens when a player is out of contract, or is considered to be too old to be sold for a transfer fee.

Full time The point when the official 90 minutes of a full match has elapsed. Time is added on by the referee to compensate for injuries to players that require treatment, substitutions or deliberate time-wasting by players (also called "stoppage time".

Goal Awarded when the whole of the ball crosses the whole of the goal-line between the posts and under the crossbar.

Goal area A rectangular area of 6 × 20yd surrounding each goal, within the penalty area; often called the 6yd box.

Goalkeeper Each team has a designated goalkeeper, whose role is to stop the opposing team from scoring a goal. The goalkeeper is the only player who is allowed to handle the ball, but this is permissible only inside his own penalty area.

Goal-line clearance When the ball is cleared to safety just as it is about to cross the goal line.

Goalpost The wooden or steel uprights marking the vertical borders of the goal, usually 8ft high and equidistant from the corner flags. The two posts are connected by a crossbar.

Halftime A 15-minute interval that separates the two halves of a match. The teams change ends before the start of the second half to negate any advantage the other team might have enjoyed in the first half in terms of wind direction or slope of the field.

Half-volley When the ball is kicked by a player just after it has hit the ground.

Handball A foul that is committed when the ball comes into contact with a player's hand. The opposing team is awarded a free kick that is taken from where the offense took place.

Header When a player propels the ball using his head.

Indirect free kick Awarded against a player if a certain type of foul or infringement has taken place. In contrast to a direct free kick, the player who takes the kick must pass the ball to another member of his team for the kick to be deemed legal.

Kickoff The start of the game, the start of the second half, or the restart after a goal has been scored. The ball must be passed to another player before the player who kicked off can touch it again.

Lancaster Gate The headquarters of the English Football Association in Bayswater, London.

League Cup An annual sponsored cup competition in English football for which only the clubs in the Premier and Nationwide leagues are eligible – in contrast to the FA Cup.

Loan transfer When a player who is unsettled or surplus to requirements moves from one club to another for a short period of time on loan, before returning to his original club.

Man-to-man marking A type of marking whereby a defender follows his opponent wherever he moves around the pitch, as opposed to zonal marking.

Marking Defenders are detailed to shepherd particular opponents, by keeping close to them and trying to stop them from getting the ball or scoring. Forwards are sometimes asked to mark opposing defenders when their side has to defend against a corner or free kicks.

Midfielder A player who generally operates in the middle of the pitch, providing a link between defense and attack and often helping out with both duties.

Net The goal is covered by a net, which is firmly attached to the goalposts, crossbar and ground behind the goals. Because the ball is restrained by the net, it is a means of telling whether the ball has actually passed under the crossbar and between the posts, so that the referee or assistant can be sure a goal has been scored.

Number 9 The number on the shirt of a player who is often the main striker or target man in a team.

Nutmeg A skillful maneuver in which a player plays the ball through the legs of an opposing player and runs on to take the ball again.

Obstruction A foul committed when a player holds back or blocks another opponent in possession of the ball.

Offside A foul committed by an attacking player who is caught nearer to the opposing goal than two or fewer opponents when the ball is played, and who was deemed to be interfering with play in the process. The defending side is awarded a free kick, to be taken from where the offense took place.

Onside Players cannot be judged offside if they were in their own half of the pitch when they received the ball, or if an opponent was the last player to touch the ball. They are also onside if they take the ball direct from a throw-in, corner kick or goal kick.

One-two A move in which a player passes the ball to a teammate and expects to receive it back again immediately. It is often used to get past an opposing player in a triangular movement.

Orange ball Used in extreme weather conditions such as heavy rain or snow, when the referee feels that a white ball would not be clearly visible to the two teams. It must have exactly the same measurements as a standard white ball.

Overhead kick An acrobatic move in which a player leaps off the ground with both feet and strikes the ball backwards over his head.

Parry When a goalkeeper blocks an attempt on goal but does not manage to hold on to the ball.

SCISSORS KICK: One of the most dramatic methods of shooting at goal, involving an athletic back-flip

Penalty area A rectangular area 18 × 44yd surrounding each goal. The goalkeeper is permitted to handle the ball only in this area.

Penalty kick A free kick given from the penalty spot when an offense is committed by a player within his team's penalty area. The only player allowed to face the kicker is the goalkeeper, who must remain on his line until the ball is kicked, and no other players are allowed inside the penalty area before the kick is taken.

Penalty shoot-out Competition used to decide the winning team if the scores are still level after extra time. The teams take five penalty kicks each, with a different player required to take each one.

The team that scores the highest number of penalties wins the shoot-out and the match. If both teams score an equal number, then the competition enters a "sudden-death" phase in which the first team to miss loses the match.

Penalty spot The mark from which a penalty kick is taken, 12yd from the goal-line directly in front of the goal.

Pitch The pitch is rectangular and must be 50–100yd wide and 100–130yd long. There is a goal and marked-out goal area in the middle of each end of the pitch.

Premier League The top division in English football, which broke away from the Football League under its own governing body in 1993. Comprising 20 clubs, with three relegated to and promoted from the First Division of the Football League each season.

Professional foul A cynical offense in which a player deliberately balks or fells an opponent who is advancing on goal. A player can be sent off the pitch for committing a foul on an opponent that prevents a clear goal-scoring opportunity.

Red card A player is dismissed from the field of play if the referee shows him a red card. This happens either because the player has received two yellow cards in the same match, or because the referee judges that he has committed a single offense that warrants a sending-off in its own right. When a player has been sent off, his team must play the rest of the game with 10 players (unless further players are dismissed).

Referee The official who is in overall control of the game. He is helped by two other officials on the field of play called the referee's assistants (formerly known as linesmen).

Replay In certain cup competitions, or in other exceptional circumstances, if a game ends tied at the end of the statu-tory 90 minutes, or after extra time, a replay between the same teams is set for a later date.

Route one Attacking tactic by which the ball is kicked far upfield, apparently aimlessly, for a team's powerful and tall striker to chase.

Scissors kick Similar to an overhead kick, this is when a player twists sideways in midair to hit the ball with one or both feet in the air.

Shin pads Protective pads which players are obliged to wear inside their socks to minimize injuries to their shins.

Shoulder charge A player is permitted to press shoulders with an opponent while attempting to gain possession of the ball. It is the only bodily contact officially allowed in the game, and a player must be within playing distance of the ball and have at least one foot on the ground.

Six-yard box See "Goal Area".

Sliding tackle A form of tackle that involves sliding along the ground to kick the ball away from an opponent. The tackling player must make contact with the ball, otherwise a foul is committed.

Squad Each manager normally has more than 11 players from whom to choose his team; this is called a squad. The best 11 players available will normally form the team.

Stoppage time Time added to the end of each half by the referee to take account of stoppages for injuries, substitutions or time-wasting.

Striker A forward player who is expected to score, and assist in scoring, goals.

Studs Attached to the bottom of a player's shoe, they must be of solid leather, rubber, plastic, aluminium or similar material. They must not be less than a half-inch in diameter or longer than three-quarters of an inch from the mounting. They provide extra grip when the field is slippery.

Substitute A player who does not start the game but may be used as a replacement for a teammate at any stage during a game. A substitute can come on the field of play only with the referee's permission, and when the ball has gone out of play. The number of substitutes a team is allowed varies from two to five players.

Substitutes' bench Area on the side of the pitch from which the substitutes and coach watch the game.

Sudden death/golden goal Rule whereby the first team to score in extra-time wins the match, if the scores are even after 90 minutes.

Suspension If a player is sent off during a match, he will subsequently have to miss a set number of games as a further penalty.

Sweeper A player who plays just behind the two center-halves and is used as a spare man. A good sweeper can read the game well, is a good passer of the ball, and sees opportunities to attack as well as providing another defensive option.

Tackle When a player wins the ball from an opponent by intercepting it without committing a foul. The tackle from behind has recently been outlawed on safety grounds, as has the sliding two-footed tackle.

Tactics The term used to describe the way in which a manager wants his side to play in a match. Tactics can apply either to defensive or attacking formations and methods of play.

Throw-in The method by which play is restarted when the ball goes out of play by crossing the touch-line at the sides of the pitch. The throw-in is awarded to the opposing team from the one whose player put the ball out of play. Play is restarted by a player throwing the ball over his head using both hands together. His feet must remain behind the line and on the ground.

SWEEPER: A player, such as AC Milan's Franco Baresi above, who plays behind the central defenders

Touch-lines The lines that border the longest sides of the pitch. When the ball crosses either of them, it is out of play.

Transfer When a player moves from one club to another, his registration is transferred to that club, normally for a fee agreed between the two parties.

UEFA Union des Associations Europ-éennes de Football. European soccer's governing body, founded in 1920.

Volley When the ball is struck in the air by the foot of any player before it hits the ground.

Wall pass Also known as a one-two or give-and-go. A triangular movement where one player gets past an opponent by making a short pass to a teammate and running toward the return pass.

Wide player A player who plays in the wide areas of the pitch (see "Winger").

Winger A player who stays out on either side of the pitch with the intention of dragging opposing defenders wide and spreading out the defense to create holes for the central strikers to move into. A winger looks to take on opposing defenders and cross the ball in to the center of the goal area to create opportunities for shots on goal.

Wings The two "wide" areas of the pitch (extreme sides) are described as the left and right wings, as seen from a defender's viewpoint.

Woodwork The term used to denote the crossbar and uprights, even if they are made of metal.

World Cup Once every four years a tournament is held between the best 32 countries of the world. The competition begins on a group basis, with the top teams progressing to a knock-out phase until only two teams are left to contest the final. The winners of the final are declared the World Cup Champions.

Yellow card Also known as a caution, a yellow card is shown by the referee to any player who commits a foul or infringement that is not within the rules of the game, and that is considered to be of a fairly serious nature. Any player receiving two yellow cards in one game is sent off the field of play.

Zone defense Type of defense in which defending players guard designated notional zones or areas, in which they guard anyone who enters the zone.

WORLD CUP: France celebrates winning the 1998 World Cup final, a tournament held every four years

Rugby League

First played in 1895, Rugby League differs from Rugby Union in several ways. The most obvious is that each team consists of 13 players, scrums are formed of six players on each side, and if a player is tackled he keeps possession after getting up. As in Rugby Union the aim of the game is for each team to score as many points as possible by touching down the ball over the opponent's goal line (called a try) or by kicking the ball between the posts. Players can carry, throw or kick the ball, and the team with the highest score at the end of the game wins the match.

Advantage Awarded to the attacking team if the referee feels that play can proceed after a foul or infringement has taken place against an attacking player. This will happen only if the referee feels it can benefit the attacking side.

Attacking team The team in possession of the ball and that is advancing toward the opposing goal-line in a bid to score a try or penalty. When a scrum is formed on the half-way line, the team that last touched the ball before it went out of play is the attacking team.

Back A player who does not participate in the scrum.

Ball The ball is oval in shape and made of leather. It has four panels and weighs 14-16oz.

Ball back A scrum will be formed from where the ball was kicked, after it entered touch on the full.

Blind-side This refers to the side of the scrum or of the play-the-ball that is closer to touch – in other words, the "open" side of the pitch.

Center spot The spot on the halfway line that marks the center of the pitch.

Charging down Attempting to block an opponent's kick as the ball rises up into the air by using the hands, arms or body to charge the ball down.

Conversion After a try has been scored, the kicker from the scoring team has the opportunity to place-kick the ball between the goalposts and over the crossbar. If he is successful, the scoring team is awarded another two points.

Corner post A post that is topped by a flag. It must not be less than 4ft high and should be made of non-rigid material. They are placed on each goal-line and touch line and help the officials and players to see where the touch lines are and when the ball has crossed out of play.

Crossbar A crossbar connects the two goalposts at each end of the playing field. It measures 10ft long, and the ball must cross over the crossbar for a penalty or drop kick to be allowed.

Dead ball This occurs when the ball has crossed out of play.

Dead-ball line The line that marks the end of the pitch. For a try to be scored, an attacker must not carry the ball over this line.

Defending team The team that is attempting to stop the attacking team from scoring any points.

Differential penalty Awarded when a foul has been committed by a player and the referee awards a penalty to the opposing team. The kicker will drop kick the ball downfield toward the opposition goal. This differs from a penalty kick in that a goal cannot be scored directly from this kind of penalty.

Drop goal Any player can score a dropgoal, gaining their side one point.

Drop kick The tactic of the kicker dropping the ball to the ground and then, as the ball connects with it, striking the ball into the air. This is similar to a half-volley in soccer.

Drop out A dropkick taken by the kicker from between the posts or from the center of the 22yd line to bring the ball back into play.

Dummy A player attempts to trick an opponent by pretending to pass or release the ball, but actually keeping possession of it. This can be very effective for an attacking player attempting to score a try.

Duration Two halves of 40 minutes each. At halftime, the teams change ends after a five-minute interval.

Facial massage Slang term for when a player grinds his opponent's head into the ground with a hand of forearm, using their full weight as they rise from the tackle.

Forward A player who helps set up play, part of a front row of forwards who form a scrum to restart play.

Forward pass When the ball is deliberately thrown forward or passed toward the opponent's goalline.

Foul The term used to describe an infringement against an opposing player. The referee will award a penalty to the opposing side.

Goal area The area of the pitch marked out by the goal line, dead-ball line and touch lines at each end.

Goal line The line on which the goalposts are situated. If an attacking player carries the ball over this line and touches the ball on the ground, he scores a try. If a defender carries the ball over the goal line and grounds the ball, then a tap penalty is awarded and play continues with a kick downfield.

Halftime The period at the end of the first half, when the players are allowed to have a five-minute interval before the second half gets under way.

Handover The attacking team has to surrender the ball to the opposition after it has been tackled the required number of times (six). The opposition then picks up play from the point at which the tackle took place.

Heeled Once a play-the-ball has taken place, the player can roll the ball back to another player with his foot, and play restarts.

Hook The act of the hooker when he attempts to reach the ball with his foot in the scrum.

Hospital pass Slang term to describe a pass that, by the nature of its trajectory (i.e. floating dangerously in front of the opposition), may draw the recipient into danger and is, as a result, likely to cause the recipient some damage.

Infringement When a player has obstructed an opposing player. The referee blows his whistle and awards a foul to the opposing side.

Kicker The specialist player in the side who strikes the ball downfield with his foot.

Kick off The term used to describe the game getting under way.

Knock-on When the ball is propelled forward (toward the opposition's dead-ball line) via a player's hand or arm.

Loose arm An offense committed by the hooker in the scrum if he "packs" with one arm loose.

Loose ball Occurs during play when the ball is not held by a player and is not being scrummaged. It is free for both sides to challenge for.

Loose head The front-row forward in the scrum who is closest to the referee.

Mark The point from which a free kick or penalty kick has been awarded or from where a scrum will be formed.

Obstruction A foul committed by a player when he blocks an opponent who does not have the ball.

Offside A player is judged to be offside if the ball is played or held by another member of his own team behind him.

On the full The ball is kicked over a given line without having first bounced.

Openside The side of the scrummage or the play-the-ball that is furthest from touch.

Pack The name given to the group of forwards in a team. When a team packs down, it also means to form a scrum.

Penalty goal If a player commits a foul, the referee can caution or dismiss the offender by awarding a penalty kick to the opposing side. This is taken from where the incident took place, and the kicker can kick the ball between the posts, which is worth two points.

Penalty try Awarded to the attacking team if a player has been fouled in the act of being prevented from scoring a try. The kicker then has the opportunity to kick the ball between the posts from the point at which the incident took place.

Pitch The pitch, or field, measures 110 × 75.5yd. The touch lines are not part of the playing area.

Place kick The kick with which the kicker, striking a stationary ball downfield, gets each half under way. Also the kick taken by the conceding team after a try or a goal has been scored.

Play-the-ball A tackled player must be released, once he indicates that he intends to play-the-ball. The player must then stand up and put the ball on the ground, and then kick or heel the ball in any direction. The team in possession is allowed five successive play-the-balls. On the sixth occasion,

providing an opponent has not touched the ball, it is handed over to the opposition for them to play-the-ball.

Prop The front-row forwards in each team, one on either side of the hooker, who take part in the scrum.

Replacement Each team is allowed to have four substitutes or replacements, with whom they are allowed to replace four of their participating players. This takes place only with the referee's permission, and when the ball is out of play.

Scrum Occurs when an infringement has taken place and the referee has not awarded a penalty kick, drop-out or a play-the-ball. The six forwards from both teams pack into a three-two-one formation on each side of the scrum, and aim to gain an advantage by pushing the defensive scrum back into its own territory as far as possible. Once there is a clear tunnel between the two front rows, the ball is played straight into the middle by the scrum-half of the non-offending team. The forwards then back-heel the ball to the scrum-half, who gets play under way again.

Sin bin The referee can dismiss a player for an act of misconduct and send him off the field of play. The player may be sent to the sin bin for five or 10 minutes.

Speculator A ball thrown in hope, which can result in an opposition intercept try.

Stiff arm A straight arm raised, usually into the face of an oncoming opponent. Also known as a coathanger.

Stoppages The term given to any period in the match where play is halted and the referee has to stop his watch. This is normally caused by an injury to a player. The referee will add on any time lost by a stoppage at the end of the match.

Tackling A player is held back by an

opposing player and either falls to the ground or loses the ball. A player can also be held to prevent him from making any progress.

Tap penalty Awarded to the defending side after an attacking player carries the ball over the dead-ball line. The kicker places the ball on the center of the 25ydline to restart the game.

Test match A game between two national teams that is not played as part of a cup competition or tournament.

Touch-down The tactic of a defender grounding the ball in his own goal area to stop play. The game is restarted by the defending side taking a drop-out from their own goalline.

Touch judge There are two of these officials who each patrol the touch-line on opposite sides of the pitch. They raise their flag when they judge that the ball has gone out of play, or if they consider that a foul or infringement has taken place during the course of play and that the game needs to be stopped.

Touch line The 110yd-long line that runs up the side of the pitch. To stay in play, the ball must not go over this line.

Try Scored by the attacking team when the ball is grounded in the opponent's goal area following an attack. The ball must touch the floor for a team to be awarded a try. A player also can score a try if he falls to the ground before he reaches the goal line but his momentum carries him over it. A try scores three points for the attacking team, with the chance of a conversion to follow.

Tunnel Once a scrum has been correctly established, there should be a clear gap in between the two lineups of players. This is known as the tunnel, and the ball is then put into this area to get the scrum under way.

Upright tackle When a player who is in possession of the ball is tackled without being brought to the ground.

Voluntary tackle Takes place when a player in possession of the ball stops play without being tackled.

TRY: The defining moment in a rugby match when a player flings himself over the line to ground the ball

Rugby Union

Rugby Union is played by two teams of 15 players. The object of the game is to score points by carrying, passing or kicking the ball over the goal line or between the goalposts. The team that gains the highest number of points at the end of 80 minutes' play is the winner.

Accidental offside If the referee is satisfied that the offside is not deliberate and that the team in possession has not gained an advantage, then he will allow play to go on with no penalties incurred.

Advantage Describes how the referee allows play to carry on, even when an infringement has been committed. The referee is allowed to use his own discretion in determining when to apply an advantage.

Ball Oval in shape, it is 11-12in long. It has a circumference of 30-31in end to end, and a circumference at the middle of 23-24in. The ball is made of four panels of leather, and normally weighs between 14-15oz. The ball can be changed if necessary, although the same ball that has been in play must be used for goal and penalty kicks.

Ball or player touching the referee As long as the referee believes no advantage has been gained, then play will continue. If he deems an advantage has been gained, then he will order a scrummage.

Bledisloe Cup Trophy awarded each year for the winner of a Test match series between Australia and New Zealand.

Bound Binding on to another player with at least one arm.

Calcutta Cup The famous trophy that is contested between England and Scotland each year during the Five Nations Championship.

Conversion A place kick awarded to the attacking team when they score a try. It is taken from the 25yd line level with where the try was scored, and is worth two points.

Dead ball Occurs when play stops or when an attempt to convert a try is unsuccessful.

Dead-ball line The line at the end of the in-goal area.

Drop goal When a player drops the ball from his hands on to the ground and kicks the ball over the crossbar between the posts on the half-volley.

Drop kick When a player drops the ball from their hands to the ground and then kicks the ball just as it is rebounding back up.

Drop out The term given to a drop kick that is taken on or behind the 25yd line. The opposing team may not move over the line until the kick has been taken. A drop out is awarded to the defending team if the opposition has committed an offense in-goal, or if the ball is made dead by the defending team once the opposition has placed it in the in-goal area.

Dropped goal Occurs when the ball goes over the opposing team's crossbar by means of a drop kick. Worth three points.

Fair catch Can be executed only by a player inside their own 25yd area or in the in-goal zone. The player must catch the ball from the direct kick and shout, "Mark", in a clear voice. If this is done successfully then a free kick is awarded. It is also a way of legally stopping play.

Field It is 109yd long and 77yd wide.

The in-goal area is 11-27yd wide. The field must be of grass, sand or clay. Touchlines are out of the playing area.

Five Nations Championship An annual tournament that takes place from January to March between England, Scotland, Wales, Ireland and France, who play against each other once in a league format. The Five Nations Champions are the team that tops the league with the most points. From 2000, Italy will join the competition to make it six nations.

Foul A foul is deemed to have been committed when a player strikes, kicks or trips an opposing player. If they perform a dangerous tackle or obstruct an opponent who is not in possession of the ball, then they will also be penalized.

Free kick Granted to a team after a fair catch or a lesser infringement. The team awarded the free kick is not allowed to score a dropped goal from it.

Garryowen The slang term given to a high lofted kick that gives the kicker's forwards time to get under the ball before it comes down. Named after the Irish club of the same name.

Goal Awarded to a team when they kick the ball over the opposing team's crossbar and between the posts, from a penalty kick, a dropkick or a conversion kick.

Heading the ball When a player their head to connect with the ball. A legal, but rarely used, maneuver.

Grand Slam A team winning all its Five Nations matches achieves a "Grand Slam".

Haka Traditional and uplifting Maori dance performed by New Zealand teams prior to matches.

High tackle A tackle carried out above the possessing player's shoulders. This form of tackle is illegal and is penalized.

Home nations The collective term for the teams of England, Scotland, Wales and Ireland.

In-goal The term used to describe the section of the field that is enclosed by the goal line, the touch in-goal lines and a dead–ball line. Included in this area are the goal-line and goalposts, but it does not include the touch in-goal line and dead-ball line.

Kickoff Always taken from the centre of the pitch. Used to start the game or restart after halftime or when a try has been scored. Once the kick has been taken, the ball must reach the opposing team's 11yd line. If this does not occur, then the kick is either taken again or a scrum is formed on the halfway line.

Knock-on When the ball is propelled forward toward the opposition's dead-ball line, either through a player losing possession of the ball or by the player hitting the ball with their hand or arm.

Line-out A set piece of play after the ball has gone out of bounds, in which a player throws the ball from the side of

LINE-OUT: When the ball goes out of play, a lineup is formed to compete for the throw-in

the pitch above and between two lines of players made up of the eight forwards from each side.

Line through the mark A line parallel to the touch line.

Lying on or near the ball This is illegal because it prevents other players from getting to the ball.

Mark The place on the pitch where a free kick or penalty kick is awarded. See "Fair catch".

Maul Involves players from both sides as they encircle the player who has possession of the ball. The maul ends when the ball either hits the floor, the player in possession of the ball emerges from the maul or when the referee calls for a scrummage.

Obstruction An offense in which a player who, while running for the ball, charges the opposition in any way other than with their shoulders; any player who is in an offside position and deliberately blocks the player from their own team who is in possession of the ball; any player who, while carrying the ball after a set piece of play, tries to force their way through the players of their own team in front; and any outside player of a ruck or scrummage who attempts to block an opposing player from moving around the ruck or scrum.

Offside Occurs when a player from the same team is in front of the player in possession of the ball. An offside is punishable by awarding either a free kick or a scrum to the opposing team at the point at which the infringement occurred. The offside player can be brought back onside once the possessor of the ball has moved back in front or kicks the ball in front of the offending player.

Onside A term that describes any player who is behind the ball and therefore behind the player who is in possession of the ball. He is not offside.

Peeling off The action used by a player during a line-out to catch the ball that has been knocked back by the player's teammate.

Penalty goal The result of a successful goalkick, and worth three points. The goal is still valid if the ball hits the crossbar or posts, or is swept back having passed through the posts.

Penalty kick Awarded to the team that has been fouled. It is normally taken from the area in which the foul occurred. The penalty kick can be taken as a kick, a drop kick or a scrum. A penalty kick can be taken by any player on the attacking team. The kicker's team must be behind the ball when it is kicked, and the opposition must be at least 11yd from the kick spot.

Penalty try Awarded to the attacking team if the referee deems that the defending team has committed foul play while the attacking team is attempting to score a try.

Place kick Made by placing the ball on the ground and then kicking it.

Playing time Full time is 80 minutes, which is split into two 40-minute halves with a five-minute interval. The two teams change ends at halftime. Any stoppage time is added on to the end of the half in which it occurred.

Playing time lost The referee can deem time to have been lost 40 seconds after a player makes a move and does not see it through. The extra time will be added on to the end of the halftime period.

Popping When a front-row player lifts an opposing player off their feet during a ruck or maul to force them out. This is illegal, and is considered dangerous.

Professionalism The sport abandoned its amateur status and became fully professional in time for the 1997–98 season.

Punt Occurs when the ball is released

from the hands and is then kicked on the volley.

Ruck A set piece of play where players from both teams encircle the ball on the ground by linking with each other using one arm. All the players must be on their feet, and are only allowed to play the ball with their feet.

Rugby boots The studs on the players' boots must be circular and not exceed 3/4in in length or 1/2in in diameter at the base. Players are not allowed to wear boots that have a single stud at the toe of the boot.

Rugby Football Union (RFU) The sport's governing body, whose role is to control the sport and ensure the laws are adhered to.

Scoring A team is awarded five points for a try, three points for a drop goal or for a goal scored from a penalty kick, and two points for a kick scored after a try (conversion).

Scrummage A scrum is formed from at least eight players from each team. They join together to close around the ball, which is placed on the ground. The front row of players must be interlocking, which serves to make a tunnel between the players. The players use their feet to control the ball. A scrummage is always used to restart play after an infringement occurs.

Substitution A maximum of three players is allowed, but they can only replace injured team members. Once a player has been substituted, he or she may not return to the pitch.

Tackle The player in possession of the ball is brought to the ground or the ball is brought to the ground by an opposing team member. If the defending player has either of his knees on the floor or lands on top of another player, then he has been successfully tackled and must give the ball up.

Team Consists of 15 players.

Throw forward See "Knock-on".

Toss Before the game begins, the two captains will toss a coin to decide who kicks off or who will choose which end of the field to take.

Touch The ball is deemed to be in touch when it connects with the touch line or goes over the touch line, either by being kicked there or carried there by a player.

Touch-down Occurs when a player touches the ball to the ground in his own in-goal. It is either done by using their hands or, if the ball is already on the ground, by falling on it and covering the ball with their upper body.

Touch judges There should always be two touch judges for a Rugby Union match. Their duties are to assist the referee, and they are positioned on either side of the field.

Tri Nations Test competition played each year between South Africa, New Zealand and Australia.

Triple Crown Any team from the Home Nations that beats the other three nations in its Five Nations matches is awarded the Triple Crown.

Try The term given to the award when a player touches the ball to the ground in the opposing team's in-goal area. A try is worth five points, and the team that scored the try is then entitled to a conversion attempt.

Wheeling the scrum If the scrum is wheeled around by more than 90 degrees (a quarter-circle), then the referee halts play and resets the scrum.

World Cup A knockout tournament held every two years. The world's top sides challenge for the trophy after qualifying matches determine which countries can take part. The 1999 finals are being hosted by Wales, with matches also played in England, Scotland, Ireland and France.

Baseball

Baseball is a team sport between two teams of nine players each played on an enclosed field. The object of the game is for one team to score more runs than the other. A run is scored by a player running around the four bases on the field. If a team has three players put out at bat, or while running the bases, they revert to fielding while the opposition bats.

Appeal When a manager claims that an umpire has made an incorrect call.

Assist Awarded to a fielder when his throw leads to a runner being called out. Assists can be awarded to two or more fielders on the same play.

Balk An illegal maneuver by the pitcher when there is a runner or runners on the base. The runners automatically proceed to the next base when a balk is called.

Ball Weighs 5–5.5oz with a circumference of 9–9.25in. The center of the ball is made of cork, which is wrapped with yarn and then covered in cow- or horsehide. The term "ball" is also used to describe a strike that the batter does not swing at, and which is outside the strike zone.

Base A marker at each corner of the diamond-shaped infield; there are four in total. The first, second and third bases are made of white canvas, and measure 15in square by 3–5in thick. Home plate is five-sided and is made of whitened rubber. In order to score a run, the runner must touch home plate.

Base coach The term given to a player who is positioned in the coaches' box at either the first or third base to direct the batters and runners.

Base hit Occurs when a batter reaches base safely on a hit without the help of an error.

Base line Measures 3ft on either side of a direct line between the bases. A runner is considered to be out if he runs outside the base line, unless he is trying to avoid interfering with a fielder who is in play with a batted ball.

Base on balls An award of first base to a batter who, while batting, receives four pitches outside the strike zone. See "Walk".

Base runner The name given to the offensive player who has just finished his time at bat until he is either called out or until the play on which he becomes a runner ends.

Bat The bat has a smooth surface and is made of wood. Its diameter at the thickest point must be no more than 2.75in and it must not be more than 42in long. The batter is allowed to treat the handle with a sticky substance in order to improve the grip, but the substance cannot extend further than 18in from the top of the handle.

Batter's box Placed on either side of the home plate, they measure 4 × 6ft.

Batter's circle Also called an on-deck circle, it is positioned between the home plate and team bench in foul territory.

Battery Alludes to the pitcher and catcher.

Batting helmets All batters must wear helmets with at least one ear flap.

Batting order This is decided by the team manager, and play must occur in this order.

Bench The area off the field where the substitutes sit throughout the game.

Bunts Occurs when the ball comes into contact with the bat to drop a soft ground ball on the infield. Can be used to try to beat out a base hit, or as a sacrifice to move your runners to the next base.

Called game The term given to a game that the umpire-in-chief has terminated for whatever reason.

Catch Occurs when a fielder grasps the ball firmly in their hand or glove following a hit by a batter or a throw from another fielder.

Catcher's box Based directly behind the home plate. Measures 43in wide by 8ft in length.

Catcher's interference When the catcher blocks the batter from striking the ball, usually by accident.

Chin music The term for a high fastball thrown near the batter and meant to intimidate him. Also called a brushback pitch.

Coach's box Placed near the first and third bases in foul territory.

Complete game Occurs when a pitcher starts and finishes a regulation game.

Curveball A pitch that is thrown with spin that causes the ball to curve as it reaches home plate.

Cut-off A throw caught by a fielder who is not the designated target of the throw. An example of this is when a first baseman receives the ball from a fielder and then throws the ball on to the second baseman to try to tag out a runner.

Defense The team or any player of that team that is in the field.

Designated hitter Does not play defense but takes the place of the pitcher in the batting order.

Dead ball A ball that is out of play.

Double play Occurs when two outs are made on the same play.

Double A hit where the batter makes it to second base without any problems.

Doubleheader Two games that are regularly scheduled or have been rescheduled and are played in immediate succession.

Earned run Every time a run scores on a hit, sacrifice, sacrifice fly, wild pitch, bunt, base on balls, stolen base, fielder's choice, put-out or balk, a pitcher will receive an earned run. Any other run is kown as an unearned run.

Error When a player misplays the ball, such as a dropped fly ball, throw or ground ball and lengthens the bat for a batter or enables a longer run for a runner. A verdict of error can be given even if the fielder does not actually touch the ball, for example if it goes through their legs.

Extra innings Occurs when both teams are tied after nine innings.

Fair ball Any ball that lands in fair territory or lands on the foul line is considered a fair ball and is played by trhe defense.

Fair territory Marked by the foul lines; anything in or between these lines is considered fair territory.

Fastball A pitch thrown as hard as a pitcher is able to throw it. The fastest pitchers in the major leagues are capable of throwing fastballs that reach 100mph.

Field The playing area is split into the infield and the outfield. The infield area is outlined by the four bases. The outfield section is marked by the extending foul lines.

Fielder Another name for any defensive player.

Fielder's choice When a fielder elects to throw the ball to a point other than first base to record a putout.

Fly ball The term given to a ball that has been hit high up into the air.

Fly out A fly ball that is caught before it touches the ground or the fence.

Force play Occurs when a player is forced to move on to the next base because the batter has become a runner. When a fielder has the ball and touches the base before the runner has reached it, the runner is forced out.

Forkball A pitch thrown with the first and second fingers spread far apart on the baseball. This pitch drops suddenly as it reaches home plate.

Foul ball Any ball that lands in or is caught in foul territory.

Foul lines The lines extend at right angles from home plate through the first and third bases to the edge of the playing area.

Foul territory The area outside the foul lines.

Foul tip A batted ball that is barely struck by the bat, and does not fly high enough to be caught for a putout.

Forfeit Occurs when the chief umpire decides to end a game in favor of the wronged team for a violation of the rules. Always awarded 9–0 in the wronged team's favor.

Gloves Catchers wear a glove or mitt that must measure no more than 15.5in with a maximum circumference of 38in. The first baseman's glove should be no more than 12in long and no more than 8in. wide. The remaining fielders' gloves should be 12in long and 7.5in wide across the palm.

Going yard A slang term for hitting a home run, short for "going out of the yard" (ballpark).

Ground out Occurs when a batter is thrown off first base because he has hit a ground ball.

Ground rule double Given to a batsman when his fair ball either goes through or under the fence, into the stands or is otherwise unplayable.

Home plate A five-sided piece of whitened rubber that is set into the ground that constitutes home base. The apex of the plate fits into the right angle of the right field foul line and the left field foul line.

Home run Occurs when a batter strikes a fair ball over the fence or circles all the bases without being called out.

Infield The 90ft square area that encloses the bases on the pitch. The first, second and third basemen are positioned here as well as the pitcher and the catcher.

Infield fly rule The ball is hit high into the air within the infield area. If the pop-up is in fair territory and if there are fewer than two batters out and runners on at least first and second bases, the umpire will rule the batter automatically out.

Illegal pitch When the pitcher releases the ball and his pivot foot is not in contact with the pitcher's plate, or when a balk occurs.

Innings When both teams have a turn at batting and fielding and each team has three putouts.

Knuckleball An odd pitch thrown by very few pitchers. It has a grip that consists of holding the ball with the knuckles rather than the fingers. The knuckleball is the slowest pitch in baseball, but the lack of spin applied to the pitch causes it it to flutter unpredictably. A difficult pitch to throw, hit and catch.

League Made up of a group of clubs who play against each other throughout a season to produce a champion team.

Line drive A hard-hit ball that flies on a lower trajectory than a fly ball.

Live ball A ball that is in play. **Losing pitcher** The pitcher who has given the winning team the lead because of the runs they received.

Mitt Worn by the catcher to catch pitches that get past the batter. It must be no more than 38in in circumference or 15.5in from top to bottom.

No hitter A pitcher who, at the end of a complete game, has allowed no hits.

Nine-inning win If the visiting team completes nine innings and is ahead then the game is deemed to be over. If the home team is ahead after the visitors bat in the upper half of the ninth inning, then they are declared the winners. Alternatively the home team can win if they score in the bottom of the ninth inning after the winning play is finished.

Obstruction Occurs when a fielder who is not in possession of the ball and is not fielding the ball blocks the progress of a runner.

Offense The team or a member of this team which is at bat.

On-deck circle See "Batter's circle".

Out Occurs when a player is released from play by a force out, a strike out, a tag out or a fly out.

Outfield The area of the field between the infield and the fence on fair territory. The players based in this area are the left fielder, the right fielder and the center fielder.

Outfielder A player who is based in the outfield, the area of the field farthest away from the home base.

Overslide When a runner slides with too much momentum so that he completely misses or loses contact with the base.

Passed ball A catcher is charged with a passed ball when he fails to catch a controllable pitch and allows opposing runners to progress to the next base.

Perfect game When a pitcher pitches a no hitter, and no runners have reached base on walks, errors or being hit by pitches.

Pinch hitter A player who is used to bat for another player. The replaced player is not allowed to return to the game.

Pinch runner The player who runs for another player. The substituted player is not allowed to return to play.

Pitch Describes a ball delivered by a pitcher to the batter.

Pitcher's mound A circular pile of dirt that measures 18ft in diameter. The mound has a rectangle-shaped rubber plate, which is known as the pitcher's rubber. This is placed in the ground and measures 6in by 24in. It is set 10in higher than home plate.

Pitcher's rubber Set in the center of the pitcher's mound and located 60ft 6in from home plate. This is the spot from where the pitcher takes his throw.

Pivot foot The player's foot that is in contact with the pitcher's plate when he delivers his pitch. Failure to do this results in a penalty being incurred.

Players A team consists of the pitcher, the catcher, first, second and third basemen, the left, right and center fielders and a shortstop.

Putout Describes when a batter runner or base runner is called out by a tag out,

PITCHER'S MOUND: The raised mound from which a pitcher throws the ball to the batter

force out or has been caught stealing.

Relief pitcher A pitcher who specializes in pitching the last few innings, or inning, of a game and protecting a small lead. Relief pitchers usually have an overpowering fastball. They are also called firemen, as they are called to put out the opposing team's offensive fire.

Run down Describes the defense trying to put out a runner in between bases.

Runs batted in Awarded to a batter who puts the ball in play and causes one or more runners to score. RBIs are not counted when a run is scored due to an error, or if the batter grounds into a double play.

Sacrifice bunt Used by a batter to advance a runner or runners. If the bunt is successful then the time is not counted as time at bat; if it is unsuccessful, then it is counted.

Sacrifice fly Occurs when a batter's caught fly ball ends in a runner tagging up and advancing to the next base.

Safe A decision by the umpire that a runner is entitled to the base for which he is trying.

Set position One of two positions from which a pitcher can deliver a pitch.

Shutout Describes when a team is held scoreless. To be credited with a shutout, the pitcher must complete a full game.

Single A one-base hit credited to the batter.

Sinker A pitch that drops suddenly as it reaches home plate.

Slider A harder version of the curveball, this pitch curves and sinks suddenly as it reaches home plate. A poorly thrown slider, known as a hanging slider, is easy for batters to hit.

Starting pitcher The player who starts the game for his team.

Stolen base The act of a runner gaining a base without the help of a hit, an error or a walk. Occurs when the pitched ball is on its way to the batter.

Strike A pitch that the batter takes in the strike zone or at which he swings and misses.

Strike zone Based over the home plate between the top of the knees and the top of the shoulders, though it can also be interpreted as only rising to the batter's waist.

Strikeout Occurs when a batter has three strikes and does not manage to get a run. A batter who tries to bunt on the third strike is considered out if the ball is picked up in foul territory.

Substitutions Can be made only when play is considered dead. Players who have been substituted are not allowed to return to play.

Suspended game A game that has to be halted and then replayed at a later date.

Squeeze play Describes a designated play when a team with a runner on third base tries to score this runner with a bunt.

Tag out Allows a fielder to record a putout. If force play is not in order then the runner must be tagged out while the player is not touching a base.

Tag up Describes the rule where a runner must be in contact with his base after a fly ball has been caught before proceeding.

Teams A baseball team has nine players.

Three-foot line This line is parallel to the first base line. It measures from halfway between the home plate and first base to beyond first base. This line is used to guide the runners.

Triple Occurs when a batter reaches third base on his hit.

Umpires Normally there are four umpires. The home umpire is based behind the catcher so that he can judge

TAG OUT: If a batter or runner fails to reach base before the ball, he can be tagged out by the fielder

the strikes. He has overall control of the game and his decisions are final. He is always dressed in protective clothing. The remaining umpires are positioned at the first three bases to ensure that the runners reach the bags safely. An official scorer is also used to record the statistical data from the game.

Walk Occurs when a batter is awarded first base for taking four balls at a time when batting against a pitcher. Is also called base on balls.

Warning track Based in the outfield, this track is used to warn fielders that they are nearing the fence.

Weather-shortened game Any game affected by bad weather and therefore canceled is completed at a later date conducive to both teams' playing schedules.

Wild pitch A pitch that the catcher fails to control, and the runners therefore proceed to the next base. This mistake is accredited to the pitcher. Any ball that bounces and allows the runners to move forward is termed a wild pitch.

Windup position One of two positions from where a pitcher is allowed to make a pitch. Usually only used when there are no runners on bases.

Winning pitcher Also the starting pitcher if he pitches at least five innings and leaves the game in the lead and remains so. If the pitcher leaves the game in the lead but the game finishes as either a tie or the opposing team moves into the lead with runs that are not charged to him, then he is neither winner or loser.

Rounders

Rounders is an English game not unlike baseball and softball. It is played by striking the ball with a bat and then running around the track to score a rounder. The team with the most rounders is the winner. The game is played mainly by women and children, and often thought of as recreational rather than competitive. But mixed-sex teams are growing in popularity.

Backward area Constitutes the area behind the front line of the batting area.

Backward hit When the ball is struck directly into the backward area.

Ball Made of leather and usually white. Weighs 21/2-3oz with a circumference of 7-71/2cm.

Batting Occurs when the batsman strikes the ball with the bat and hits the ball forward into play.

Batting square The area in which all bats must be taken. Measures 61/2ft by 61/2ft. All of the lines are considered part of the square.

Bowling square All bowls must be performed from within the square. Measures 8ft × 8ft. All the lines are considered part of the square.

Duration There is no set time limit, and the game is officially finished after all the batters have been struck out over two innings. Alternatively, the team that leads by five rounders or more can decide to make the other team bat on, forfeiting their own second innings.

Half-rounder Scored when the batter successfully gets around the track but without hitting the ball.

Innings Each match is made up of two innings. The inning begins when the first ball is bowled and ends when the batters have been declared out.

Kit All players must be clearly numbered and the vests must be of different colors for each team. Players are not allowed to wear spiked boots.

No-ball Occurs in the following situations: when the bowler's under-arm action is not considered to be continuous; when the bowler does not keep his feet inside the bowling square before releasing the ball; when the bowler directs the ball on to the wrong side of the batter or at the batter's body; if the bowl reaches higher than the batter's head or lower than the knee.

Obstructions Classed as a fielder blocking a batter's hit or run, or a batter deviating from the track and therefore interfering with a fielder's play.

Officials There are two umpires. The first is the batting umpire, who must have a clear view at all times of the batting square and the first post without having to turn their head. The second official is the bowler's umpire. They may consult each other, and their decisions on the state of play are final. After the first inning is complete, the two umpires swap positions on the pitch in the interest of fairness.

Outs A batter is considered out when his or her feet are not fully inside the batting box before the ball has been struck or, while making a run, they are on the inside of the post. It also happens when a fielder, or the ball the fielder has thrown, reaches the post before the batter, or if they are caught out, or if the batter deliberately blocks a fielder, overtakes another batter or moves from a post before the ball has been thrown.

Penalty half-rounder Awarded to the batting team when the bowler throws two no-balls in a row, or if a batter's play is blocked by an opposing fielder. Can also be awarded to the fielding team if they are obstructed by the waiting batting team.

Posts Four vertical posts, 4ft high, supported on bases and placed at the corners of the running track.

Rounder Awarded when a batter-strikes the ball and reaches the fourth post before another ball is bowled.

Running track The area used by the batter when running. It extends 6 1/2ft beyond the fourth base.

Runs While making a run the batter must always pass on the outside of the post. In order to reach the fourth post the batter must stop at each post on the way round while still carrying the bat. When stationary at a post, the batter should remain in contact with the post at all times either by hand or bat until the bowler has put the ball into play. At no time must more than one batter be at a post, and a run is invalid if the player leaves their post before the ball has been bowled.

Side out Occurs when there is no batter waiting to bat and all the running batters are out due to a fielder throwing a full pitch, or the ball is placed into the batter's square before any batter reaches the fourth post.

Start of play The two captains toss a coin to see who will take the first inning. The batters must stay in the same order throughout both innings.

Stick Made of wood with a length of 18in. It has a round cross section and must be no more than 6 1/2in in circumference at the thickest part.

Substitutes Two substitutes are permitted at any dead-ball situation as long as they have been named before play begins. Any player substituted is not allowed to return to the game.

Teams Each team is allowed a minimum of six players and a maximum of nine. In a mixed team, the maximum number of men allowed is five.

ROUNDERS: A popular recreational sport in England, particularly with children and families

Softball

Softball is an outdoor sport that was originally played indoors. The team that scores the most runs wins the game. There are two types of softball: fast-pitch and slow-pitch. The game is played by both men and women.

Altered bat An illegal practice, involving adding material or extra grips to the bat, including more than two layers of tape.

Appeal play A rule introduced if a player or coach requests the umpire to resolve a dispute. This must be done before play continues, or before the players have stepped over the foul line.

Assist Can be awarded to two or more players when their pitch results in a run for a fellow team member.

Ball 11–12in in diameter with a weight of 5.9–6.1oz.

Base hit When the batter reaches first base safely. Can also apply to forced play at another base, or through a fielder's choice of base.

Base path Is always a direct line that measures 3ft wide between each base. If a runner makes a run outside the base path, then they are automatically out unless their run puts them in the way of a batted ball being fielded by another player.

Batter A batter can be out if the ball is legally caught on the fly.

Catch When a player grabs the ball in their hand or glove.

Chopped ball An illegal shot in which the ball is deliberately hit hard downward so that it bounces into the air in an attempt to avoid being caught.

Crow hop Action used by a player to pitch the ball by springing off the player's plate and then hopping into a new position to complete the throw.

Dead ball A ball not in use during play and is not considered in play again until the pitcher has possession and the umpire declares "play ball".

Double A strike that allows a player to arrive at the second base safely.

Double play A device used by the defense to register two outs that are made on the same play.

Error A penalty incurred when a player loses a ball and consequently aids his or her fellow teammates by giving them extra time to reach a further base or allowing the batter an extended bat.

Extra-inning victory Once the game goes into extra time, both teams have a chance of winning until one side scores the most runs in an extra inning or until a winning run is scored by the home team.

Fair and foul territory The two areas on the pitch that are separated by the two foul lines. Anything on or between these two lines is known as the fair territory, and anything outside this is called foul territory.

Fake tag The title given to a player who deliberately impedes an opposition player who is without the ball. The usual umpiring decision given in these circumstances is to award the obstructed player the base at which they would have arrived had they not been tagged.

Force play Happens when a batter becomes a runner and forces the other runner on to the next base. In the case of a fielder reaching second base with the ball before the runner, then the runner will be forced out of play.

Forfeit A penalty imposed by the referee for one of several reasons, such as a team refusing to play, rushing or delaying play or deliberately breaking the rules, or if a side does not show up. If a player has been thrown out and does not leave the field within the allotted time of one minute, his team forfeits the game. A forfeited match will always result in a 7–0 score being awarded.

Foul ball Any ball that is struck into foul territory.

Ground rule double When a batter's ball goes under or over the fence, the ground rule double is given as compensation.

Home run When a fair ball is hit over the fence or alternatively circles the perimeter of the bases without going out of play.

Illegally batted ball Results when the ball is hit and the batter's foot is either touching home plate or is entirely outside the batting box. It is also deemed illegal when struck by an illegal bat.

Infield The section of the pitch enclosed by the four bases.

Innings Made up of seven segments that comprise the whole game.

Interference Pertaining to any physical or verbal abuse given to an opposing player.

Leaping Describes the pitcher's action while delivering the ball in the air to the batter.

Legal touch An action taken by a defending player marking an opposition runner who has possession of the ball that results in an out.

Obstruction Occurs when a defending player hampers a batter from striking the ball or interferes with a base runner when the fielder is not in possession.

Out The four main outs are: a strike out, a force out, a tag out and a fly out.

Outfield The section of fair territory between the infield and the fence.

Overslide When a runner overslides on the second or third base they are in danger of being out, but that is not the case for a batter on first base.

Passed ball Occurs when a catcher falters on a strike that should have been contained with minimum effort.

Quick-return pitch A pitch made by the pitcher before the batter is ready.

Runner A runner is out if the fielder touching the base receives the ball before the runner reaches the base.

Runs batted in The points collected by a batter when their strike leads to a runner scoring.

Sacrifice fly Given to a batter whose caught fly ball ends in a third base player tagging up and scoring.

Seven-inning win – home side If after the visitors have batted in the remaining slot of the seventh innings and the home side is in the lead, then it has won. Alternatively, if the home side strikes a run in the lower slot of the last innings and then scores, the game is won.

Seven-inning win – visitors If after complete innings, the visitors are in the lead, they have officially won the game.

Shortened game If one side has scored more points after five innings, then the game can end. If the home side has more points after four and a half innings, then the game can end.

Team Slow-pitch, 10 players; fast-pitch, 11 players.

Triple A system of scoring that is awarded to a batter when they successfully reach third base on their strike.

Triple play Points given to the defending side when it gets three outs on the same play.

Wild pitch A pitch that a catcher misses, resulting in one or more runners progressing to the next base. The blame for this always lies with the pitcher.

Cricket

Cricket is played on grass between two teams of 11 players, the aim being for one side to score more runs than the other team. A specially prepared rectangular wicket (very level, and with close-mown grass) is placed in the center of the cricket ground with a set of three stumps (a wicket) at either end, exactly 22yd apart. The captains of each team toss a coin to decide who is going to bat first and who will field first. Two batsmen from the same team take turns facing six consecutive balls from the same bowler, until either of them is out. Meanwhile the 10 remaining players on the other team are positioned tactically around the cricket field to try to prevent the batsmen scoring runs and to try to catch him out.

All-rounder A player who is considered to be of a high standard at both batting and bowling.

Appeal If a member of the fielding side believes that a batsmen should be out, they must shout "How's that?" (or "Howzat"). An appeal of this nature must be made before the umpire can order a batsman out.

Averages Throughout the season, both the batsmen's total number of runs scored and the amount of wickets a bowler has taken are added together and then divided by the number of games they have played in. This will give a clear idea of how well they are playing and if they are being consistent.

Backlift Describes the way in which the batsman who is facing the bowler raises his bat in readiness to hit the ball.

Backward defensive The batsman will normally play this shot against a short ball from the bowler. They will take a step backward and wait for the ball to pitch up against the bat before striking it into the outfield.

Bad light When the umpires judge that the light is too poor to allow the game to continue in safety. Nowadays, automatic light meters indicate when the light level is acceptable for play at top-level matches. A batsman can appeal to the umpires if he feels it is too dangerous to play on.

Bails Two cylindrical pieces of wood laid across the top of the three stumps at each end of the wicket. Grooves are set into the top of the stumps to prevent the bails rolling off or being blown off by the wind. For a batsman to be given out by being bowled, one or both bails must fall off the stumps. If the ball hits the stumps and the bails stay on, then the batsman cannot be out. The same applies to a run out.

Ball The ball is normally made of red leather with a stitched seam running down the middle. It must weigh 5.5–5.75oz and has a circumference of 8.8–9in. If the ball is lost during a game, then a replacement of similar condition must be used. A new ball is always used at the start of each innings.

Bat Used by a batsman to strike the ball. It is made of wood (traditionally willow) with a rubber grip at the top. It measures 3.1ft in length and its usual weight is about 2.6lb.

Batsman The player who is facing the bowler at the wicket and is trying to score as many runs as possible. He wears protective gloves and leg guards called pads. Also refers generally to any player who is a specialist at batting.

Beamer A fast, head-high delivery, which the umpire will normally deem a no-ball.

Bouncer A delivery that is short and fast, and flies up toward the batsman's head. If the ball bounces too high, then the umpire calls a wide.

BOUNCER: A fierce, short-pitched delivery that bounces high over the batsman's head

Boundary A description of a hit from the batsman that crosses the boundary line for four or six runs.

Boundary line The line, normally forming an oval shape, that defines the limits of the playing area. If the batsman hits the ball across this line, the team is awarded four runs. If the batsman strikes the ball over the boundary without it hitting the ground at any point, then he scores six runs.

Bowled A batsman is out if the ball delivered by the bowler hits the wicket and dislodges the bail(s), even if the ball first hits the bat or any part of the batsman's body.

Bowler The player in the non-batting side who runs up to the wicket to deliver the ball to the batsman.

Bowling crease A line that runs 4ft behind the popping crease. The wickets are set on this crease.

Bye A run the batsman can take when

the ball has not touched the bat or any part of his body.

Captain The leader of the team. He tosses a coin with the opposing captain at the start of the match to determine who bats first. During the game, he will decide which player will bowl, and the positioning of players in the field.

Catch A batsman is out if he strikes the ball directly in the air to any fielder and they catch the ball in their hands without dropping it.

Caught and bowled When a bowler takes a wicket by catching a hit in the air from the batsman to whom he bowled.

Century Scored by the batsman when he gets 100 runs in one inning.

Crease The line in front of the wickets. A batsman can be stumped by the wicketkeeper if he stands in front of the line ,and is run out if the ball hits the stumps before he crosses the crease.

Cut A shot taken by the batsman against a delivery that is short and wide of the off-stump. He uses the ball's momentum to deflect the ball at an angle behind him, glancing the face of the bat rather than using force.

Cutter A medium-paced delivery by the bowler that spins or bounces into or away from the batsman.

Dead ball Called by the umpire if he feels that the batsman is not ready to face the bowler, in the case of a serious injury to a player, or if the bowler drops the ball in the process of a delivery. No runs can be scored from a dead ball, and if the bowler has delivered the ball, it is not included in the over count.

Dead pitch A pitch on which the ball bounces low and straight.

Declaration Made by the batting side when they believe they have scored sufficient runs to win the game. A declaration can be made by a captain before all his team's batsmen are out. It is normally called so that it allows them enough time to get all the opposing batsmen out within the allotted time or number of overs available.

Delivery One bowl by the bowler.

Dismissal When a batsman is out.

Driving An attacking form of hitting the ball with the bat. To achieve it, the batsman lifts the bat behind him and then takes a long, smooth swing to follow through the ball rather than just applying the bat to the ball.

Duck When a batsman is out without scoring a run.

Duckworth–Lewis Method of scoring a rain-affected one-day match.

Duration of the day's play There isn't a strict limit of six hours (*see below*). Play will finish when the correct number of overs has been bowled. This could be the result of the players having been taken off the field due to rain or bad light. It is up to the umpire's discretion as to what time play can continue to.

Duration of the match This varies according to the standard of the match. In Test Match cricket, each side has two innings over a five-day period, each day's play lasting for approximately six hours (*see above*). In domestic cricket, league matches are played over a three- or four-day period. One-day games are played over two innings, one for each side, and each team has the same number of overs (often 55) to score more runs than the other side.

Extra Run scored without the batsman hitting the ball with the bat. This can be the result of a wide, bye, leg-bye or a no-ball.

Fall of wicket The term describing when a batsman is out.

Fielder Every player in the non-batting side who is not the bowler or wicket-keeper takes up a position in the field to try to stop a batsman from scoring any runs.

Fine leg A fielder who stands on the leg-side of the wicket, but behind where the batsman stands in relation to the wicket.

Flipper A ball from a spin bowler that comes out of the back of the hand like a top spinner, except that when it lands it gains speed and stays low, making it difficult to play. Australia's Shane Warne is most famous for bowling it.

Follow on Takes place when the team batting second fails to score at least 200 runs fewer than the opposition in a Test Match, or 150 runs in a three- or four-day game. The opposing captain can ask his opponents to bat again.

Forward defensive When a ball is pitched up close to the stumps, the batsman will normally move his front foot forward toward the pitch of the ball, bending his knee in the process. This forms the basis of all drives.

Four Four runs are awarded to the batsman when he strikes a ball across the boundary line that bounces before it does so.

Full toss A delivery by the bowler that reaches the batsman without first bouncing. The batsman may swing his bat using a hook shot or a drive in an attempt to score a boundary.

Golden duck Term used for the score of zero when a batsman is out on his first ball without scoring a run.

Googly An off-break delivery bowled by the bowler to a right-handed batsman that is delivered with an leg-break action in an attempt to deceive the batsman.

Grubber A delivery by the bowler that rolls along the ground.

Guard At the start of his innings, a batsman will ask the umpire to help him mark a point on the crease so he can judge where his stumps are. This is normally done by the batsman calling out "middle" or "two legs".

Gully The fielder who stands behind the slips to field deeper-hit shots from the batsman.

Half-century A score of 50 runs by a batsman in one inning.

Handling the ball If the batsman stops the ball with his hand without his opponent's consent, he can be called out by the umpire for handling the ball.

Hat trick When a bowler takes three wickets in three consecutive balls. A player is "on a hat trick" when he has already taken two wickets with two balls and is hopeful of gaining another wicket on the next delivery.

Helmet Worn by a batsman to protect his head from bouncers or other dangerous deliveries.

Hit wicket A batsman is out if he knocks the bails from his own wicket with his bat or body while playing a shot or setting off for the first run. See

GOOGLY: The art of pretending to bowl a leg-break ball, but actually turning it the other way

also "Playing On".

Hook A shot played at shoulder height by the batsman against any short delivery, or any ball that is on a line just outside the off-stump. Good footwork is essential for this shot. The back foot is normally well back, enabling the front foot to be moved to open the body further. This gives the batsman the chance to meet the ball with his arms at full stretch.

How's that? For a batsman to be called out, the bowling side must shout an appeal of "How's that?" for the umpire to dismiss the batsman. This appeal must be raised before the bowler comes in to deliver his next ball.

Innings This is when 10 batsmen on one team have been dismissed by the opposition, or a specified number of overs has been bowled. Each match consists of one or two innings per team, depending on the standard of the match.

Innings defeat When a team is bowled out twice for fewer runs than the other team scored in a single inning.

Kit Players are expected to wear white or cream shirts and trousers, except in some one-day matches where colored clothing is permitted. The wicketkeeper and batsmen wear gloves and padded leg guards called pads.

Last over The final over delivered by a bowler before an interval or at the close of play. The last over can be started if the umpires arrive in position at the bowler's end before time is called.

LBW Short for leg-before-wicket. A batsman can be called out if any part of his body, clothing or equipment intercepts a ball that would have hit the wicket, providing the ball pitched, or would have pitched, in a straight line between the wicket – even above the bails.

Leg-before-wicket See "LBW".

Leg-break A delivery by the bowler that spins into a right-handed batsmen from his leg side.

Leg-bye A run taken by the batsman when the ball does not come off the bat but has deliberately been pushed away by a part of his body.

Leg glance If the batsman is having trouble playing the ball through the on-side, he can use the side of his body or hip to deflect the ball away.

Leg stump The pole of the wicket that is closest to the batsmen's legs when he takes guard.

Limited-overs match A cricket match played in a restricted number of overs. This can apply to a standard one-day game or to a match that has been shortened due to the intervention of the weather.

Lofted drive An attacking shot used by the batsman. The ball is struck high into the air in an attempt to score a boundary.

Long off A fielding position that is set straight on from the wicket and is positioned on the boundary line. This position is directly behind the wicket and just to the right as the fielder prepares to come in and stop the batsmen from scoring any runs past them.

Long on A fielding position that is set straight on from the wicket and is positioned on the boundary line. This position is directly behind the wicket and just to the left as the fielder faces the batsmen.

Long Room A famous viewing gallery that is situated inside the Lord's pavilion. It is for members only and the players always pass through this historic room to walk out onto the field.

Lord's The home of English cricket, in St John's Wood in central London, where all major domestic finals are played, as well as major Test matches.

Lunch Taken at the end of the morning session – normally at about 1pm. The players come off the field for a 40-minute interval before the afternoon session takes place.

Maiden An over in which no runs have been scored.

MCC The Marylebone Cricket Club, established in 1787, which was responsible for the laws of the game in England until 1968 and worldwide until 1993. It still owns Lord's cricket ground, its headquarters.

Medium pace A delivery by the bowler that does not have the intensity of a fast delivery but is quicker than a spinner's ball.

Middle stump The middle of the three stumps forming a wicket.

Mid-off See "Point".

Mid-wicket A fielder who stands on the on-side or leg-side of the field in the center to try to stop the batsman scoring a boundary.

Mid-on A fielder who stands on the on-side, but farthest from the striking batsman.

New ball A new ball can be taken at the start of each inning, and in matches of more than three days, after a set number of overs (usually 75) depending on the competiton. The new ball should favor fast bowlers because it has more shine and bounce.

No-ball This is an illegal delivery by the bowler and is called for one of two reasons: either the umpire has deemed the bowler to have thrown the ball instead of bowling it; or the bowler has no part of his front foot grounded behind the popping crease in his delivery stride. The batting team is automatically awarded a run and an extra ball in the over.

Off-break A delivery by the bowler that, on pitching, spins into the batsmen from his off side.

Off side The side of the field to the

right of the batsmen as they take up their stance sideways to the bowler.

Off stump The stump of the wicket that is farthest from the batsman's legs when he takes guard.

One-day match A variation of cricket played in a single day with a restricted number of overs for each side.

On side The side to the left of the batsman as they take their stance sideways onto the bowler.

Outfield The section of the playing area outside the wicket.

Over A set of six fairly delivered balls by the bowler toward one wicket. The direction of the deliveries switches to the opposite wicket each over.

Over the wicket An approach whereby the bowler delivers the ball from the hand nearest to the stumps.

Overthrows Runs scored when a fielder inadvertently throws the ball beyond the wicket having fielded the ball from a stroke.

Pad The protective guard used by batsmen and the wicket-keeper to protect their legs.

Pitch This is the area between the two bowling creases. It extends 5ft on either side of a line joining the center of the wickets. The rest of the playing area is enclosed by a boundary line.

Play At the start of the game or a new innings, when the umpires are happy that everything is in order, one will shout, "Play", to signal to the bowler to come in with his first delivery.

Playing on When a batsman knocks the ball on to his own wicket and the bails fall off. He is called out.

Point A fielder who stands on the off side, about 15yd from where the batsmen are.

Popping crease This runs 4ft in front of and parallel to each wicket. The batsman must stand within this area, or he can be called out by the umpire. If any

part of his body or his bat is behind the line, then he cannot be called out.

Retiring A batsman can leave the field of play at any time during his time at the wicket. He can return to the wicket later, but only at the consent of the opposing captain.

Return crease This intersects the popping crease and consists of two lines that are 8.6ft apart. It is used as a guideline for the bowler, who must not overstep the second line before releasing the ball. If he oversteps the line, then the umpire calls a no-ball.

Round the wicket An approach whereby the bowler delivers the ball from the hand farthest from the stumps.

Run Taken by the batsman after he has hit the ball to the outfield. Both batsmen at the wicket have to run toward the opposite wicket, crossing in the middle, and touch the popping crease, and every time they make it safely from one wicket to the other while the ball is still in play, the batsman who struck the ball scores one run.

Run out A player can be run out if the ball, having been thrown by any fielder, directly hits the wicket before the batsman reaches the popping crease while the ball is in play.

Runner A player who runs between the wickets for a batsman who is unable to take the run himself due to injury.

Shooter A fast delivery by the bowler, which stays low.

Short run A quick, riskier run taken when the ball is played not very far away from the wicket.

Sight screen There are two screens, one at each end of the field behind the wickets and on the boundary, that are used as a blank background to help the batsmen see the ball more clearly. Spectators are not allowed to move in front of them during play.

Silly mid-off A fielding position close

to the wicket on the off-side, square of the batsman.

Silly mid-on A fielding position that is set close to the wicket on the on-side, square of the batsman.

Silly point A fielder who stands very close to the wicket on the off-side, slightly forward of square.

Six Six runs are awarded to the batsman when he hits the ball in the air and it crosses the boundary line before coming into contact with the ground.

Sledging A euphemism of Australian derivation for the barracking of the batsman by the wicket-keeper and/or other fielders close to the wicket as the bowler comes in to bowl – a form of gamesmanship designed to distract the batsman.

Slip One or more of these fielders plays behind or next to the wicket-keeper, and to the offside of the field. They stand around 5–10yd apart from each other in an arc, hoping to catch a batsman out.

Spinner A bowler who delivers a slower ball, spinning it so that the bounce deceives the batsman.

Square leg A fielder who stands on the leg side of the wicket and quite close to the striking batsman.

Stance The way in which the batsman positions himself as he prepares to face the incoming bowler. Batsmen normally place their feet about 6–8in apart, on either side of the popping crease, with their weight distributed evenly for good balance and mobility.

Sticky wicket A damp surface that leads to the ball bouncing erratically. The batsman usually finds it extremely difficult to hit the ball as a result.

Stone-walling Batting defensively with the intention of not getting out rather than trying to score runs. A tactic used by a side that is unlikely to match the other team's run total but could force a draw instead.

Strike rate The average number of runs that a batsman makes per 100 deliveries.

Stumping If a batsman misses the ball and moves out of his ground, other than to attempt to play the ball, the wicket-keeper can break the wicket, without another fielder's intervention. The decision over whether to call the batsman out is then made by the umpire, and in some cases may be referred to the third umpire.

Stumps Three long, thin cylindrical pieces of wood that are placed together at opposite ends of the wicket. They are 28in high and a total of 9in wide, and the bails are placed in shallow grooves in the top of them. The bowler aims to bowl the ball past the batsman and to hit the stumps to get the batsman out.

Substitutes Each side is allowed to bring a player onto the field to replace a participating player who is ill or injured. Substitutes are allowed to field, but not to bat or bowl.

Sweep A shot taken by the batsman in which he helps the ball on its way rather than fiercely striking it. The batsman will bend his right leg to drop his body close to the ground and then swing the bat around to play the ball behind square, where the bowler is only allowed two fielders.

Tea Break taken midway through the afternoon session. The players leave the field for a 20-minute interval and then return for the final session of the day.

Teams There are two teams of 11 players, normally consisting of specialist batsmen, all-rounders, bowlers and a wicket-keeper.

Test match This takes place between two international sides over a maximum of five days. Each side has two innings in which to score more runs than the opposition. The number of overs is not limited, but matches can finish early if a result is achieved inside five days.

Test series Number of Test matches between two countries, usually a rubber of three or five games.

The Oval The home of Surrey County Cricket Club in south London and a famous Test match venue.

Third man A fielding position close to the boundary, on the off side behind the wicket.

Third official An official not on the field of play who is called upon to determine whether a batsman has been run out, if it is a close decision. The third official watches an action replay of the incident in the stand, and then flashes a green or red light to show his decision. A red light means the batsman has been called out.

Time At the end of the last over, the umpires will call "Time" to halt play for the day.

Toss At the start of the match, the two captains toss a coin to decide who will bat first. This decision is considered extremely important, and is made according to the prevailing wicket and weather conditions, and the weather forecast for the remainder of play.

Twelfth man The player who misses selection in the final 11 but is still part of the team. Can replace one of the playing 11 as a fielder but cannot bat or bowl.

Umpire Two umpires control play on the field; one stands behind the wicket at the bowler's end and the other at square leg. They are responsible for deciding whether or not a player is out, and for deciding if conditions are fit enough to play – if not, they may take the players off the pitch because of rain or bad light.

WACA One of the most famous cricket grounds in Australia, in Perth, which stages leading domestic and international games.

Whites This relates to the attire worn by players. Men are expected to wear white shirts and white trousers, while women are allowed to wear white skirts. Colored clothing is now common on one-day matches.

Wicket At each end of the field is a wicket consisting of three stumps, which are placed in a line next to each other; two bails are placed on top of each wicket. The wickets are 28in high and 9in wide, and each bail measures 4.38in long. Also the generic name for the field including the sets of stumps at both ends.

Wicket-keeper The only player on the fielding side who wears gloves; he is similar to a baseball catcher. He positions himself behind the batsman's wicket, and tries to catch any balls from the bowler that beat the batsman. He also normally receives the ball from a fielder after the batsman has hit the ball away from the wicket, at which point the ball is no longer in play. He can stump a batsman out by knocking the bails off with the ball in his hand when the batsman's feet are not in his crease.

Wide Awarded against the bowler if he sends the ball so wide of the wicket or so high over the batsman that he cannot reach the ball. The umpire signals a wide as soon as the ball has passed the line of the striker's wicket, and the batting team is awarded one run as well as an extra delivery in the over.

Yorker A bowled delivery that lands at about the batting crease so that the batsman is hitting the ball as it bounces. A difficult delivery to play.

Highland Games

The Highland Games have a long and proud history. Played mostly in Scotland, competitors in the heavy events compete in the traditional costume of kilt and sporran. The games are made up of athletic events, including the triple jump, the high jump and pole vault. The heavy events include putting the shot, throwing the weight, throwing the weight over the bar, throwing the hammer and tossing the caber. There are also cycling, wrestling and tug-o'-war events.

Abuse Any entrant who uses physical or verbal abuse against any official will be reported to senior officials.

Bibs Must be worn by all athletes involved in the games; they must have clearly marked numbers on both the front and back.

Bicycles In all the cycling events, the bikes must have fixed wheels. All loose fixtures such as speed gears, brakes or mudguards are illegal. Handlebars must be plugged.

Catch-as-catch-can style Wrestling method in which both wrestlers are allowed to take hold of their opponent in any way except by the hair, flesh, ears, private parts or clothing. No kicking is permitted, nor are strangleholds, flying mares or hammerlocks. A wrestle is deemed a valid win when the opposing wrestler is pinned by the shoulder to the floor for three seconds.

Costume In all the heavy events, competitors must wear Highland attire, i.e. kilt and sporran. In the athletic events, competitors must wear bibs and are banned from advertising on their clothes except for the sponsoring companies. In the catch-as-catch-can style of wrestling, competitors must wear jock straps and shorts with stockinged feet or rubber gym shoes.

Cumberland and Westmoreland wrestling To start off, both wrestlers must hold each other by standing chest to chest and placing their chins on each other's shoulders with their right arm wrapped around the opponent's body. The wrestlers are not allowed to kick, and a successful wrestle is called when any part of the body besides the feet is on the floor.

Dead heat If two or more competitors are deemed to have tied in a qualifying race, then they will both go through to the next round.

Finish line Fabric is stretched over the finishing point and tied to two posts, one on each side of the track. A competitor is judged to have finished a race when their torso crosses the line.

Heavy events The shot put, throwing the weight, throwing the hammer, throwing the weight over the bar and tossing the caber.

High jump Each competitor is allowed three attempts at each height. Diving or somersaulting is illegal.

Judges All judges should be placed at least 4.4yd from the winning post in line with the finish.

Light field events Include the high jump, pole vault and triple jump.

Obstruction Any competitor who is deemed to have blocked or jostled another entrant will be disqualified from their race or game and reported to the general council, who will then decide on disciplinary action. Any competitor in a track event who is placed on the inside and then runs wide to prevent another runner from passing will be penalized in the same way.

Pegs All starts must be pegged down, and the pegs should be clearly marked with the distance of the race on them.

Pole vault Each competitor is allowed three attempts at each height.

Putting the ball The ball should be made of stone or metal and be round in shape. It should weigh between 16 and 22lb. The ball is thrown from the shoulder with one hand, and is taken from behind the trig.

Rope The rope used in the tug-o'-war should be a maximum length of 12ft.

SGA The Scottish Games Association, the governing body that ensures adherence to the rules in all events.

Spiked shoes All entrants for races up to and including the 43yd must wear spiked shoes for their races.

Starter's orders For sprint events, the starter's orders are: "Get to your marks", "Get set", and "Go", the last of which will be signaled by the shot of a pistol. Any competitor who goes over the mark with hands or feet when under starter's orders will be penalized. For all races up to and including the 437yd the penalty is to be put back 3.3ftm, for the 875ydm the penalty is 6.5ft and for the one mile the penalty is 16ft. If a second offense is committed, then the penalty is doubled, and a third offense results in disqualification.

Stopped race Officals have the power to stop an event for safety reasons.

Throwing the hammer The hammer should weigh between 16 and 22lb. It should have a round metal head and a wooden or cane handle. The hammer should measure no more than 4ft 2in. When making the throw, the competitor should be positioned behind the trig and in a standing stance.

Throwing the weight The weight is made of metal with a ring and chain attached. It should weigh between 28 and 36lb and should measure no more than 18in. The throw is taken from behind the trig, and only one hand is allowed to be used.

Throwing the weight over the bar The maximum weight is 56lb. The competitor must use one hand, and can choose the height of the bar to throw over; however, once chosen, the bar must then be kept at that height.

Tossing the caber There is no standard length or weight for the caber. The competitors can choose from where they take their throw, and can take any length of run that they want.

Trig Made of wood, it measures 6in high and is 4.5ft long. In the shot put, hammer and weight for distance games the competitors must make their throws from behind this point. They should have one foot behind the trig prior to making their throw, and both feet behind the trig on completion.

Triple jump The jump is made into a sandpit. Each contestant is permitted three attempts and can take any length of run. If they fall back after taking a jump, it is deemed a foul.

Tug-o'-war Teams are made up of five or eight players. The anchor man is the only team member allowed to put his heel in the ground. The remaining players must have their heels raised at a height of 0.25in at all times. The players must remain standing, and no hand-over-hand pulling is allowed. A yellow card is given for any infringements of the rules. Any further fouls result in disqualification of the offending team.

Youth races The minimum age for entry is 10 years old and the maximum age is 16. In open events, entrants must be no younger than 17.

Hurling

Hurling is a Gaelic field game contested between two teams of 15 players. Players attempt to score a goal using a hurley to strike or carry the ball toward their opponent's goal. A goal is scored when the ball enters the goal between the two goalposts and under the crossbar.

71yd line The line behind which the players must stand when the game is kicked off. It is also used for a free puck after the ball has been played over the end line by a defender.

Ball The ball has a cork center with a cover of horsehide. It weighs 3.5-4.5oz and has a circumference of 23–25in.

Caman Another name for the hurley stick.

CAMAN: The paddle-like stick, larger than a hockey stick, used to hit the ball in hurling

Carrying The method of taking more than three steps while in possession of the ball.

Crossbar The horizontal pole connecting the two goalposts. It measures 7yds

Disallowed The term used to describe a goal that has been ruled out. The referee has either seen an infringement, or one of the attacking players has entered the parallelogram before the ball. The goal does not stand, and play restarts from where the incident took place.

Duration The game lasts for 70 minutes with a maximum interval of 10 minutes at halftime, when the teams change ends.

End line The line at the end of the field. If the ball runs over this line, then play stops and the ball is awarded to either the defensive or attacking side, depending on who touched it last.

Expulsion A player can be sent from the field of play if they are found guilty of violent or threatening conduct. The whole team can be disqualified and suspended for rough play.

Free puck This is awarded if the referee feels that an infringement has taken place. It is taken from where the infringement took place, unless the offense was committed by a defender in the 22ydarea, or if a player was fouled after delivering the ball.

Goal Scored when the ball is hit under the crossbar and between the goalposts.

Goalkeeper The defensive player who stands in the parallelogram trying to stop the attacking side from scoring a goal.

Goalpost There are two goalposts at each end of the field, each measuring 16ft high. The crossbar connects the two goalposts.

Goal umpires There are four of these officials in a hurling match, with one standing next to each goalpost, and they determine if a goal has been scored. If the ball passes beneath the crossbar, the attacking team gains three points.

Halftime The period during which the game is stopped, exactly midway through the match. Teams are allowed a maximum interval of 10 minutes, after which they change ends for the start of the second half.

Hurley A curved stick with a broad blade that is used to strike the ball. It measures 36in long and 4in at its widest, tapering to each end. It weighs 20-24oz

Linesman One of two officials who control half of each sideline. They determine when the ball has run out of play and change ends at halftime.

Parallelogram The area directly in front of goal. Attacking players are not allowed to enter this zone without the ball, and the goalkeeper cannot be charged within this area, unless he has the ball or is obstructing an opponent.

Pitch A standard playing surface measures 159x98yd.

Point A point is scored when the ball has passed between the goalposts but over the crossbar.

Puck-out When an attacker runs the ball over the end line, the defending side is awarded a puck-out. It is taken from within the parallelogram, and all opponents must be beyond the 71yd free puck. When a defender runs the ball over the end line, the attacking team is awarded a free puck on the 71yd line, opposite where the ball crossed the line.

Referee The official who controls the game on the pitch. He makes all final decisions and keeps track of the time.

Sideline The line that runs up the length of the field. The ball remains in play as long as it does not cross this line or the player with the ball does not cross over the line.

Side puck Given against a player who runs over the sideline with the ball. It is then taken as a free puck from where the ball crossed the line.

Sliothar Gaelic name for the ball.

Solo run A distinctive feature of the game where a player runs as far as he can get with the ball balanced or teed up on the stick.

Stoppage A period in which the referee halts the game and the clock is stopped.

Tackling A player is permitted to charge an opponent shoulder to shoulder. They can also strike another player's hurley, but only if both are striking the ball at the same time.

Team Each side consists of 15 players, and can have three substitutes.

Throw-in The referee throws the ball in between opponents to start play again after the interval. A throw-in also occurs after simultaneous fouls by opposing players, and if play has been interrupted.

Shinty

Shinty is a Gaelic field game played between two teams of 12 players. The aim of the game is to use a caman to hit the ball and score as many goals and points as possible. A match lasts for 90 minutes, and the team that scores the most points wins the game.

10yd area The area that an attacker is not allowed to enter without the ball. The goalkeeper is not allowed to go out of this area.

10yd hit Awarded to the defending side if an attacker has run the ball over the byline without a goal being scored.

Attacker A player whose role is to score as many points as possible.

Ball The ball is made of cork and fabric with a leather covering. It weighs between 2.5 and 3.5oz, and has a circumference of 7.5–8in.

Byline The line that runs along the width of the pitch and signals the end of the playing surface. Once the ball crosses this line, play is stopped.

Caman The club used to hit the ball. It is wooden and should not stand higher than hip level. The head of the club (otherwise known as the *bas*) must pass through a ring 2.5in in diameter. The *bas* is triangular.

Caution The referee can warn a player for an act of misconduct committed on the field.

Center spot The spot in the center of the pitch from where the game is started.

Corner hit If a defender runs the ball across his own byline, the attacking side is awarded the ball from the 2yd quarter-circle. A goal can be scored directly from a corner hit.

Crossbar A pole connecting the front two goalposts at each end of the field. It measures 12ft long and is 10ft above the ground.

Defender A player whose role is to try to stop the attacking players from scoring a goal.

Duration The game lasts for 90 minutes, with a halftime interval of five minutes. Extra time is permitted for a penalty hit to be taken.

Extra time The period at the end of the match that is added on for a penalty hit to be taken.

Field The field is rectangular and normally measures 80 × 110yd.

Flag post There are four flag posts positioned at each corner of the rectangular field. They must measure no less than 3.5ft high.

Goal A goal is scored when the ball is placed between the goalposts and under the crossbar and has gone fully over the goal line.

Goal judge One of two such officials who stand at each end of the playing field. Their role is to observe goal scoring, fouls from within the 10yd area, and to judge whether the ball has crossed the goal line.

Goalkeeper The player whose role is to stop the attacking team from scoring a goal.

Goal line The line marking the end of the 10yd area. It is the area from where the goalkeeper aims to defend his goal. An attacker is not allowed in this area without the ball.

Goalpost There are four goalposts at either end of the field measuring 10ft high. The fronts of the goalposts are white.

Hit in Awarded to the opposition if the ball is accidentally hit over the sideline. The hit is taken from where the ball went out of play. The ball is put back into play by an overhead hit with the back of the caman. A goal can be scored directly from a hit in.

Linesman Four of these officials are each responsible for one half of each sideline. They determine when the ball has crossed the sideline and which player has hit it.

Offside An attacker is offside if he is caught inside the 10yd area without the ball.

Penalty hit Awarded against a defender for a foul in the 10yd area. All players, except the striker and goal-keeper, must stand at least 5yd from the ball. The striker places the ball on the penalty spot and hits the ball directly toward goal.

Penalty spot The spot from where a penalty hit is taken.

Players Each team has 12 players, with a maximum of two substitutes.

Set blow Penalty imposed for any kind of infringement committed against their opponents. The ball is placed on the ground at the point at which the infringement took place.

Sideline The 160yd-long line running up the length of the field. The ball has to stay within the sidelines in order to remain in play.

Suspension A player can be ordered off the field by the referee for rough or reckless play.

Throw up Taken directly after a goal has been scored and to restart a half. The referee starts the game by blowing his whistle and throwing the ball to a minimum height of 12ft between two opposing players who are stood on the center spot.

SHINTY: A Gaelic stick and ball game of Scottish origins

Lacrosse

Lacrosse is played by men and women; for a women's team there are 12 players on each side, and for a men's team there are 10 players. The game is played using a stick with a triangular-shaped net on the end, and play is conducted by catching, throwing or carrying the ball. The team scoring the most goals is declared the winner of the match.

9yd arc The section of the field directly in front of the goal circle joining the circle and goal lines to an extended area that is linked by an 9yd arc.

13yd fan The area measuring 13yd and shaped in an arc from the goal circle.

Ball Made of rubber with a circumference of 7.75–8 in and weighing 5–5.25oz.

Blocking When a player gets in the way of a defending player who is in possession of the ball without giving them the opportunity to move clear and avoid bodily contact.

Body checking The action of a defender who, without physical contact, makes the opposing player change direction.

Critical scoring area Measures from 16yd in front of the goal circle to 10yd behind the goal circle with a width of 16yd either side of the goal circle.

Crosse-checking The action of a defender who uses their crosse to try to remove the ball from the opposing player's crosse.

Deputy A player on the defending team who is permitted to enter the goal circle when the goalkeeper is outside the goal circle, providing their team is in possession of the ball.

Draw The point at which the game begins. Two players from each team stand at the center line with their crosses held high, parallel to the center line.

Expulsion foul Applies to any player caught fighting. The offending player is

sent off and barred from the next game.

Field This area usually measures 120 × 70yd and is divided into two main halves encompassing three main areas: the defensive area, the wing area and the attack area.

Field crosse Usually made of wood, leather, nylon, rubber, plastic, fiberglass or gut. The crosse is 36–44in long and the pocket is made up of four or five thongs that are cross-laced with 8–12 stitches. The pocket has a maximum depth of 2.5in. The total weight of the field crosse must be a maximum of 20oz.

Free position The term given to a foul. It is always awarded to the player who is fouled, and must be taken with all other players at least 4.4yd away.

Free space to goal Not marked on the field, but a space delineated by two invisible lines drawn from the ball to the outside perimeter of the goal circle. This area defines the lane to goal within the scoring area.

Goal crease A circle of 9ft radius. The middle point of the crease is the center of the goal line.

Marking When a player shadows an opposing team member within the length of a stick.

Penalty lane The area used by the attacking team to take up a free position, given to them because of a foul. The area must be free of all other players. The area is measured within the scoring area in front of the goal line.

Personal fouls Covers slashing, cross-checking and any general roughness that the umpire deems excessive. The penalty includes being suspended for one to three minutes and the ball being given to the opposing team.

Pick In which a player without possession of the ball forces an opposing player to move in a differing direction.

Playing time Consists of 50 minutes' full time split into two halves, with a 10-minute interval at halftime.

Signal flag Used by the umpire to indicate to the players any fouls that have been committed.

Slashing An aggressive technique involving the use of a crosse to swipe at an opposing player, aiming for either physical contact or impact with their crosse. An umpire can rule that a foul has been made without actual contact.

Slow whistle Describes a foul committed against the attacking team in the scoring area. A foul is given only if the attacking team has not scored a goal.

Substitutions May be made any time during which the ball is not in play. There is no limit to the number of substitutes allowed, and players who have been substituted may re-enter the game at any point.

Technical fouls These encompass such actions as interference, stalling, pushing or holding. The sanction for these offenses is a 30-second penalty against the offending player if the affected team had possession of the ball during the foul; if the offending team had possession of the ball when the foul was committed, then the ball is passed over to the other team.

Throw Occurs when the ball has gone out of play. Two players from opposing teams stand 1yd apart while the umpire, at a distance of 4-9yd away, throws the ball into the air to continue play.

Uniform All players must wear rubber-soled shoes, a helmet with a face guard and mouthguards, a throat protector and chest protector. Goalkeepers are allowed to wear padding on arms, legs, shoulders, chest and gloves.

LACROSSE: Players use a stick with a net on the end to catch the ball and then pass or shoot it

Field Hockey

Field hockey is played with 11 players on each team. Players use their hooked hockey stick to control, dribble and hit the ball. The object is to score goals by putting the ball in the opposing team's goal. The team to score the most goals wins the match.

Aerial Used to propel the ball over a greater distance and usually to pass it over defenders for the forwards. An aerial is not allowed to land in the opposing D. It is sometimes also nick-named Bold or Daz.

Aerial pass Playing the ball in the air rather than along the ground.

Aluminium Recently introduced alternative to wooden or kevlar sticks. Banned at some levels of the game.

Astro Short for Astro Turf (that's trade-marked), the artificial playing surface used for most senior hockey matches in place of grass fields. Astro-Turf ensures a consistent and level playing surface, particularly during the winter months when grass fields could be unplayable. Astro-Turf fieldsare one reason for the gradual eclipse of Asian nations at international level.

Back pass Enables the game to move more smoothly and helps a team put itself into a better position by passing the ball backward to another player before attacking.

Back stick An illegal shot in which the ball strikes the rounded face of the hockey stick.

Ball The hard ball has a circumference of 8.8–9.2in and weighs 5.5–5.75oz. It is normally white.

Bully The name for the set play that is used to restart the game, similar to a drop-ball in soccer, from where the infringement took place. Two opposing players stand facing each other and tap each other's sticks and the ground three times. All other players must be at least 16ft away until the ball goes into play.

Center pass A set piece used to start a game and to resume play after a goal has been scored. It is always played from the center line and the ball must be passed back to a teammate.

Closing down Method used against an opposing player in possession of the ball to maneuver him into position in order to make a tackle. The tackling player should force the opposing player into as small as space as possible to limit his room for maneuver in order to try to take the ball from him.

Corner hit Taken on the back line by an attacking player within 5yd of the corner flag but nearest to where the ball crossed the back line. Once the ball has been struck, this player may not touch the ball until it has been played by another player of either side.

D The semicircular area around the goal. In order to score a goal, an attacker must shoot from within this area, or the ball must come off a defender's stick within this area.

Dangerous play Fouls consisting of a dangerously raised ball, playing while lying on the floor, tackling from the wrong direction and any other action that threatens another player. It is penalized by temporary suspension from the game.

Dribble Skillful, fast run with the ball kept close to the hook of the stick.

Duration The game is split into two 35-minute halves with an interval of 5–10 minutes. The teams change ends at half-time to even out any advantage gained in the first half due to wind direction, sun low in the sky or other factors.

Feet The gaining of an unfair advantage by use of a foot. It does not have to be intentional.

Field The field is rectangular in shape and has a length of 100yd with a width of 60yd. The field is split in two crossways by a center line and then split again with a 25yd line in each half of the pitch and nearest to each goal. The shooting areas are 16yd semicircles.

Flick An action where the ball is pushed with the stick along the ground or raised into the air. It can be used to put the ball over an opposing player's stick or to raise the ball when taking a strike at the goal. It is also used to take a penalty stroke.

Formation The lineup of a team during the game according to the tactics of the coach. The most popular formation used to be 1–2–3–5 involving five forwards, three half-backs, two full-backs and the goalkeeper. However, more common formations are now 1–1–3–3–3 or 1–3–5–2.

Fouls A player is not allowed to lift his stick above shoulder level when playing or about to play the ball, block an opposing player with his stick or body, push or shove, charge or trip the opposition, stop the ball or catch it, strike the ball with the rounded face of the stick or touch the ball unless using the stick.

Free hit Awarded to the other team for any foul committed outside of the goal area.

Goal The goal is 4yd wide, 7ft high and 4yd deep. A goal is scored when the ball is put into the net from within the 16yd circle. For a penalty corner, the shot must hit the back board, otherwise the goal is disallowed.

Green card A warning card issued to a player for foul play.

Helmet Worn by a goalkeeper with a face-grille for protection of the face, along with gauntlets, leg, chest and abdomen guards.

Hit Used to move the ball long distances such as when shooting at goal, taking free hits or passing cross-field.

Indian dribble A dribbling method originating from Asia in which the left hand rotates the stick while the right balances it.

Kevlar A composite material providing greater strength than traditional willow for field hockey sticks.

Knuckle wrap Half-glove made of synthetic material used to protect a player's left hand on Astro Turf.

Long corner Taken on the back line by an attacking player within 5yd of the corner flag, but nearest to the point where the ball crossed the back line. Once the ball has been struck, this player cannot touch the ball until it has been played by another player of either side. A hit taken on the sideline.

Man-to-man marking This involves defending players each being responsible for defending against specific attacking players from the opposing team.

Misconduct Applies to time wasting, dangerous behavior or any other general bad behavior. If a captain is deemed not to be fulfilling his role satisfactorily, he can be penalized for misconduct.

Obstruction Blocking another player's passage to the ball. This rule is upheld much more stringently than in soccer.

Officials Two umpires on the field of play who are responsible for half the field each diagonally, and stay in their own half for the entire game. They use a whistle to control the game. Either one or two timekeepers can be used.

Offside Occurs when a player is positioned in front of the ball and player at the moment the ball is played within their opponent's 25yd area. A free hit is awarded to the defending team.

Pass back Always taken from the center of the field and used to start the game, restart after halftime and after a goal has been scored. All players must be in their own half of the field, and opposing team members must be at least 5yd from the ball. See "Center Pass".

Penalty corner Awarded to the team that has been fouled within the circle. The corner can be taken anywhere along the goal line, but it has to be at least 10yd from the goalpost. Infringements that merit this award include deliberately playing the ball over the back line, and fouls committed within circle, at a corner or within the 25yd fix.

Penalty stroke Awarded to the attacking team when they have been intentionally fouled in the circle. The ball is placed 7yd away from goal on a marked penalty spot, and a designated attacker attempts to score against the goalkeeper. The attacking player is allowed only one stroke, which can be a scoop, push or flick – but not a hit.

Playing distance The term used to describe the distance within which a player is able to play the ball.

Playing the ball Players are allowed to control the ball only with the flat side (left side) of their sticks. The only exception is the goalkeeper, who can kick or move the ball with their feet or pads when in their own circle.

Push-in Occurs when a team puts the ball over the sideline, leaving the opposing team to take the push-in. All players must be at least 5yd away. They are often taken quickly to surprise the opposition.

Push pass Used to move the ball speedily over shorter distances. With no backlift, the stick stays in contact with the ball as the stick is followed through.

Red card Denotes instant dismissal for serious foul play for the rest of the match. Also usually followed by a long suspension.

Reverse-stick push The stick is reversed to propel the ball to the right, usually over short distances.

Rolling substitutions The continuous replacement of one player by another throughout the game, as long as each side has only 11 players on the field at once.

Scoop An aerial stroke played with the body facing the direction in which the ball is propelled.

Scoring For a goal to be valid, the ball must have been hit by an attacker from within the circle and have fully crossed the goal line between the goal posts and the crossbar.

Shorty Slang name for short corner. A hit taken from the back line within the D. A maximum of five defenders including the goalkeeper is allowed on the goal line. The remainder must be beyond the halfway line. Attackers must stop the ball outside the D before shooting from inside it.

Sin bin Area where a player sits when he has been shown the yellow card and been temporarily suspended from the match. The sinbin is usually behind a goal or by the corner.

Sixteen-yard hit Taken at or within 16yd of where the ball went out of play on the end-line. The ball must be hit or pushed at ground level, and all players must be at least 5yd away until the ball has been struck.

Specialist Until a recent rule change, this was a player who came on merely to hit short corners. This is no longer permissible in the rules.

Square pass A pass across the field of play to change the point of attack.

Starting play The two team captains toss a coin to decide who will start the game or which end of the field they will defend in the first half.

Stick The left-hand face of the head is flat, while the right-hand side is rounded. Players may only strike or touch the ball with the left (flat) side of the stick, otherwise a foul is called. The total weight of the stick must not exceed 28oz or be lower than 12oz, and the diameter of the shaft should not be more than 2in.

Sticks A foul tackle caused by one player's stick hitting another's instead of the ball or when a player raises the stick above the shoulder when attempting to play the ball, which is also an infringement.

Substitutions The maximum number of substitutions allowed is three.

Suspension The referee can send a player off the field for five minutes' playing time for certain offenses. Also refers to a ban received by a player for subsequent matches following the award of a red card against him.

Teams Each team is allowed 16 players, but only 11 at a time are allowed on the field.

Through pass Used to get through the opposing team's defense. The attacking player passes the ball between defenders to a team member or into a space for them to move on to.

Triangle A formation used by three midfield players as part of their defensive strategy.

Umpires The two officials who stand on the field of play to officiate in a match. Each umpire is responsible for half the field split diagonally and can stop the game when a foul takes place.

Wall pass When a player passes the ball to a team member, who immediately passes it back in order to pass a defending player.

Yellow card Awarded for foul play that places the offender in the sin bin for a period at the umpire's discretion.

Zonal marking Describes a tactic in which members of the defending team defend a specific area of the field by creating a zone. The zone's focus is on the area of greatest danger and each defending player is responsible for a specific attacking player's movements in their own area of the zone.

2

Court Games

This section includes those games played on courts, either indoor or outdoor, as well as table tennis, which is not played on a court but is closely related to tennis. They are mostly played with rackets or hands hitting balls through or over nets or against walls.

Sticks and Balls

Baseball Has a cork center that is surrounded by yarn and two strips of either cowhide or horsehide that is stitched together.

Caman The stick used to play hurling and shinty with. Curved in shape with a broad blade which is used to hit the ball.

Cesta A wicker basket that is made of a chestnut frame and covered with woven reed. A leather glove is sewn to the outside so that a pelota player can wear it and is fastened with tape wound round the glove.

Cheese A thick flat disc that is made of a hard wood and is used in skittles to knock over the targets.

Club There are three main types that golfers use to play with, a wood that is used for long shots, an iron that is used for shorter shots and a putter that is used for playing the ball on the putting green.

Cue Must be of a traditional shape and a minimum of three feet. Used to play snooker, billiards and pool.

Mallet Used to play croquet with. Can be any length. The head is made of wood but metal may be used to weight and strengthen the mallet.

Paddle Made of wood and is either oval or square in shape. A leather thong is attached to the handle and worn around the wrist. Used to play paddleball.

Pelota Has a hard rubber core which is covered with a layer of linen thread and several layers of goatskin. It has a diameter of 2in and weighs 4.5oz.

Puck Made of vulcanized rubber or other approved material. Weighs 5.5-6oz.

Shuttlecock Usually made of 16 feathers that are fixed into a cork base. A combination of natural and synthetic materials are used.

Basketball

Basketball is a fast indoor game played with two teams of five players each. The object of the game is to score as many baskets as possible by shooting the ball through a hoop high up at both ends of the court. The winning team is the one that has scored the most points after two halves of play.

Air ball A missed attempt at shooting a basket that fails to touch the rim or backboard

Alley-oop pass When the ball is passed to a team member positioned near the basket who, on receiving the ball, scores in a smooth and fluent style.

Assist A pass to a team member that directly results in a basket.

Ball Round, and made from leather, rubber or synthetics, it should have a circumference of 30-31in and weigh 21-23oz.

Backboard Supports the basket, and normally made of hardwood or clear plexiglas. It can measure either 6 × 4ft or 6 × 3.5ft. The bottom and sides of the board are normally padded to prevent injury to players when jumping up to score a basket.

Backcourt violation When the team in possession passes the ball back into their own half of the court or fails to advance the ball past halfcourt in 10 seconds.

Bank shot When the ball rebounds off the backboard and into the net.

Baseball pass A one-handed over-head pass.

Baseline The end line, situated 4ft behind the backboard.

Baseline drive When a player makes a drive along the baseline to attack the opposing team's basket.

Basket The orange hoop through which the ball must go for a player to score. A net underneath slows the ball,

to confirm that the ball has indeed passed through the hoop. The net is made of white cord hanging from small metal rings. A basket is also the name given to the score awarded for putting the ball through the hoop, worth two points on most shots.

Bench Situated on the sidelines of the court, this is where the substitutes sit throughout a game.

Between-the-legs-dribble When an offensive player dribbles the ball between his own legs to keep a defensive player from being able to steal the ball.

Blocking An illegal move by a defender to impede the ballhandler by making contact.

Bounce pass Used to get the ball past a defender to the receiving player. The bounce can be made with one or two hands. Ideally the pass should be bounced quickly and hard to prevent the ball from being intercepted by the opponent.

Boxing out A strategy used to prevent opposing players benefiting from grabbing rebounds.

Bucket Slang term to describe a basket.

Centers Usually the tallest players on the court, whose role is to score from close range. They play in the key area, and must therefore be good rebounders and passers.

Charging foul When an attacking player charges into a stationary defender.

Charity stripe Another name for the free-throw line.

Chest pass One of the most commonly used passes. The ball is held between the finger pads, with the thumbs meeting at the back of the ball. The ball is held against the chest with the elbows extending outward. The ball is then thrown in a straight line to the receiver. This can be a powerful pass, as the player is able to put their full weight into the throw.

Court The size of the court varies according to the level at which the game is being played, but the features of the court remain the same for all. The court is split into two by a center line, around which are two center-circles. Each end of the court has a free-throw line, bordered by free-throw lanes. These lanes both have a semicircle with a 6ft radius from the center of the free-throw line. The boundaries of the court are marked by the sidelines and end lines, and there should be at least 3ft of unobstructed space beyond them. The court must have a hard surface.

Crossover dribble When an offensive player dribbles the ball from one side of his body to the other, as if he is going to move in that direction, then switches the ball back to the other side of his body to catch the defensive player off balance.

Dead ball Describes when the player has been whistled dead by the referee.

Double dribble This ballhandling offese occurs when a player dribbles the ball, stops dribbling by holding the ball with one or both hands, then resumes dribbling. The opposing team is awarded possession of the ball.

Double foul When two players commit a foul at the same time, resulting in a jump ball.

Double team Also known as a trap. Occurs when two defensive players cover one offensive player.

Downtown The slang name given to the area outside the three-point arc. Placed 8yd from the basket, shots from this area are worth three points.

Draft System used by the National Basketball Association in America to sign up amateurs from colleges and high schools to the professional game.

Dribble Using one hand at a time, the ball is bounced onto the floor. The player can remain still or move across the court while dribbling. The dribble ends when the player catches the ball. They are not allowed to start dribbling the ball again until another player has touched the ball.

Dunk A one or two-handed shot where the player jumps to reach above the level of the basket and slams the ball into the hoop. One of the most exciting shots in the game.

Elbow A player is penalized for use of the elbow by the opposing team being awarded two free throws. If the elbow comes into contact above the shoulder, then the offending player is often ejected from the game.

Fake When a player pretends to make one move but actually makes another to trick an opponent. Similar to a dummy in soccer.

Fast break Taken from a defensive position, this is a quick counterattack with the aim of scoring before the opposition have had a chance to regroup.

Field goal Also called a basket, and worth either two or three points depending on where the shot was taken.

Forfeited game A game is conceded if a team does not have five players ready by 15 minutes after the official start of play, is not on the court within one minute of the referee's signal, or does not have at least two players on the court.

Forwards Aim to score as many baskets as possible during a game. Forwards play close to the basket, and must be good shooters and rebounders. They are usually taller than guards, but shorter than centers.

Free throw A shot taken from the free-throw line that has been awarded for a penalty. Worth one point.

Front court The half of the court where the offensive team needs to be in order to score a basket.

Full-court press When a team aggressively defends the whole of the court area and not just its own half.

Goaltending When a shot is blocked by a defensive player as it is on its way down toward the basket, or when a defensive player touches the ball as it is directly above the basket or on the rim. This is illegal and gives the offensive team an automatic two points. Offensive goaltending occurs when an offensive player touches the ball as it is directly above the basket or on the rim. The penalty for offensive goaltending is loss of possession of the ball.

Guards Usually the shortest players on the court, but also the quickest. They need to shoot from long distance, and excel in dribbling and passing.

High post The spot taken up by a player at the top of the key area, farthest away from the basket.

Hook shot The player starts with his back to the basket. He quickly pivots around in a continuous movement before jumping and extending his shooting arm to flick his wrist to release shot toward the basket.

Incidental contact When two opposing players come into contact without a deliberate foul or violation.

Intentional fouls When a player commits a personal foul without attempting to play the ball, such as pushing an opposing player. Two free throws are awarded to the opposition.

Interference If the ball is on or above the basket, it is illegal for any player to touch the basket or backboard.

Jump ball The ball is thrown into the air by an official between two opposing players to start the first or second half, or after a double foul has been committed or if two players from opposing teams have gained possession of the ball at the same time. The two players must stand in the half of the circle nearest to their own baskets.

Jump shot A one-handed shot that is released while the player is at the top of a jump.

Key The keyhole-shaped area extending from the baseline under the basket to just beyond the free-throw line.

Lay up Occurs when a player runs through the key area and lays the ball into the basket with a one-handed shot, which often rebounds off the backboard before going into the basket.

Legal guarding position The position a defensive player will adopt against an opposing player by placing both feet on the floor in a normal straddle position.

Live ball The ball is deemed live when it is first tapped from the starting jump ball. Also when it touches a player on the court, when it has been thrown in and when it is shot on a free-throw attempt.

Low post Taken up by a team's center, they situate themselves at the lowest point of the key area nearest to the basket.

Man-to-man A defensive strategy in which a player directly guards an opposing player instead of an area on the court.

Motion A style of offense where a group of players all move together at the same time to create scoring opportunities.

MVP An award given to the "most valuable player".

NBA The National Basketball Association, which is in charge of the professional league in the USA.

No-look pass A flashy play where an offensive player looks in one direction as a fake, then throws a pass in another direction without looking at his actual target.

Officials The referees, the scorer, the timekeeper and the shot-clock operator.

One-on-one A single offensive player taking on a single defender during play.

Outlet pass Develops a defensive rebound into a fast break.

Out of bounds A player is out of bounds if he touches or goes beyond the boundary lines. The ball is deemed out of bounds if it touches any player or object in this area. The ball is then awarded to the team not in contact with the ball before it went out.

Overhead pass The ball is held in the same way as for a chest pass, but is thrown from over the head.

Overtime Five minutes of extra play are added on when the game ends in a tie.

Pass The movement of the ball from one player to another.

Passing lanes The area that is difficult for a defensive player to defend with his hands. These include over the top of the head, either side of the defender's head, either side of the defender's feet and under the defender's arms.

Personal fouls Includes a wide number of contact fouls, such as pushing, tripping or holding.

Pivot The action a player will use while in possession of the ball to move in any direction while still keeping one foot in contact with the floor.

Playmaker Another name for the ball-handling guard, also known as the point guard.

Possession indicator Displays and indicates which team will gain possession of the ball in the next held-ball or double-foul situation.

Rebound When a player gains control of the ball after a missed shot.

Scoring If a player's feet are on or inside the three-point line when scoring a goal, they receive a two-point field goal. If a player's feet are not on or inside the three-point line, then a three-point field goal is awarded. Free throws are worth one point each.

Screen When an offensive player reaches a spot first and remains stationary, leaving the defending player to maneuver around him and therefore slowing his progress.

Shot clock Rules how long a team is allowed to be on the offense before attempting to score a goal. The clock is stopped at the end of each period of

LAY UP: A short-range shot flicked toward the backboard and basket

play, and when the whistle is blown for a foul, a violation, a held or jump ball, suspension of play or time-outs. The shot clock is reset after each made or missed shot.

Slam dunk A player jumps spectacularly into the air at a considerable height and throws the ball down hard into the basket to perform a slam dunk (see also "Dunk").

Starting The visiting team chooses the end from which to start, and the teams change ends at halftime. The game is started with a jump ball, and both teams must have five players on the court.

Strong side The side of the key area into which the attacking team has passed the ball.

Substitutes Substitutes are allowed to sit on the bench. They can enter play only during a dead ball and when the clock has been stopped. Substitutes are not allowed to take over from a player shooting a free throw unless he is injured.

Technical fouls Fouls that have to do with behavior rather than play, such as arguing with referees or fighting between plays. Players and coaches are ejected from the game after two technical fouls each.

Ten-second rule A team in possession of the ball in the backcourt has 10 seconds in which to move forward with the ball into the frontcourt. They are not allowed to return to the backcourt with the ball.

Three-point play When a player who is fouled while scoring a two-point basket goes on to score one more point from the free-throw line.

Three-point shot A shot taken from outside the arc that scores a basket.

Three-second rule No player is permitted to stay in the restricted area between the opposing team's end line and free-throw line for longer than three seconds at a time when his team is in possession.

Time The game is split into two halves of equal time, with a break for halftime. If the game ends in a tie, then an extra five minutes are added at the end.

Traveling When a player carries the ball rather than dribbling it correctly.

Uniform Players must have their numbers clearly marked on both the front and back of their jerseys.

Verticality Used to ensure that a player has a legal position. A defender who already has moved into a position and raises his arms and hands within the vertical plane is in legal position, and therefore should not be charged with a foul if an offensive player comes into contact with them.

Violations When a player breaks the rules without physical contact being involved. Includes double dribbling, kicking or hitting the ball. No foul is charged for a violation, but the team in possession of the ball loses it. Any time the ball goes out of bounds, it is automatically awarded to the opposing team of the player who last touched the ball.

Weak side Describes the opposite side of the key area from which the attacking team has the ball.

Zone Used as a defensive strategy to cover areas of the court rather than individual players.

SLAM DUNK: A player jumps high above the basket and slams the ball home in dramatic style

Netball

Netball is predominately a women's game, and is played between two teams of seven players. Players score points by putting the ball through a ring at the opponent's end of the court. Players are not allowed to run with the ball, but can pass it by throwing it to their teammates.

Airborne throw When the catching player grasps the ball while in the air, and then releases the ball before their feet have relanded on the court.

Attacking team The team in possession of the ball attempting to score a goal.

Back-line The boundary lines at each end of the court.

Back-line throw-in Takes place when the ball has gone out of court and is taken from the back-line.

Ball Weighs 14–16oz and has a circumference of 27–28in. Either made of rubber or leather.

Banding The term used to describe the strips that divide the court.

Bending The movement of a player when taking a curving course.

Center circle The marked circle in the centre of the court where play is started and restarted after a goal has been scored.

Center court The middle third of the court.

Center pass The name given to the pass used to start the game and restart play after a goal has been scored.

Chest pass A fast, two-handed pass delivered from the chest area.

Clearing When a player moves to clear space for another player to move into.

Court Measures 100ft long by 50ft wide. It is divided into three equal sections with a center third and two goal thirds. Each goal third contains a goal circle, which is a semicircle with a radius of 16ft. The center third contains a center circle which is 3ft in diameter and is placed in the center of the court.

The goalposts are 10ft in height and the rings have a diameter of 15in.

Court linkage Used by the players to make the most of the space on the court and the position of team members by passing the ball down the court.

Cues Used by players to signal to one another the best time to pass the ball, and when and where to reposition on the court.

Dead-ball situations When play is stopped and then begun again from a stationary position, in other words at a throw-in, a center pass or a free pass.

Defending team The team without possession of the ball, and which is trying to prevent the opposition from scoring a goal.

Double marking When two players guard a single opposing player to ensure that the player remains without the ball.

Dummy run When a player moves into a space as if to receive a pass to fool the opposing team, but is really creating space for another player to receive the ball.

Feed An exact pass made into the shooting circle.

Feint pass When a player pretends to aim a pass in one direction while actually releasing the ball into a completely different area.

Footwork rule Applies to the player in possession of the ball who is limited in movement.

Free pass Awarded to the opposing team for a penalty incurred.

Goal-circle The name given to the

semicircle that marks the shooting area at each end of the court.

Holding position Where a player in possession of the ball is deciding in which direction to pass, while in a static position.

Lunging Using one leg to make a long stride while the other leg remains still.

Man-to-man Used as a defending tactic where each player is assigned to a single opposing player and is expected to mark them continuously throughout play.

Marking Used by both teams to prevent the opposing team from gaining possession of the ball by closely monitoring each player.

Obstruction When an opposing player blocks any movements that interfere with a pass or shoot. A penalty pass or shoot is awarded to the offended team.

Officials Two umpires who each take half of the court, two scorers who keep a record of the score and a timekeeper.

Offside When a player enters a part of the court that is off limits to the position in which they are playing. A free pass is awarded to the opposing team.

Overhead pass A two-handed pass that is taken from above the head. Effective in delivering the ball over the opponent's head to another team member.

Penalty pass Awarded to the opposing team for any penalty incurred involving obstruction or contact. The offending player must stand to the side of the opposing player and is not allowed to move until the ball has been released.

Penalty shot The same rules apply as for a penalty pass, but if the penalty occurs in the shooting circle then a shooter can either shoot or pass the ball.

Pivoting When the player keeps one foot on the ground and swivels on it to point in a different direction.

Rebounding When a player jumps to recover the ball after a missed shot at the goal.

Repositioning Moving to another position having passed the ball.

Reverse handing When a player uses the hand farthest away from the opposing player to reach toward the ball to try to make a deflection.

Reverse pivot A maneuver used to change direction in which the player swivels on the foot nearest to the opposing player and therefore moves in a different direction.

Rolling off Describes a movement in which a player will bend away from the opposing player and quickly turn their back while moving in a different direction.

Shooting circle The goal circle from where players can take a shot at goal.

Shoulder pass Taken from shoulder height and used by a player to project the ball accurately across a long distance.

Substitutes Up to three players are permitted in the event of injury or illness. Substituted players are not allowed back on court.

Throw-in Used to put the ball back into play when it has gone out of the court.

Toss-up Used to put the ball back into play when the referee is unable to award possession to either team.

Transverse lines The two lines that divide the court up into thirds.

Teams Each team has seven players.

Under-arm pass A one-handed pass that is taken from below the waist area and is used to pass the ball to a fellow team member who is close by and unmarked.

Zone defense The name given to the method a team will use to defend a specific area of the court by trying to intercept the ball when it moves through the zone.

Korfball

Korfball is played between two teams, each positioned within a zone on the court. Each team contains four men and four women, and a player scores a goal by throwing the ball into the opponent's basket. It is a passing game, and physical contact is not allowed.

Attacker A player whose objective is to score goals.

Ball The ball is very similar to a size 5 soccer ball. Its weight at the start of the game must be 15-17oz and its circumference must be 27-28in.

Basket A long, cylindrical post made of wood or metal with a net attached to it at the top. Players throw the ball toward the basket in an attempt to score a goal. The posts are fitted into the ground or a base. The basket measures 15.7in wide and 10in deep. The goalposts measure 12ft high.

Boundary line The line marking the end of the playing field. For play to continue, the ball must stay within this line.

Center line A line running down the center of the court. The throw-off is taken from this line to get each half under way.

Court The court is divided into two equal zones. It measures 44yd by 22yd and is marked out by clearly visible tape. A grass court is marked by white tape, while other types are marked by yellow tape.

Cutting An attacker runs so close to another attacker that the defender cannot follow the first attacker without the risk of colliding. This is deemed to be an offense only if the first attacker goes on to throw for goal.

Defender A player who tries to stop the opposition from scoring.

Dribble Bouncing the ball while moving down the court.

Duration There are two halves of 30 minutes, with a halftime interval of 5–15 minutes, after which the teams change ends.

Extra time The period added on at the end of the game to compensate for any stoppages that have occurred during the game.

Flags Positioned at each corner of the playing field, they mark the end of the playing surface and measure about 5ft high.

Foul The referee awards a free pass against the team whose player has been penalized.

Free pass Awarded to the opposition after an offense has been committed or if the ball has gone out of play. The pass is taken from where the offense took place, or where the ball went out of play. Players from the opposing side must keep a distance of at least 8ft until the player has taken the free ball.

Halftime The period separating the two halves, lasting 5–15 minutes.

Interference Otherwise known as hindering. Players are not allowed to prevent the free movement of other players by physical contact or other forms of obstruction.

Linesmen Two of these officials judge when the ball has crossed over the sideline and out of play. They will also signal to the referee if they feel a foul has been committed.

Moving with the ball Players are not allowed to run with the ball. If a player stops with the ball they can pivot on only one foot.

Out of play Once the ball has crossed the boundary line, the ball is deemed to be out of play and a free pass is awarded against the side that last played the ball.

Penalty Awarded against a team for any kind of offense that stops an attacker from scoring a goal. The penalty is taken from the penalty spot, 8ft in front of the opposing team's post.

Penalty spot The mark from which the penalty is taken.

Playing areas Each time a team scores two goals, the players move into the other zone. After the players have moved into the other zone, defenders become attackers and attackers become defenders.

Playing the ball Players can use their hands to catch and pass the ball. They cannot use their fists, legs or feet to play the ball and must not play the ball while they are lying on the ground. Players are not allowed to play the ball outside their own zone, unless they play the ball in the air after jumping from that zone.

Stoppages Periods in the match when play comes to a halt and the referee stops the watch – for example, when a player is injured. Any time lost in the game is added on in an extra-time period.

Substitute A team is allowed to bring in two substitutes for tactical reasons. If a player is injured, then the referee can allow further changes.

Teams A team consists of four men and four women. During the match, two men and two women are positioned in each zone.

Throw off At the start of the game and at the beginning of the second half, the ball is thrown off from the middle of the center line in the attacking zone. After a goal has been scored, the team that conceded the goal takes a throw off.

Throw up The method of restarting play by the referee. The referee throws the ball up between two members of opposing teams, who jump up in the air to challenge for the ball.

Zone The court is split into two separate zones, the defending zone and the attacking zone.

KORFBALL: Using a ball similar to a soccer, teams attempt to score goals by throwing it into a basket

Volleyball

Volleyball is a court game played by two teams of six players who use their hands or arms to hit the ball over a net. The winning team is the one that scores the most points – achieved by making the ball touch the ground on the opposition's side of the court.

Assisted hit A player is not allowed to be helped by a team member or object in order to reach the ball, but if they are about to commit a fault then they will not be penalized if a teammate pulls them back to prevent them doing so.

Attack hit A hit aimed into the opposing team's court. Serves are not considered attack hits.

Attack lines These separate each side of the court into a front zone and a back zone. The lines are parallel to the net, and are 10ft from the center line. A player in the back row may try for an attack hit if they are behind the attack line or when they are in front of the line, providing that the ball is lower than the top of the net.

Back row Consists of three players who are placed in the back zone when the serve is made.

Ball Round and made of leather, with a circumference of 25.5–27in and weighing between 9 and 10oz.

Beach volleyball Version of the game played on the beach, generally with only two or four players per side. It was a demonstration sport at the Atlanta Olympic Games in 1996.

Block When one or more players stop the ball before or just after it crosses over the net.

Change of court After each set the teams change sides of the court. Their fellow team members have to change benches as well.

Combination attack Used by two or more players to confuse opposing play-ers. They approach the net together, and the opposing team will not know who is going to attack and from which area.

Court The area is divided into two by the center line that runs under the net. On either side there is an attacking line that is 10ft from the net. The court is 20yd in length with a width of 10yd.

Covering the smash Occurs when a player is smashing the ball. Their fellow teammates close in around the player in case the opposing block sends the ball

BEACH VOLLEYBALL: A glamorous outdoor version of the sport, rapidly growing in popularity

back into their court, giving them a better chance of playing the ball before it reaches ground level.

Dead ball When the referee blows the whistle or when play stops.

Delay When a team takes too long to substitute a player or delays play for other reasons. The penalty for a first delay is a warning by the referee, and the penalty for a second delay is the loss of the rally.

Dig The term given to the action by a player who first puts the ball over the net unless the player is making a block.

Dig or bump pass When the ball is played on a player's outstretched fore-arms. This move is used when the ball is either traveling very low or moving very fast.

Double foul When players from both teams commit a foul at the same time. The point will be replayed.

Double touch When the ball touches two parts of a player's body in succession, or when a player touches the ball twice in a row.

Dump The action of a player tipping the ball with their fingertips just over or to the side of the block.

Fault Results in either a lost serve or the opposing team being awarded a point.

First referee Positioned at one end of the net.

First pass Once the ball has been received by a serve or a smash, the first pass is the one made to the setter.

Floating service When the ball moves through the air without any spin, giving it the appearance of floating in the air. The serve can dip or swerve suddenly when the speed of the ball drops.

Foot fault Occurs when a player while serving places a foot over or on the back line or when any player puts a foot over the center line into their opponents side of the court.

Front-row A player positioned in the front zone between the attacking line and the net.

Hand grip The hands must be kept together with the fingers of the right hand placed across the fingers of the left hand. The thumbs should then be touching along the outside edges.

Held ball Occurs when two players hold the ball at the same time above the net during a blocking maneuver. The point is replayed.

Hit Any contact that a player has with the ball.

Hook serve When serving the ball, a player may make a circular arm movement, which starts from the thigh area and finishes in contact with the ball above the head.

Interval The break separating the sets of play, each lasting for three minutes.

Kill A spike that cannot be returned, giving the attacking team a point or a sideout.

Line judges Either two or four used, positioned either at the corner of the court or at the service area. They decide whether balls are in or out, signal when a ball crosses the net outside of the crossing space and when a server foot-faults. They also authorize game interruptions, substitutions and time-outs.

Match The best of three or five sets.

Net Placed over the center line, the mesh net is 3.3ft deep and 31ft long. The height should be 8ft for men and 7.3ft for women, and it has a 2in canvas band at the top.

Overhead serve The ball is held directly in front of the hitting arm just above shoulder height. The ball needs to be only a short distance from the net to clear it.

Penetration Involves moving a back-row setter into the front court in order to perform a set. A front-court setter can then act as a third smasher.

Playing fault Any breach of the rules by a player taking part in a game. Always results in a loss of rally.

Point cap Used when a game ends without a clear winner. A team wins by being ahead by two points or reaching 17 points first.

Rally The complete number of hits between the teams. The team that wins the rally wins the serve.

Recovery dive Enables a player to put the ball in front or to the side of the opposing players. The point is saved by diving toward the ball and playing it on the back of the hand before landing.

Red card Penalty given by the referee for a more serious offense, resulting in a loss of serve.

Rotation order When a team gains serve they must rotate their players one position clockwise so that a new player is in the serving position. Failure to do so results in a fault.

Sanctions Given for any penalties, usually in the form of a red or yellow card.

Scorekeeper Sits facing the first referee. Logs points and time-outs, and ensures that substitutions are legal.

Screening Involves the serving team blocking the opposing team's view of the server or the trail of the ball. This includes jumping, arm waving or moving sideways as the serve is being made. Also occurs when the server is hidden behind two or more players.

Second referee Positioned near the post outside the playing court opposite the first referee.

Serve This action puts the ball into play. The server uses the hand or any part of the arm to send the ball over the net and into the opposing court.

Service area The server must be in this area when in contact with the ball. The area is bound by the right sideline and the serving line.

Service order Players must follow the service order written on the lineup sheet.

Set A strike that sets up a spike.

Set pass A volley pass that must be played near to and above the net for the smasher to strike.

Setter Normally a specialist player whose purpose is to set up the ball for a spike.

Shoot set Also known as the parallel set. Played fast and low for the smasher to strike.

Short set Played near to the setter and a short distance from the net.

Side out Happens when the serving team does not score and the serve goes to the opposing team.

Spike A hard-driven ball that is hit when trying to score or gain a side out.

Spiker The title given to the player who finishes the attack by hitting the ball across the net fast and hard.

Substitutes Six players are allowed to be used as substitutes, who may only come on to the court when the ball is dead.

Switching System used by the players to change position during the rally to ensure a more effective lineup.

Team A squad of 12 players, only six are allowed on court at any one time.

Three-ball system Three balls in total shall be used during a match.

Time-out Usually used tactically by the coach to give his team advice in between play. Each team is allowed to stop play during any set for two intervals of 30 seconds each.

Tip When a player tips the ball with their fingers; permitted, as long as the player does not throw or hold the ball.

Toss The ball must be thrown up into the air by approximately 20in. The hitting hand is drawn back as the ball is thrown up by bending it at the elbow and then bringing it forward to connect with the ball.

Under-arm serve One arm holds the ball out in front of the body while the other arm is swung back and then forward, making contact with the heel of the hand or a closed fist to loft the ball over the net.

Volley pass Describes the main pass used throughout play. The fingers on both hands are used, ensuring that the ball does not stay or get stuck in the hands.

Yellow card Used by the referee to signify a fault has been committed. If a referee holds up both the red and yellow cards, the offending player is sent off for the rest of the game.

SPIKING: The most dramatic method of winning a point, jumping high to thunder the ball to the floor

Badminton

Badminton is played using strung rackets (similar to tennis rackets, but smaller, more flexible and much lighter) and a feathered shuttlecock by either two or four players on a marked rectangular court. It can be played indoors or outdoors, although games normally take place in a draft-free indoor environment. The object of the game is to score points by hitting the shuttlecock over the net into the opponent's half of the court, so that it hits the ground before they are able to return it.

Backhand strokes Shots that are played to the left of the body for a right-handed player, or to the right of the body for a left-handed player. A backhand may be played from in front of the player for delicate shots at the net.

Basic strokes Six basic strokes can be played: overhead, shoulder high and under-arm, on both the forehand and backhand. From these basic shots come a vast range of variations.

Block return A shot with very little follow-through, which drops steeply once over the net.

Brush Similar to the "Tumble" but played when the shuttle is high to the net and generating greater, point-winning pace.

Changing ends Players change ends after each game, and in the middle of the third game – when the leading scorer reaches six points in an 11-point game or eight in a 15-pointer. If the players forget to change ends, they must do so as soon as they remember and all points remain.

Clear A difficult shot played from the back of the court to the back of the opponent's court.

Court The size of the court is different for singles and doubles matches: 17 × 44ft for singles matches, and 20 × 44ft for doubles.

Doubles A game of badminton between four players, two on each side, played on the larger-sized court.

Doubles sideline This marks the width of the court to 20ft and the inbounds area for doubles matches.

Fault Occurs when the shuttle: lands outside the court; passes through or under the net; does not pass over the net; touches the roof, ceiling or any side walls; touches a player or player's clothing; touches any person or object out of bounds; is caught, held and slung on the racket; is hit twice in a row by the same player on the same play; or if both partners in doubles hit the shuttle before it is returned to the other side. A player also commits a fault if the shuttle is in play and he: hits it when it is on the opponent's side of the net; touches the net or posts with his racket, clothing or any part of his body; has his racket or any part of his body over or under the net; or obstructs an opponent's stroke.

Forehand strokes Shots played in front of or to the right of the body for a right-handed player, or in front of and to the left for a left-handed player.

High-lift A shot played from around the middle of the court high and to the back of the opponent's court.

In-play A shuttlecock is in play until it: hits the floor; hits the ceiling or goes outside the court; hits a player or a player's clothing; hits the net or post and drops on the hitter's side of the court; or gets stuck in the net or suspended on top of it.

Left service court One of two boxes on both sides of the net marked by the boundaries of the short service line, long service line (doubles), center line and singles sideline. When facing the net from either side, this is the box to the player's left.

Length of play The match is continuous, ending only when one player or team has won the required number of games. A rest of five minutes is normally allowed in international matches between the second and third games.

Let A call that halts play when: a shuttle is suspended on the top of the net,

NET: The net in badminton is much higher than in tennis, some 5ft above the ground at its top

passes the net and then becomes caught on the other side of the net; a player touches the net or posts with his racket, clothing or any part of his body; a player has his racket or any part of his body over the net, or obstructs an opponent's stroke.

Long service line The line from within which serves must be made. The line for doubles matches is 19ft from the net on both sides. The line for singles matches is a further 2ft from the net and also marks the back boundary.

Love The zero score from which all competitors begin games and matches. This is termed "love-all". When one player or team has won a point the score moves on to "one-love" or "love-one" – the first score in each case being that of the serving player or team.

Markings The court is normally marked by white or yellow lines. Their 40mm width is included within the overall court dimensions.

Net Stretches across the middle of the court, and over which players must hit the shuttlecock. It is stretched between two posts so that the top of the net is 5ft high with a mesh 2.5ft deep.

Net return Played close to the net, a shot that is lifted just over the net and drops steeply on the other side.

Overhead shots Played when the racket makes contact with the shuttle above the player's head.

Overhead smash When above the player's head, the shuttle is struck powerfully and steeply downward either in front of or to the side of an opponent. An attacking move intended to win the point.

Position of readiness A position on court to which all players should return between each shot. Usually in the middle of the court, it enables them to deal quickly and appropriately with their opponent's return.

Racket foot The right foot for a right-handed player or the left foot for a left-handed player.

Rally A series of shots between opposing players, starting with a serve and ending when the point is won.

Receiver The player in a singles or doubles match who returns the opening shot of the server.

Scoring Only the player or team serving can score a point. Women's singles games are normally scored to 11; men's singles and doubles games to 15. If a women's singles game is tied at 9–9 or 10–10, the side that reaches that score first may "set" the game. When a game is set, the score is known as "love-all" and it is the first player to reach either two or three points (as agreed) who wins. If the game is not set, then the winner is the first player to reach 11 (women's) or 15 (men's and doubles) points. Matches are normally decided by the best of three games.

Server The server is the player who starts off the point by hitting the shuttlecock over the net to their opponent.

Service The service is the shot that starts a play or rally. When the server is serving even points (e.g. 2, 4, 6), he must stand in the right-hand half of his service court; when the server is serving odd points, he must stand in the left-hand half. In doubles, the non-server can stand anywhere on his side of the net. The receiver must not move until the server has served. The server must: keep both players apart while serving, as must the receiver while receiving; be within the boundaries of the service court, touching no lines; hit the base of the shuttle first; make initial contact with the shuttle below the server's waist; have all the racket's head clearly below the hand that holds the shuttle at the moment of contact; serve in a continuous motion.

Short service line A line 6ft from the net on both sides beyond which all serves must land.

Shoulder-high shots Played to the side of the body when the racket makes contact with the shuttle at the height of the player's shoulder.

Shuttlecock The feathered object that players hit back and forth over the net with their rackets, also known as the "shuttle" or the "bird". It is made from 16 feathers in a cork base, and there are various weights available that determine the speed of its flight. Synthetic feathers are also used.

Singles sideline Marks the width of the court to 17ft and the in-bounds area for singles matches.

Slice Achieved by angling the face of the racket when it makes contact with the shuttle.

Stab A shot played at the net designed to fall steeply and tight to the net on the opponent's side.

Starting the match The winner of the toss of a coin or shuttle, or of the spin of a racket, chooses whether to serve or receive first, or from which end of the court to begin.

Top slice A way of top-spinning a driven shot so that the shuttle loops downward as it passes over the net.

Tumble Another shot designed to drop suddenly and tight to the net. Played when the shuttle is close to and low to the net. The shuttle "tumbles" head over tail.

Umpire The official in charge of the match who may also be assisted by a service judge and a line judge.

Walls In international competition, the recommended space between the perimeter of the court and any surrounding walls is 7.5ft from baseline to the wall and 7.2ft from sideline to the wall. In any other form of competition the distances are 5ft and 4ft.

Tennis

Tennis is a racket game played on a court of two halves, separated by a net. It is played by individuals (singles) or pairs (doubles) whose object is to hit the ball over the net, landing within the confines of the court with the aim of preventing your opponent from being able to hit it back.

Ace A winning service shot on which the receiver is unable to hit the ball.

Advantage The player who wins the point after deuce has "advantage" and will win the game if he wins the following point. The name of the player with advantage is called to indicate who has the point (e.g. "Advantage Brown").

All The score indicating that both players or partners have the same score (e.g. "30-all").

All England Lawn Tennis Club The most prestigious club in world tennis was founded in 1874 from the All England Croquet Club, and boasts Wimbledon as its home.

Association of Tennis Professionals (ATP) Founded in 1972 by leading men's professionals to represent the interests of professional players.

ATP Tour Formed in 1988 as a joint venture between the players and tournament directors of nearly every major men's professional event except the four Grand Slams. There are now over 80 tournaments in the Tour's calendar. Players earn ranking points reflecting their success in each tournament.

ATP Tour World Championship Located in Hannover, Germany, this year-end final features the top eight ranked players of the season competing for the prize fund of $3.3 million (1999).

Backcourt The area between the service line and the baseline.

Backhand A stroke played across the body with the back of the hand facing the direction of the strike. For a right-handed player this would be a shot playing a ball in front of or to the left-hand side of the body.

Ball Made of hollowed rubber, covered in a variety of colors (traditionally yellow or white).

Ball boy/girl Retrieves balls during the match and supplies them to the players.

Ball-in-court A ball that lands on a line is considered to have landed within the area of the court, even if it only touches the outside edge of the line.

Ball-in-play This is the time from the moment of a serve until the point has been won.

Baseline The line marking the back of the court.

Baseline player A player whose style is to play ground strokes from the backcourt and who avoids approaching the net.

Break point The point on which the receiver can win the game. If the receiver wins a game they are said to have "broken serve".

Cat gut Material from which racket strings were originally made. Now almost all are synthetic.

Centerline A line that runs through the centre of the court connecting the two service lines on either side of the net.

Chalk On a grass court, the lines are marked with white lines, known as "chalk". If a ball from the opponent lands on the line, there is often a puff of white powder from the line marking, known as "bringing up the chalk".

Changing ends Players change sides

on the court after the first game of every match and every two games thereafter, and in the middle of a tiebreak.

Chop A stroke that generates large amounts of backspin.

Chopper grip Also known as the frying-pan grip, this refers to the way the racket can be held when serving.

Court The playing surface can be made of grass, clay, varieties of concrete and carpet. It is divided by white lines which are part of the official playing area. The lines denote the left and right service court, the backcourt, the baseline, the service line, the singles sideline and doubles sideline. It is 78ft long, 27ft wide for singles and 36ft for doubles.

Covered court An indoor court with an artificial surface.

Cross court When the ball is hit from one side of the court diagonally to the other (right to left or vice-versa).

Cut A quick stroke that produces under spin on the ball.

Cyclops The electronic device which monitors the service line. It beeps when the ball lands beyond the line allowing the line judge to call "fault".

Davis Cup A challenge cup contested for by men's national teams comprising four singles and one doubles match. The competition is based on straight elimination, although there are regionalized preliminary rounds before the top eight national teams join the fray during the latter stages.

Deep shot A shot that lands at the back of the court near the baseline.

Deuce Deuce is reached when both players have 40 points (i.e. 40-all). To win the game from this point, a player must win two consecutive points or the score will keep returning to deuce.

Double bounce When the ball bounces twice before a shot is played, the receiver loses the point.

Double fault A player who serves a fault on his second serve is said to have made a double fault and loses the point.

Doubles Played under the same rules as singles, but with two players on each side on a wider court and with a different order of serving and returning. Partners take turns serving (once every four games therefore) and can change their order only at the start of a new set. Similarly, partners decide whether to receive serve from the left or right-hand service court for the duration of a set. Players can hit in any order during a rally.

Drive Usually played from the back of the court, this is a stroke that is played after the ball has bounced once.

Drop volley A cushioned volley played close to the net causing the ball to just clear the net and drop with very little pace on the opposing side.

Eastern grip Another name for the grip required to play a forehand shot.

Fault A fault is called when the rules of play are broken. A point is lost by failing to hit the ball before it has bounced twice, hitting the ball out of the court, failing to hit the ball over the net (a player is allowed to play the ball around the net), hitting the ball more than once (deliberately or otherwise), if a player touches the net, ball or net post, or hits the ball by projecting the racket.

Federation Cup This is the women's equivalent tournament of the Davis Cup, and is an elimination event competed for by national teams.

Final set The third or fifth set of a match. Whoever wins the deciding set wins the match.

First service The first of the two allowed attempts to serve at the start of any point.

Flushing Meadows Synonymous with hosting the U.S. Championships Grand Slam tournament.

Follow-through This is an essential

part of any shot, and refers to the swing and motion of the racket after initial contact has been made with the ball. The follow-through affects the direction and power of the shot.

Foot fault Called when either foot touches on or inside the baseline or is on the wrong side of the baseline center mark at the moment of serving.

Foot-fault judge An official who rules whether a foot fault has been committed.

Forehand The forehand is played with the palm of the hand facing the direction of the strike. For a right-handed player this would be a shot in front of or to the right of the body.

Game "Game!" indicates the end of a game and is called when a player scores the winning point of a game.

Game point The point being played that will result in one of the players winning a game.

Grand Slam The Grand Slam events are the four most prestigious on the professional tour: the Australian Open, French Open, Wimbledon Championships and U.S. Open Championships.

Grand Slam Cup An annual tournament for the 12 men and eight women who performed best during the four Grand Slams of the year.

Grip The leather or synthetic-covered handle of the racket.

Ground stroke A shot played after the ball has bounced on the ground, usually made at the back of the court.

Half volley A shot that is played just as the ball hits the ground.

Head The area of the racket that is strung and used to strike the ball.

International Tennis Federation (ITF) The worldwide governing body for tennis with authority for the game and its rules.

Kick serve A serve that is hit with topspin, causing it to bounce high upon hitting the ground. This type of serve can be difficult to return with accuracy.

Let Called when it is judged that the point should be played again. This is most commonly called on a serve if the ball hits the net but lands within the appropriate service court.

Linesman An official who observes a line and decides whether a ball has landed in play or not.

Lob A high, looping shot designed to clear an opponent who has advanced toward the net, and which lands at the back of the court.

Love Zero score for either player (e.g. 15-love or love-15).

Lawn Tennis Association (LTA) British tennis's governing body.

Match A tennis match is decided over the best of three or five sets.

Match point The point on which a player may be able to win the whole match if he wins the next point.

Mixed doubles One man and one woman on each side contest a match over the best of three sets.

Net Suspended between two 3.5ft posts, and reaching 3ft in height at the centerline, the net divides the court into two symmetrical sides. This is also the term given to a shot that hits the net.

Net cord A taut piece of cloth strung over the middle of the net and fixed to the ground.

Officials An umpire, a net-cord judge, a foot-fault judge and linesmen.

Out Called by a linesman when the ball lands outside the boundary lines of the court without first bouncing into play.

Overhead A shot played when the ball is above the player's head. The most common overhead shot is the smash.

Passing shot A shot played to either side of an opponent that looks as if it ought to be retrievable, but that passes them. As long as the ball is not called out, this is a winning shot.

Poach In a doubles match, you poach a shot if you play one that your partner should have played.

Post The support for the net at either side of the court.

Racket A racket can be a maximum of 29in long and 12.5in wide. They are made of a variety of materials and can be of any weight. The surface is strung with a pattern of crossed strings.

Racket abuse When a player slams their racket into the ground or net in frustration. Can result in a warning from the umpire or docking of points.

Racket tension The tautness of the strings on the racket. Different players prefer different tensions.

Rally The term describing the series of shots once a point has begun. A rally continues until the point contested has been won or lost.

Rankings The list of players sorted according to success. Tour rankings are headed by the player who has scored the most competition points over the previous 12 months.

Receiver The player who is receiving the shot from the server.

Referee The official who has overall authority for a tournament.

Return of service The first shot of a point played by the receiver of the service.

Reverse shot A shot that deflects to the side when it bounces.

Roland Garros The stadium made famous for hosting the French Open – one of the four Grand Slam events.

Rough or smooth? When deciding who will serve first or to select initial ends of court, a racket is normally spun and a player calls either "rough" or "smooth". Whether the strings fall rough side or smooth side up determines who makes the choice. Also known as "up or down". The alternative is to toss a coin.

Scoring The scoring comprises points, games and sets. Play begins with no points (love-all). The first point scores 15, the second 30, the third 40 and the fourth the game. If play reaches 40-all (called deuce), the next point won is called advantage to the winning player, and the game is then won by winning the subsequent point. The score can return to deuce indefinitely if a player keeps losing the point that would win them the game.

Second serve After a service fault on the first serve, the server is given a second chance to make a good serve, the "second serve". This is normally a softer serve than the first one to give the server a higher chance of the serve going in.

Seed There are normally 16 seeds in a competition. A seed is a player who is considered to be among the most likely to win that tournament. The draw for a tournament is arranged in such a way that the seeds cannot play each other until the later rounds. In theory, the first and second seeds should play each other in the final.

Serve Every point is started with a serve. Each game begins by hitting from the right side of the court into the left-hand service court and from alternate sides from then on. Both feet must be either behind the baseline when the serve is struck. The ball is tossed into the air and is struck in a similar manner to an overhead smash. The server has two chances to make a good serve.

Service break A serve is broken when the receiver wins the game.

Service court On each side of the net there are two service courts: left and right. These are boxes bounded by the singles sidelines, the service line and the center line. As a player faces the net, his left service court is to his left and his right service court to his right.

Service fault Can be for a foot fault, not serving into the correct service court, hitting the net with the ball, or running or walking while serving.

Service line Marks the back edge of the service courts and lies between the net and the base line.

Set A set consists of up to 12 games and a tiebreak – except for the final set, which must be won by two clear games, and therefore has no limit. A set is won when a player has won six games with at least a two-game advantage. If the score is 6–5, then the set can be won 7–5; at 6–6 the set goes to a tie-break.

Set point A player is said to have "set point" if he is in a position to win the set on the next point played.

Shake-hand grip Another name for the grip on the racket required to perform a forehand shot.

Singles A singles match is one played between two players.

Slice A stroke that applies spin to either cause the ball to swerve in the air and/or stay low after bouncing.

Smash A powerful attacking shot played when the ball is above the head.

Straight sets A player is said to have won a match in straight sets if he wins without conceding a set.

Tiebreak To prevent long matches, a tie-break is played to decide the winner of the set when the game score is six-all. The first player to score seven points, with a minimum two-point lead, wins the tie-break and the set. They are not normally played in the final set.

Top spin The ball is hit with a rising action and an exaggerated follow-through, causing the ball to dip in flight and drop into the court sooner than it would otherwise have done; this increases the speed and bounce of the ball on striking the ground.

Top-spin lob A lob that has had top-spin applied in order to make the ball fly high, then drop into court beyond the opponent.

Toss The way in which a player throws the ball up for a serve.

Tramlines The parallel lines that run the length of the left and right-hand sides of the court. The outer line is the "doubles sideline" and the inner line is the "singles sideline". The ball must not bounce within the tramlines during service or during run-of-play in a singles match. In a doubles match the ball may bounce within the tramlines but only during run-of-play.

Two-handed A grip using both hands to hold the racket. It is normally used to get extra power on backhand shots.

Umpire The official who sits in a raised chair in line with the net and who is in overall charge of the match.

Volley Striking the ball before it has bounced.

Wimbledon The home of the All England Tennis Championships, the grass-court tournament held every summer.

Winner To play a shot that is impossible for the receiver to return.

Winning a point The server wins a point by hitting an unreturnable serve or shot. The receiver wins if the server fails to serve the ball in play two consecutive shots (a double fault).

Women's Tennis Association (WTA) This is the equivalent of the ATP for ladies' tennis.

WTA Tour There are more than 50 tournaments in the tour's calendar, and players collect ranking points reflecting their success in each tournament.

WTA Tour Championships The equivalent of the ATP Tour World Championships on the women's tour. The top 16 ranking points-earners over the year compete for the prestigious and lucrative title in New York.

Real Tennis

Real tennis has been played for many centuries, having been enjoyed at Hampton Court Palace by Henry VIII. Although it has been marginalized by lawn tennis, it is still a popular game in some quarters. It is played indoors on a special court as either singles or doubles. The game is scored by sets, and the player to average the most points is deemed the winner.

Ball Between 2.4- 2.5in in diameter, it should weigh between 2.5 and 2.75oz.

Back walls The walls between the floor and the penthouses that join the main wall.

Bandeau The strip of wall situated below the penthouses.

Batteries The name given to the walls between the floor and openings.

Better A chase is deemed as "better" if it is a greater distance from the net and on the same side of the court.

Bisque A stroke that is granted to the opposing player.

Boast A return that strikes a wall on the same side of the net as the striker.

Bobble service A strike taken slowly, which bounces on the penthouse and lands near to the grille wall.

Boomerang service A service that moves from the service penthouse to the grille penthouse to the back wall, and then rebounds to the service penthouse before dropping to the grille wall.

Chase Occurs when a ball drops into the hazard court or anywhere on the service side or in the gallery area.

Coup de cabasse A straight force that falls into the dedans by one of its outside edges.

Coup de chandelle A high return that falls into the dedans.

Coup d'Orléans A return shot that hits the service wall before falling directly into the dedans.

Coup de temps A stroke taken off the back wall, because the ball is too close to the floor for a normal strike.

Court Real tennis uses a four-sided court divided into two areas by a net: the service side and the hazard side.

Cramped odds Handicaps that ban certain services or strokes.

Dedans The openings of the service side, positioned at the back.

Deuce The score when both players have won three strokes.

Double Describes the ball when it falls before being hit.

Drop Occurs when the ball first comes into contact with the floor after passing over the net, or goes through an opening without having touched the floor.

Drop service A high service taken near to the main wall, which lands next to the grille wall.

Du tout When a player has to take only one stroke in order to win the set.

Fault line Placed nearest to the grille, and stretches from the service line to the grille wall.

Galleries Placed opposite the main wall, they are openings that are below the penthouses. On the service side of the court are the line, first, second, door and winning gallery; and on the hazard side of the court are the line, first, second, door and last galleries.

Gallery post Positioned between two galleries, and deemed to be part of the one that is closest to the net.

Giraffe service High underhand shot taken from the side penthouse.

Grille The opening in the grille wall.

Grille penthouse Placed above the grille wall.

Grille wall The back wall that is positioned on the hazard side of the court.

Half court line The line that separates the hazard side from the service side of the court.

Hazard chase/hazard side chase A chase that is made on the hazard side of the court.

Joues The inside vertical walls of the winning and last galleries, the dedans and the grille.

Ledge The horizontal part of the wall that forms an opening.

Love The score held by a player who has not yet won a stroke in the game or a game in the set.

Love game A winning set in which the opposing player did not score a stroke.

Love set A winning set in which the opposing player did not win a game.

Main wall The only wall on court with no penthouse.

Net Measures 3ft at the center and 5ft at the main wall.

Nick Describes when a returned ball touches the wall and floor at the same time when it falls, and is also the name given to the junction of the wall and floor.

Odds Any handicap is called odds.

Out of court Occurs when the ball comes into contact with the walls above the area marked out for play, or if it touches the rafters of the roof or lighting equipment.

Penthouse The name given to the sloping roof of dedans, galleries and grille that reaches along three sides of the court.

Pique service An overhead shot that is taken from the main wall next to the second gallery line. The ball should land near the grille wall and fault line.

Play line This line is marked on the walls to indicate the upper limits of the play area.

Railroad service Taken from the side wall between the last gallery and dedans wall, the railway service is an overhead shot.

Rough The side of the racket where the knots are.

Rest A stroke that starts when the ball is served and ends when it is dead.

Racket A bat made of wood that is used to hit the ball.

Return When the ball moves from one player to another.

Service Used to start a rest.

Service line Nearest to the grille wall and parallel to it.

Service wall Placed above the side penthouse.

Set Each set is a separate unit, and the player has to win a pre-agreed upon number of sets to win the match.

Side wall Positioned under the side penthouse.

Smooth The side of the racket where there are no knots.

Striker The last person who hit the ball.

Striker out The player taking the service.

Tambour The projection on the main wall close to the grille.

Tray The inside part of the lower opening behind the ledge.

Twist service A service that is played underhand and is taken from near the side penthouse. Once the ball hits the grille wall, it moves back toward the side wall.

Wing net Used to protect the marker that is placed in front of the net or post.

Winning gallery Positioned on the hazard side, it is the last gallery.

Winning openings Consists of the winning gallery, the dedans and the grille.

Worse A chase is deemed "worse" if it is made on the same side of the court and nearer to the net.

Table Tennis

Table tennis is played between two players (singles) or four players (doubles). Players use solid paddles to hit a small white ball back and forth across a table divided by a low net. Players take turns to hit five serves in a row, and win a point if their opponent fails to return the ball. The first player to reach 21 points wins the game.

Anti-loop A shot that tends to lessen the effect of spin, and is particularly good against a loop or heavy chop.

Backhand drive A shot with the paddle held at a slightly closed angle so that, using the elbow, the player can move the paddle forward in an upward position hitting the back of the ball at the peak of the bounce.

Backhand push Hit with an open paddle angle putting a slight backspin on the ball. The stroke is short, with movement coming from the elbow, and the player will play a short follow-through. This shot is used to return backspin services and to return short balls.

Backspin A player will purposely put spin on to the ball to make it spin back as it hits the table on the other side of the net, deceiving the opposing player.

Ball The ball is made of celluloid or similar plastic, weighs 0.09oz and has a diameter of 1.5in. It must be white or yellow, with a matte surface.

Base line The white lines around the edges of the table.

Block A stroke a player uses in returning the ball using hardly any movement. They will use the spin and speed already on the ball from the opposing players's shot to get the ball back.

Center line This line defines the area of serve in a doubles game.

Change of service The serve in singles and doubles changes from one player to another after every five points

are scored (by either player or pair). The only time this rule changes is if both players score 20 points, in which case the service changes after every point.

Chop A downward stroke used by a player that produces backspin.

Choppers Players who use a chopping action to hit the ball.

Combination paddle A bat with different textures of rubber on each side.

Controller A stroke enabling the opposing player to perform set exercises or practices.

Counterhit An attacking stroke used against a topspin, drive or loop shot.

Doubles Two players stand at each end of the table and take alternate shots in a rally.

Drive A forceful shot that relies heavily on speed.

Duration A game normally consists of the best of three or five games. There are no stoppages during the game, unless a player claims a two-minute rest period between games.

End line The line at each end of the table. For the ball to remain in play, the ball must not carry over this line.

Expedite system Introduced if a game exceeds 15 minutes in length. It then applies to the rest of that game and the rest of the match. In this system the serve alternates after each point. If the service and 12 successive strokes of the server are returned by the receiver, the server loses a point.

Flick A player uses their wrist as the

main force in the stroke.

Float A shot that produces little or no spin, but has a similar action to that of a chop or backspin.

Forehand drive A shot that is generated from the shoulder, with the elbow held at a slight angle and the paddle slightly closed. The paddle moves in an upward direction to hit the back of the ball at the peak of its bounce.

Forehand push A shot used to play short, low balls and to return backspin serves. The player will play a short stroke with an open paddle, putting slight backspin on the ball.

Free hand The hand with which a player does not hold the paddle, but nevertheless still very important when serving the ball. It must stay behind the end line, or an extension of it, until the receiver has hit the ball back over the net.

Half-volley A player will strike the ball early just after it has bounced.

Hammer grip When a player holds the paddle with no fingers running up the blade of the bat.

High defense A player will play the paddle back with considerable height; this is much more effective when given a large degree of spin. It might be played if a player gets in trouble and wants more time for the next shot.

Inverted rubber Rubber put on to the bat with the pimples facing inward.

Kill A stroke in which a player will aim to win the point using the maximum possible power, so that his opponent has no chance of reaching the ball.

Let A rally between the players from which no points can be scored. This can be due to any number of incidents, but it will be up to the umpire's discretion to call a let when he sees fit.

Loop This stroke produces a very heavy backspin, and the ball travels in a loop before bouncing on the opponent's court. The idea of this stroke is to confuse the opponent with spin and different speed variations at an intense level.

Minute rally Played with two members per team. The number of strokes hit within a timeframe of a minute are then counted, the winners being those with the highest number of strokes.

Net This is stretched across the centter of the table by a cord attached to a post at either end. It measures 6ft long, and the ball must pass over it for a rally to continue.

Obstruction Takes place when the player's paddle, or any item of his/her clothing touches the ball in play when it has not passed over the court.

Out of play As soon as the ball touches any object other than the playing surface, or crosses over the end line, then it is ruled to be out of play.

Paddle This can be of any weight, size or shape. Each side must be of a uniform dark color. For international standards, one side must be red and the other black. The blade should be made of wood and should feel continuous and of even thickness. It is then covered by a rubber surface, no greater than 4mm thick.

Paddle edge A variation of the game where the ball is first hit on the blade of the paddle before then hitting the ball on the edge. The number of successes is scored in three attempts.

Paddle hand The hand in which the player holds the paddle.

Pen grip The grip most used by Asian players, who hold the handle between the thumb and forefinger in a manner similar to that of a pen.

Piggyback singles A game involving two teams with a minimum of two members. One team member climbs on to the back of another player, and each time a point is scored the teams change ends or reverse piggybacks.

Playing area Not less than 15yd long and 8yd wide. The minimum height above the table is 12ft. The minimum area required at the sides of the table is about 3yd at each side and 6yd at the ends.

Playing surface It should be dark colored, normally green, and matte painted with white marking lines around the edge of the table.

Point A player loses a point if he fails to make a good service, return the ball legally, or if the ball bounces twice. A player wins a point if he wins the rally.

Push A stroke used to control and place the ball on the table.

Rally The time during which the ball is in play. The two players will continue to alternate hits until a point is scored. There is no time limit on how long a rally can last, but as soon as the ball goes out of play or hits the net, the rally comes to an end.

Ready position The position a player takes up when they are preparing themselves to take a shot. Normally, a player will stand an arm's length from the table edge.

Receiver The player who strikes the ball second in a rally.

Roll A stroke in which the player uses the wrist to "roll" the bat to return the ball to an opponent.

Sandwich paddle A bat that uses sponge and rubber rather than just rubber as the playing surface.

Scoring A player scores a point by winning a rally. The game is won by the first player to score 21 points. If, however, both players score 20 points, then the winner is the first player to score two more points than the opposition.

Serving The ball is placed in the open palm of the free hand. The ball must be stationary, above the level of the playing surface and behind the serving end line. The server will then throw the ball up into the air without spinning it. It must travel at least 6in. The server can then strike the ball on its descent, but the paddle must stay behind the server's end line. The ball must touch the server's court first, pass over the net and then touch the receiver's court. The receiver will hit the ball to begin a rally.

Shakehands grip This method of holding the bat is most common in the Western world. You can use both sides of the bat when playing a stroke.

Sidespin A player will deliberately put spin on to the ball to make it revolve horizontally when traveling toward the opponent, causing it to curve in the direction of spin.

Smash A forceful shot with an emphasis on speed. It is a power stroke that will have the intention of winning the point. Also known as a flat hit or kill.

Spoilers Defined as players with unusual strokes that do not conform to predetermined guidelines.

Stroke counter The official who counts the number of strokes under the expedite system.

Table This can be made of any material, but it is normally of wood. It must give a bounce of 9in to a standard ball, when the ball is dropped from a height of 12in. It is 9ft long and 5ft wide.

Topspin The spin put on the ball to make it turn in a clockwise direction vertically, away from the striker.

Unforced error An error in which a player loses a point because of his own lack of judgement or skill, rather than through his opponent's attacking.

White line A 0.75in white line around the edges of the table.

Rackets

Rackets is a court game played with a racket and ball. It is generally accepted as the fastest of the traditional court games, and is played by either two or four players.

Appeal Used by a player to request the adjudication of an official when they feel they have been treated unfairly by an opponent.

Bully Another name for a rally.

Court An enclosed four-walled area with a floor space measuring 60ft long by 30ft wide. The back of the court is separated by a half-court line which divides the right-hand side forehand court and the left-hand side backhand court.

Duration There is no set time for each match; the game ends when a pre-agreed score is reached.

Double fault Occurs when a player serves two consecutive faults.

Fault A service is a fault for four reasons: a foot fault; if the ball, when served, first bounces on or before the short line; when the served ball goes on to or under the service or cut line on the front wall; if the ball bounces in the wrong receiving part of the court.

First serve The player who will serve first is decided before the game begins by spinning the racket.

Foot fault When a player, at the moment of hitting the ball, fails to place one foot on the floor within, but not touching, the line that encloses the service box.

Good return Occurs when the player hits the ball above the board without it first having come into contact with the floor, the back wall, any part of the player's body, and before it bounces twice, has been struck twice or flies out of court.

Half-court line Marked on the floor, measuring from the short line to the back wall.

Hand in The player who is serving.

Hand out The player who is receiving serve.

Let The term used when a point is replayed, and the way in which a player can gain recompense for a fault or unfair behavior from an opposing player. These incidents include: preventing a player from gaining a clear view or having a chance to hit or reach the ball; if the ball touches another ball; if a player is prevented from touching the ball due to either being blocked or through fear of injury to himself or the opposition.

Marker The marker is there to assist the referee and take over from the referee if necessary. His job entails calling faults, calling play after a good stroke, calling the score after each rally and calling not-up or out-of-court and keeping a record of the score.

New ball A new ball is used at the start of each game, and at other times if the ball is deemed unfit to play with.

Out ball The ball is deemed out of court if it touches the front, sides or back of the court above the areas marked out for play, or if it touches or moves any of the light fittings or roof area.

Players The game can be played as either a singles (two players) or a doubles (four players) match.

Queen's Club Considered the "home" of rackets since 1887.

Referee The leading official who rules on good returns, lets, foot-faults, continuous play, obstructions and overcut service.

Rally The act of hitting the ball back and forth once the ball has been put into play. A rally is won when an opposing player fails to serve or return the ball. A rally won when by "hand in" is worth one point. A rally won by "hand out" makes that player "hand in".

Serve Striking the ball with a racket and putting the ball into play.

Service board The board positioned across the lower part of the wall. The ball must hit the front wall above this line.

Service box A rackets court has two service boxes, one on either side of the court. The players take alternate serves from each box. At the start of the game and each hand, the server is allowed to serve from either box.

Short line Placed parallel to the front wall and marked on the floor.

Single-service rule Employed in America and Canada, where a server does not receive a second serve after committing a fault on the serve.

Striker The player who returns the serve after the ball has hit the front wall.

Scores The first player to reach 15 points is the winner, except when the score reaches 13-all, when the receiver may decide to "set" the game at five or three. This means that the first player to reach either of these scores is then the winner. Likewise if the game reaches 14-all for the first time, then the receiver may again decide to set the game at three, meaning that the first player to reach three is the winner. In both these instances, the receiver is also allowed to decide to elect no set. If this occurs then the first player to reach two points at 13-all or one point at 14-all is the winner.

T&RA The Tennis and Rackets Association, which is the governing body of the two sports.

World Rackets Championships The premier title in the sport, which has been contested since 1820 and takes place every year.

Squash

Squash is a racket sport that is played on an enclosed four-walled court. The ball can be bounced off any wall within the marked lines, but every shot must come off the front wall before hitting the ground. It is normally played by two players, but doubles squash is also a recognized sport. The object of the game is to win points by ensuring that your opponent is unable to return your shot before the ball bounces twice.

Appeal A player's means of asking the referee for an on- or off-court ruling, either for a change in the marker's finding or for a let to be allowed. This is a relatively frequent occurrence in squash matches, because of the confined nature of the game and the close proximity of the players to one another.

Ball Squash is named after the ball used to play it, which can be squashed between finger and thumb. It weighs 12.7–13oz and is made of rubber. The degree to which the ball will bounce is indicated by a colored spot: yellow is the slowest, followed by white, blue and red, which is the fastest.

Boast A shot played to the front wall via a side wall or the back wall.

Cutline The middle line on the front wall above which the ball must travel, without first hitting a side wall, when a serve is made.

Court Measures 32ft long by 21ft wide. The backcourt is divided by a short line and then divided again by the half-court line. The front and side walls are used during play to rebound the ball.

Down Expression used when a serve strikes the board or tin or fails to reach the front wall. It is also used when the ball strikes a player before it has bounced more than once.

Drop shot A shot hit softly just above the tin, landing close to the front wall

Duration There is no set time limit, as the winner is the player who gets the best from five games. There is a 90-second break between each game in competitive matches.

Fault Occurs when the ball comes into contact with the walls, floor, ceiling or any other objects before being served, or if the ball is served against any part of the court before coming into contact with the front wall. Also if the ball is served on to or below the cutline but above the board, if the ball's first bounce lands on or outside the short or half-court lines of the quarter court opposite the server's box.

Foot fault When the player who is serving fails to have one part of their foot on the floor within the service box but without coming into contact with the service box line.

Game ball When the server needs one point to win the game.

Good return When the ball, having bounced only once, is struck against the front wall above the board without previously coming into contact with the any player's body or clothing.

Half-court line Marked on the floor, it runs parallel to the side walls. It divides the back of the court into two displaying a T-shape where it comes into contact with the short line.

Hand in When a player has the serve.

Hand out Occurs when a change of server is made.

Interference A player must make every effort to give his opponent the opportunity to hit the ball without obstruction or hindrance of movement. If there is interference, a let is given, but not if the player does not make an effort to return the ball.

Losing serve A server loses serve in the following circumstances: when the serve first hits a side wall, floor or ceiling; when part of one foot is not on the floor in the server's box, with no part of that foot on the box line when he strikes the ball; when the ball bounces on or outside the short or half-court line of the quarter court opposite the service box; when the server fails to hit a serve; when the server does not strike the ball correctly, when he hits the ball more than once or carries the ball with the racket; when he serves the ball out; when he is struck by his own serve before the opponent can strike at it.

Let An undecided point that is replayed. Rallies are replayed when a striker hits the ball in a manner that does not ensure the safety of his opponent; a player is distracted by an occurrence off the court; the receiver is not ready for the serve and doesn't attempt to return serve; the ball breaks during play; or court conditions affect play. A let is also given if a player cannot get to the ball because of obstruction, or he fears for the safety of his opponent if he attempts to hit the ball.

Marker The second official whose job is to aid the referee. His duties include calling play, the score, faults such as a foot fault, a not-up, a down, an out or a hand out. The marker must repeat all of the referee's decisions.

Match ball When the server needs one point to win the match.

Nick The junction between the side or back wall and the floor. If the ball lands on this point it can often stop dead.

Not up A call of not-up applies when the striker does not hit the ball properly, when the ball bounces on the floor more than once before being struck, when the ball comes into contact with a player's body or clothing, or the server attempts to hit the ball but fails to do so.

Knock-up Period directly before a game when the players hit the ball to each other to warm up both themselves and the ball.

Obstruction Occurs when a player deliberately blocks the opposing player and hinders their play. The referee can award the rally to the opposing player in this instance.

Out A ball that hits the out line or the wall or fittings above the out line.

Out line Top line of the court below which the ball must remain. If a player hits the ball above the out line, the ball is out and the point is lost. It travels around the front, side and back walls.

Penalties These include a warning by the referee or awarding a stroke, game or match to the opposing player. Behavior that will incur penalties includes obscene language or gestures, any kind of verbal or physical abuse, being argumentative with the officials, abusing the racket or ball, dangerous play, unnecessary physical contact, returning late to the court or taking too much time to warm up.

Points Can only be awarded to the server. When the server wins a stroke, he gains a point; when the receiver wins a stroke he becomes the server.

Quarter court One half of the back part of the court, divided into two equal parts by the half-court line.

Rally A series of shots by players during a game that begins with a serve and ends with the ball no longer in play.

Racket The maximum length of the racket is 27in with the strung area being no bigger than 7.25in wide by 8.5in long. The string is made of gut and the rest of the racket was traditionally made of wood – although most modern rackets include at least some composite materials.

Reasonable backswing The act of moving the racket away from the body before making contact with the ball; a backswing is deemed reasonable when the movement is not excessive. An extreme backswing occurs when the player's racket arm is held extended toward a straight-arm position.

Reasonable follow-through The reasonable continuation of movement by a player after the racket has come into contact with the ball. An excessive follow-through occurs when the player's racket arm is extended in a straight position with the racket also extended straight, or when in that position the player swings the racket into a wider arc than that of the line of flight of the ball.

Singles A game of squash between two players who play up to nine points, with the best of three or five games. Players take a 90-second break between games.

Set one When the score reaches 8–8, the receiver may call "set one"; the first

NOT UP: Is called by the referee when the striker fails to hit the ball correctly

player to reach nine points wins the game.

Set two When the score reaches 8–8, the receiver may call "set two"; in this case, the first player to reach 10 points wins the game.

Server The player who begins a rally with the opening shot. Only the server can score points. When the receiver wins a rally, he wins serve. The server may choose which service box he starts serving from.

Service The act of putting the ball into play to begin a rally. The right to serve first is decided by the spin of a racket.

Service box The area on each side of the court in which the server must have at least one foot as he first strikes the ball.

Short line Parallel to and 18ft from the front wall, and extending over the full width of the court.

Striker Player whose turn it is to hit the ball after it has rebounded from the front wall, the player who is in the process of hitting the ball or who has just hit the ball.

Stroke Gained by the player who wins a rally. Results in either a point won or change of service hand.

Tin The strip at the bottom of the front wall above which every shot must go. The strip is normally made of metal, and produces a hollow sound when hit to indicate to the players and referee when a shot is down.

Tin line/board The bottom-most line at the front court wall.

Volley The ball played before it has bounced on the floor.

Volley boast The ball played to the front wall via a side wall on the volley.

Walls The walls are painted white or off-white and are smooth to provide a true bounce for the ball.

Fives

Fives is played on a four-walled court by two players (singles) or four players (doubles). Players wear gloves on their hands to strike the ball. A player can score points only if they are receiving the serve.

Ball It is hard and white, has an inner core of cork and string and an outer skin of leather. It weighs 1.5oz and has a circumference of 5.75in.

Blackguard A service that hits the front wall without hitting the side wall. The receiver can hit the ball, providing he states he intends to before doing so.

Board A wooden board across the front wall measuring 2.5ft from the floor. Players must hit the ball over this line for the rally to continue.

Court Fives is played on a four-walled court measuring 18ft in width and 28ft in length. Its height is 15ft. The walls of the court should be black, and the floor red. The floor is made of stone and has no markings.

Duration The first player to score 15 points wins the game. If the score reaches 14-all, then the first to reach 16 wins. This is known as "game-ball all". If there is more than one game in a match, then a three-minute interval is allowed between the games.

First cut The first stroke that the first receiver of the ball makes. It is either a stroke that hits first the right-hand wall and then the front wall above the ledge, or a stroke that hits first the front wall above the ledge between the right-hand wall and the vertical line marked on the front wall.

Fives Originally derived from the slang expression "bunch of fives" describing the five fingers on the hand.

Front wall The wall that faces the two players. The server has to hit the ball against this wall for a rally to begin.

Pepper box A buttress placed at the end of the step and which projects out of the left-hand wall.

Preliminary rally Held before the game to decide which player starts the game off as receiver. The winner of the rally becomes the receiver.

Receiver The player who receives the serve. This is otherwise known as the "first cut". Only the receiver can score a point by winning a rally.

Returning service The ball can bounce off any of the four walls before being returned by the receiver as long as it touches the floor only once. The ball can then be hit to any other walls before striking the front wall.

Round Word used by the players to tell another player to duck their head out of the way of the ball, or to move to the other side of the court.

Scoring Only the receiver is allowed to score points. When a receiver wins a rally, he gains a point. If the server wins a rally, then he becomes the receiver.

Scraper A first cut stroke that will hurt the fingers.

Serving Play begins with the server, who will throw the ball so that it hits the front wall and then a side wall before falling into court. Once the ball has bounced, the server then hits the ball against the same side wall and onto the front wall above the board.

Shooter A stroke that, on its rebound, hits the exact angle that divides the court into two portions.

Slogging The name given to the serve received by the opposing player.

Court Handball

Court handball is played on a walled court between two single players or two double teams. The ball is hit with a gloved hand. The winning player or team is the first to win two games of 21 points each.

Ace The term given to a legal serve that the receiver misses.

Back wall shot The action of the ball rebounding off the back wall.

Ball Normally made of rubber with a diameter of 1.9in, weighing 2.3oz. Two balls should be made available at the beginning of the game. The chosen ball for play should be used for the whole game unless there are compelling circumstances.

Ceiling serve The ball hits the ceiling before landing on the floor.

Ceiling shot A shot that is hit directly toward the ceiling.

Cutthroat The term given to a game of handball with three players.

Court Four walled and measuring 20ft in width and 40ft in length with a height of 66ft.

Court hinder When an erratic bounce is caused by either an obstacle or a wet court.

Crotch ball When the ball hits any two walls, the wall and the floor, or the wall and the ceiling.

Defensive shot Used to make sure that the opposition is kept clear from the defensive area. This shot is not used to try and win the rally.

Dig Used by a player who receives a low shot.

Duration The first player or pair to win two games is the winner. They are allowed three one-minute time-outs and a five-minute interval between the first two games, and a 10-minute rest between the second and third games.

Equipment time-outs Allowed at the referee's discretion for either team. They may last for two minutes and are usually taken for broken laces, wet gloves, lost shoes and so on.

Fault A ball that is illegally served.

Fly shot A shot that is played before the ball bounces.

Foot fault Happens when a part of the server's foot is outside the service zone before the served ball has passed the short line.

Hinder The term used to describe the blocking action of a player by either hindering a shot or the flight of the ball. Hindered play is always replayed.

Hit Only the front or back of the hand are allowed to hit the ball.

Hop serve When a serve has a spin on it that makes the ball hop to the left or right.

Kill shot Occurs when the ball hits the wall at such a low angle that the opposing player has no chance of reaching the ball to return the shot.

Long serve The serve hits the back wall before touching the floor.

Offensive shot Used to try and win a rally.

Officials The referee has the final call on all decisions and keeps records of all points, protests and hinders. For larger games a linesman and a scorer are also used.

Out-of-court serve The ball bounces off the front wall and then out of the court.

Passing shot When the hit is driven past the opposing player's reach on either side.

Players Two, three or four players can play handball.

Point Can only be scored by the server or serving team.

Rally Describes the movement of the ball back and forth between the players until one side cannot legally return the ball. The winning team or player of the rally wins the serve.

Service line Measures 5ft from, but parallel to, the short line.

Service zone The section of the court that is marked by the short line and service line.

Short line The halfway line on the court between the front and back walls.

Short serve The first bounce of the ball must hit before or on the short line.

Side out Describes the action of the receiving player or team winning a rally and gaining a serve.

Technicals A technical is deemed to have occurred if any unsportsmanlike behavior is displayed. This includes arguing, swearing or any violent conduct. The punishment for a technical is the loss of one point.

Time-outs Each side is allowed three one-minute intervals in games that go to 21 points, and two one-minute intervals in games that go to 11 points. They are only allowed to be taken before the referee declares the score after a rally, or calls second serve.

Two consecutive screen serves Serves that pass too close to the server and obstruct the receiver's sight.

VOLLEY: Each player is allowed only one touch of the ball at a time and only one hand. no other part of the body can be used

Team Handball

Team handball is played by two teams of 12 players each, five of them being substitutes. The object of the game is to score as many goals as possible while passing and dribbling the ball with the hand.

Court Measures 44yd long by 22yd wide. The court is divided by a center line, and is marked by the goal areas and the sidelines. The goals measure 3.3yd wide by 2.2yd high.

Duration The game is split into two 30-minute halves with an interval of 10 minutes.

Extra time Occurs when there is a tie-break, and consists of two halves of five minutes each. If there is still a tie after the second overtime period, then a penalty shootout is used to decide the winners.

Free throw Given to the team that has suffered an infringement from the opposing team. Occurs either at the point of the violation or, if it happened between the 10yd line and the goal-area line, then the throw is taken from the nearest point outside the 10yd line.

Free-throw line Also known as the 9m line. It is placed 10yd away from the goal-area line but is parallel with it.

Goal area Marked out by the goal-area line. It is semicircular in shape and is placed 3.3yd away from the goalline.

Goalkeeper's restraining line Also labelled the 4.4yd line. Placed directly in front of the goal, 4.4yd away from the rear goal line.

Goalkeeper's throw Given to the goalkeeper when the ball crosses the outer goal line. The goalkeeper must take the throw from the goal area and beyond the goal-area line.

Officials Two referees are aided by a timekeeper and a scorekeeper.

Penalties Punishable by a warning, suspension or expulsion.

Referee throw Taken from the center of court, the referee will throw the ball vertically between two players of the two teams. Occurs when two opposing players commit a violation, the game is interrupted and nobody is in possession of the ball, or if the ball comes into contact with the ceiling or fixtures.

Seven-meter line Measures 3.28ft in length and is placed 7.6yd away from the rear edge of the goal line. It is directly in front of the goal mouth.

Seven-meter throw Taken at the 7.6yd line, and the player has three seconds to take an attempt at goal. This throw is awarded when a defending player makes an illegal maneuver and therefore destroys the opposing team's chance of scoring.

Starting The game is started by the two captains tossing a coin to decide who will have possession of the ball first. The starting player will begin with a throw-off at center court.

Throw in Used when the ball goes out of bounds and is taken from the point at which the ball went out.

Teams Each team consists of seven players, plus five other squad players who act as substitutes.

Paddleball

Paddleball is a court game that uses either one, two or three court walls. A small paddle is used to hit the ball off the wall or walls. The game can be played with two, three or four players, and the winner is the first to reach 21 points. A match is based on the best two out of three games.

Ball The ball is black and almost 2in round. When dropped from a height of 6ft it should rebound approximately 3.5ft.

Court measurements One- and three-wall courts are typically 34ft long and 20ft wide. The front wall is 16ft high with 4ft wire fencing on top of it. On four-wall courts the length is 40ft long and 20ft wide. The front and side walls are 20ft high and the back wall 12ft high.

Doubles Played with two players per team. Generally conforms to the rules of singles.

Doubles service After the first serve is out, the service passes to the other side. After this point both partners are allowed to lose their serve before passing over.

Dress Players must wear white shirts, shorts, socks and shoes.

Duration There is no official time limit to a match, which consists of the best of three games. A two-minute break is allowed between the first two games, and a 10-minute break after the second. During this time players may leave the court.

Foot fault Given if a player is not standing between the short line and the back line when the ball crosses the short line.

Four-wall court Has three high walls, a ceiling and a lower back wall. A line midway between the front and back wall is called the short line, and in front of this is the service line. The space between is the service zone. Each zone is marked off to form a service box.

Illegal serves A serve is illegal if the ball hits the floor before crossing the line, the ball rebounds from the front wall to the back wall or over the end line before hitting the floor, or if the ball goes out of court.

Loss of service A player loses service if he makes two consecutive illegal serves or he bounces the ball more than twice before striking it. A player also loses service for dropping the ball and hitting it in the air, if he strikes at the ball and misses the serve, or the ball goes out of court.

Obstruction Players must not prevent their opponents from seeing or playing the ball. They must not make any physical contact on an opponent.

Officials A referee is assisted by a scorer.

One-wall court Has a 4ft wire fence along the top of the wall. The sidelines are extended beyond the line at the back of the court to help in judging long balls and serve-outs. Markings are different from those of a four-wall court, in that the service line is behind the short line.

Paddle Made of wood, the paddle may be oval or square. A leather thong is attached to the handle and must be worn around the wrist during play. The paddle is approximately 8in wide and 1.3ft long, and weighs about 1lb.

Partners' positions (four wall) The server's partner must stand in the service box with his back to the wall and both feet on the floor until the ball crosses the line.

Partners' positions (one wall and three wall) The server's partner must stand outside the sideline between the short line and the back line until the ball has crossed the short line.

Players Played by two, three or four players, known as singles, cutthroat and doubles, respectively.

Playing the ball When returning an opponent's service or shot, a player may hold the paddle with one or two hands but may not switch it from hand to hand. The thong must remain around his wrist at all times and he must not hit the ball with any part of his body.

Return of serve (four wall) The receiver must remain at least 5ft behind the short line until the ball is struck by the receiver.

Return of serve (one wall and three wall) The receiver must remain behind the service line until the ball has passed the short line. A legally served ball may be returned to the front wall before it bounces or after it has bounced once. The ball may touch the side walls, back wall or ceiling and still remain in play.

Referee Stands in the center and above the back wall in four-wall courts; on the side near the end of a side wall in three-wall courts; and on the side toward the front of the court on an elevated platform in one-wall courts. He umpires the game.

Scorer Keeps a record of play and announces scores after each exchange.

Scoring Only the serving player or side can score points. These are obtained when the opposition is unable to return a volley or serve or deliberately hinders the serving player or side. A point is lost if the ball goes out of court. The first side to get to 21 points wins a game.

Serve-out A single action that causes loss of service.

Service Service is decided by the toss of a coin. The server for the first game also serves first in the third game. Before each service the server calls the score, giving his own score first. He may not serve until his opponent is ready.

Service box Marked off at the end of each serving zone.

Service line Situated in front of the short line. Players must serve from behind this line.

Service method The player drops the ball on the floor within the service zone, and strikes it with a paddle on the first bounce so that it hits the front wall and rebounds. The server must remain in the service zone until the ball has crossed the short line.

Service zone The space between the short line and service line.

Short line Halfway between the front wall and back wall.

Thong Attached to the handle, it must be worn around the wrist during play.

Three-wall court Similar to the one-wall court, although the side walls extend as far as the short line.

Time-outs Play is continuous except for time-outs. Teams or players are allowed two time-outs per game, and they must not exceed 30 seconds. Play may be suspended for 15 minutes for an injured player.

Jai alai

Originating from Northern Spain, Jai alai (also known as pelota) is a game played with a ball and hand basket on a three-walled court It is usually played by singles, doubles or triples.

Arriere The player on the court whose job is to stand at the back and hit the deep volleys that come across from the opposing team.

Atchiki To hold or wait. Describes the moment between the ball being caught in the cesta and then thrown back out. When first introduced, this technique made the game much faster and more spectacular.

Cesta A wicker basket worn on the hand like a glove. It is measured to fit each individual player. The materials that make up the cesta are chestnut, leather and reeds that are woven around the wooden frame. A piece of tape is used to tie the glove to the hand.

Court It is oblong in shape and surrounded by four walls, one of which is made of a clear screen so that spectators can watch. The other three walls are the frontis, which is the front wall; the lateral, which is the side wall; and the rebote, which is the back wall. The court is separated into 15 different sections with areas 4–7 being the serving area. The court measures 59yd long by 13yd wide with a height of 40ft.

Dress A player's shoes must be made of rubber and are white. The jerseys must be a differing color for each player, as must the belt or sash worn around the waist. The players wear helmets for safety reasons.

FIPV The Federacion Internacional de Pelota Vasca is the official governing body of the game, based in Madrid.

Frontis The Spanish term given to the front wall of the court. It is made of granite blocks and is square in shape.

Fronton A two- or three-walled court that can be either covered or uncovered. The area of the court has varied measurements.

Itzia Means "the nail", and describes the piercing pain that players receive when they are hit on the hand by the ball at the base of the fingers.

Jeux directs Describes games where the ball moves freely between the players. They are scored the same as in tennis: 15, 30, 40, game. The two main games are rebot and pasaka.

Jeux de blaid Describes those games in which the players face a wall where the ball is struck directly or off another wall; they are scored by points. There are 11 games in this category: main nue, cesta punta, pala larga, yoko-garbi, grand chistera, pala corta, raquette, remonte, sare and two types of palette.

Lateral Spanish word for the side wall of the court. It is oblong in shape and is made of a cement called gunite.

Main nue Means "bare hand", and is one of the most popular forms of jai alai played today.

Officials There are three judges in total who spread themselves over the court in order to ensure that the rules of the game are adhered to. They are situated opposite sections 4, 7 and 11. Each judge carries a bat to protect themselves from the ball, as it moves at great speed throughout the court.

Pala The Spanish word for spade. The game is played two a side, and is one of the fastest forms of jai alai played. A long wooden bat is used, made from either beech or ash.

Pasaka Means "to pass". Played two a side, the competitors use either their bare hands or a short, heavy and slightly curved glove that is made of leather.

Pelota The ball weighs 4.5oz and has a diameter of 2in. It is made of a hard rubber in the center, which is surrounded by a layer of linen thread and then covered in two layers of goatskin.

Pik A high shot that is usually untakeable, as it pounds against the back wall

JAI ALAI: Players have a long wicker basket glove taped to their arm to play the game

to fizz along the floor.

Place libre An open outdoor court with a single wall. The dimensions of the court are varied.

Players The game can be played as singles, doubles or triples.

Playing the ball The ball is hooked into the cesta and then thrown in one motion to the area called the frontis. The ball must be played on the green parts of the wall for the play to be legal. The ball may be returned either before or after it has bounced.

Quiniela Is the term given to the betting version of the game. It can be played with either singles or doubles

with a maximum number of eight players. The first team starts play, with the number-one side serving. It continues until one team loses a point. The losing team then leaves the court and is replaced by the number-three team, and so on. The team in the lead always stays on the court until the maximum score has been reached, then the game is over unless a tie-break is required, in which case a further game is played.

Rebot The Spanish term for "to reverse" or "turn back". The game is played five a side, and is performed on an open court.

Rebote The Spanish word for back wall, square in shape and made of gunite.

Scoring The number of points available to be scored during each match is between 7 and 35. Points are accumulated when an opposing player: hits the ball back after it has bounced more than once; misses the ball entirely; when returning the ball does not hit the frontis, or fails to catch and throw the ball in one smooth movement.

Serving Taken from the serving zone, the ball must rebound off the frontis and then land back into the serving zone.

Serving zone Positioned between the spaces marked 4–7 on the court.

Seven-points system This system is used when there are eight teams or players on the court who play for seven points. One point is given for each win scored until every team or player has had their first turn, then the points system doubles to two points per win.

Trinquet A small covered court that is rectangular in shape. It encompasses a gallery and a penthouse, and usually has a dedans net on the penthouse side.

Yoko-garbi A three-sided game that is named as "a clean game". It is played on an open court with one wall.

3

Target Ball Games

These sports involve using a ball to hit a target, whether it be knocking over skittles or trying to get a golf ball into a small hole. Some of them, such as snooker and pool, are played on tables with pockets as targets, while others are played outdoors, with the golf course being one of the biggest arenas in sport.

Sports Footwear

Bowling shoes Have soft soles so as to not damage the bowling surface. Shoes for a right-handed bowler should have leather on the left shoe sole and rubber tipped with leather on the right sole. Heels are made of hard rubber.

Cleat Another name for stud.

Crampons Spikes that can attach to the shoe. Used in mountain climbing to gain a good grip in differing terrain.

Ice skates Used in ice hockey, ice skating, bandy and speed skating. The boot is attached to the blade and covers the ankles for support. Their are different styles but the basic boot remains the same across the board.

Roller skates Used in roller hockey and artistic roller skating. Although there are varying types a few rules apply to all. The boot must be bolted to the skate. The boot usually reaches up to the ankles to give support and there are normally four wheels on each skate.

Skis Varying types such as downhill skis, slalom skis, giant slalom skis, Super G skis, cross-country skis and ski-jumping skis. All are made of synthetic materials.

Spikes Positioned on the heel and sole of training shoes. Used to give grip on differing surfaces in athletics. A maximum of 11 spikes on each shoe is allowed.

Studs Must be made of leather, rubber, aluminium or similar material and round in shape. Placed on the sole and heel. Used in sports such as football.

Waders Worn by anglers to keep themselves dry. Made of rubber they cover the leg and thigh.

Billiards

Billiards is played between two players on a special table covered in green felt to make it smooth. Players use a cue to strike the cue ball across the table in a bid to hit one of the three balls placed on the table – the white, spot white and red. A player can score points by pocketing the balls (hazards), or by hitting both other balls (cannons).

Anchor cannon A shot that is rarely played in a game of billiards. The red and the object white are jammed together between the upper and lower jaws of the top pocket, and the cue ball is rolled against them, touching both at the same time.

Baulk The area at the top of the table from which the game gets under way, and where players frequently leave the cue ball for safety.

Baulk line The line from where the baulk line spot is situated. It is this spot that marks from where each frame gets under way. The player must place the cue ball behind this line and in the D, and strike it toward the red ball on the spot.

Balls They must all be of the same size and weight. The white and spot balls are the cue balls. The red ball can only be hit by other balls knocking against it, and is never touched by the cue.

Balls touching If the striker's ball is resting up against another ball, the red ball is automatically replaced on the spot. The non-striker's ball, if on the table, is then placed on the center spot.

Bottom pocket Applies to the two pockets at the baulk end of the table.

Break The term used to describe the number of points a player scores in one turn at the table. Each time a player scores from a shot, he is allowed to take another one. Only when the player misses does he forfeit his turn.

Cannons Two points are awarded to a player if the cue ball strikes both other balls. An additional two points can be scored if the cue ball falls into a pocket after a cannon. A player can also score two points if the white ball is struck first, or three points if the red ball is hit first.

Center pocket Applies to the two pockets in the middle of the table.

Center spot Used to spot the ball if two balls are touching on the table. The non-striker's ball is placed on the center spot in the middle of the table.

Chalk Applied to the cue to improve contact when striking the ball.

Cue A long, thin piece of wood with a special tip that is used to strike the cue-ball. It must not be less than 3ft long.

Cue ball The ball used to strike the red ball.

Cushion The padding around the edge of the table. It measures 2in in width.

D The area in which the striker must place the cue ball to get the game under way, or to restart the match after a foul has been committed.

Duration The game is played for an agreed length of time or until a player scores an agreed number of points.

Fouls Awarded against a player for any infringement that is not within the rules of the game. The striker automatically loses his shot and any score made in that break.

Frame The term used to describe a game.

In-off white A player can make his

own white enter the pocket after making contact with his opponent's white.

Losing hazards Two points are awarded to a player if the cue ball is pocketed "in off" the white ball. Three points are given if the cue ball is pocketed "in off" the red ball. Players are allowed to score only 15 consecutive hazards whether winning, losing or both.

Nursery cannon Occurs when cannons are close together.

Pocket A gap in the cushion supporting a small net into which the balls fall. There are six pockets on a table.

Pocketed ball If the red ball is sunk into the pocket, then it is automatically replaced on the spot. When the cue ball is pocketed, the striker brings it back into the D to restart play. If the non-striker's cue ball is pocketed during a break, then it remains off the table until the break has finished.

Pot white A player can strike his opponent's white into a pocket.

Rests Used to support the cue for a shot that would otherwise be out of reach. These can be a long butt cue (9ft), a half butt cue (7ft), a rest (8ft) or a half butt rest (5ft).

Start The game gets under way by the red ball being placed on the spot and the striker putting the cue ball any-where in the D. They are then ready to take the first shot, and must hit the cue ball toward the red ball. The second player will then bring his cue ball into play.

Stringing Players can try to beat each other for choice of balls or the order of play that they will take. This can be by them each playing the cue ball from the D, and the choice will go to the player whose ball finishes nearer to the bottom cushion. The same playing order is kept throughout the game.

Table A slate bed covered with green felt. It measures 12ft long and 6ft wide. It is supported by eight legs that are 2ft 11in high.

The spot At the start of a game the red ball is placed exactly at this point on the table, and the striker hits the cue ball toward the spot.

Top pocket The two pockets at the end of the table nearest to the spot.

Scoring The striker scores points for winning hazards, losing hazards and cannons. All the points accumulated in a shot are counted.

Winning hazards Two points are awarded to a player if the cue ball strikes the other white ball into a pocket. Three points are awarded if the cue ball hits the red ball into a pocket.

Snooker

Snooker is played between two players on a billiards table. Players use a cue to strike the white cue ball toward one of the 15 red or six other colored balls on the table. Players score points by pocketing balls in a certain order, and by forcing their opponents to give away points by missing the target ball. Each game is called a frame, and the player with the highest score at the end of the frame is the winner.

147 The maximum break that a player can score. To reach 147, a player must pot the black ball after potting each red, up to where the colored balls are pocketed (which must be done in a certain order).

Angled The cue ball is obstructed by the jaws of the pocket in such a manner that a player cannot hit the object ball.

Baulk area The area at the top of the table from where the game is started, and where players will try to position the cue ball to put it as far away from the red balls as possible.

BRIDGE: The player bridges their free hand to ensure a secure grip of the cue.

Balls There are 22 balls on the table at the start of a frame. They are all of equal size and weight. English snooker balls are 2.5in in diameter.

Break The shot(s) that make up a player's turn while at the table. Each time a player pots a red ball, they are allowed to take another shot, this time on a colored ball; if they pot that, they attempt to pot another red, and so on. When that player fails to pot a ball, their opponent takes the following shot. The points tally up to that time for the first player is called the break.

Bridge To play a controlled shot, it is important for a player to provide a steady support for the cue. A player uses their non cueing hand to create this support, called a bridge. This is achieved by the player placing the spread fingers of their non playing hand on the table, then lifting the wrist up while keeping the fingers in contact with the table to form a bridge. The thumb is then extended outward to provide a firm base for the cue.

Century When a player reaches 100 points in a break.

Chalk A small cube of compacted chalk that a professional player usually keeps handy in their waistcoat pocket in order to improve the contact of the cue with the cue ball.

Clearing the table A series of shots in which a player comes to the table and is able to pot all the remaining balls to win the frame.

Colors The name for all the colored balls in snooker except the reds and the cue ball. When potted, the colours score the following: yellow, two points; green, three points; brown, four points; blue, five points; pink, six points; black, seven points. Once all the reds have been potted, the players must pot the colored balls in this order. If any reds still remain on the table, the players can nominate which color they wish to attempt to pot, when they have potted a red.

Cue The long wooden stick used to strike the cue ball.

Cue ball The white ball. The cue ball is the only ball a player may strike directly with his cue.

Cushion The inside edges of the table against which the ball can be played. The cushion curves outward above the six pockets around the table.

D The area in which the cue ball is placed to get the game under way. The cue ball is also placed here after a foul has been committed (for example, when the cue ball has been inadvertently potted). The D has a radius of 11.5in.

Double When a player strikes the target ball toward a cushion at such an angle that the ball rebounds into the opposite pocket.

Duration When all the balls (except the cue ball) have been cleared from the table, the player with the highest score wins the game. If the scores are level after the last black has been potted, then the black ball is respotted and the players draw lots for the choice of playing at the black from the D. Alternatively, the frame may end when a player is ahead of his opponent by a greater number of points than is left on the table, were the other player to pot all the remaining balls.

Extension A tubular device added on to the cue in order to lengthen it, so that a player can reach the cue ball when it is awkwardly placed.

Forcing shot A shot that is considerably above medium pace.

Foul Awarded against a player who plays a foul shot – for example, missing their designated ball, failing to hit any ball or pocketing the cue ball. The striker automatically loses their turn and any score they may have made on that shot. Their opponent receives the appropriate score and then has the choice of playing the ball from where it has come to rest, or asking their opponent to play again.

Frame A professional snooker match is normally made up of the best of an odd number of games, known as frames. The number of frames played depends on the competition. It will vary from the best of 9 frames up to 35 in the World Championship Final.

Free ball When a player is snookered on the reds after a foul shot by their opponent, they can nominate any colored ball on the table as a red. If that ball then gets potted, it counts as one point, it is respotted in its correct place on the table, and a color can then be nominated in the normal way.

Full-ball A shot in which the tip of the cue, the center of the cue ball and the center of the object ball all form a straight line.

Half-ball A shot in which half the cue ball covers half the object ball at the moment of impact when striking the ball.

Half butt rest Players use this rest to play a ball that is not within arm's length. It measures 5ft.

In hand A player can replace the cue ball in the D after their opponent's ball has either gone "in off", or they have forced the ball off the playing surface.

In off A foul stroke when the white ball cannons into a pocket after hitting the "on ball". The opposing player will be awarded four points (or the value of the on ball, if it was worth more than four points).

Jump shot When the cue ball jumps over the object ball or any intervening ball. The referee will call a foul and the opposing player takes the next shot.

Kiss A foul awarded against a player who makes a second contact on the object ball.

Long butt cue Used for an extremely long shot at the other end of the table. It measures 9ft.

Natural angle The angle that the cue ball takes after hitting the object ball at medium pace, without a player putting screw- or sidespin on to the ball.

On ball The term given to the ball that is next to be struck.

Plant Two object balls that are not touching. The cue ball will be struck toward them at such an angle that they will strike each other and the second object ball will be potted.

Pockets Small holes at the edge of the table into which the balls can be potted. There are six pockets on a standard table and they vary between 2 and 4in wide.

Pyramid The 15 reds are formed into a triangle of five rows at the start of the game, with one red at the top of the pyramid and five at the bottom. The cue ball must strike the pyramid to get the game under way. Skilled players often strike the cue ball with heavy side-spin at the start of a frame, so that it rolls past the pyramid of reds and spins back behind the base of the pyramid to gently split the reds, leaving very few options for their opponent.

Red There are 15 reds in a game of snooker. A player must always pot a red ball before trying to pot one of the colored balls to score more points. A red ball is worth one point.

Respotted ball If a colored ball is potted while any reds remain on the table, or is illegally potted at any stage, then it is respotted at its starting point at the beginning of a frame. If the appropriate spot is covered by another ball, then the color is placed on the next available spot in descending order of value.

Rests Players can use a rest to support the cue for a shot. There are a number of different rests for this purpose.

Running side Spin put on to the cue ball to make it travel down the table.

Safety shot There are a number of occasions when a player will find themselves near to the pack of reds, but have no chance of potting a ball. In this situation, the player will normally strike the cue ball toward the baulk area of the table, so that it hits a red ball on the way but then ends up as far away as possible from the remaining red balls. This makes it difficult for their opponent to score points themselves.

Scoreboard A traditional snooker scoreboard resembles an abacus, and records units, tens and hundreds via horizontal sliding pointers.

Screw A shot in which the cue ball spins backward after it has made contact with another ball. This is executed by aiming the cue at the very bottom of the cue ball.

Set Two object balls are touching in such a manner that when contacted by the cue ball, at any angle, the second object ball will be potted.

Shot to nothing When a player attempts to pot a ball in a bid to continue the break, knowing that the cue ball will run to safety regardless of the outcome.

Side When a player strikes the ball to the left or right of the center of the cue ball to apply spin on one side or the other. This is vital for a player in positional play. Side applied to the right of the cue ball will make the ball spin counter clockwise, and therefore curve slightly to the left and shoot off the cushion when it strikes it.

Snooker The description applied when a player cannot see a straight-line path between the cue ball and the ball that is "on", because another ball that the player must not hit is obstructing the cue ball. This is called "being snookered". A player must attempt to get out of a snooker by playing the cue ball off

SPIDER REST: A raised rest that allows players to cue over the top of another ball or balls

a cushion or cushions and hitting the target ball before any other ball. If they miss the on ball, a foul is awarded against them.

Spider A type of rest with an elevated head containing three grooves that helps a player to take a shot where intervening balls would obstruct the normal rest.

Starting play The game begins with the first player placing the cue ball in the D and striking it toward the reds.

Stun When a player has a straight shot, they can stop the cue ball dead on impact to prevent it following the target ball into the pocket, or to position the cue ball precisely for a subsequent shot. The cue ball need be hit only slightly below center for the ball to stop dead.

Swerve When a player has been comprehensively snookered and cannot use the cushions to escape, they may attempt to swerve the cue ball by applying an extreme amount of side-spin so that the cue ball curves around the obstructing ball and hits the object ball.

Table A snooker table consists of a flat and level bed of 2in thick Italian or Portuguese slate. It has a green cloth surface, called baize (felt) and has cloth-covered rubber cushions. Snooker can be played on any standard billiards table.

Touching ball Two balls that are resting against each other. With the referee's permission, a player can play the white ball away to safety without hitting another ball.

Triangle The rack used at the start of the game to position the red balls in a pyramid.

White See "Cue ball".

Pool

Pool is played on a pocketed billiards table, normally smaller than a traditional snooker table. The object of the game is to pocket all your own balls first before finishing with the black ball. All in all there are 15 colored balls and a white cue ball, which must be used to strike the other balls.

Balls The balls must each weigh between 5.5 and 6oz.

Ball bouncing from pocket When a target ball rebounds from a pocket, it is not considered to have been pocketed.

Ball falling without being hit If a stationary ball falls into a pocket without being hit by another ball, the player at the table is credited with pocketing it.

Ball frozen to a cushion If a player stops the cue ball in front of a target ball frozen against a cushion, one point is lost whether or not the cue ball touches the target.

Ball off the table A foul is called if a ball jumps from the table and does not return into play.

Bank shot A shot where the cue ball strikes a colored ball into a cushion on one side of the table with the intention of making the ball rebound into a pocket on the table's opposite side.

Break The target balls are arranged using the rack, with the number-eight ball arranged centrally and on the spot marked on the table. The opening player must start with the cue ball behind the head string. The cue ball must make contact with the racked balls, either directly or via one or more cushions.

Continuous play A player may pocket 14 object balls successively.

Cue ball within the string A foul is committed if a player, with the cue ball in hand, fails to shoot from within the head string after a warning from the referee.

Disqualification Players can be disqualified by the referee for unsportsmanlike conduct.

Duration A match is made up of an agreed number of "blocks". Each block is played to an agreed number of points, usually 125 or 150 in title play.

End of block The first player to reach the agreed number of points must continue to play until all but one of the target balls on the table are pocketed.

Foot on floor At least one foot must be touching the floor when playing a shot. Failure to adhere to this rule results in the loss of a turn and of one point.

Foul snookers When a foul occurs and the next player is snookered, he is described as being "foul snookered".

Free ball When a player cannot see both sides of the object ball they are about to strike after a foul has been committed, they are allowed to hit any other ball on the table and count it as one of their shots.

Head string The line that runs across the baulk end of the table.

Impossible shot It is possible for a player to be unable to play a shot without fouling. In such a situation the player must concede a foul.

Interference by a player A player commits a foul when accidentally disturbing a ball with any part of his body or clothing, ending his turn and losing one point.

Interference from another person If anyone other than a player disturbs a ball, it must be replaced as near as possible to its position before the interference.

Jump shots If the cue ball leaps from the table it is considered a jump shot. A jump shot is legal if the player causes the cue ball to jump as the result of a legal stroke.

Lagging Players "lag" to decide the order of play. The choice goes to the player whose cue ball comes to rest nearest the head of the table after being stroked against the bottom cushion from behind the head string. The cue ball may touch the side cushions.

Legal shot On all shots, the player must cause the cue ball's initial contact with a ball. Failure to play a legal shot is a standard foul.

Misses A player's turn ends if he misses the shot called. There is no penalty as long as the cue ball hits a cushion after hitting a target ball, or drives at least one object ball to a cushion or into a pocket.

Non standard fouls Failure to perform a fair break; failure to play the ball within 60 seconds of the ball coming to rest; pocketing the cue ball on a fair break. Non standard fouls are called by the referee as soon as they occur, and the offending player loses control of the table.

Order of play Determined by the toss of a coin or lagging. The winner decides whether to break or not.

Penalty Following any foul, the offending player's opponent is awarded two shots.

Pocketing balls A player must always call the ball he is aiming to pocket, and in which pocket.

Push shots or double hits Any shot played with speed will not be deemed a push shot, regardless of whether the cue tip may have come into contact with the cue ball more than once.

Racking The highest-numbered balls should be placed near the foot of the triangle, the lowest numbers near the side.

Safety play When attempting to play a safety shot, a player has three options: to play the target ball to a cushion; to hit a cushion with the cue ball after a target ball; to pocket a target ball. A player is not obliged to declare his intentions before playing a safety shot.

Scoring A point is scored for shooting a nominated ball into a called pocket, with an additional point scored for every other object ball pocketed in the same stroke.

Scratching A player may scratch the cue ball into a pocket at the break shot or during continuous play. At his first scratch a player ends his turn, loses one point, and has one scratch marked against him.

Serious fouls Committed when the player plays a shot out of turn or strikes any ball other than the cue ball with the cue. When this happens, the balls must be replaced as close as possible to their positions before the foul.

Snooker A player is snookered when it is impossible to play a particular shot legally in a straight line.

Solids The term given to one set of balls on the table that are fully colored.

Standard foul A standard foul is committed if the player fails to hit the designated ball they were supposed to strike.

Strings Imaginary lines through spots and parallel to the ends of the table.

Stripes The term given to a set of balls on the table that has striped markings.

Table A slate base covered in green felt. There are six pockets. Tables range from 3.5 × 7ft to 5 × 10ft. The length is always twice the width.

Time limit on protests If a player considers that an opponent is guilty of a foul, he may ask the referee for a ruling.

Total snookers A player is in a total snooker when it is impossible to play any legal shot in a straight line.

Touching balls If the cue ball is touching an object ball, the player is obliged to play away from that ball at an angle of more than 90 degrees.

Boules

Boules is played between two players or two teams. The aim of the game is for each player to place their boule nearer to the target jack than their opponent's boule. The player who manages this scores a point. The player with the most points at the end of the game wins.

Advantage The opposing team can accept the position of all the objects, or may have the objects repositioned. The fouling boule can either be left in its place or taken off the pitch.

Baguette A long stick used to measure and evaluate distances. It is also used for tracing lines and marks. It measures 2in in length and its width is 2in. Both teams' baguettes must be identical.

Boule A round ball used by a player to get as near to the jack as possible. It must be made of metal or a synthetic material. It must be 3.5-4.3in in diameter and weigh 1.5-2.8lb. The boule must not be nailed or weighted with lead.

Boule pointée A boule thrown from a standing position to travel along the ground and aimed to stop as near to the jack as possible.

Boule portée A boule thrown into the air in a parabolic arc that aims to finish as near to the jack as possible.

Boule tirée A boule thrown from a run into the air in a parabolic arc, which aims to dislodge another object while it is landing.

Buried boule If a boule is more than half buried after a regular point, then it automatically remains in play.

Buried jack After a regular *tir*, if the jack is more than half buried then the advantage rule applies.

Chance disturbance This can be caused by a non-player. If a *boule pointée* is blocked by a disturbed object, then the object is repositioned and the point is retaken.

Delays If a team holds up the start or resumption of play, then the opposing team receives one point for each five minutes, or part of the five minutes after a 10-minute period. The opponents can win the game if they reach six points just from the other delaying play.

Designating Before a *tir* can be used, a player must choose one target object within the 5.5yd rectangle. This can be either the jack or an opponent's boule.

Disturbance A player interfering with a boule or accidentally disrupting their own teammate. The advantage rule will normally be taken in this circumstance, or all the objects can be replaced and then the player can retake his boule.

Footline The line over which a player must not put their feet when throwing the boule or jack.

Foul The referee can award a foul against a player for any kind of offense that is against the rules of the game. This could be anything from unsportsmanlike conduct to a player deliberately prolonging a match.

Interfering The throwing team is allowed to remove obstacles from the pitch, move the boundary lines, and smooth and level the surface. Once the jack is thrown, the pitch can be touched only to mark positions. Nobody is allowed to touch the pitch while the boule is moving.

Inversion Takes place when a fouling boule is blocking the former position of another object. With the advantage rule, the opposing team can ask for the removed boule to be repositioned and the fouling boule can be left in position.

Irregular point A point is deemed to be irregular if a foul has been committed.

Jack A small white ball used as a target toward which the players throw their boule. The jack must be made of wood, and cannot have ridges, hobnails or lead weighting. It is 1.5in in diameter and can be colored to make it easier to see.

Marking objects The position of all the boules and the jack must be marked before each throw. The baguette is used to draw all the lines at 90 degrees. The jack is marked by the team that threw or placed it. If the jack gets displaced, then the scoring team does the marking.

Measuring If a team feels they have scored, they will measure the distance between the boule and the jack. A boule can be temporarily lifted while the scoring team is doing this.

Misuse When a player does something wrong with the boule that is not met within the rules of the game. For example, accidentally hitting another player's boule. The opposing team can then put the correct boule in the position of the boule played in error.

Out of play If the boule runs over the endline, it is ruled to be out of play.

Out-of-play line If the boule crosses this line, it is adjudged to be out of play.

Penalties The umpire awards a penalty for any unsportsmanlike conduct.

Pitch Any kind of surface is allowed. The standard measurement of a pitch should be 30yd in length. The minimum pitch width for an international match is 3.3yd and there must be end banks at least 0.8in high. The pitch is surrounded by lines which must be visible and can be retracted if necessary.

Positions As soon as the jack is thrown, all of the other players must stand behind the same footline as the thrower. If one of the teammates is out of position, the throw is disallowed and that team loses the right to a second throw.

Regular point A player is awarded a point when the boule does not go out of play, does not travel more than 3.3ft after hitting a boule or jack on the pitch, or it lands within at least 2.2yd of the front edge of the far 5.5yd rectangle.

Repositioning If any kind of disturbance or foul takes place, a player is allowed to move their object and place it in a new position.

Scoring Once both teams have played all their boules, one team is awarded a point for each of their boules that is nearer to the jack than that of their opposition's boules.

Sideline point A point falling near a sideline is deemed to be regular if over half the landing mark is within the line.

Target jack At the start of the game, the right of first throw of the jack is decided by lot. The jack is then thrown from behind the footline. A throw is deemed valid when the jack comes to rest in the 5.5yd rectangle at the far end.

Throwing To throw a boule, a player must have both feet behind the footlin except for a *tir*, when one foot may be put on the line. The team that threw the jack throws the first boule. The first opponent then throws their first boule.

Tir Used to trace arcs using a baguette.

Tracing arcs Before a *tir* is made, the opposing team traces arcs with a baguette. Arcs are normally 6-8in long, but an arc in front of a designated target can be extended.

Bowls

Bowls is played by either two players or two teams with up to four players each. One point is scored by positioning the bowl as near to the jack as possible. The winning team or player is the one to have accumulated the most points or ends during a game.

....

Across the head When a shot arrives narrowly off the head. If the shot is made deliberately, then this is usually done to try to make the opposing players bowl out of the count, but if it is done unintentionally, it is seen as a wasted shot.

Aiming point The visual mark that may be concrete or imaginary, at which a player will aim his or her bowl in order to achieve the best result.

Arc The curve that the bowl makes as it responds to the bias.

Athletic stance The most common position used to bowl with. The feet should be in line with the intended delivery. The knees should be bent, and the follow-through should be fluid and natural.

Attacking bowl A bowl used to try to gain the advantage by either disturbing the head or an opposing player's bowl.

Back bowl A bowl that is deliberately played behind the jack with the intention of securing the place when the jack is moved on. The best place to position a back bowl is nearest to the ditch.

Banks The raised area of the green beyond the ditch that is out of bounds.

Bias The lateral force of the bowl while moving, which gives it the arc.

Block shot A position shot that is designed to block the path of the opposition, and therefore deprive them of access to the head.

Boundary jack If a jack hits the boundary, it is still in play. Players can still play toward it, but their bowls must stay inside the rink.

Bowl It can be black or brown in color, and is usually made of wood or rubber. Each set must have a distinguishing mark, and must be officially tested for bias. Wooden bowls must have a maximum weight of 5in and a maximum diameter of 13cm. Rubber bowls must be 3–3.5lb in weight, with a diameter of between 4.6-5in.

Claw grip The most common way of handling the ball. The thumb must be positioned high up on the side of the bowl. This leaves the bowl resting forward onto the palm, with most of its weight being deflected onto the fingers.

Count The number of shots scored on an end.

Cradle grip The bowl is cradled in the palm of the hand with the thumb dropped. This maneuver allows maximum power with minimum effort, but gives the player less control than the claw grip.

Crouch stance When the bowler crouches on the mat before rising to deliver the bowl.

Damaged jack Once this occurs the end is dead, and the jack is replaced with another one.

Dead bowl A bowl that either stops completely outside the rink boundaries or within 15yd of the mat, or is moved beyond the rink boundaries by another bowl. Also if the bowl stops in the ditch without having made contact with the jack while on the green, or rebounds from the far bank without having touched the jack on the green. All dead bowls are removed from the rink immediately and put on the bank.

Dead end An end is deemed dead when the jack is moved beyond the boundaries of play. The end is then replayed in the same direction.

Dead jack Occurs if the bowl moves the jack over the bank, side boundary, into a hole or so that it rebounds within 60ft of the mat. These actions make the end null and void, and it must be replayed in the same direction.

Delivering the jack The first bowler of the game delivers the jack. The jack must land at least 70ft from the mat to be legal.

Displaced jack or bowls Describes the jack or bowl being moved by the opposition's jack or bowls.

Ditching the jack When the jack is driven into the ditch.

Draw shot The most important shot in the whole game, where the ball is sent as close to the jack as possible.

Dress It is mandatory for players and officials to wear footwear with smooth rubber soles and no heels.

Drive shot Used to remove one or more bowls from the head. Also known as a firing shot, it can be a very effective bowl but should be used sparingly. This shot negates the bias on the bowl.

Duration Games are played for either a specific amount of time, a specific number of ends or until a certain number of points have been won by one team.

Fast green Little effort is needed on a fast green, as the surface provides little resistance to the bowl.

Finger grip The bowl is held completely clear of the palm with the fingers taking all the weight. The thumb comes right to the top of the bowl. It is usually used on fast greens.

Firm wood This bowl is quite forceful but, unlike the drive shot, is affected by bias.

Fixed stance This is a restricted stance with the arm and shoulder taking the responsibility for the delivery. The knees are bent, with the free hand holding on to a knee to steady the stance.

Fours The main form of bowls, with each of the four players taking two bowls each.

Foot faults One foot must always be on or above the mat when a bowl or jack is released for play to be legal. When a foot fault occurs the umpire will warn the player, but if it happens again then the umpire can declare the bowl stopped and therefore dead.

Full-length jack A jack that is delivered within 2yd of the ditch and then centered on the 2yd mark.

Grassing the bowl When the bowl is placed smoothly on the green during delivery.

Green Square or rectangular in shape, but both must have side measurements of 33–44yd in length. The green is restricted by a ditch and a bank.

Green speed The time that it takes a bowl to move 30yd to the jack and stop. It is measured in seconds.

Head The name given to the bowls that congregate around the jack while an end is in progress.

Heavy green A slow green that resists the movement of a bowl, normally found in Scotland.

Jack Must be white with a weight of 8–10oz and a diameter of 2–2.5in.

Jack high bowl A bowl that is level with the jack on either side.

Lignum vitae The dense wood that bowls used to be made of.

Live bowl Any bowl that is within the boundary of the rink, or any toucher in the ditch between the strings.

Master bowl The bowl used to test all

other bowls to ensure the correct arc and bias. This must be done for any bowls used in competition.

Mat Black in color and made of rubber. It measures 1.17in in width with a length of 2ft, and has a 2in-wide border in white.

MAT: A black rubber mat marks the spot where players bowl from, aiming for a white jack ball

Offenses Any behavior that is deemed to be unsportsmanlike and illegal during the course of play. This includes playing on the same rink on the day of a competition, placing any object on the green to assist in play that is not authorized, distracting any player while they bowl, playing a bowl out of turn, standing less than 1yd behind the mat or changing a bowl for no valid reason.

Pairs Two teams of two players each. Four bowls per team, with the winners reaching the highest score after 21 ends.

Placing the mat The mat is placed at the start of each end and cannot be removed until the end is finished. The first end has the mat put in the center of the rink with its front edge 6ft from the rear ditch, while all following ends must have the front edge at least 6ft from the rear ditch.

Positional shot A tactical shot played not to the jack but to a preplanned position on the green in order to gain the maximum advantage later on.

Rest shot A bowl played to another bowl in the head that will rest there.

Result A game is decided after one player or team reaches an agreed number of points, after an agreed number of ends or after a set time limit is reached.

Rinks These divide the green and measure 14–19ft in width. They are numbered in order and their boundaries are marked by green threads that are linked by pegs at the rink corners. The center of each rink is also marked by a peg on the bank at each end. Each end ditch is 75ft apart, and this is indicated by a white marker on the side banks.

Running Used to describe the desired weight of shot.

Running shots The term given to all shots that are played with greater force than a normal draw shot.

Scoring The bowl that lands nearest to the jack is valid for one point. If the opposing team's bowls are equal in distance from the jack, then the end is drawn and no points are awarded. The first player to score 25 points wins.

Semi-crouch stance Occurs when

the bowler bends the knees or back prior to taking a bowl.

Shot bowl The bowl that is closest to the jack within the head.

Shoulder of the arc This point is at the extreme width of the arc where the bowl turns inward toward the head. The imaginary shoulder of the arc is the point at which the bowler must aim toward to reach the true shoulder.

Singles Two players who each have four bowls. The winner is the first to reach 25 points.

South African clinic The title given to a variation of the fixed stance. The front foot moves forward while the body weight is taken by the back foot prior to delivery.

Springing the jack When the bowl played hits another bowl that is touching the jack, and therefore moves the jack away.

Start Rinks are drawn for by the teams. The winner of the toss decides who will play first at each rink. A trial end in each direction is allowed.

Straight hand So called because the forehand or backhand are straighter than the opposing hand.

Tap and lie shot Also called the wrest shot. Describes the action of tapping a bowl out of the way and remaining on that spot.

Tied end Occurs when two bowls cannot be separated and the measure for shot is equal. The end is then declared a draw.

Toucher Describes a bowl that touches the jack while still in motion. This bowl is then marked with chalk until the end is finished. This bowl will stay live even if it ends up in the ditch, as long as it is between the strings.

Tracking Occurs when the playing area is flattened, making the bowls move faster.

Trail shot A running shot that removes the jack through the head.

Triples Three teams with two players each. The game lasts 18 ends, with the winning team having scored the most points.

Weight The gait of the bowl during delivery of the shot.

Wick shot The term used to describe the deflection that occurs when a bowl comes into contact with another bowl.

World Bowls Board The governing body of outdoor bowls whose responsibility is to ensure adherence to the rules.

Wrong bowl When a player delivers a bowl out of turn.

Yard on shot A shot that is played with a yard more than draw weight.

Bowling

Bowling is played by between one and five people at a time. A plastic ball is pushed or thrown down a lane, at the end of which are 10 wooden pins that need to be knocked over.

Alley/lane Measures 60ft from the foul line to the center of the head pin. The width of a lane is 41–42in. The surface is generally either of wood or plastic.

Approach Otherwise known as the runway, it is a minimum of 15ft long and ends at the foul line.

Ball Of nonmetallic material with a circumference no greater than 27in and a weight no more than 16lb. It can have up to five holes for finger grips.

Bowling The object of the game is to score the most points by rolling a ball down the alley and knocking down pins. Played by individuals or teams of up to five players per team. Players take turns bowling one frame at a time.

Channels (gutters) Grooves on either side of the lane to catch errant balls.

Dead ball When a dead ball is called, the delivery does not count. Any pins knocked down must be replaced.

Dead wood When a pin leans and touches the kickback or side partition, it is considered to have legally fallen. These pins are "dead wood" and must be removed before the next delivery.

Double A player has rolled two consecutive strikes.

Foul When any part of the player touches any part of the lane or the foul line during or after delivery. The delivery counts, but any pins knocked down are not recorded.

Foul line The point by which the player must have bowled the ball. Stepping over the line is a foul.

Frame Consists of two deliveries by a player. If a player scores a strike on his first shot, the frame is over.

Illegal pinfall A pinfall is not legal if the ball leaves the lane before reaching the pins, a bowler fouls or a ball rebounds from the rear cushion and knocks down any pins.

Pin deck Where the pins stand. The headpin is 60ft away from the foul line. The pin deck is 2.85ft from front to back.

Pinfalls These are legal when pins are knocked down by the ball or another pin, including a pin that rebounds from a side panel, rear cushion or sweep bar.

Pins Made of wood, plastic-coated wood or synthetic material. Each pin is 15in tall and weighs between 3.4lb and 3.6lb. Pins are set 12in apart from each other in a triangular pattern.

Scoring The number of pins bowled down in one frame is the number of points scored. However, this does not apply for strikes. In this instance, an "X" is marked and your next score is added to your strike score.

Spare Scored by a player who knocks down any remaining pins on the second delivery of the frame. The player scores 10 points plus the number of pins he knocks down on his next delivery.

Split A set up of pins left standing after the first delivery, when the headpin is down and the remaining pins far apart.

Strike Recorded by a player who knocks down all the pins on their first delivery. A strike cannot occur on the second delivery, even if no pins were knocked down the first time.

Turkey The term for successive strikes by one player.

Skittles

Skittles is played with an even number of players ranging from two to 24. The players roll or throw a ball or disc toward the nine skittles at the end of an alley and score a point for each one they knock down. The player with the highest score at the end of the three chalks wins the match.

Alley The area from which the ball or cheese is rolled toward the skittles. It is 3ft wide and must be 21ft long from the front of the first plate.

Ball Made of wood or molded rubber. It has a diameter of 5in.

Chalk A player is allowed three throws when hoping to strike the skittles down. If a player knocks down all his skittles before the three throws, the skittles are set up again.

Cheese The cheese is a thick, flat disc usually made of a very hard piece of wood. It can be used as an alternative to the ball when attempting to strike the skittles. It weighs between 10 and 12lb.

Duration The scores for each player are totaled after each leg has been completed. The player with the highest score wins the leg. A game is the best of three legs.

Floorer This takes place when all nine skittles are knocked to the ground by hitting the head pin with considerable force at exactly the right angle.

Foul throw Awarded against a player if they run over the line, or if the ball or cheese hits the side of the alley before connecting with the skittles.

Frame The area in which the skittles are set up. It is made of hornbeam and measures 4.5ft square. One plate is the center of the frame from which the other eight skittles are then 3in from the edges of the frame and 1.9in from the center.

Headpin The pin that is in the center at the front of the frame.

Heel The front of a player's foot. This must not go over the line when the playing is releasing the ball or cheese.

Leg Three chalks from each player make up a leg.

Line A black line is marked on the alley that a player must not go over when releasing the ball down toward the skittles. It is 15.5ft from the frame.

Metal plate Circular base on which the skittles rest, 3in in diameter.

Padded area At the end of the frame there is a protective area to stop any damage from occurring.

Repositioned If any of the skittles has been knocked down, they need to be replaced by the setter-up.

Run A player will run toward the line before releasing the ball to get more power on the ball. However, they must not run over the line.

Scoring A player receives one point for every skittle they knock over. Each player is allowed three throws, and can score a maximum of 27 points.

Setter-up At the end of a chalk, each team provides a setter-up who will set up the skittles again and remove any balls or cheeses after a foul throw has been committed.

Skittles An object that a player will attempt to strike down with either a ball or the cheese. There are nine skittles in a frame and they are normally made of wood. Different shapes and sizes can be used. Skittles measure 14.5in in length and have a radius of 6.8in at the top of the pin and 3in at the bottom.

Croquet

Croquet is played between two or four players, who aim to score points by striking the balls with a mallet through a course of hoops and against a center peg. The winning team is the one that finishes the course first with both balls, or that scores the most points in an agreed period.

....

Aiming point The point at which to aim the ball when the two balls need to be sent in different but predicted directions, as well as the point at which to aim in an angled hoop shot.

Baulk A line that is placed yard from the boundary line along the yard line. It is used as the spot for starting a game and for lift shots.

Bisque The name given to an extra turn in a handicap game, and the term used for the stick to indicate the presence of a turn.

Boundary line The line that forms the limits of the playing area or lawn. Usually indicated as such by chalk or string.

Break A turn containing more than one stroke.

Continuation stroke An extra stroke that comes after a croquet stroke or running a hoop.

Corner The joining parts of the four boundary lines.

Corner area Cover all four one-square-yard areas of the court.

Corner spot The inside spot of the corner area. A ball that goes out of court within at least a yard of the corner area will be replaced on this spot.

Croquet stroke The name given to the stroke that hits the roqueted ball.

Croqueted ball The opposing ball that you hit with your ball and mallet in a croquet stroke.

Crush A crush is a fault in which the ball is forced against a hoop or the peg with a mallet.

Doubles A game of croquet between four players who play as two pairs.

Double target Occurs when two balls are close together, giving the striker a wide target to aim for.

Drive shot A croquet stroke that is played without a roll or stop.

Either ball rule The rule that allows a player to choose which ball would be most beneficial to play between the two balls on court.

Error The term used to describe any action that is deemed illegal that does not include the use of a mallet. Usually incurs a penalty.

Fault Includes any form of play with the mallet that is deemed illegal. The majority of faults result in a penalty being awarded.

Four-ball break Uses the striker's ball plus three others.

Free shot If a shot is missed then the ball goes to a safe place on the court.

Full game A 26-point game in which six hoops are run in both directions by both balls.

Guarded leave Means that a player will leave his or her balls in as awkward a position as possible at the end of his turn for the opponent to play against.

Half angle The method for calculating the aiming point for a stroke that sends the two balls in different directions.

Hoop point The point scored from running a hoop.

Innings The term used for a player who is in control of the situation.

Jaws The space in between the

uprights of the hoops.

Join up When your turn is finished and the balls are close together.

Lift shot A player is allowed to lift the ball and play it from baulk.

Peel When a ball other than the striker's scores a hoop point.

Pegged-out ball Occurs after a peg out.

Peg out Occurs after a ball has scored all of its hoops and then hits the peg. The first player to peg out both balls is the winner.

Penultimate The second-to-last hoop in a full game.

Pioneer When the ball goes to the next hoop but one, in three- and four-ball breaks.

Pivot The primary ball in a four-ball break.

Push shot Describes the shot that maintains contact with the mallet and ball. This pushes the ball along rather than striking it.

Roll shot A stroke that results in both balls moving the same distance.

Roquet When you hit another ball with your own.

Roqueted ball The ball that you have just hit.

Rover The name given to the ball that has run all of its hoops.

Running a hoop When a ball has passed through the correct hoop in the correct direction.

Rush The movement of another ball that has been roqueted.

Safe shot Where, despite a shot being missed, it gives little away to your opponent, even if it ends up near your opponent's ball.

Scatter A strike that ensures your ball hits another ball on which no roquet can be made.

Scoring a hoop Means the same as running a hoop.

Sequence game The old style of cro-quet where the balls were lined up in a strict sequence.

Setting The term given to the placing of the hoops and peg on the lawn, and describing the adjustment of the hoop to the correct width.

Singles Play between two players using two balls each.

Stalking Describes the striker follow-ing the line of strike to the ball so as to be correctly positioned to take the strike.

Stop shot Occurs when the striker's ball moves only a short distance in com-parison with the other ball.

Take-off A stroke that involves your ball moving to the required spot while the other ball remains almost stationary.

Taking croquet Placing two balls in order to play a croquet stroke.

Three-ball break Occurs when the striker's ball plus two others are used to make a break.

Tice A ball that is placed so as to entice the opposing players to shoot and miss. Usually tried at the beginning of a game.

Tie The situation that happens at the end of play when both sides have equal points.

Time The duration of play and the call used to indicate the end of play.

Two-ball break Occurs when a player uses the striker's ball plus one to make a break.

Wiring Occurs when a player cannot use a ball to hit any other ball. If the wiring was caused by an opposing player, then the injured party may claim a lift shot.

Yard line Placed one yard inside the boundary line. Also the area where balls are placed when they go out of court.

Yard line area The section of the play-ing area lying between the yard line and the boundary line.

Golf

Golf has been described as a sport played 95 per cent with the mind and five per cent with the body. The simple objective is to use a series of clubs to propel the ball, both through the air and along the ground, into a series of 18 holes in as few strokes as possible.

19th hole The clubhouse bar. When players go for a drink after a game, they are said to be playing the 19th hole.

Address The term given to the way in which a golfer stands to play a shot.

Albatross A score of three under par for any given hole. It is a rare sight on a scorecard, but can occur when a player holes an approach shot to a par five.

Apron Where grass is cut lower than the fairway on the immediate approach to the putting surface. You can putt from it, but the grass is still slightly longer than that on the green itself.

Augusta National Golf Club The Georgia golf club that hosts the Masters every year. The course is renowned for its remarkable beauty and its vivid array of flowers.

Back nine Golfing parlance for the closing nine holes played on a standard 18-hole course.

Ball The size of the standard ball is 1.68in. in diameter, and it should weigh no more than 1.6oz.

Ballmarker When the ball comes to rest on the putting green, a player can mark his ball and clean it if he so wishes. When you do so, however, you need to place a marker behind the ball before lifting it up.

Bare lie This is when the ball comes to rest on a piece of terrain that has little or no grass beneath it. It is an awkward situation, and restricts the types of shots you can hit from it.

Barranca Spanish term for gullies or ditches that occasionally have water in them.

Birdie A score of one under par on any given hole. For instance, if a player takes three shots to complete a par four, then he has recorded a birdie.

Bite A term used when a player has managed to get the ball to stop quickly on the green.

Bogey A score of one over par for any given hole. For instance, if you take six shots on a par five.

British Open The oldest of the four major championships, first held in 1860.

Bunker A hazard that more often than not contains sand. You must not ground your club in a hazard before playing your shot.

Caddie The person who carries a golfer's clubs around the course. He or she may also, upon request, assist with club selection, course information such as yardages, and help read greens.

Casual water Any water on a golf course that is not part of a hazard. You can claim relief from casual water.

Chip A type of shot that is often played around the green. It can be played with virtually any club in the bag. The backswing is minimal, as is the follow-through.

Clubs A player may use a maximum of 14 clubs. There are three types of clubs: woods, irons and a putter. Each has a grip, a shaft and a face.

Course A standard golf course consists of 18 holes, each of varying length.

Divot The piece of earth dug up as a player strikes the ball. Etiquette requires that players replace divots.

Dormie In match play, if leading an

opponent by the number of holes remaining, you are said to be dormie.

Draw A shot where the ball is drawn deliberately from right to left in the air.

Drive When you are playing a par four or par five, the shot off the tee is called a drive.

Driver The club that has the longest shaft but the least loft of all the clubs, except the putter, and is used to hit the

CADDIE: The golfer's constant companion during a round of golf. Their job is not only to carry clubs but also to give advice on club selection, warn of obstacles ahead and help judge the slope of the greens

ball the farthest.

Drop The action a player takes after striking the ball into water or into an unplayable lie. It is also done when you are taking relief (from casual water). It is done by extending the arm at shoulder height and simply dropping the ball to the ground.

Eagle A score of two under par on any given hole. For instance, if you take three shots to complete a par-five hole.

Etiquette Golfers are expected to treat their fellow players on the course with courtesy and to behave responsibly toward the course.

Fade A shot that is deliberately shaped from left to right; the opposite of a draw.

Fairway The mown area between the tee and the green.

Fairway woods Woods (most often made of metal now) that are meant primarily for use off the ground instead of off a tee. The three-, five-, and seven-woods are good examples. All have smaller heads than a drive, and have weight concentrated in the bottom of the club to help get the ball airborne off the fairway or out of the rough. These clubs are used when a golfer is too far from the green to reach it with an iron.

Fat A term used when the club digs into the ground significantly before making contact with the ball.

Flag A banner that is attached to the top of a stick to demonstrate where the hole is located on the putting green.

Fourball A format used to play a doubles match where each golfer plays a ball from tee to green. The best ball from each partnership is the one that counts at the end of every hole.

Foursomes A format used to play a doubles match where only one ball is played per partnership. Each duo plays alternate strokes with their ball.

Front nine Golfing parlance for the opening nine holes to be played on a standard 18-hole golf course.

Gimme The term used for a putt conceded by an opponent without having to hole it because it is so short. There are no gimmes in professional golf or most club competitions.

Grand Slam The term for the four major tournaments in modern professional golf: the Masters, The U.S. Open, the British Open and the PGA Championship. Only four players (Gene Sarazen, Ben Hogan, Jack Nicklaus and Gary Player) have won the modern Grand Slam.

Greens in regulation A statistic used for describing in percentage terms the number of times a player gets his ball onto the putting surface in two shots fewer than the par for the hole.

Ground under repair Any area of the course where repair work is being carried out. It is shown by the white sticks surrounding the area. If your ball ends up in it, you may take relief, but no nearer to the hole.

Handicap A handicap is an allowance given to players to help them compete on an equal level, whatever their ability. A player's handicap is arrived at after consideration of his recent rounds.

Hazard A hazard is any bunker or water hazard. Roads, tracks and paths are declared not to be hazards.

Hole Each putting green has a 4.5in diameter hole into which players aim to hit the ball in as few strokes as possible from the tee.

Hole in one A tee shot that ends up in the hole. Also known as an ace.

Honor The player that has the honor on each hole is the one that tees off first. It is decided by whoever completed the previous hole in the fewest shots.

Hook A shot that curves in an out-of-control manner from right to left.

Iron A term used to describe the smaller-headed clubs that are mainly used on shots from the fairway and rough.

Lag putt A long putt that the player tries to hit near the hole, rather than aggressively trying to make the putt.

Lateral water hazard A water hazard, defined by red stakes, that runs alongside the line of play.

Lie The angle at which the clubhead lies in relation to the club's shaft.

Links A golf course constructed on land by or reclaimed from the sea.

Loft The angle at which the club face falls away from the designated target.

Lost ball When you lose your ball, you must go back to the place from which you played your previous shot and play it again, adding on one penalty stroke.

LPGA The Ladies' Professional Golf Association governs events played on the LPGA Tour in America.

Masters An invitational tournament and the first men's major to be contested in the year, taking place in April. It is always staged at Augusta, unlike the other three majors, which rotate between locations.

Match play A format of golf in which golfers compete to win as many holes as possible rather than counting the lowest number of shots.

Net Your net score is the final one when your handicap is taken away from the gross number of shots you have taken.

Old Course This is found at St Andrews and is reckoned to be the place where golf was first played. It is the most celebrated venue at which the British Open is played.

Order of play The farthest from the hole should play first. When players are on the teeing ground, the player who shot the lowest score on the previous hole tees off first.

Out of bounds This is an area not deemed to be inside the perimeters of the course, and is marked with white sticks. If your ball finishes out of bounds, you must return to where you played your last shot and play it again, taking a penalty of one shot.

Outside agency A term used by the Rules Book to describe a factor that may cause a ball to move – for example, people, but not weather conditions.

Par If you take four shots on a hole that is designated a par four then you are said to have parred the hole or played the hole to par.

Penalty In stroke play, violations of the Rules of Golf are penalized by adding shots to a player's total. In match play, he is likely to lose the hole.

PGA Championship The last of the four majors played each year.

PGA of America The Professional Golfers' Association, the organisation that administers the PGA Championship and the Ryder Cup.

PGA Tour Coordinates and runs the majority of events for top professionals in the United States with the exception of the Masters, the US Open and the PGA Championship.

Pin Golf jargon for the flag stick.

Pitch A high-flying shot, often played with a short-iron, to land the ball softly on the green.

Pitch-and-putt A scaled-down golf course where all the holes are par threes.

Pitch mark The mark the ball leaves when it lands on the green. Golfers are expected to repair their pitch marks.

Playoff If players' scores are tied at the end of a tournament, they enter a playoff to determine a winner. It can be sudden death or over a designated number of holes.

Preferred lie Winter Rules can come into force when courses deteriorate through adverse weather. To counter this, players are permitted to improve their lie – hence a preferred lie.

Presidents Cup A competition played every four years between the United

States and a "Rest of the World" team, not including players from Europe.

Provisional ball If a player believes a ball to be lost, another one may be taken after telling their opponent that they are about to play a "provisional". If, after searching for the original ball, it cannot be found, one penalty-stroke is added and the provisional ball becomes the ball in play.

Putt The type of shot played when the ball is on the putting green. It is hit along the ground with a putter.

Putter The club used by players when on the putting green. It has minimal loft.

Putting green The closely mowed area where each hole is located.

Relief Granted to a player when the shot he is trying to play is prevented by certain impediments, such as casual water, ground under repair and golf car paths. A player granted relief usually is entitled to drop the ball nearer the hole with no penalty.

Rough The part of the golf course that is not cut and where the grass and other foliage is not closely mowed.

Round A full 18 holes is referred to as a round of golf.

Royal and Ancient Golf Club This is the most famous golf club in the world (see "St Andrews"). Its rules are those used by golfers worldwide, except in the United States and Mexico.

Rules of Golf Administered by the Royal and Ancient and the USGA.

Ryder Cup A competition played every two years between professional golfers from Europe and the United States. It was first contested in 1927.

Sand save The term given when a player lands in a greenside bunker but still saves par by hitting the ball on the green, then making his first putt.

Sand shot Any shot played from a bunker is a sand shot.

Scorecard The card on which a player writes down his score as the round progresses. Players should exchange scorecards with an opponent to mark each other's card.

Scrapes Instead of greens, some courses, particularly in dry areas of Australia, use a thick dirt that needs to be scraped before each putt.

Scratch When a player has his handicap down to zero.

Shaft The part of the golf club that links the clubhead and the grip. In the past, shafts were made of hickory, but now the three most common materials are steel, graphite and titanium.

Shank The worst type of golf shot you can hit. The ball comes off the hosel at the base of the shaft instead of the club face, causing the ball to fly wildly off-line.

Short game The part of the golf perceived by top professionals to be the most important. It incorporates chipping, putting, pitching and bunker play around the green.

Slice An exaggerated left-to-right movement of the ball in the air is a slice.

Spoon Golfers often refer to their three-wood club as a spoon.

Stableford The scoring system where the winner is the golfer who has scored the most points. You get one point for a net bogey, two points for a net par, three points for a net birdie, four points for a net eagle and five points for a net albatross.

St Andrews A small town on the east coast of Scotland widely regarded to be the home of golf. The town is the home of the Royal and Ancient Golf Club and the Old Course.

Sticks A colloquial term for a set of golf clubs.

Stiff If a ball is hit onto the putting green so close to the flag that the player will not be able to miss the putt, then he or she is said to have "knocked it stiff".

Stimpmeter A handheld device that measures the speed of greens or how

ST ANDREWS: The golf course on the east coast of Scotland where many believe golf was first played

fast a ball will roll across them.

Stroke play The scoring format where the winner is the golfer who has taken the least number of strokes to get around the course.

Stymied A phrase that is used to describe when a player has his path to a target blocked.

Tee A wooden or plastic peg in varying sizes that the golfer may place his ball upon at the start of each hole.

Teeing ground Each of the 18 holes to be played must start from the teeing ground. This is a rectangular area defined by markers.

Tee off Striking a shot off the tee is said to be teeing off.

Thin Players hit the ball thin when the leading edge of the club fails to slide under the ball completely.

Unplayable ball If a player's ball is in an unplayable lie, there are three options after a one-stroke penalty has been added to your score. You can either replay the shot from its original position; drop the ball within two club lengths of the unplayable ball but no nearer the hole; or move the ball back as far as you want on a straight line with the original unplayable lie between you

and the hole.

US Open The national championship of the United States. It started in 1895.

Utility wood A wood that has been constructed with the specific purpose of troubleshooting. It has plenty of get to help loft the ball out of tall rough or bunkers.

Walker Cup A team tournament for amateurs contested every two years by teams from the United States and Great Britain and Ireland. First played in 1922.

Water hazard A body of water that is marked with yellow stakes. If you play into one, there is a one-shot penalty and you will either have to play the shot again or drop the ball no nearer the hole directly in line with the point at which the ball entered the hazard.

Winter Rules When adverse weather conditions affect the state of the course, clubs may use Winter Rules. This permits a player to improve his lie by placing the ball in an unaffected area no nearer to the hole.

Woods A group of clubs that were originally made with wooden heads. Through technological advances, most woods are now made out of metal. These clubs are used to hit the ball long distances.

4 Athletics

This area comprises running, jumping and throwing events, either in a specialized stadium or on more open terrain (cross-country running, for example). It also includes multi-discipline events such as the modern pentathlon, triathlon and ironman, which include swimming, but are grouped here because they are chiefly races between athletes.

The Olympic Games

Amateur Describes anyone who does not make any money for taking part in a sport.

Anthem The official Olympic anthem was composed by Spyros Samaras with the words written by Costis Palamas, the Greek poet laureate.

Olympic rings Made up of five rings and six colors, blue, yellow, black, green and red on a white background. First used in 1913 to represent all the nations involved in the games. At least one of the colors from the flag of every nation is included in the six colors of the flag.

IOC The International Olympic Committee who were founded in 1894 when they started the Modern Olympic Games.

Medals Are awarded to the first three winners of each discipline, with gold for the first, silver for the second and bronze for the third.

Museum The Olympic Museum is based in Switzerland and was opened in 1993.

Olive wreath The original prize given to the winner of the original games.

Olympiad Ancient Greek term that is still used today to describe the interim period between the games.

Olympic flame Originally lit at Olympia in Greece and carried to the site of the games across national barriers. It is seen as a symbol of International unity and the eternal sporting spirit of the games. Made its first appearance at the modern games in 1928.

Olympic motto The Latin motto for the games is *Citius, Altius, Fortius* which translates as "Swifter, Higher, Stronger".

Olympic village The area where all competing athletes stay during the duration of the games.

Paralympics A separate competition that is held after the Summer Games with various sports for the physically disabled.

Summer Games These are held every four years and include the track and field events.

Winter Games These are held every four years but with a two-year separation from the Summer games. This has been the case since 1994.

Track Events

Track events consist of sprint, middle- and long-distance races that take place on the athletics track as well as walking and marathon events that take place off the track, and the relay, steeplechase and hurdles races. Most of these events are run by both men and women.

GENERAL TERMS

Assistance Deemed illegal and punishable by disqualification. Assistance is taken to mean any direct help that a competitor receives during a race – except for medical help.

Barging Describes when one runner makes contact with another by bumping into them when the athletes are not confined to their own lanes. Can result in disqualification.

Beating the gun When one (or more) competitor takes off from their starting position before the gun has been fired. Can result in disqualification.

Bell Used to signal to competitors that they have begun the final lap of a middle- or long-distance race.

Bend On the usual 400m track, the bends are the curved running sections at each end. On these sections, runners are said to be running the bend.

Boxed in Occurs in middle- or long-distance races when a runner is closely surrounded by other runners and is unable to get away without having to change the rhythm of his running.

Direction of running All track events are run counterclockwise on the track.

Dip finish When the runner pushes their chest forward to touch the tape when taking their final stride in order to try to finish as well as possible.

Doping All competitors are required to make themselves available for random drug testing. If any prohibited substance is found to be present within body tissue or fluids, the competitor is immediately suspended until a hearing at which the officiating body will make a final decision on the competitor's fate. If found guilty, a competitor faces a minimum ban of four years and a maximum of a life ban from the sport.

False start When a competitor fails to comply with the starting orders after a reasonable time, or if a competitor disturbs their opponents after the on-your-marks order has been given. Also occurs when a competitor moves or starts before the gun has been fired but after assuming the full and final set position. A competitor who has made one false start is warned; two false starts result in disqualification.

Finish line A competitor is deemed the winner if their torso has crossed the finish line first. The line should be at least 2in wide and is held across the track by two posts positioned at least 12in from the edge of the track. The posts should measure approximately 4.5ft high with a width of 3in and a thickness of 0.8in.

Footwear Footwear must not have any aids to assist the athlete, such as a spring in the shoe. There must not be more than 11 spikes on the shoe and they must not exceed 9mm in length.

Heats A series of qualifying races to decide who will race in the final of an event, as there are only eight lanes on a track. The winner and second-placed contestants qualify for the next round.

IAAF The International Amateur Athletics Federation, the governing body of athletics.

Lanes Each competitor in sprint and middle-distance events is assigned a lane at the start of each race. In races up to and including the 400m, competitors are given their own lane for the whole race. In 800m events, runners run in lanes until after the first bend, when they can cut to the inside lane. Races over 800m are not run in lanes. Each lane should measure between 4ft and 4.1ft wide. Each lane is "staggered" in relation to the next, so that athletes do not stand alongside each other at the start. This ensures the overall distance run by each competitor is the same.

Lap scorer Keeps count of laps run by each competitor in races over 1500m. Appointed by the referee to assist in ensuring the rules are adhered to.

Marksmen Assistants to the starter. Their job is to ensure that competitors are placed in the correct stations, which are 3.3yd behind the starting line. Once this has been done the marksmen will signify to the starter that all is ready.

Number cards All competitors must wear number cards on both the front and back of their torso. If photographic equipment is in use at the finishing line to determine the result of a photo finish, then the judges may require competitors to wear additional numbers on the side of their shorts facing the camera.

Obstruction Any competitor who impedes a fellow contestant by jostling, running or walking across their path or in any way blocking their progress is liable to be disqualified.

Pacesetter A competitor in long-distance races who sacrifices his own chance of winning by running faster than usual in the early stages of a race so as to create a fast-paced race. Often used to help a top athlete aim for a world record time.

Pain barrier The physical pain an athlete may have to overcome when pushing themselves hard during a race.

Photo finish When two or more athletes finish so close together that their times may be identical, photographic evidence is necessary to decide the winner. The victor is the competitor whose torso crosses the finish line first.

Rest time between heats When qualifying heats are being run, competitors are entitled to breaks between successive heats in which they are competing 20 minutes for races up to and including 100m; 40 minutes for races of greater than 100m and up to the 200m; 60 minutes for races of greater than 200m and up to 400m; 80 minutes for races of over 400m and up to 800m; and 100 minutes for races greater than 800m.

Revolver The gun used to signal the start of a race. It must be fired up into the air and give off a flash that the manual timekeepers can see clearly, as the time is counted from when the flash goes off.

Sex test Introduced into competition in 1966 to ensure that women athletes are medically female.

Sitting in Describes the positioning of a long-distance runner who is running slightly behind and outside the shoulder of another runner.

Spiked When an athlete has his legs unintentionally caught by the spikes of another athlete.

Starter The official who ensures that every race is started correctly. The starter's decisions are final.

Starting blocks Allowed only in races up to and including 400m. Competitors have the choice of whether to use them or not. All starting blocks must be made of rigid materials and have no springs or other artificial devices to aid a competitor. They must be fixed to the track, and when the athlete is in position both hands must be in contact with the floor.

Starting orders For races up to and including the 400m, the starting command is as follows "On your mark", "Set", and then the gun shot signals "Go". For distances greater than the 400m, the starting command is "On your marks", which is the signal for the competitors to approach the starting line without actually touching it. Once the steady position has been assumed by all the competitors, the gun is fired to signal "Go".

Stations Stations for all competitors are chosen by drawing lots. In straight sprint races the competitor drawn first is placed on the left of the track facing the finishing line (known as lane 1) and all other competitors are placed outward from there. In races on a spherical course the competitor drawn first is placed nearest the center of the track and the others follow from there.

Surging A tactic used by long-distance runners to upset the rhythm and pattern of the other runners by quickening their pace and then slowing it again.

Tartan tracks Those that have been laid with a resilient synthetic surface to make the track usable in all weathers.

Ties In the event of a tie occurring in qualifying heats, the two tied competitors both go through to the next round. If a tie occurs in a final, the referee can decide to let the two tied competitors rerun the race. If this is not a practicable option, the tie will stand.

Timekeepers Employed to keep a manual record of all times and laps run, even if automatic equipment is being used. They should stand in line with the finish and be at least 5.5yd from the outside track.

Timing Carried out by fully automatic equipment, or by timekeepers using a stopwatch.

Track The eight-lane course on which races are run. Competitors always run round the track in an counterclockwise direction.

Wind assisted In races of 200m or less, the wind speed and direction during the race must be recorded, as this information is a factor when validating record claims. The gauge should be placed parallel to the track and at least 50m from the finishing line. If the wind speed exceeds 2m/s in the direction in which the athletes are running, any record time achieved is not valid. The wind speed is not taken into consideration if a record is achieved into a headwind.

RELAY EVENTS

In athletics, relay races are run for both men and women over 100m (4 × 100m) and 400m (4 × 400m). Each relay team consists of four competitors. A baton is passed from one team member to another in succession, and the team that completes the race first is the winner. In the 4 × 100m, the race is run strictly in lanes; in the 4 × 400m, however, only the first leg is run in lanes, and on the second and subsequent legs the runners are allowed to break to the inside lane once the first bend has been run. The team in the lead at each changeover point is allowed to take the inside lane.

Acceleration zone Also known as the pre-changeover zone, the section of the track leading up to the changeover zone that enables the receiving athlete to accelerate to racing speed.

Alternative method A method of baton changing in which the carrier transfers the baton into the opposite hand of the outgoing runner.

Anchor leg The last leg of a relay race.

Baton A smooth, hollow, cylindrical tube normally made of metal used for all relay races. It measures a maximum of long and must weigh no less than 1.8oz. Each team's baton should be a different color to assist the judges.

Changeover When one team member hands the baton to another.

Changeover zone There are three change over zones during a race, and competitors are not allowed to pass the baton on unless the incoming and out-going athletes are both in these areas. Each changeover zone is 20m long.

Check or cue mark Used to mark the track with either a scratch or a sprinkling of powder to guide the runners at the changeover. It must be within a runner's own lane.

Disqualification A team is disqualified if any member impedes or blocks another competitor during the race, or if a change over is not started or completed within the change over box.

Dropped baton If a competitor drops the baton, only they may pick it up.

Down sweep A method of baton changing that involves the incoming runner placing the baton into the upturned palm of the receiving runner.

Final leg See "Anchor leg". When the final competitor reaches the finishing line, he or she must hand the baton over to the waiting official. Throwing or dropping the baton will result in dis-qualification.

Free distance The space between the incoming and outgoing runners at baton changeover.

Handover The term used to describe the passing of the baton from one team member to another. The handover must take place in a 20m changeover zone. If the handover takes place outside this zone, the team is disqualified. The baton's position, not the runner's position, determines whether the handover was legitimate.

Heats If a team qualifies for the next round of a relay event, they are not allowed to change their team members for any other race unless one of them is injured or ill.

Incoming runner The runner who is in the process of finishing his leg, and is either ready to pass the baton on or cross the finish line. The incoming runner should maintain maximum speed until the baton is safely in his team-mate's grasp.

Lanes All 4 × 100m relay races are run in lanes. In 200m races the first two legs are run in lanes, as is the first part of the third leg, up to the first bend. In 400m races, the first lap and first part of the second lap up to the end of the first bend are run in lanes.

Leg The section run by one runner in a relay event.

Marks Placed on or beside the track for relay races only, they mark the zones in which the team members are allowed to pass the baton.

Outgoing runner The runner who collects the baton from his teammate. The outgoing runner should aim to be at maximum speed as he is receiving the baton. He should watch the baton until the last possible moment before sprint-ing away.

Procedure Each team member runs one leg of the race. They carry the baton with them as they run and can only hand it over to their team member once they reach the changeover zone. Once they have handed over the baton, competitors should remain in their lanes until the course is clear to avoid imped-ing other competitors.

Running order A team is allowed to change their running order.

Start The start is staggered as the track is oval-shaped; this ensures that all competitors run the same distance.

Substitutions May be made only with athletes named before the race.

Team members Each team has four members of the same sex. There are no mixed-sex relay events.

Upsweep Involves the incoming runner bringing the baton up into the palm of the outgoing runner.

HURDLES EVENTS

The hurdles events in athletics consist of the men's and women's 400m, the men's 110m and the women's 100m. The decathlon and heptathlon competitions also involve hurdles events. In each hurdles event, the athletes must run over 10 hurdles.

Chopping Shortening the length of one's stride in order to position oneself correctly for the next hurdle.

Decathlon A competition of 10 events for men that includes the 110m hurdles.

Disqualification Occurs when a hurdler drags their foot or leg below the top of the bar of the hurdle at the moment of clearance, if they deliberately knock the hurdle over with their foot or hand, if they run around a hurdle, or if they jump a hurdle that is not in their lane. However, a hurdler is not disqualified for unintentionally knocking hurdles over.

Height of hurdles For the 100m hurdles, they are 33in high; for the 400m women's hurdles they are 30in high; for the 110m men's hurdles they are 42in high; and for the 400m men's hurdles they are 36in high.

Heptathlon A competition of seven events for female athletes that includes the 100m hurdles.

Hurdles The hurdle consists of two uprights, which support a rectangular frame with a level top rail. The minimum weight of the hurdle should be 22lb. The hurdle should be of either wood or metal, with the top bar colored for maximum visibility. The maximum width of the hurdle should be 4ft.

Lanes Each competitor must stay in their own lane throughout the race.

Lead leg/arm Describes which leg or arm goes over the hurdle first.

Stride pattern The number of strides taken by a hurdler between hurdles. Eight strides are usually taken to the first hurdle, three in between hurdles.

Trailing leg The leg that goes over the hurdle second.

STEEPLECHASE

The steeplechase is considered a long-distance event, and the standard Olympic distance is the 3000m. It is run over seven and a half laps of the track, with four hurdles and one water jump on each lap. The event originated from cross-country events, with the water jump representing a ditch.

Check or cue mark Competitors can place a sprinkling of powder or a scratch on the track to help their lead-up to the water jump.

Disqualification Occurs when a steeplechaser either steps to one side of a jump, fails to go over or through the water in the water jump, or trails a foot or leg below the top of the hurdle to one side of it.

Hurdles They must weigh between 80 and 100kg. Men's hurdles are 91.5cm high, women's hurdles are 76cm. Each hurdle is 4m wide and the bar on the top of each hurdle is a 13cm square section. After the competitors have run the first 200m on the flat, they then have to cross five hurdles per lap, positioned across three inside lanes. Competitors may jump, vault or stand on hurdles.

Markers Some runners place these 15m from a hurdle so that they can pace their run-up to it. No solid object can be placed on the track.

Walk-overs A basic exercise regularly

practiced by steeplechase runners where low hurdles, set 3.3-5ft apart, are walked over.

Water jump The fourth jump in every lap, it is the same height as the other hurdles and 12ft long, but has a water-filled trench on the far side. The water depth nearest the hurdle is 28in, sloping upward to track level.

WALKING EVENTS

Walking events are some of the most underrated in terms of difficulty for the athlete. They require strength, discipline and concentration for races of up to 31 miles in length.

Action Walkers must maintain unbroken contact with the ground. The rear foot must not leave the ground before the front foot has made contact with it. While a foot is on the ground, the leg must be straightened.

Disqualification A competitor is allowed one caution for incorrect action. A caution is signaled by an official using a white flag. Any further cautions result in disqualification, signaled with a red flag.

Refreshment stations These contain approved refreshments for races exceeding 12 miles. The first refreshment station is situated 6 miles from the start, and subsequent stations every 3 miles.

Road walks Most often included in international competitions, 12 miles and 31 miles for men, and 6 miles for women.

Sponging points These supply water, but only after a distance of 12 miles.

Track events The distances in this type of event are 12 miles and 31 miles for men, and 6 miles for women.

MARATHON

The marathon is a long-distance race based on an ancient Greek event, contested over a distance of 26 miles and 385 yards (42.2km). Marathons are run mostly on road surfaces, with the start and finish being staged in the stadium during major championships.

Arena The venue for the start and finish of the event in major championships such as the Olympic Games.

Clothing Marathon runners are advised to wear lightweight vests and shorts to allow air to move freely around the body. Athletes can lose up to 14lb in weight through sweating during a marathon.

Fuel depletion and sweat loss These pose major problems and can seriously hinder a runner's progress in a marathon. Regular intake of water is therefore strongly advised.

Medical staff Officials who monitor races and have the power to withdraw competitors should they require urgent medical attention.

Refreshment stations Approved refreshments may be taken from these stations, which are located after the first 7 miles and then at every3 miles. No other form of refreshments are permitted.

Sponging points These supply water and are situated midway between the refreshment stations.

Wall Description applied to the sensation marathon runners often experience toward the end of a race when their legs become heavy and they feel they can run no farther.

World best performances Only these performances, rather than world records, are recognized because of the varying terrain of marathon races.

Field Events

Field events, which take place away from the track in an athletics stadium, encompass the long jump, high jump, triple jump, pole vault, shot put, discus, javelin and the hammer events. All of these demand different skills from the participants and have their own sets of rules.

LONG JUMP

In the long jump, athletes attempt to jump as far as possible into a sandpit from a takeoff board following a sprint run-up.

Failures A jump is considered a failure when a competitor does any of the following treads on any ground beyond the takeoff line; takes off from either side of the takeoff board, even if this is before the takeoff line; walks back through the landing area; touches the ground outside the landing area closer to the takeoff line than to the impression in the sand from where any measurement would be made; or performs any kind of somersault.

LONG JUMP: In order to further their distance, the athlete must ensure that their run up and take-off is as fast and as possible

Landing area A sandpit, which begins approximately 3.3ft from the takeoff board and is approximately 10ft in length. The sand must be raked level with the height of the takeoff board and moistened before the competition to allow accurate measurement.

Markers Competitors may leave marks alongside the runway to assist with their approach, as long as they do not use an indelible substance to make them. No marks may be placed beyond the takeoff line.

Measurement Made between the break in the sand nearest to the takeoff line that has been caused by any part of the competitor's body, and the takeoff line itself. The direction of measurement must be parallel to the direction of the runway.

Red flag Shown for an illegal jump.

Rounds Sometimes also known as "trials". A round constitutes one jump in competition. There are two ways a competition can be conducted (a) Each competitor takes part in between three and six rounds; (b) Each competitor takes part in three rounds, with the best three to eight competitors progressing to a further three rounds.

Runway The straight length of track along which a competitor sprints toward the takeoff board. The runway is level and at least 44yd long, although there is no maximum length.

Takeoff board A piece of wood about 8in long across the track marking the point at which competitors must take off. Beyond this is a 4in Plasticine board that captures the footprint of any athlete overstepping the takeoff board.

Takeoff line The far edge of the takeoff board beyond which the competitor must not tread.

Tie If there is a tie for the final place(s) for the next round of a long-jump competition, all competitors who are tied with each other progress to the next round regardless. In the case of any tie at the end of the entire competition, competitors' second-best jumps will be decisive. If there is still a tie, then it is the third-best jump that counts, and so on.

White flag Shown when an athlete has completed a legal jump.

Wind assisted Instruments placed by the side of the runway to record wind speed. If the wind speed is greater than 2m/s, a record-breaking jump cannot be ratified as an official record.

Windsock Positioned near the take off board, this enables competitors to judge the strength and direction of the wind before beginning their approach.

HIGH JUMP

In this event, competitors attempt to jump over a crossbar that is supported between two vertical poles set 13ft apart, known as uprights. When a competitor successfully clears a height without knocking the crossbar from its supports, the height is increased for the next jump.

Approach The length of the approach for a jump is unlimited, the minimum length is 16yd.

Bar The rod of metal balanced between the uprights.

Elimination A competitor is eliminated from the competition after three failures at the same height.

Failure A jump is classed as a failure if the jumper knocks the bar from its supports; takes off using both feet; or touches an area beyond the uprights before clearing the bar.

Fan Also known as the apron, a semi-circular area within which competitors must make their running approach. Its outer edge is at least 16yd from midway between the two uprights.

HIGH JUMP: Athletes begin with a run-up and then leap high into the air, flipping their body over a bar

Fosbury flop Method of high jumping in which the jumper clears the crossbar by arching their back over it.

Judges Two or three judges ensure that jumps are legal and that all apparatus is properly set up.

Landing area This is a mattress made of cushioned foam rubber that breaks a competitor's fall after a jump. There should be a gap of at least 4in between the landing area and the uprights to prevent the crossbar being knocked down by movement of the mattress.

Markers Competitors may place marks on the runway to assist with their approach, as long as they do not use an indelible substance.

Measurements The height of a jump is measured vertically from the ground to the lowest part of the top of the bar.

Passing A jumper may "pass" at any height (sit it out) and attempt the next height.

Rounds A competitor completes a round when successfully clearing a height. When all competitors have cleared that height, passed at that height or been eliminated, the competition progresses to the next round. The bar must be raised at least 0.8in from one round to the next.

Tie In the event of a tie, the jumper who made the fewest attempts at the winning height is declared the winner. If this is indecisive, the jumper with the fewest total failures wins.

Time allowed The time allowed to make a jump varies according to the stage of the competition. When there are more than two or three competitors in the event, each jumper is allowed around two minutes to make a jump. When fewer competitors remain, this increases to four minutes.

Winner The competition continues until only one jumper is left in the event.

TRIPLE JUMP

The triple jump is made up of a hop, a skip and a jump before the competitor lands in a sand area. The winner is the competitor who jumps the furthest after completing this sequence successfully. Each competitor has six attempts. If there is a tie, the winner is decided by comparing the relevant competitors' second-best jumps.

Hop A competitor completes his approach before raising one foot in the air; he must then land on the foot from which he took off.

Judging Five judges ensure the competition is run properly. One watches for any failures and has two flags – one white and one red to signal good jumps or no jumps. Two judges mark and measure the actual jump. One judge calls up the competitors and clears the runway, while the other judge stands between the takeoff board and landing area to watch the competitors' feet.

Jump After completing a hop and a step (skip), the competitor again raises both feet into the air and attempts to gain as much distance as possible into the landing area.

Jumping area The area between where the competitor starts the initial takeoff and the start of the landing area. It measures 14yd in length.

Landing area The landing area is filled with sand and should be moistened before the competition begins. It has to be raked level with the takeoff board before every jump.

Measuring The judges measure a jump from the nearest break in the landing area made by any part of the competitor's body. Distances are measured to the nearest 0.4in, and the measurement is taken right up to the takeoff line and at right angles to it.

No-jump When a competitor makes a

foul jump that counts toward his total.

Red flag Shown by the official when he judges that a no-jump has been made.

Run-up A competitor can have an unlimited approach. Marks are allowed to be placed alongside the runway, but not actually on the surface itself. They may not be placed beyond the takeoff line.

Shoes Heel spikes are recommended for use on grass. Plastic heel cups may be used to protect the heel bones.

Step (skip) After completing a hop, the competitor raises both feet in the air before landing on the opposite foot to that on which he landed for the hop.

Takeoff board The platform from which the athlete attempts his approach. This is made of wood and is sunk level with the runway.

Tie If the distances are level after six trials, than a tie is decided by comparing the tying competitors' second-best trials.

Trial A single jump that is deemed to be fair by the judges. A competitor normally takes six trials, and the athlete with the best distances over the six attempts wins the triple jump.

White flag Shown by the official when a jump is judged to be legal.

POLE VAULT

An event in which competitors have to vault over a high crossbar using a flexible pole as a lever. The heights are much greater than for the high jump, but the principles are the same. After successfully clearing a height without knocking the crossbar from its supports, the height is increased for the next jump.

Approach The length of the run-up is unlimited, although the minimum is 16yd.

Binding One or two layers of adhesive tape can be used at the lower end of the pole up to a depth of around 12in.

Elimination A competitor is eliminated from the competition after three failures at the same height.

Failure A jump is classed as a failure if the jumper knocks the bar from its supports; touches an area beyond the uprights, with either himself or the pole before clearing the bar; moves his lower hand above his upper hand or his upper hand off the pole.

Judges Two or three judges ensure that jumps are legal and that all apparatus is properly set up.

Landing area This is a mattress made of cushioned foam rubber that breaks the fall of competitors after a jump.

Markers Competitors may leave marks alongside the runway to assist with their approach as long as they do not use an indelible substance to make them. No marks may be placed beyond the takeoff line.

Measurements The height of a jump is measured vertically from the ground to the lowest part of the cross bar.

Passing A jumper may pass at any height and attempt the next height, but he may not then return to the previous height.

Pole Can be made of any material, and be of any length or diameter.

Resin Resin or an adhesive substance may be applied to hands to aid grip.

Round A competitor completes a round when successfully clearing a height. When all competitors have cleared that height or passed at that height, the competition progresses to the next round. The bar must be raised at least 2in each round.

Runway The straight length of track along which a competitor sprints towards the takeoff board. The runway is level and at least 44yd long, although there is no maximum length.

Takeoff board A piece of wood about

8in in depth marking the point at which competitors must take off. Beyond this is a 4in-deep Plasticine board that captures the footprint of any athlete overstepping the takeoff board.

Take-off box At the end of the runway in front of the crossbar is a box sunk into the ground where vaulters plant their pole after their approach. Competitors may place sand in the box when it is their turn to vault.

Take off line The far edge of the takeoff board beyond which the competitor must not tread.

Tie If there is a tie for the final place(s) for the next round, all tying competitors progress to the next round. In the case of any tie at the end of the competition, competitors' second- best jumps will be decisive. If there is still a tie then it is the third- best jump that counts and so on. If this process is unable to determine a winner for first place in the competition, there will be additional rounds between those tying until a winner becomes apparent. If this process is unable to determine any other positions, then those competitors will be awarded the same position.

Windsock Positioned near the takeoff board allowing competitors to judge the strength and direction of the wind.

Winner The competition continues until only one jumper is left in the event.

SHOT PUT

The shot is a spherical metal ball that a competitor must "put" (throw) from their shoulder as far as possible into a marked sector. Each competitor must put the shot from within the circle, and it must land within a marked sector. Each competitor normally has six puts, and the athlete who puts the shot the farthest wins the event. In the event of a tie, the competitor who has thrown the second-

best throw is declared the winner.

Circle The area from which the competitor puts the shot. It is bounded by a white-painted band of iron, steel or wood. The surface of the circle is usually concrete, and there is always a raised stopboard, which the competitor must not step on before completing their throw.

Foul Awarded against a competitor if they cross over the line or commit any kind of infringement.

Ground outside The area outside the circle. If a competitor enters this zone, the put is considered invalid.

Judging At least two judges keep a record of all trials, and show a white flag to indicate a fair throw and a red flag to show a foul. They will also check the recordings at the end of each round.

Landing The shot must finish within the inner edge of the sector lines.

Measurement Each put is measured immediately after it has taken place. The judges measure each put from the nearest mark made by the shot to the inner edge of the ring bounding the circle. Distances are recorded to the nearest 0.4in.

Putting action The competitor stands in a stationary position to begin the put, and must be within the circle. They are allowed to use only one hand, and throughout the putting action must not drop their hand below its starting position. The shot cannot be brought behind the line of the shoulders. A put is deemed invalid if, after starting his action, the competitor touches the top of the stopboard or the ring bounding the circle.

Sector lines The lines marking the edges of the field. The shot must land within these marked sectors for a shot to be deemed valid.

Shoes Competitors wear shoes without spikes, as a concrete surface is recommended for the area within the circle.

Shot The shot put is a solid metal ball, which the competitor throws as far as possible from within the circle. It must be spherical in shape and smooth-surfaced. It is made of solid iron, brass or any metal that is not softer than brass. The minimum weight of the shot in the men's event is 16lb and 8.8lb for the women's event.

Stopboard At the front of the circle is a raised arc, which the competitor is not allowed to touch when throwing the put. It is 4in high and 4.3in wide.

Tie If the scores are level after six trials, the winner is decided by the competitors' second-best throws.

Trial The term given to a single shot thrown by a competitor.

DISCUS

The discus is a round metal object resembling a flying saucer that is thrown from a circle into a marked-out area of the field. The winner is the competitor who achieves the best distance in six trials.

Cage Made of a metal frame with netting covering the whole frame.

Circle The area on the field from where the discus is thrown. The throw will be classed as illegal if the competitor does not have both feet in the circle at the time of release. For safety reasons, the circle should be surrounded with netting so that if the discus is accidentally released, it will do no harm to other competitors or spectators.

Discus Generally made of wood with a metal rim and a weight attached in the middle. The minimum weight of the discus should be 4.4lb for male competitors and 2.2lb for female competitors. The diameter should be 8.6-8.7in

for men and 7.0-7.1in for women.

Foul A competitor is deemed to have committed a foul while making a throw if they touch any part outside of the circle or the top of the circle rim with their body.

Heats Each competitor is allowed six trials if there are fewer than eight competitors, otherwise three trials each are taken with the best eight gaining another three. The winner is the competitor with the farthest throw out of the six heats.

Kit Shoes should not have any spikes. Fingers are allowed to be taped up individually to provide better grip.

Landing The discus must land within the inner side of the sector lines.

Measuring Distances are measured to the nearest 1.5in below the distance thrown.

Officials There should be five judges, two of them positioned on their own side to watch for infringements that may occur within the circle; the other three are spread out randomly on the field, as nobody knows where the discus will land.

Throwing The correct way to hold the discus is to grip it with one hand while twisting the body and then releasing while still in the circle. The competitor must begin their throw from a stationary position. Any throwing technique is

DISCUS: Competitors whirl around in a circle to gain momentum before throwing the discus

allowed as long as it conforms to the official rules of the event.

Tie A tiebreaker is decided by the competitors' second-best throws. Whoever has achieved the farthest throw will progress to the next round or will win if it is a final.

Time Each competitor is given one and a half minutes in which to perform their throw. If they go over this time limit they will be disqualified.

JAVELIN

The javelin is a spear-like instrument that individual competitors throw as far as possible within a marked area. The athlete who throws the javelin the farthest is the winner.

Arc This is made of wood or metal and is painted white. It can also be just a painted white line marking out the area of the arc.

Fouls Indicated by a red flag, a throw is deemed illegal if the competitor's body comes into contact with the ground, scratch line or arc.

Grip The javelin should be gripped in one hand only with the fourth finger nearest to the point and the hand on the grip. Competitors are allowed to use a sticky substance to enhance their grip on the javelin.

Javelin The minimum weight of the javelin for men is 1.8lbg and 1.3lb for women. The tip of the head should be metal and the rest made of wood, with the cord grip placed in the center of gravity. The men's javelin measures 8.9-9ft in length, whereas the women's javelin measures 7.2-7.5ft in length.

Kit Shoes should be spiked with a maximum of 11 spikes permitted. They should measure no more than 0.5in in length and 0.2in in diameter. Gloves are forbidden. Competitors are allowed to wear a leather belt to protect their backs

if they wish.

Landing The tip of the javelin must land first, although it does not have to stick into the ground. It must land within the marked area and leave a mark that is visible to the judges.

Marks Used to show where the javelins have landed. They should be placed outside the sector lines.

Measurements Distances are recorded to the nearest even unit of one inch below the distance thrown.

Officials There should be at least two judges whose job is to keep a record of all trials and results. A white flag is used to indicate a fair throw and a red flag to indicate a foul.

Practice throws Each competitor is allowed two practice throws in the arena before the competition starts. These must take place within the arc, and the javelin must be returned by hand. No practice throws are allowed after the competition has started.

Throw The correct way to throw a javelin is with one hand at the grip while the arm is raised over the shoulder and then released. It is illegal to sling or hurl the javelin.

Ties These are decided by the relevant competitors' second-best throws. Whoever has the highest scored throw either goes through to the next heat or is declared the winner if the tie occurs in a final.

Trials Each competitor is allowed three trials (attempts), with the best eight of those competitors gaining an added three trials to go through to the finals.

HAMMER

The hammer event is decided within six trials. The hammer is a round ball and chain made of metal and is one of the heavier throwing events.

Broken hammer If a hammer breaks

while a competitor is making a throw then the attempt is not counted. The same rule applies if a foul is committed; it will not be counted if the foul occurred because the hammer broke.

Cage A cage is placed around the circle for safety reasons. The frame should be metal and covered with netting to ensure that a wild shot does not harm anybody.

Circle The area from which the throw is taken. The competitor should have both feet inside the circle until the throw has been completed.

Foul A foul is committed if a competitor, while taking their throw, puts any part of their body on the outer edge of the circle or on the ground outside it.

Hammer The hammerhead is made of metal and is spherical in shape, measuring 4.3-5in in diameter. Attached to the hammer head is a handle and chain that is 0.1in thick and 4.6-4.8in long.

Hammer glove Competitors are allowed to wear a glove to protect their hand. A right-handed competitor should wear a glove on their left hand.

Landing For a throw to be valid, the hammer must land within the inner lines of the marked sector.

Measuring Distances are measured to the nearest one inch below the distance thrown.

Officials There should be five judges in total. Two judges near the cage ensure that the throwing procedure is followed, and three judges out on the field see that the hammer lands in the correct place.

Throwing The throw begins with the competitor inside the circle in a stationary position. The hammer is allowed to rest on the ground either on the inside or outside of the circle. The competitor makes a swinging action with the hammer before releasing it. The competitor must stay inside the circle until the hammer has landed.

Tie A tiebreaker situation is decided by competitors' second-best results.

Time Competitors are given one and a half minutes to make their throw. If they exceed the time limit, they will be given a fault against them; if they offend a second time, they will be disqualified.

Trials Each competitor is allowed three trials, but if there are more than eight entrants, then the best eight will go on to have three more trials, making six in total.

Cross Country Running

Cross country is a pursuit in which runners race over courses set on natural terrain as opposed to a running track or road. The runner who completes the course in the quickest time wins. In team competitions, the winning team is the one whose aggregate placings of team members totals the lowest.

Artificial obstacles Although man-made hurdles and obstacles can be used on the course, they should be kept to a minimum and used only where absolutely necessary.

Assistance Assistance or refreshments must not be given to runners during a race.

Clerks of the course A set of officials who should be present at any major cross-country event. Clerks of the course help guide the runners in the designated direction.

Distance There are recommended distances for international competitions: men, 7.5 miles;juniors, 5 miles; women, 3.8 miles; junior women, 2.5 miles.

Dress Normal athletics clothing is worn, usually comprising running vest, shorts and shoes with or without spikes according to the ground conditions. Runners wear numbers on their chests and backs.

Funnel The accepted method of finishing a cross-country race is by using a funnel that narrows down the runners into a single line, and makes it easier to determine the finishing order of the runners. Funnels are 55yd long and run parallel to each other.

Funnel judges They record the finishing order of all competitors in their allocated funnel.

Funnel stewards Ensure the finishing funnels are kept clear of spectators and other personnel not required at the finish, while ensuring the smooth flow of competitors into the funnel in the order in which the judge placed them.

IAAF The International Amateur Athletics Federation has overall authority over the rules governing cross-country competition.

Individual For many local and national races, runners may compete individually. However, for international races, runners must enter as part of a team.

Markings Courses must be clearly marked with red flags on the left-hand side and white flags on the right-hand side. The flags must be appropriately positioned and proportioned to ensure that they are clearly visible from a distance of 1136.6yd.

Obstacles Part of the natural terrain within which the course is set, such as ditches, hills and heavy ground, and are an essential part of cross-country running. However, there should be no excessively difficult obstacles such as deep ditches, dangerous hills or thick undergrowth. The course should allow runners an unhindered run and be free of obstacles for the first 1640yd.

Officials All major events employ the following officials a referee; a judge; a timekeeper; a starter; clerks of the course; points men; umpires; funnel judges and funnel stewards; result recorders and assistants.

Pointsmen These officials tally the points scored by a competitor and the total of points attained by a team.

Race The race itself should be run on

open country, fields, uncultivated land and grassland. Only a very limited amount of plowed land is permitted.

Referee Has overall charge of a championship and settles any disputes.

Refreshments Although these races can take place over long distances – often 6.2 miles for men – refreshments are not allowed during a race.

Result recorders A set of officials who record the final results.

Road running The amount of road running on the course should be kept to a minimum.

Scoring At the conclusion of the race, the placings of the scoring team are added together. The winning team is determined by who has the lowest points aggregate. In the event of a tie, the higher place is awarded to the team whose final scoring runner finished highest up the order.

Start A pistol shot signals the start of a race, although a five-minute warning may be given if there are a large number of competitors. Runners line up at the starting line, with members of the same team lined up behind each other.

Starter A course official who signals the start of the cross-country race with a flag or pistol.

Teams Cross-country races are normally organized as team competitions over and above individual competition. Regulations differ regarding the number of teams, reserves and number of runners who can score depending on the event. A standard guide is the IAAF cross country championship ruling, which states "For men's races a team cannot enter more than 12 competitors, with no fewer than six and no more than nine permitted to start, only six of whom will score points for the team. For women's races, junior men's and women's races, no more than eight competitors can enter and no fewer

than four. No more than six of these are permitted to start, of whom four can score points."

Tie A term used to describe when two or more competing teams have the same number of scoring points.

Woodland These sections or areas must be clearly marked.

MOUNTAIN/FELL RUNNING

Checkpoints For all courses not marked out clearly with flags, runners must pass through checkpoints, which are normally found at mountain summits, and find their own way between the checkpoints.

Distance Distances can be anything from 0.9 miles to 25 miles depending on the course.

Dress Dress is normally standard athletic clothing, although special mountain shoes and protective clothing can be used, usually dictated by the weather and ground conditions.

Locations These races take place in particularly hilly or mountainous areas, which often are unsuitable or have limited facilities for other sports but are ideal for fell runners.

Markings All courses in international competition should be clearly marked with flags along the route, although they are not necessarily marked for local competitions.

Up and down One of two types of mountain race, predominantly contested in the United Kingdom, where runners have to tackle climbs as well as descents.

Uphill only One of two types of mountain race, predominantly contested in alpine regions, and where runners make their way to a summit finish, climbing all the way.

World Cup The inaugural mountain and fell running World Cup competition took place in 1985, and it is now held annually.

Orienteering

Orienteering is a running sport in which competitors use a map and compass to find a certain number of set control points around a designated course. The person or team to do this in the correct order and in the shortest amount of time is deemed the winner.

Aiming off This is a navigation technique that is safe and saves time. It aids the competitor in finding a point on a long feature. The method of aiming off is to aim deliberately to one side, so that when you come to the line feature and cannot see the control marker you know which way to turn to locate it.

Attack point Placed within 164yd of a control. It is used to choose a route so that the control can be located much more easily.

Base plate The part of the compass that encases the compass housing.

Bearing The term given to the direction in which you want to go.

Bramble bashers Socks that are used to protect the legs. They are knee-high and have a layer of rubber facing on the outside.

Cartography The correct name given to the art of map drawing.

Collect Allows the competitor to move quickly and ignore irrelevant details by marking off large features on the route.

Collecting feature A large feature used as a checking-off point while the competitor travels along the route.

Contact The act of relating the ground to the map and vice versa so that the competitor can see exactly where they are.

Control A control marker is a three-sided prism that measures 12in on each side. Each control is numbered and split into two by color, one half being white and the other half orange.

Control card Used by each competitor to mark at each control, proving that they have reached every point.

Control code Each control is marked with its own identification number. Each number is given to the competitors on their description lists to ensure that they are at the right control.

Control descriptions Used by the competitors to see where each control is marked on the course. Also displays their codes.

Control flow The act of arriving at a control, marking and then leaving.

Corridor A confined space on the map or terrain that links the controls.

Course Encompasses the start, controls and finish that each competitor must complete.

Duration Generally there is no set time limit, as the winning runner is the first one to finish the course with all the controls in the correct order.

Elite The term used to describe the top class at national and championship events. Only a small number are chosen and they are all seeded.

Fight Impenetrable forest, shown as dark green on a map.

Fine compass Used for fine orienteering.

Fine orienteering Also known as precision orienteering. The competitor should know where he or she is at all times and follow the compass carefully.

Following Following other competitors is illegal and considered to be cheating.

Form line Displayed as a broken

brown line, showing ground detail.

Handrail Used by the orienteer to make his route safe and simplify map reading. It is a long or line feature.

Index contour Every fifth contour line is drawn more heavily to make the height and shape of the ground stand out on the map.

Line features Used to show certain features on the map, or terrain such as walls, streams, etc.

Master maps Used by the runners to copy the course onto their own maps. This is normally done after the start, and is included in the total time.

Misconduct Competitors will be disqualified for missing a control or for not stamping their control cards correctly. Any form of cheating is also illegal.

Mountain orienteering Normally held over one or two days, the courses encompass rugged mountain terrain and are a real test of fitness and navigational skills.

Night orienteering Orienteering that is done at night. Competitors are allowed to use a flashlight to see their maps.

Officials The meet director is in charge of the event, and is assisted by a jury of at least three people who will act as course planners and organizers.

Photogrammetry Describes photographs taken from the air that are used for surveying.

Premarked maps Used when there are no master maps.

Prestart The few minutes before the start.

Punch Used by competitors to mark their cards at each control point. Each punch is different with its own distinct shape to ensure that no cheating occurs.

Re-entrant A small valley shown by one, two or more contour lines.

Relay orienteering Usually carried out with three or four people in each team. Each member runs their own part of the route.

Rough compass Running on a compass bearing without sticking precisely to the line of travel.

Rough orienteering When the competitor runs very quickly, collecting the major features along the way.

Runability The term used to describe how easy or hard it is to move through the terrain.

Score orienteering Usually consisting of 30 controls, which are worth several points each. There is normally a time limit of an hour, and the winner is the one who gains the most points.

Start Competitors start at one-to two-minute intervals to prevent cheating.

Straight-line route The shortest path between control points.

String courses Used by young competitors, the course is short and is marked by string all the way along.

Stub Part of the control card. It is used to record who is in the forest and for showing the results after the competition has finished.

Tags Short brown lines that show the downhill side of a contour line in areas where this might be confusing.

Thumbing The act of placing your thumb next to your current location on the map while running to save time hunting for your position.

Vegetation Term which describes whatever is growing in the area, displayed on the map using different colours. White shows runable trees, green less-runable trees and yellow shows open ground and no trees. Blue displays water and black shows rock features and roads, etc. Brown displays contour lines, and red or purple shows the course and out-of-bounds areas.

Whistle A whistle is used by competitors for safety reasons to help alert others of their location.

Triathlon/Ironman

Triathlon is a three-part discipline comprising swimming, cycling and running. The three sports are contested as a continuous event without a rest. The triathlon can be an individual or team event over varying distances, and ironman is a variation on the event.

··

GENERAL TERMS

Competition timing The competition begins when the competitor has begun swimming and ends when the competitor has reached the finish line after running.

Courses Each course has a start, finish and transition area that is normally situated on a circuit. The start and finish area can be situated in different places with two transition areas.

Finish The end of the race from which the competitors will either reach a finish line or complete a certain distance, depending on the sport.

Funnel judges Officials who check the placing of competitors at the finish.

Ironman The longest and hardest of all the triathlon courses. Competitors swim 2.4 miles cycle 112 miles and run 26.2 miles (the marathon distance).

Long course The triathlon is contested over a much longer distance than the short course swimming 2.5km, cycling 80km and running 20km.

Marshals Officials who direct competitors on cycle and running circuits.

Race director The official who controls and organizes the triathlon.

Rescue canoeists Officials who watch from a canoe and come in to save a competitor if they need be.

Rescue powerboat crews Boats follow competitors around on the swimming circuit to ensure their safety.

Safety officer Ensure competitors do not face any dangers while they are competing.

Short course This race is contested over the shortest distance for the triathlon swimming 0.9 miles, cycling 25 miles and running 6.2 miles.

Timekeepers There are eight timekeepers whose main job is to keep a check on all the competitors and the time it takes them to finish the race.

Transition area The area in which the competitors can change from their swimming gear into their cycling kit and can go to collect their bicycles from pre-prepared racks.

Transition time The time given to the competitors to change clothing and their equipment from one sport to another. This is included in the total competition time.

SWIMMING

Buoys Floats that mark the course at 55yd intervals.

Clothing Competitors must wear swimming caps with their competition number attached. They have the option of wearing a wetsuit, which must not have a thickness of more than 0.1in.

Lead boat A boat runs 27yd ahead of the leading competitor as a guide for all the swimmers.

Safety Competitors wear colored caps so they can be easily identified in the water. Powered safety craft and canoes patrol the course to check on safety. If a swimmer needs rescuing, they should raise one hand. If water temperatures are too low, then the event will not be held.

CYCLING

Bicycle All lightweight and fitted with gears. Low-profile machines are allowed, but not with wind-reducing protective shields.

Clothing A specialized triathlon suit or cycling shorts and a suitable shirt can be worn, along with cycling shoes or running shoes.

Course The race normally takes place on public asphalt roads. All sand and grit on the road has to be removed from the curves. The competitors must follow the rules of the road.

Disqualification A cyclist can be eliminated if they are caught drafting or not following the rules of the road.

Draft busters Race officials who patrol the course ensuring that the drafting rule is not broken.

Drafting Competitors are not allowed to be paced by another rider or by a car. Riders must keep a minimum distance of 5.5yd behind the rider in front of them. When overtaking they must move out by at least 2.2yd.

Pushing Slow pedaling with a high gear (as few as 60 pedal revolutions per minute).

Spinning Fast pedaling with a low gear (up to 120 pedal revolutions per minute).

Transition The period in which the competitors change from swimming to cycling sections.

RUNNING

Clothing A specialized triathlon suit may be worn with the race number attached to the front. Alternatively, a competitor may wear a vest, shorts and running shoes.

Course The running circuit usually takes place on public roads and streets.

Disqualification A runner can be disqualified if they have been paced or receive assistance for any reason.

Transition Competitors can start the running section as soon as they have racked their bicycle. They can also take this opportunity to change their shoes and clothing.

TRIATHLON: Massed ranks of swimmers at the start of a triathlon race, with a cycle and run to follow

Modern Pentathlon

Modern pentathlon involves fencing, swimming, shooting, cross-country and riding events. All classes are both team and individual events, with men and women competing, but the Olympic class is for men only.

FENCING

Absence of blade Fencer's weapons that are not in contact.

A droite To the right.

A gauche To the left.

Advancing When the front foot takes a small step forward and the rear foot immediately follows with an equally small or smaller step forward.

Advertisement A warning.

Après la parade After the parry has occurred.

Arrêtez To halt the action.

Balestra The action of making a short jump before making a lunge.

Bind A way of removing an attacking blade by making a half-circular movement with the tip of the sword when the blades are already in contact.

Ceding parry When the defensive fencer gives up their sword to the attacking fencer.

Circular or counter parry When the tip of the weapon completes a full circular movement without moving forward toward the opponent. Used as a defensive device to deflect or block.

Compound attack A method of attack that uses at least two movements that have followed a feint each time.

Compound riposte A riposte that is made up of at least one feint.

Counter riposte An attacking motion made after a successful parry of the opposition.

Dérobement Evading an attack on the blade of the defender.

Detachment parry A sharp parry that leaves the blade immediately after deflecting the movement.

Engagement When both blades are in contact.

Envelopment Using a circular movement to take the opponent's blade to the original line of engagement done on an opponent's straight arm.

Feint A deceiving movement that is seen as threatening. Can be made with the foot, the arm or the hand.

Foible The name used to describe the weakest part of the blade.

Forte The name used to describe the half of the blade nearer to the guard.

In quatata Used by a defending fencer to dodge an attack by side-stepping the blade.

La belle Describes the deciding touch or sudden death between two fencers who are tied at the end of their bout.

Lunge The most basic movement used to attack. The fencer takes a step forward with the weapon-wielding arm extended to carry the blade to the target.

On guard Used as an instruction by officials to warn the competitors to get ready. If used as an instruction by a teacher, the students are expected to guard in some way. This position is a balanced one from which you either attack or defend.

Parry A defensive movement used to deflect an opponent's strike with their foible by using their forte.

Pas de touche Means that no touch has occurred.

Piste The French word for path, but meaning the fencing strip. It should be of a flat and even surface made of wood, linoleum, rubber, plastic and metallic mesh, indoors or outdoors.

Quarte Used to block the opponent's blade by hitting high toward the inside so that the blade points past the chest or stomach.

Riposte The attacking action that a fencer will use after successfully parrying an attack.

Touche Describes when a hit has been scored. To score a touche the point must touch the target, which is the trunk of the opponent.

(*see also* "Combat Sports," pages 212–215).

SWIMMING

Alternate strokes Describes both front and back strokes.

Breaststroke At all times the arms and legs remain underneath the water in this stroke. The arms pull back at the same time in a circular movement and are pushed forward together from under the chest. The legs are drawn up together with the feet facing outward, then they kick out and back.

Butterfly The arms pull back and recover above the water while the legs simultaneously perform a vertical dolphin movement.

Crossover kick Occurs with one leg crossing over the other.

Dolphin kick A flexible vertical kick where both legs and lower trunk wave through the water just like the movements of a dolphin.

Flutter kick A vertical leg movement in which the legs move alternately.

Freestyle A race in which competitors are allowed to use any stroke they want.

Negative split Swimming the second half of the race faster than the first.

Pull The part of the stroke performed by the arms.

Touch Each swimmer must touch the end of the pool at the end of a race to show they have finished.

SHOOTING

Action The mechanism that is fired on breech-loading and bolt-action rifles.

Aiming off A technique whereby a competitor allows for the effect of the wind on the bullet in his aim.

Backsight Eyepiece with a small circular hole for aiming. Placed behind the breech and can be moved vertically or horizontally.

Course of fire In a competition, a shooter has a set number of shots he can fire and a time limit in which to fire his bullets.

Drag Occurs after a bullet is fired. The subsequent air turbulence causes the bullet to slow down.

Foresight To help with the shooter's aim, this instrument is placed on the front of the barrel.

Hangfire The unusually lengthy time between the firing pin hitting a bullet's percussion cap and the propellant charge catching alight.

Stop-butt Term used to describe a mound rising at the rear of the targets.

RIDING

Deep going Describes soft, wet ground into which hooves sink.

Gait The pattern of a horse's stride.

Get under Occurs when a horse misses its stride and therefore takes off too close to an obstacle.

Good going Means that the ground condition is perfect and doesn't jar the horse or cause the horse's hooves to sink into the earth.

Hard going Describes bone-dry earth that jars the horse.

Napping Describes a horse's unwillingness to go beyond a certain point.

Override To tire out a horse and force it beyond its capabilities.

Peck To stumble on landing.

Run out To miss an obstacle by going to one side or the other.

5

Gymnastics

....

This category involves sports which require competitors to perform set moves either on the floor or in the air, requiring a high level of flexibility, suppleness and strength. Trampolining is included because it is a form of gymnastics performed in the air, and the same applies to acrobatics to some extent.

Sports Psychology

Aggression Used by the athlete to channel their will to win at all odds and the determination to sacrifice their own or their opponents, bodies in the cause of victory.

AMT Anxiety Management Training. Used by the athlete to recognise early physical-muscular signs of tension build-up and the tools needed to perform deep muscle relaxation wherever and whenever they are needed.

Behaviorism The study of observable behavior, response to stimuli and objective variables.

Ideomotor Training Performed by the athlete visualizing in the mind a clear picture of the task ahead, leading to the brain registering it as an instruction to be carried out.

Motives Range from self esteem gained when winning a competition, the sense of allegiance and camaraderie with fellow teammates, the pleasure gained from being the best at your discipline and the stature and rewards gained from being the best.

Outside stress The added stress of the media and loss of privacy when having been successful.

Playing out of your skin Adage used by athletes to describe a perfect performance that feels like it had nothing to do with themselves.

Psyching Method of unnerving your opponent with a war of words or any method that will affect their concentration.

Psyching up Method used by coaching staff to get athletes focused and determined to succeed.

Split mind Means to unsettle your opponents, confidence in their own judgement. See psyching.

Stage fright The sense of fear felt before the start of an important competition. Symptoms range from nausea to temporary paralysis or breakdown.

Success phobia Occurs when an athlete will unconsciously fail, therefore saving themselves from the added stress that success brings.

Termination symbolism Describes the fact that there has to be a winner in most cases. Sudden death is a crude example used when speaking of this.

Will power The use of mind over matter where a competitor is determined to succeed at all costs.

Men's Gymnastics

Gymnastics consists of six separate events: the floor, pommel horse, rings, vault, parallel bars and high bar. All events require competitors to show varying levels of agility, strength and flexibility.

Acrobatic element Describes a somersault or handspring, performed from either a standing position or a run.

Apparatus The equipment that the gymnasts use for their exercises. These include the pommel horse, the vault, the rings and the horizontal bar.

Bonus points Earned if the gymnast performs a very difficult routine or movement combination.

Ballet Used by gymnasts as an intrinsic part of their training to improve their posture, flexibility, coordination, agility, balance and strength.

Clothing Clothing should be close fitting to avoid becoming entangled with the apparatus. Regarding footwear, athletes have the option of going barefoot, or wearing socks or gym shoes. Handguards are also allowed to protect the gymnast from blisters. They should be made of suede, leather or any synthetic materials, although leather seems to work best as it retains the hand chalk.

Dive roll Similar to a forward roll, taking off from two feet and diving into the roll.

Element Describes the smallest independent movement with both a definite start and end to the movement; usually 10 elements make up an exercise.

Events Include individual, combined and team competitions.

Exercise Describes the complete presentation by the gymnast. Can consist of compulsory or optional exercises.

Faults Range from small to major. Faults are deemed to have occurred when the gymnast breaks form, uses the floor or apparatus for balance, positions hands or feet wrongly, either loses balance or doesn't complete a dismount, during a handstand either bends the arms or falls out of the handstand, falls off the apparatus, steps outside the floor area during a floor exercise or fails to start on time.

FIG The Fédération Internationale Gymnastique, based in Switzerland.

Flexibility Enables the gymnast to work through the whole range of movement of the joints.

Gymnastic element Any movement made by the gymnast that is not counted as being acrobatic, such as rolling or jumping.

Hand chalk Used to absorb perspiration and reduce friction between the hand and apparatus, therefore helping prevent blisters and aiding the gymnast's grip of the apparatus.

Handstand A basic movement. The gymnast balances on both hands with the body in a vertical line.

Hold part Occurs when the gymnast has to hold a position for a minimum of two seconds.

Individual combined events The maximum points that can be gained for this event is 60. The leading 36 competitors must all perform an optional exercise on each of the apparatus.

Individual event The maximum score to be gained from this event is 10 points. The eight leading gymnasts from the team event will compete in the final of this event.

Officials Four judges are used to score each individual event that is supervised by a senior judge. Two senior judges are used in the men's individual finals.

Optional exercise Allowed in competition to permit the gymnast to show off their own area of expertise.

Salto Another term for a somersault.

Team competition Each team consists of six members (except in European Championships). An optional exercise is performed on each apparatus. The maximum amount of points a male team can reach is 300.

Value groups Based on the difficulty of the element, movement or exercise, they are split into five categories A, B, C, D and E. Also considered are the strength and physicality of the movements when deciding into which group the gymnast's performance should be graded.

FLOOR EXERCISE

The gymnast's routine must consist of a forward acrobatic series, a back acrobatic series and one other with one held position. The event differs from the women's event in that it is not performed to music.

Back flip A backward moving accelerator from feet to hands to feet that usually precedes a somersault.

Cartwheel A sideways moving element from feet to one hand to the other hand to feet with the legs in a wide position.

Deductions These are made for small, medium and large errors on all of the apparatus.

Floor area A matted area measuring 13yd by 13yd. During their routine each gymnast should use the entire floor area.

Fly spring A forward accelerator from two feet to two hands to two feet; usually precedes a forward somersault.

Head spring A forward moving element from feet to hands and head to feet. The arms are bent and the element is performed by closing the heels and straightening the arms.

Round off A premovement for a backflip. Transfers momentum from a forward to a backward direction.

Routine Each routine should consist of three different acrobatic movements, one forward, one backward and one other. These parts can be used in any order during the floor exercise.

Time The time given to each gymnast for their floor exercise is between 50 and 70 seconds.

Voluntary exercise Each competitor will use this exercise to demonstrate the area in which they are most skilled. It must show a rhythmic and harmonious whole while incorporating acrobatic and gymnastic elements that display the gymnast's abilities of strength, balance and flexibility.

RINGS

The object of this exercise is to display the gymnast's abilities in strength, swing and hold. It is important to have upper body strength for this event.

Backward swing The gymnast should get into a downswing position with his body straight at the hips and his arms straight at all times. Once he is near the hanging position, he should use his feet to propel his body upward into a position where his hips are above his shoulders and his legs are parallel to his arms. The next stage is for the gymnast to turn the rings so that his thumbs are pointing outwards and then move the rings backward while simultaneously using the arms and legs to complete the turn.

Complete swing Consists of both the forward and backward swing, and once the gymnast has mastered this he should be able to apply it to more

RINGS: An excercise that demands great upper body strength, the rings are 8.4ft above the floor

advanced skills on the rings.

Deductions Handstands with bent arms and touching the ropes with the arms lead to a deduction of between 0.3–0.5 points, handstands with bent arms or touching the ropes with the arms lead to a deduction of 0.2–0.3 points, the swinging of the ropes leads to a deduction of 0.1–0.3 points, a fall from a handstand that is not planned is deductible by 0.2–0.5 points and a cross or inverted cross, or free support scale with a bent body or not in a completely horizontal shape, is deductible by 0.5 points.

Drop Starts with the gymnast in an inverted hang position, which then turns into a deep pike with the hips held just above shoulder level. As the body moves upward, the gymnast pulls downward and outward on the rings to make the shoulders rise. The rings are then turned to make the body rise through the rings and toward the legs. Once this is achieved, the gymnast will push the rings downward to the side of the body, which serves to lower the body from a pike to a dish, thus completing the movement.

Forward swing During the downswing phase, the body should be held in a dish shape, with the rings turned so that the heels of the hands face the feet. The next stage is the vertical hang position where the heels are accelerated backward and driven upward until the hips are above the shoulders.

Height of rings The rings are placed 8.4ft from the mat.

Routine The rings routine should consist of one forward long swing, one backward long swing and one strength hold.

PARALLEL BARS

The parallel bars display the gymnast's ability to swing in support above the bars moving to and from handstand, and swing under the bars in hang.

Back uprise The gymnast starts from a dish shape and then raises his hips and legs above bar level to gain momentum while then swinging backward so that his entire body is behind him but parallel to the bars, before raising his entire body into a straight line in the air. The next stage is to maneuver into a full handstand on the bars to complete the movement.

Backward roll The gymnast moves from the hollow back position into a dish shape. He then lowers his shoulders on to the bars while simultaneously raising his legs into a straight position with his hips above his shoulders. The next stage is to maneuver into a handstand while swinging the body back into a downswing.

Bars Measure 19ft high and 38ft long. They sit parallel to each other and are made of wood.

DISMOUNT: Each movement should be tight and controlled with the gymnast landing on sure feet

Deductions A competitor will be penalized for including more than three pronounced hold parts.

Drop upstart Maneuver started with a forward swing that moves into a deep pike by raising the legs toward the chest. The shoulders are then dropped backward with the body fully turning while underneath the bars, to then move into a deep pike again before going into an upswing that lifts the body high into a "V" support with the hips extended to bring the back down.

Forward roll Once the hips are above the shoulders in the upswing, the arms are bent with the elbows rotating forward and outward. The gymnast continues to swing forward with the arms lowering the shoulders on to the bars, which push the elbows downward and outward. In the next stage, the gymnast moves into a dish shape with the head

in a position to be able to see the feet, while the hands are moved to regrasp the bars so that the body can go from a high shoulder support position into a downswing.

Routine Consists of one move above bars, one release and regrasp, and one move from hang to support.

VAULT

The vault uses a vaulting horse and springboard to display the gymnast's flight and somersaults. Each vault has a set tariff up to 10 points. Each competitor must perform one chosen vault.

Apparatus The horse vault is set at a height of 55in. A springboard is used to assist in flight and is placed in line with the long axis of the horse.

Approach The maximum length that the gymnast is allowed to use in their approach is 27yd. Once the run has been made the gymnast will take off from both feet while momentarily using both hands to gain support on the horse.

Deductions Made if the gymnast makes a run of more than 27yd, or departs from the line of the long axis of the horse during the flight phases or bends his arms when they should be straight.

Handspring vault On takeoff the gymnast should use the legs to drive the body upward, while the hands should reach along the horse with the chest in a low position to thrust the body off the horse while the body is in a horizontal position.

Landing Must include the gymnast landing firmly on both feet with the arms raised above the head in order to help steady the body and produce a stable position.

Rotational vault The flight from the springboard should be low, with the body in a horizontal position so that there is a slight angle between the arms and body when the hands come into contact with the horse.

Scoring A maximum score of 10 points can be gained for each vault. All the vaults have a founding score that can be altered according to the level of difficulty of the vault.

Somersault vaults There are two types the singular rotational, such as the handspring vault, which uses the rotation in the same direction both on and off the horse; and the counter-rotational, in which the direction off the horse differs in rotation to the flight on to the horse, such as squat and straddle vaults.

Straddle vault The flight, contact and thrust are the same as the squat approach. When the thrust occurs, the gymnast will snap his feet down wider so that they straddle the horse and

create a slight dish position in the body before closing the legs together in order to land safely.

Straight leg squat vault The flight should be aimed low with the gymnast leaning forward at the point of takeoff. The arms should be straight ahead of the shoulders with the hips horizontal to the shoulders.

HORIZONTAL BAR

The horizontal or high bar uses the gymnast's swinging skills and is a highly artistic event. Each competitor gets two turns to display their achievements in this field.

Deductions Given as a penalty for using hold or strength parts, for missing a requirement or for failing to dismount correctly.

Drop upstart The movement starts with the gymnast in a dish shape with the hips pressed against the bar in a downswing motion until the hips become level with the bar. The legs then squat quickly with the ankles and shins almost touching the bar to then move the bar down the line of the leg so that the shoulders rise above the bar.

Float upstart Carried out with straight legs used to push the hips up and behind the bar, while the gymnast presses down on the bar to lift the shoulders. The legs are then lifted into a dish shape as the forward swing begins to extend the body to the height of its swing before then bringing the ankles to the bar and pressing the bar along the line of the legs.

Forward hip circle The gymnast grasps the bar in the overgrasp position while leaning slightly forward over the bar. The body is then turned forward in a downswing motion before bringing it into a piked position with the hands regripping the bar. With the body in a deep fold, the movement is kept rotating until the gymnast begins to extend his body and slow down the motion by pressing the bar into his hips.

Forward seat circle The gymnast begins by sitting on the bar with his hands in undergrasp. He then lifts his seat above his shoulders before bringing his thighs in to his chest and squatting his legs downward between his arms. The body should be in a deep fold under the bar. He then goes into upswing, pressing down on the bar while still in the pike position, then extending the body to slow down the motion.

Grasp There are a number of different grasps. These can include the overgrasp with a backward rotation and the undergrasp with a forward rotation; the mixed grasp, which has one hand in overgrasp and the other hand in undergrasp; the crossed grasp, which has the arms crossed with both hands in overgrasp; and the elgrip grasp, which has the arms rotated to grasp the bar backward with the fingers over the bar and the thumbs under the bar.

Routine Must include forward and backward giant swings, movements close to the bar, flight elements that recatch on the bar and elements with turns around the long axis. All these elements must be swinging movements that are performed without interruption.

POMMEL HORSE

Also known as the side horse, the pommel horse event is made up of measured movements that the gymnasts have to incorporate into their routines.

Deductions Gymnasts can be penalized for not using the scissor maneuver, for mainly using only one part of the horse or for not using a part of the horse at all.

Double leg circle Keeping the legs together at all times, the gymnast will start off by leaning on both arms while the legs are leaning out and away from the body to perform this exercise. As the gymnast swings his hips and legs around, he will lift his arm and switch to the other as his body passes around, so that he is always supported by one arm as his body moves in a full circle.

Front shears From the pendulum swing position, the left leg is swung upward behind the left shoulder then across the horse to create a straddled pendulum swing. The weight is then put onto the left arm, and the right leg can then swing upward and behind the right shoulder. The left leg is then taken back across the horse and the right leg crosses the horse to start the downward swing in front of the horse.

Pendulum swing The upper leg is swung upwards into a vertical position but still behind the line of the shoulders for this exercise. The body weight should go onto the supporting arm while the other arm can be lifted from the handle. The lower leg should move the lead leg at the same time to reach a horizontal line through the elbow of the support arm.

Pommel horse This piece of equipment measures 3.4ft high and 5.3ft in length, normally made of wood. The horse is separated into three sections by two handlebars, which are evenly spaced.

Routine A gymnast's routine on the pommel horse must include different types of circular and pendulum swing on different parts of the horse, as well as at least two scissor connections, an element that is performed on one handle only and double leg circles that must dominate throughout.

Women's Gymnastics

Women's gymnastics involves a number of different forms of human movement and dance. They all have their own specific requirements in terms of the apparatus that is used and the way in which the gymnasts are marked according to the style of performance and the judging criteria.

Aerial A movement that a gymnast performs into the air without using her hands or feet on the apparatus.

Arabesque A gymnast takes two steps before stretching forward to complete a jump forward with an arch. She will then cross-step over with a quarter turn and continue to turn until she has completed a half turn.

Astride sitting A gymnast can sit astride on the floor by rolling forward, backward or sideways from a previous move. While she is on the floor the positions for the upper body and arms are endless.

Back flip A movement that starts with both feet together. A gymnast will bend her knees and lean backward with her shoulders in line with her hips. She will push her hands toward the ground and then pass through a momentary handstand.

Backward roll A gymnast bends down into a crouch position with her back to the mat. She will then proceed to roll backward in a tucked position with her palms facing upward so that her hands can be placed flat on the floor. She will then push strongly from her hips to land in a crouch position.

Backward walkover A movement in which the gymnast pushes all of her weight onto one leg with the other stretched forward. The head is kept between the arms and the body bent backward to bring the hands to the floor. The legs are then pushed into the air through the splits position to land on one leg and the other leg is pushed backward in preparation for the next move.

Balance beam The beam measures 17ft long, 4ft high and 4in wide. It is covered with vinyl or leather and is made of wood padded with foam rubber. A gymnast will approach the beam from the board or floor and the exercise must last from 70 to 90 seconds. She can use two static holds on the beam.

Beam A piece of apparatus used as one of the four exercises on which gymnasts are expected to perform. It has adjustable supports to suit the height of competitors.

Bonus points Awarded to a gymnast if she performs a high routine exercise, which can gain her extra points from the judges.

Bridge position This movement involves a gymnast lying on her back with her knees bent and hands flat on the floor, close to her ears. She will then push up strongly from her hands and feet until the arms and legs are straight and she has managed to reach a fully arched bridge position. It is also another name for the crab position.

Boundary line This marks the outer limit of the floor. If a competitor steps on or over this line, she can be penalized by a deduction of points.

Cabriole A gymnast jumps onto the beam or the floor and takes off from one leg. Both legs are then brought together in the air before landing separately.

Cartwheel A complete inverted sideways wheel of the body to an even-rhythm count of four. A gymnast will push her hands and roll her head downward to the ground before lifting both feet into the air and landing on the ground with both feet together.

Cast A varied movement that takes place on the parallel or asymmetric bars in which the body is moved from a support position.

Cat leap Jump that requires the gymnast to push her legs in front of the body.

Chalk Used by gymnasts to keep their hands dry before they conduct their routine.

Clothing A gymnast is expected to wear a leotard, which must be made of a nontransparent cloth. Footwear is optional.

Compulsory exercise These are set for a period of four years, and are devised to test the gymnast's control and knowledge of specific skills.

Connecting move When a gymnast makes the transition from one move to another. Precision is necessary in order to effect a smooth transition.

Crab A move that requires the gymnast to have both her hands and feet on the floor with the tips of her fingers pointing down toward her feet.

Dismount A method by which the gymnast leaves a piece of apparatus at the end of a performance or an exercise.

Dive handspring Another name given to a fly spring.

Double back somersault A gymnast uses a rotation through 720 degrees to jump backward to complete this somersault.

Double leg circle This move takes place on the pommel horse where both the gymnast's legs are passed around the body of the horse under the left and right hands in succession.

Elbow lever Area in which the arms are bent at the elbows. A single and double elbow lever can be performed.

Element The smallest independent movement that a gymnast can use.

Face vault The front of the body moves over the apparatus.

Fall When a gymnast falls to the ground, she has a set time in which to recover and continue her performance. It is 10 seconds for the beam exercise and 30 seconds on the uneven bars.

Faults Gymnasts can be penalized for demonstrating a movement or exercise that is not deemed valid within the rules of the sport. This can be for either a general fault, which is caused by a lack of assurance or elegance, or for faults this were specific to the apparatus.

First flight The second part of a vault in which the gymnast arrives on the horse after taking off from the springboard.

Flank vault The side of the body moves over the apparatus.

THE BEAM: One of the four exercises for female gymnasts, and possibly the most difficult

Float The gymnast's body swings under a bar, straightening up as she comes out the other side.

Floating support A gymnast will only use her hands to come into contact with the bar. No other part of the body is permitted to do this.

Floor exercise Performed by a gymnast on a specially strung matted area measuring 13yd x 13yd. She will perform to music and will have to perform the most current compulsory exercise, which has been laid down by the FIG. Each gymnast can then perform an optional exercise, which is made up of elements chosen by them that meet the relevant guidelines.

Fly spring A handspring from which the gymnast takes off on both feet. This is also referred to as a dive handspring.

Forward roll A gymnast bends down into a crouch position and places her hands on the floor with her fingers placed forward. She then places her head between her arms. As she lifts her hips, she pushes her feet and rolls forward into a standing position.

Forward somersault A gymnast will always use a springboard to perform this move properly. She needs a high upward jump at the start with her arms reaching forward and upward. When the gymnast has reached the height of the jump, she can pull her arms down and rotate forward.

Forward walkover A gymnast will use the same starting-off procedure as for the handstand, but in this movement allowing the leading leg to pass over the head to the floor, with the legs going through the splits position. The leading foot is then pressed hard into the ground with the hips being lifted upward and the other leg should be raised as high as possible.

Free cartwheel A move that needs a strong thrusting action to begin with from the gymnast's leading leg. She will push hard against the ground while the back leg lifts into an upward direction.

Free forward roll The gymnast begins in a crouch position with her arms overhead. She will then lift her hips and push from the feet to stretch her arms forward and downward. The head is then tucked between the legs and the back rounded. As soon as the feet leave the beam, her shoulders come into contact with the beam to complete the move.

Free walkover Starts in the same way as the free cartwheel. The gymnast makes a strong push from the floor and an upward thrust with the legs. The arms should be swung downward and backward to assist the lift upward. When learning this move, a gymnast can use a springboard for assistance.

Front support A position the gymnast uses to support the arm with her front facing the apparatus.

Full turn As the gymnast springs off the horse with a strong thrust from the hips, she will attempt to gain as much height as possible and complete a 360-degree turn in midair.

Giant swing With her body straight, a gymnast swings around the bar.

Glide forward The movement gymnasts use to raise their body from a hanging position into a support position. They swing underneath the bar and end up in a front support position on top of the bar.

Half turn A gymnast can move her body 180 degrees to face the other direction by stretching her arms out and bending her knees facing forward or turned out. The gymnast's legs can be either bent or straight when performing this move.

Handspring Referred to as a fast handstand – the speed of the legs and push from the hands give it the necessary momentum for the gymnast to land on her feet. In terms of the vault, the gymnast will strike the horse in a stretched position with both feet stretched upward and the hands supporting the horse.

Handstand A movement in which the gymnast places both her hands on the floor and then kicks to an inverted position. They will be shoulder-width apart and her back and arms straight throughout the movement with her head moving naturally in line with the rest of the body.

Hecht half-turn A movement that a gymnast performs on the airbars. It has a swinging element, release and then a half-turn before capturing the bar again.

Hip circle A movement that can be performed both backward and forward. A gymnast performs a circle on a bar through 360 degrees with her hips in contact with the bar throughout.

Horse vault The vaulting horse is 4ft high, 5.3ft long and 14in wide. It is made out of wood on a metal frame, and has a very thin layer of padding, which is covered with leather or vinyl. The springboard is placed in line with the short axis of the horse. The gymnast runs down a runway releasing both feet off the springboard, and vaults crosswise over the horse. Gymnasts get one attempt in compulsories and two attempts in optionals.

Individual events The eight competitors with the highest score on each individual apparatus from the team competitions take part again for the individual apparatus title. The maximum score women can gain is 10 points.

Kick uprise The movement in which a gymnast moves from an inverted hang position to a straight-arm support. She can do this by moving her legs out, while at the same time bringing herself

up on her arms.

Landing Following a move that includes a jump into the air, a gymnast will always want to come back onto the mat without falling over. A good landing is vital for a high score, and they will aim to jump back to the ground with both feet firmly together. The gymnast will sometimes have completed a 180-degree turn about the long axis prior to the landing.

Longswing The gymnast moves between two posts to jump straight with a full-turn dismount to land to the ground.

Lunge position One of the most versatile links that a gymnast can use. They can move their arms, upper body and head to any position, but their legs can only be positioned by adjusting the width of their feet.

Neckspring A movement whereby the gymnast puts all of her weight on to her neck and follows it through with a spring to the handstand position.

Officials There are four judges who score each event independently. They are supervised by one superior judge.

Optional exercise The 36 leading gymnasts in the team competition demonstrate an optional exercise on each apparatus.

Overgrasp The term given to a grip on the bar where the palms always face forward.

Palm strap A leather device that is used to protect the hands from friction. Also referred to as a handguard.

Peach basket Another name given to an underbar somersault.

Phases For purposes of evaluation the vault is divided into four phases (1) First flight phase; (2) Support/strike phase; (3) Second flight phase; (4) Landing. All vaults must be demonstrated with the support of both hands on the horse.

Pike The body is bent forward from the hips with the legs stretched forward.

Planche A support position from where the body is horizontal and facing downwards. It is supported from straight arms above the apparatus.

Push-off The point in a vault at which a gymnast pushes herself from the horse with her hands.

Reuther board The springboard that the gymnast jumps off to get onto the vaulting box.

Ribbon The hand apparatus used in modern rhythmic gymnastics.

Round-off Another movement that starts very much like the fast cartwheel. The legs are put together in a vertical position, and the body makes a quarter-turn inward. The gymnast should be in a position to land facing the direction of the approach run. The gymnast needs to have strong hands in order to land on her feet with her arms pushed upward ready for the next movement. This will always change a forward movement into a back movement.

Round-off dismount A gymnast stands at the end of the beam and will take up the same procedure as that for a cartwheel. She raises her arms into the air and lifts one leg before facing downward and making a quarter turn inward.

Run-in A gymnast will always take a short run before jumping to gain some momentum.

Scale A gymnast balances on one leg and holds the other one in a number of positions.

Scoring Each exercise is scored from one to 10. The highest and lowest scores of the four judges are ignored and the middle two are then averaged to give the recorded score. Deductions can then be awarded by the judges of a whole, half and one-tenth points. For some events there is starting score with a pos-

sible bonus to create a maximum of 10 points – this can be for originality, risk or virtuosity.

Second flight The second part of a vault from a push-off to landing.

Set exercise All gymnasts performing in the competition perform the same routine.

Shoulder stand A move that is very similar to that of a handstand. However, the weight rests on the shoulders.

Side splits A process of doing the splits whereby the legs are pushed out to the side with the body facing forward.

Splits A movement whereby the body faces forward with the legs outstretched and completely in contact with the floor.

Squat vault A movement in which the gymnast's legs are tucked up over the apparatus.

Straddle A position a gymnast uses that involves her legs being pushed wide apart as in a straddle vault.

Straddle forward The gymnast moves her legs forward to upstart on the high bar and then progress to do a handstand on the half turn.

Stretched first flight The gymnast will employ a strong, fast, powerful approach, which will be combined with the efficient use of the Reuther board.

Support Any position from which the body weight is supported on the arms.

Support seat The body is in a seated position in one of a number of angles and is then supported on the arms.

Swan dive Movement in which a gymnast jumps from a standing position and then dives into another position. Anything from a handstand to a roll.

Swing down A gymnast moves down between the poles and then swings forward on the half-turn.

Team competition Six members of

each team demonstrate a compulsory and an optional exercise on each apparatus. The total for each team is then worked out by adding together the five highest scores. The maximum points are 600 for men and 400 for women.

Tucked backward somersault The gymnast begins in a standing position and jumps into the air swinging her arms upward and keeping the body tight. At the height of the jump, she will rotate backward into a tucked position and extend her legs and arms in order to land properly.

Twist A rotation around an imaginary axis running down the length of the body, using both the head and arms for the turn.

Two-legged squat A short run is needed before the gymnast places both hands on the beam and springs from both feet onto the top of the beam, before squatting both legs between her hands over the beam into a sitting position.

Undergrasp A gymnast holds on to the bar with the palms of her hands facing backward.

Underswing A gymnast performs an underswing with both legs together as they exercise a half-turn with flight over the low bar to catch the lower bar in momentary support.

Uneven bars Gymnasts swing from one bar to another in an attempt to score as many points as possible. The upper bar is 7.75ft high while the lower bar is 5.2ft high. The bars running along the two poles are 11.4ft long. They have a metal support and are made of wood or fiberglass. The elements comprising the compulsory exercise are the same as for the optional exercise. A gymnast is allowed to perform only four consecutive elements on the same bar.

Upper-arm support The term given to a gymnast who uses the top of the parallel bars to support her arms.

Upward swing The gymnast faces the bars from the stand and floats upstart. They lay away clear with their hips circle backward and their Hecht half-turn to catch the upper bar and then swing backward.

Vaulting box A layered wooden box that is padded with leather.

Vaulting horse Used by men and women in the vaulting competition. The gymnast can twist and turn before landing upright.

Vault marking A vault is graded A, B, C or D for difficulty, and is then divided into eight groups by type. The gymnast must show the number of the vault they are about to perform. Each judge will score the vault by making a deduction from a maximum possible of 10 points for a vault.

Voluntary exercise This gives the gymnast the opportunity to test out her own field of expertise and to show her individual talents by devising her own routine.

Rhythmic Gymnastics

Rhythmic gymnastics is a floor-based discipline that is set to music and involves the manipulation of small hand apparatus. Exercises are performed by individuals or by groups of six depending on the competition.

Adage Slow, controlled movement.

Allegretto Cheerful interpretation.

Allegro Quick, lively movement.

Amplitude Fullness of movement.

Andante Slow, flowing movement.

Apparatus Five pieces of apparatus, recognized by the international federation, are used for competition rope, ball, hoop, clubs and ribbon.

Arabesque A balance on one foot with the other leg lifted high at the back.

Assemblé A jump from one foot, landing on both feet.

Balance Transfer of weight from one foot to the other.

Ball Made of rubber or a similar material. It should weigh a minimum of 14oz and have a diameter of 7-8in. Associated movements are throws, bouncing, rolls over the body or on the floor, circles, spirals and figure eights.

Base mark In scoring, this is the average of the score awarded to a gymnast and the score of the head judge.

Battement Beating of the foot with the feet coming together sharply.

Bourrée Several small, quick steps on the run.

Cabriole A lively jump with the feet clicking together.

Cat leap A jump from one foot to the other with knees bent and high to the front, one after the other.

Changement A jump with the leg position changing in the air.

Chassé A three-step move step, close feet together and step again.

Clothing Leotards are the proper apparel, and may be worn with bandages and slippers or socks.

Clubs Can be made of wood or be synthetic. Each club is 16-20in long and weighs at least 5.2oz. Associated movements are mills, rotations while in flight, throws, asymmetric movements, swings, circles and tapping.

Code of points The International Gymnastics Federation judging rules and regulations.

Dégagé One leg stretched away from the other with toes pointed and touching the floor.

Demi-pointe Standing on toes with the balls of the feet raised.

Developpé Bending and then straightening the knee.

Elements The smallest gymnastic movement with a noticeable start and finish point. The difficulty of an element is classified as A, B, C, D or E, with E being the most difficult.

En tournant Any move performed with a turn.

Entrechat A jump with feet moving forward and back twice while in the air.

Fine The end of an exercise.

First position With heels touching and feet turned out, the arms are at shoulder height, forward and curved.

Fish spring A jump from two feet with the back arched and one or both legs bent and feet touching the back of the head.

Glissade A sliding or gliding step movement.

Grand battement A high kick of the leg in any direction.

Grand jeté A large leap from one foot to the other.

Groups Six gymnasts may perform together. They should use six identical pieces of apparatus, or three pieces of one and three of another.

Hoop Made of wood or plastic. The diameter inside the hoop is 32-35in and it should weigh a minimum of 10.5ozAssociated movements are rolls on the floor or body, rotations, swings, circles, figure eights, throws and passing through or over the hoop.

Jeté A jump from one foot to the other.

Komat jump The same as a cat leap.

Lunge Can be made forward or to the side. A forward lunge is made with the feet pointing forward and wide apart with the front knee bent and the back knee straight.

Mills Small circles made with clubs.

Needle scale Balance on one foot with the other leg lifted high behind in the vertical splits position. The body is dropped forward with hands on the floor or gripping the ankle.

Pas de bas Low steps derived from Scottish dancing.

Pirouette A turn made on the toes.

Pivot A turn made on the ball of the foot.

Plane The area of space around the body described as frontal, sagittal or horizontal.

Plié A bend of the knees with feet on the floor.

Ports de bras Movement of the arms.

Relevé A rising or lifting movement snapping on to the ball of the foot.

Retiré Lift one leg with knees bent until the toes touch the inside of the opposite knee.

Ribbon The ribbon, made of satin or a similar material and 13-20ft long, is attached to a stick made of wood, plastic or fiberglass, which is 20-24in long and has a maximum diameter of 0.4in. Associated movements with the ribbon are snakes in different planes, spirals in different planes, swings, circles in different planes, figure eights, throws and small tosses.

Rope Made of hemp or a similar material, it has no handles and is proportionate to the size of the gymnast. Associated movements with the rope are jumps and leaps, skips or hops, swings, circles, rotations, figure-eights and throws.

Scissors jump A jump from one foot to the other making a scissors action with straight legs.

Second position With feet apart, sideways and turned out, the arms are out to the side at shoulder height in the second position.

Spiral A continuous spiraling movement with either the body or apparatus.

Split leap A leap forward from one foot to the other, performing the splits position while in the air.

Stag leap A leap made with one leg bent and toes touching the knee of the other leg, which is straight.

Temps levé A hop movement.

Tendu Referring to the position of the leg being stretched tight.

Third position With one foot in front of the other and the heel of the front foot touching the instep of the back foot and feet turned out. The arms are at shoulder level with one to the side and one forward.

Time limit In individual competition, each exercise lasts for between one and one and a half minutes. Group exercises last for between two and two-and-a-half minutes.

Tour jeté A turning jump with a leg swing.

"V" sit A sitting position with the body in the shape of a V. The legs are lifted straight and the back is straight.

Wave A movement that starts at the feet and ripples up through the body.

Sports Acrobatics

Sports acrobatics is a gymnastic event with sections for individuals, pairs and group exercises. It is made up of two main elements, which are tumbling and group work, and is performed by men and women.

Approach run For tumbling routines, there is an approach run of at least 11yd before the specially sprung track on which tumbles are performed.

Balance routines These are exercises where gymnasts perform elements without flight, but which require great balance such as creating pyramids and performing handstands.

Choreography Most group exercises require an element of choreography, involving putting together a routine that is smooth in its performance and reflects the music to which it is being performed.

Combined routines These are made up of at least five pair and group elements. Two or more of these must be balance routines and at least two must be tempo routines. There are also at least three individual elements.

Combined run A run must include at least two somersaults – one without a twist and one incorporating a twist.

Compulsory exercises Although most gymnastic events involve an element of compulsory exercises, this is not the case in sports acrobatics.

Faults Faults are errors made in the execution of tumbles, exercises or routines. Points are deducted from an individual and overall team score for any faults.

Floor area All pair and group work is performed on a square, matted floor area as in rhythmic or artistic gymnastics.

Group work Balance routines and tempo routines are at the core of group work. There are also combined routines

that involve elements from both categories.

IFSA International Federation for Sports Acrobatics. Sports acrobatics is the only form of gymnastics to have its own governing body. The IFSA was formed in 1973.

Landing area There is a landing area at the end of the track on which tumbles are performed, and it is at least 16ft in length.

Men's four balance routines The men's four balance routine requires gymnasts to form one or two pyramids and hold them for at least four seconds. Because of the height involved in these exercises, there is no music and safety mats are used.

Men's pairs Two men performing balance, tempo and combined routines.

Mixed pairs One man and one woman perform balance, tempo and combined routines.

Music In pair and group work, all routines are performed and choreographed to music except for men's four balance routines.

Pair work Balance routines and tempo routines are at the core of pair work. There are also combined routines, which involve elements from both categories.

Presentation This is the performance of a pair or group routine involving the choreographed integration of a number of exercises. This should last less than 20 minutes for balance and tempo routines and three minutes for combined routines.

Scoring routines The following categories are considered for scoring composition, difficulty, execution, general impression and whether balances are held for long enough. Faults are then taken into account.

Scoring tumbles Composition, difficulty, execution and general impression must be taken into consideration when scoring tumbling routines in competition. Once these marks have been added, points for faults are deducted.

Straight run There must be at least three somersaults in a run. A double somersault is counted as two separate somersaults, and a triple somersault is marked as three. Somersaults with 180 degrees twist or more are not permitted in this section.

Tempo routines Tempo routines involve a mixture of different skills and elements – flight phases; turns and somersaults; at least two moves where the partner is caught; a set of tumbles; some individual exercises, and some choreographed elements.

Track Tumbling runs are carried out on a specially sprung track that is 27yd long, and also involves an approach run and landing area.

Tumbling Tumbling routines are performed by men or women with three tumble runs being performed – one involving somersaults without twists; one involving somersaults with a twist and one that combines somersaults with and without twists.

Twisting run One or more somersaults are required in a run, each with at least a 360-degree twist.

Women's pairs Two women performing balance, tempo and combination routines.

Women's trio Very similar to women's pairs, only these routines involve three women performing balance, tempo and combination routines, as well as the forming of pyramids in the same fashion as men's four balance routines.

SPORTS ACROBATICS: Balance routines, especially in group work, form an important part of competition

Trampolining

Trampolinists perform athletic and gymnastic movements while jumping on the trampoline. There are individual, team and synchronized competitions. Competitors attempt to maintain form, rhythm, height and synchronization during their routines.

Adolph A forward somersault with three and a half twists.

Aeroplane A half twist to a front drop.

Arbitration jury The officials who settle any dispute at a competition include a member of the organizing committee, the president of the technical committee, the referee and two judges.

Back drop A basic landing with only the back in contact on the trampoline.

Back full A backward somersault with full twist.

Back pull over A back drop where the legs are pulled over the head into a three-quarter somersault to feet.

Ball out A one-and-a-quarter forward somersault originating from a back landing.

Barani in A multiple forward somersaulting movement with a half twist in the first somersault with a back somersault out.

Barani out A multiple forward somersaulting movement with a half twist in the last movement.

Barrel roll A side somersault.

Bed The name given to the jumping and landing part of the trampoline.

Bluch A front drop, half twist to front drop.

Break The gymnast flexes at the hips, knees and ankles to stop the recoil from the bed.

Cast Describes a sideways movement across the bed.

Cat twist A back drop, full twist to back drop.

Checking Absorbing the recoil of the bed by flexing hips, knees and ankles.

Cody Also known as a cote. It is a forward or backward rotation from a front drop takeoff.

Compulsory routine The moves that constitute a compulsory routine imposed upon competitors at a competition. All trampolinists therefore perform the same routine.

Corkscrew A back drop, one-and-a-half twist forward to back drop.

Corpse A flat back drop.

Cradle A back drop, forward half twist to back drop.

Crash dive A three-quarter forward somersault with the body fully extended during its descent.

Dismount Describes the movement of going from the trampoline to the floor.

Dorso ventral axis The imaginary line that passes from the front to the back of the body that the trampolinist rotates about when performing side somersaults and turntables.

Double full A backward somersault with a double twist.

Double twister A back somersault with a double twist.

Early twist fliffis Any fliffis movement where the twist is performed in the first somersault.

Final round The 10 best gymnasts progress to the final round where they must perform a voluntary routine.

Fliffis Any double somersault with a twist either forward or backward in either or both somersaults.

Free bounce A straight bounce where

no movement occurs while the trampolinist is in the air.

Front drop A basic landing made on the stomach while the body is fully extended.

Judges There are five judges for the execution of jumps, two for difficulty and another three for synchronized jumping.

Jumping zone The area within which all jumps must be performed is clearly marked out in red on the middle of the trampoline bed.

Knee drop When the trampolinist lands on their knees with shins and feet horizontal and trunk vertical.

Layout When the trampolinist lands on the trampoline with their body fully extended (laid out prone).

Log roll A front drop, full twist to front drop.

Mount The first movement performed in a routine, and the method of getting onto the trampoline.

Out bounce A free bounce performed at the end of a routine to show judges that the trampolinist is still in control.

Piked In the piked position, the legs are straight with thighs close to the upper body. Feet and legs are kept together with toes pointed. Arms are kept straight and close to the body .

Preliminary round Gymnasts perform one compulsory and one voluntary routine. The 10 best trampolinists at the end of the round progress to the final round.

Randolph A forward somersault with two and a half twists.

Repetition If a jump is repeated in the voluntary routine, the degree of difficulty for that particular move is only scored once.

Scoring The highest and lowest marks of the execution judges are ignored and the middle three marks are summed. The difficulty mark is added and in syn-

chronized competition the mark for synchronization is added.

Seat drop A basic landing on the seat with the legs fully extended in front of the body.

Second attempt If the arbitration jury feels that a competitor was suitably disturbed during a routine, they can allow that competitor a second attempt at the routine.

Spotters A spotter must stand at each side of the trampoline for the safety of trampolinists. They are not allowed to speak to or touch competitors unless they are falling off the trampoline. They must wear tracksuits and gym shoes.

Springs The springs connecting the trampoline bed to the frame should be covered with a shock-absorbing padding.

Swingtime A movement performed immediately after another movement with a free bounce in between.

Swivel hips A seat drop, half twist to seat drop.

Synchronized competition Pairs of trampolinists perform the same routine simultaneously on two trampolines.

Team competition Three or four team members perform one compulsory and two voluntary routines.

Triffis A triple somersault with a twist in any or all of the somersaults.

Tucked In the tucked position the thighs should be close to the upper body with knees bent and hands touching the legs below the knees. Feet and legs should be together, toes pointed.

Turntable A side somersault performed in the horizontal plane from stomach to stomach or back to back.

Voluntary routine The moves that constitute a voluntary routine are decided by individual competitors. More difficult elements carry a higher potential score.

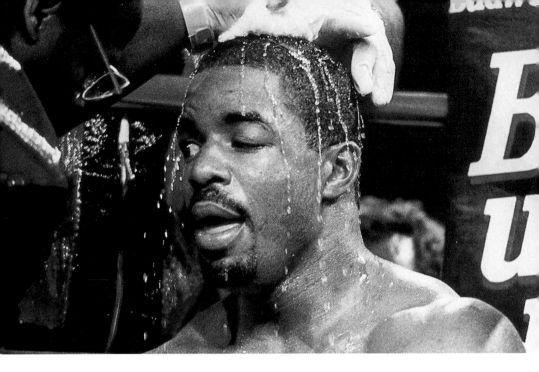

6 Combat Sports

Most of these sports are derived from genuine forms of combat but have been refined to make them highly-formalized disciplines with the element of danger reduced as much as possible. They are mostly performed between two competitors, with the object being to score points rather than to hurt or maim the opponent.

Sports Injuries

Achilles tendon The large tendon that joins the calf muscles to the heel. The tendon becomes inflamed and causes great pain in the heel of the foot.

Bruises A discoloration of the skin caused by blood leaking into the fat layer under the skin. Expect to gain many when practicing and competing in martial arts.

Complicated fracture Describes a fracture where major blood vessels or nerves are involved. Can affect the limb below as it will be deprived of blood. Nerve damage can mean paralysis of the limb.

Compound fracture Describes a fracture where the fracture site and air connect. Meaning that infection is likely, therefore slowing down the healing process.

Concussion Any state where the brain function has been noticeably altered by injury to the head. Can affect memory, balance and co-ordination.

Dislocation Occurs when the surface of the bones which form a joint are forced apart. You can tell a dislocation has occurred because a deformity can be seen, i.e. the bone sticking out at an odd angle.

Ice pack Should always be kept close at hand during training or competition as it can greatly aid in stopping swelling or numbing an area.

Internal bleeding Occurs in a closed cavity and is therefore very dangerous as no blood loss is displayed, making it hard to diagnose.

Face lacerations Usually occur due to either a punch or kick. Can range from a black eye or cut lip to more serious injuries such as a cheek bone fracture or broken nose.

Fractures Encompass a small crack to a full-blown break. There are three main types of fracture, simple, compound or complicated fracture.

Shock There are two types, physical– where the heart cannot maintain blood pressure and mental- where the injured party can be affected after the event.

Simple fracture The most common type where the bone is not completely broken. Usually a lot of bleeding as the ends of the bone are sharp and therefore damage the surrounding tissue and muscle.

Spine injuries Can include sprains, tears or in extreme cases breaks. Generally cause pain in the lower back, buttock, thigh or leg.

Sprains Are fairly common in any type of sport and cause a loss of flexibility and minor pain. The problems occur when they are ignored before they have had ample time to heal and the injury re-occurs.

Boxing

Boxing is based on the rules drawn up by the Marquess of Queensberry in 1865. They encompass the present-day rules that are governed by the World Boxing Council. The bout takes place in a ring between two competitors whose main objective is to gain the most points by landing punches on their opponent. The match is held over various rounds (depending on the weight category). Contestants either win by points, stoppage or, the most spectacular way, a knockout.

AIBA The Amateur International Boxing Association.

Bantamweight Must weigh between 112lb and 118lb if professional, or 112lb and 119lb if amateur.

Bag A padded bag that is suspended from the ceiling and is used by the boxer for practicing his punching.

Bell Rung at the start of each contest and at the end of each round.

Below the belt Any area below the hips. It is a foul to hit in this area.

Block A defensive move in which a boxer deflects punches by blocking with the arms, elbows, hands or wrists.

Bobbing and weaving The act of ducking out of the way of intended hits, and then moving into a position of attack.

Boxing The word comes from the Latin term *boxus*, meaning to box. It is so-called because the hand is put into a clenched fist with the thumb laid over the fingernails to form a box.

Break A command used by the referee to tell the two boxers to end a prolonged clinch.

Butt When a boxer places his head beneath his opponent's chin and jerks it upward. This action is deemed a foul.

Button Also known as "the point", it is the place on the jaw or chin that, if hit directly can floor an opponent.

Caution A boxer is given a caution when he commits a foul. The referee does not have to stop the fight to give a caution. Once cautioned three times for the same foul, a boxer will be given a warning.

Clinch When fighters grab each other in order to trap the opponent's arms so that he cannot use them. A prolonged clinch can lead to disqualification.

Count The referee will begin a count one second after a fighter has been knocked down. The boxer has until the count of 10 to get up and carry on, or he is out.

Counter The follow-up action by a competitor after he has thrown a punch or missed a punch.

Cruiserweight A category that exists only for professionals, with competitors weighing between 174lb and 195lb.

Decision A fight can be decided by a win on points, retirement, stoppage, disqualification or walkover.

Disqualification A fighter will be disqualified for having received three warnings, or for any behavior that the referee deems to be unacceptable.

Down A boxer is considered down if he touches the floor with any part of his body (apart from his feet), hangs on the ropes or is outside the ropes. Also applies if the boxer is still standing and the referee feels it is impossible for him to carry on.

Draw When both competitors have equal points at the end of the bout.

Duration For amateur bouts the standard length of a match is three rounds of three minutes each. For professional title fights there are typically 12 three-minute rounds. All contests have a one-minute break between each round.

Elbowing The act of using the elbows to strike an opponent. A foul.

Featherweight Must weigh between 118lb and 126lb for both amateur and professional categories.

Feint When a competitor pretends to hit his opponent in one place while trying to land the punch in another.

Fix The illegal, prearranged action of the fighters and/or management to ensure the fight ends with a particular outcome.

Flyweight Amateur contestants in this weight category must weigh 106 to 112lb – professionals 108 to 112lb.

Fox To pretend to be hurt or injured while luring your opponent into a position where he is vulnerable.

Glass jaw The name given to a boxer who has a weak chin. Usually one who has been knocked out several times.

Gloves Weigh 10oz for weight classes up to 156oz, and 12oz for heavier classes. All professionals wear 12oz gloves regardless of the weight class.

Golden Gloves Amateur tournament held in the United States. The winner receives a gold medal and a diamond-studded Golden Gloves trophy.

Gumshield Worn by all boxers to protect their teeth and gums while fighting.

Handshake Boxers must shake hands at the beginning of the bout as an act of sportsmanship. Professionals must also shake at the start of the final round.

Haymaker A colloquial term for a punch with a huge windup. Normally thrown in desperation.

Heavyweight If amateurs, boxers in this class must weigh between 178lb and 200lb, and if professional they must weigh over 195lb.

Hook A short-arm punch that is thrown with the wrist turned at the point of impact and the arm curved rather than bent.

IBF International Boxing Federation.

Infighting Takes place when the two boxers are very close to each other. They use short-arm punches, hooks or uppercuts. It is illegal to hold on to your opponent and hit him at the same time.

Irishman's confetti The name given to the illegal holding of a metal item in the hand to add power to the punch.

Jab A short, sharp punch with little windup. Usually used to soften up an opponent or distract him before a bigger punch is thrown.

Judges These officials score the fights. Five are used for amateur bouts and three for professional fights.

Junior lightweight Only exists as a professional category. The competitors must weigh between 126lb and 130lb.

Kidney punch An illegal punch thrown at a boxer's kidneys.

Knockout When a boxer is knocked down and cannot recover to carry on within a count of 10. The boxer does not have to be unconscious, or so dazed that he cannot get up, for it to be considered a knockout.

Light flyweight Fighters in this category must weigh no more than 107lb if professional or 106lb if amateur.

Light heavyweight Fighters in this category must weigh between 165lb and 178lb if amateur, and between 160lb and 178lb if professional.

Light middleweight Fighters in this category must weigh between 148lb and 156lb if amateur, and 147lb and 154lb if professional.

Lightweight Fighters in this category must weigh between 130lb and 135lb if professional, and 130lb and 132lb if amateur.

Light welterweight Fighters weighing 140lb for both codes.

Lonsdale Belt A boxing award created by the National Sporting Club of London. Lord Lonsdale lent his name to the championship belts for each weight class.

Low blow An illegal punch that lands below the belt.

Madison Square Garden New York venue that has hosted some of the greatest boxing matches in history.

Mandatory eight count Given to a boxer after he has been knocked down. If he is ready to resume before the count of eight has been completed, the fight can restart, but not until the referee has finished the count.

Mark A punch that lands on the solar plexus (between the ribs and the navel).

Middleweight Fighters in this category must weigh between 154lb and 165lb if amateur, and 154lb and 160lb if professional.

Milling Used to describe boxing, fighting or exchanging blows.

Mufflers The earliest form of boxing glove. They were formed by wrapping cloth around the hands in an attempt to minimize the damage resulting from the impact of a punch.

Neutral corner A corner of the ring that is not occupied by either of the boxers or their seconds. The referee will usually use one of the two neutral corners to add up his scorecards.

No contest A decision made by the referee to end a fight if he feels that the competitors are not giving their all, or if he feels that the fight has been fixed.

One-two punches Two punches that are thrown one after the other. Also known as the postman's knock because of the rat-a-tat-tat sound when the punches land on their target.

Open-glove punch When a boxer strikes his opponent with the inside of the glove or slaps instead of punching – both of which are illegal.

Palming An illegal action when the boxer uses his palm to rub his opponent's face upward when in a clinch.

Parry A defensive action that involves pushing the opposing fighter's glove away by hitting it, or moving inside the offensive arm to turn it away from its target.

Pivot punch A backward stroke that uses the knuckles to hit the target. This punch is deemed a foul.

Points decision In each round of a contest a boxer earns points according to the punches he lands on his opponent. In amateur boxing the total for each round is 20, and for professional bouts the maximum is 10 points per round. In the event of no knockout occurring, the fighter with the most points wins.

Pulling a punch Used in sparring and when a boxer might feel compassion for his opponent. The act of pulling a punch softens the blow received and is illegal.

Purse The amount of money paid to the boxers by the promoter of the fight.

Rabbit punch An illegal hit that lands on the back of the neck.

Referee The official in charge of ensuring fair play occurs and that the fight remains active. He has the authority to stop the contest if he sees fit.

Ring The place in which the fight takes place. It has a canvas surface and is enclosed by three or four thick ropes. It must measure no more than 20ft square and be no less than 14ft square.

Ropes The ropes that enclose the boxing ring. A boxer is thought to be in trouble when his opponent has him pressed against the ropes.

Round A boxing contest is divided into

several equal periods called rounds. Rounds vary in length and number depending on the competition.

Roundhouse A punch thrown so that the arm comes around and hits the opponent side-on.

RSC (Referee Stopping Contest) If the injuries a boxer receives are bad enough, the referee can stop the contest and award the match to his opponent.

RSCH (Referee Stopping Contest for Head Injuries) If a boxer's head injury is serious, a match can be stopped and the bout awarded against him.

Seconds Helpers who assist boxers with treatment of injuries and offer advice after each round. They are only allowed to enter the ring at the end of a round, and normally sit on the outside of the ring by their boxer's corner. They cannot coach boxers during the contest.

Shadow boxing Used by the boxer in training when he fights an imaginary opponent. Aids him by working on his footwork and speed.

Southpaw The name given to a boxer who stands with his right foot forward and leads with his right hand rather than vice versa. He normally has more power in his left hand than his right.

Spar A training boxing match used to gain practice. Special sparring gloves, which are larger than usual, are used to minimize the power of the punches.

Speed bag A small bag hung from the ceiling and used by boxers to practice their rhythm when punching.

Sucker punch Any punch that is completely unexpected. Usually directed toward an overconfident opponent to take them by surprise.

Super heavyweight Category for amateurs only. Competitors must weigh at least 200lb.

Swing A sweeping punch that uses the full curve of the arm. A difficult punch to throw successfully.

Swinging bag Placed on a flexible spring stand. The boxer uses the swinging bag to practice his aim and judgement of distance. Also used for counter punching and dodging.

Toe the line The practice of meeting in the middle of the ring at the beginning of each round. Also describes the practice of the boxers conforming to the rules and generally exhibiting good behavior.

Unification fight Describes a fight between two fighters who hold different belts under the jurisdiction of two different governing bodies.

Uppercut Aimed at either the solar plexus or the chin. This punch can be devastating and is delivered using the front knuckles in an upward motion.

Walkover A boxer can win a match when his opponent fails to appear within three minutes of the bell.

Warning Given to a boxer who has already received three cautions. Three warnings in one fight leads to disqualification.

WBA The World Boxing Association, the second most important controlling body of boxing after the WBC.

WBC The World Boxing Council, the boxing authorities who cover the largest area of the world in terms of membership. They are responsible for the WBC championships.

WBF The World Boxing Federation, a governing body of boxing that holds its own championships.

Weigh-in Competitors must be weighed on the day of the competition. They must weigh no less and no more than the weight for which they are entered.

Welterweight Fighters in this category must weigh between 140lb and 148lb if amateur, and between 140lb and 147lb if professional.

Thai Kickboxing

Thai kickboxing dates back a thousand years and is growing in popularity all the time. Competitors use varying kicks and punches in order to gain points and be declared the winner. A match comprises five three-minute rounds that are separated by two-minute rest periods.

Attention stance Used by students before they begin training. It is a formal stance.

Back kick Beginning from the fighting stance, the competitor shifts their weight to the front foot. They then move their right foot across while looking over their shoulder, thrusting their foot heel-first into the opponent.

Ball of foot The pad of flesh on the bottom of the foot that is exposed when the toes are drawn back.

Crescent kick A circular kick that moves the sole of the vertical foot across the front of the opponent's body.

Duration The contest lasts for five three-minute rounds, with a rest period of two minutes between each round.

Edge of foot Very effective when kicking an opponent. It is usually aimed at the opponent's instep, knee, hip, ribs or face.

Elbow strike A very effective blow which is used in a downward movement to strike the crown of the head. Thai boxers like to use their elbows, as the blow is normally more powerful.

Fighting stance A position that enables a competitor to gain a good balance of stability and movement. It is suited to fast maneuvers.

Flying kick Performed with both feet off the floor simultaneously.

Focus The concentration on a particular part of the opponent's body to generate maximum impact.

Forward stance Used for most punch and kick maneuvers. The hips are turned to the front, with the front knee bent and the rear knee straight.

Foul A boxer commits a foul if they bite or spit, strike their opponent while still holding the ropes or strike them when they are down, or use hip throws or pushes.

Freestyle sparring Practicing without prearranged moves.

Front kick Beginning from a fighting or forward stance, a competitor raises the knee to the correct height and pulls back the toes. The next stage is to thrust the foot into the opponent's body by fully straightening the knee joint.

Full contact Any fighting technique in which full body power is put into contact with an opponent.

Gloves Similar to normal boxing gloves, they weigh 4–6oz and are made of leather.

Guard The position of the boxer's hands in relation to his stance. They can either be defensive or used before a

FORWARD STANCE: Hips face forward with front knee bent and rear leg straight

KICKING: Thai boxers can kick as well as punch, and even knee an opponent in the groin

counterattack. The different guards allow the boxer to use his body to its maximum potential while making things awkward for his opponent.

Heel The back of the foot used to strike an opponent.

Heel kick Any kick that uses the heel of the foot to strike an opponent.

Instep The top of the foot used to strike in an upward snapping movement to the groin or above.

Knees A powerful weapon, generally swung upward into and opponent's groin area.

Long-handed boxing When punching, the thrusting arm is fully extended.

Lunge punch Taken from a forward stance, the punch is struck as the competitor advances forward, giving more power.

Mongkon A ritual headband worn during the ritual dance, but which is taken off before the fight begins.

Muay Thai Another name for Thai boxing.

Ram muay A ritual dance performed by both boxers before the start of a contest. It is symbolic of each training camp.

Reaps Taking the opponent's supporting leg away.

Reverse punch A punch from the opposing hand to the leading foot.

Reverse roundhouse kick A kick delivered in a moving horizontal arc with the sole of the foot rather than the instep. It is aimed no higher than the chest area.

Reverse turning kick Made using the rear leg, which is fully straightened. The target is the shin.

Ritual An important part of this martial art. At the beginning of a match the fighters walk around the whole ring while holding the top rope. This is done to seal off the ring against evil forces.

Roundhouse kick Made using the instep as the point of contact with the target. The kick is directed in a horizontal arc.

Roundhouse punch Using a relaxed action, the punch is thrown in a circular direction.

Shins The part of the leg between the ankle and the knee, used as a striking weapon.

Side kick With a competitor turned sideways to his opponent, he thrusts out a kick using the heel and edge of the foot to make contact with the target.

Snap kick A kick that brings the leg back to the body in a very quick movement.

Sparring When two boxers practice their moves on one another.

Stamping kick Used to full effect by thrusting the heel of the foot downward into the opponent.

Weight categories There are 12 weight categories in total for Thai boxing, ranging from 112lb atd one end of the scale to 175lb or more.

Wrestling

Wrestling is an individual combat sport fought between two men on a mat or in a ring. They can use different styles and techniques in a bid to throw their opponent to the ground and pin him down to register a fall. The wrestler who achieves the fall is declared the winner of the bout.

Ankle and leg drive A standing throw used by a wrestler that takes their opponent off balance by grabbing one leg and bringing them down to the mat. This move is also known as a leg snap.

Body press A wrestler uses all his weight against his opponent lying on his back to help him secure a fall.

Bout The time period during which the two wrestlers have to fight each other and aim to score the most points against each other. They normally last for three minutes with a minute's rest between each bout. The bout ends in the event of a fall or a disqualification.

Breakdown A wrestler brings their opponent to their side or stomach by removing their hand and/or knee support.

Bridge The term used to describe a movement by a wrestler to support himself on his head, elbows and feet. This prevents his shoulders from touching the mat.

Brutality Unnecessary roughness by a wrestler with the intent to injure an opponent, resulting in disqualification.

Catch-as-catch-can Another name for freestyle which a wrestler uses against any part of their opponent's body.

Cautions A referee can warn a wrestler about his conduct – including aspects such as lack of sportsmanship, passive obstruction or arguing with the judge or the mat chairman.

Competition A number of wrestlers take part in a series of matches and the wrestler who wins the most matches and then picks up the most points among the finalists is declared the overall winner.

Contestants Individual wrestlers who take part in a competition.

Correct hold A well-executed throw used by a wrestler on their opponent that does not result in a take-down.

Counter move Used by a wrestler to block or stop their opponent from attacking them. They can be awarded points for this type of move.

Cradle A ground hold used by a wrestler when applying a cross-face hold with one arm, while bringing the other arm through the opponent's crotch.

Cross-buttock A wrestler employs a standing throw with which his opponent is forced over the hips or lower back. This move will normally come after a head-hold.

Cross-face A ground hold secured by putting one hand across the side of their opponent's face and grasping his opposite arm above the elbow.

Danger position When a wrestler's shoulder or back forms an angle with the mat that is less than 90 degrees, and they resist with the upper body to avoid a fall, they are considered to be in a dangerous position.

Default Occurs when a bout is ultimately decided by an injury to one of the players. The opposing player automatically wins the match.

Disqualification A contestant can be thrown out of a competition for committing a serious offense or for being disqualified twice for passivity.

Double A hold secured by both arms, or on two of the opponent's limbs.

Double-thigh pick up A standing throw used by a wrestler that puts their opponent on the mat by hooking them behind the legs.

Drawn The two wrestlers have the same number of points at the end of a bout.

Dress Wrestlers wear tight-fitting one-piece singlets. Wrestlers are permitted to wear light knee guards and their shoes must not have any heels, rings or buckles.

Duration The bout lasts for five minutes without any interruption. The timekeeper will announce the time every minute and rings the bell to signal the end of the bout. The referee will then blow his whistle. Any action that takes place between the bell and the whistle is not deemed valid.

Elimination After a wrestler has suffered two losses, they are withdrawn from the match. Elimination rounds continue until only three wrestlers are left in each pool.

Escape point Awarded to a wrestler after they have escaped from the bottom position and stand up again to face their opponent.

Fall A wrestler brings their opponent down to the mat and pins both their shoulders to the ground long enough for the referee to count one and then strike the mat with his hand. They are then declared the winner of the bout by the referee.

Fall-back A wrestler will successfully achieve a take-down by holding their opponent from behind and falling backwards.

FILA The Fédération de Lutte Amateur-the International Amateur Wrestling Federation, founded in 1921.

Final This is fought out between the last three contestants remaining in the competition. If any of the finalists has not met each other before in a previous round, they will fight each other in a final bout. If they have met each other before, the penalty points from that bout are carried forward and they will not meet again.

Finalists The last three contestants remaining in the competition who will compete in the final itself to determine the winner of the competition.

Five points Awarded to a wrestler for a high throw on their opponent that places them in an immediate position of danger.

Fleeing a hold A wrestler performs this move after refusing contact to prevent the opposition from executing a hold.

Fleeing the mat A wrestler can avoid an opponent's attack by going off the mat. This can result in a caution or a penalty point.

Flying mare A standing throw used by a wrestler that uses their opponent's arm as a lever to hurl them over their back.

Forfeit When a wrestler fails to show up for a bout, the match is abandoned and the opponent is automatically declared the winner.

Fouls Awarded against a wrestler by the referee for any act of misconduct that is not within the rules of the game. This ranges from stepping on an opponent's feet to lifting an opponent from a bridge to throw him on to the mat.

Freestyle Classified as one of the three official FILA styles, and one of the most popular moves a wrestler can use on their opponent. This includes using a hold, throw or trip.

Full nelson A ground hold used from

a position behind the opponent by putting both arms under their armpits and fastening the hands or wrists on the back of his neck. This move can be performed only from the side and without any use of the legs. This is also known as a double nelson.

Grand amplitude A movement used by a wrestler that involves them using a high, sweeping throw in which the opponent is lifted off the mat.

Greco-Roman One of the three official FILA styles. It is played under the same rules as freestyle, except that a wrestler is not allowed to grasp below the hips or use the legs to effect a take-down or to hang on to an opponent.

Gut wrench A hold used by a wrestler which is applied to their opponent's torso in an attempt to turn him to score points.

Half nelson A ground hold used by a wrestler who places one arm through their opponent's corresponding armpit and then around his neck.

Head-hold A wrestler puts one arm around their opponent's head. If they attempt to use both arms, a foul will be awarded against them.

Hook A wrestler reaches around or under an opponent's arm or leg to grasp him with the hand or crook of his arm. This term is also associated with a wrestler putting his leg or foot behind an opponent's leg to carry out a take-down.

Judge The official who determines when a wrestler merits a point.

Kneeling position A wrestler has been forced to the ground, but can counter his opponent and get up with his hands and knees, which must be at least 8in apart. They can change position only after the referee has blown his whistle.

Mat The area on which the two wrestlers fight each other. It can be square (no less than 11yd or no greater than 13yd on all sides) or, for international contests, has a circular area which measures 10yd in diameter. There is a center circle 3.3ft in diameter and a mat area around the wrestling area which is at least 5.5yd wide.

Mat chairman The chief official.

One point Awarded to a wrestler if he takes his opponent down to the mat with no back exposure, or applies a correct hold that does not cause his opponent to touch the mat with his head or shoulders.

Par terre position A starting position for a wrestler, who begins the bout with his hands and knees on the ground, and his opponent begins with his hands on the back of the wrestler on the ground.

Passive obstruction A wrestler continues to obstruct an opponent's hold or lies flat on the mat.

Passivity zone The outermost part of the mat that is still deemed in bounds. The referee calls "zone" when the wrestlers move into this area and they need to return to the center of the mat.

Penalty points When a bout has finished the points are converted into classification points using the classification table.

Pin A wrestler can win a fall by forcing his opponent down to the ground and holding his shoulders on the mat.

Placing in danger The term used when a wrestler goes beyond 90 degrees with his back turned toward the mat. He will resist falling completely to the ground with his back pointed upward.

Red card The referee will show this to a coach for unsportsmanlike behavior. The coach is then expelled from the match.

Referee The official who is in charge of the bout and who stands on the mat with the two wrestlers. He will raise the appropriate arms and fingers to indicate points for the wrestlers.

Reversal A move used by a wrestler who comes out from below his opponent and then gains control of him. He can be awarded one point for successfully completing this move.

Sambo One of the three official FILA styles. The wrestler will attempt to throw his opponent on his back while remaining standing himself.

Slam A wrestler throws his opponent down with unnecessary force without falling to the mat himself.

Slipped throw Unsuccessful attempt by a wrestler to throw from the standing position or the par terre position.

Standing arm-roll A standing throw employed by a wrestler in which he grasps his opponent's arm, and then puts it around his own body so that he can then be rolled on to the mat.

Start of bout The two wrestlers shake hands in the center of the mat and are inspected by the referee before returning to their respective corners. The referee blows his whistle and each round starts with the two wrestlers in a headlock position.

Take-down A wrestler brings his opponent down to the mat in a position not considered to be dangerous. A wrestler is awarded one point for this maneuver.

Technical points Points awarded to a wrestler for certain holds and moves. Penalty points can also count as technical points.

Termination A bout finishes when both shoulders of one wrestler are touching the mat at the same time, when his opponent is in control. It can also be terminated when there is a difference of 15 points between the two wrestlers.

The fall The term given when both shoulders are in contact with the mat. The referee will hit the mat with his hand to signify the fall, and then blow his whistle.

Three points Awarded to a wrestler for bringing his opponent from a standing position into an immediate position of danger.

Tie When the points are level between the two wrestlers at the end of the bout.

Timekeeper An official who keeps a check on the time during the bout. He announces the time every minute and rings a bell at the end of the bout to signal to the referee that it has finished.

Tomber The French word for "fall". The referee will say this word when counting the time during a fall.

T-sign A signal made by the referee with his hands to inform judges and the timekeeper he is stopping the round.

Two points Awarded to a wrestler if his opponent has been placed in a rolling fall or he rolls from side to side to form a bridge using both the elbows and shoulders.

Verbal warning The referee verbally warns a wrestler about his conduct and will award a caution if the incident happens again.

Wing A wrestler holds his opponent on the ground by locking his arm tightly and then rolling him over.

Sumo Wrestling

Sumo wrestling was the first recognized martial art, originating in Japan as long ago as 23BC. It incorporates ceremonial rituals as well as wrestling, and is the national sport of Japan. The average weight of a sumo wrestler is 280lb with an average height of 6ft.

Banzuki The title given to the list of rankings.

Basho The name of a sumo tournament.

Bintsuke Hair oil used by all wrestlers to hold their hair in place when taking part in competition.

Butsukari-geiko The pushing technique used during competition. It is one of the most common techniques used.

Chankonabe The high-protein diet the wrestlers eat in order to keep up their weight.

Chaya A sumo tea shop.

Chon-mage The top-knot sumo wrestlers wear in their hair to keep it out of the way.

Danpatsu-shiki The haircutting ceremony.

Deshi An apprentice wrestler.

Dohyo The sumo ring. It is a hard clay platform measuring 18ft square with a height of 2ft.

Dohyo-iri The ceremony during which the wrestlers enter the ring.

Dohyo-matsui A ring dedication ceremony, performed the day before a basho, with three referees asking for a blessing.

Gyoji The referee.

Hataki-komi Slap-down technique.

Heya Also called beya. This is the stable where the wrestlers live together and train together.

Hidri A left-hander.

Hikkake Description for the pulling technique.

Jinku A sumo song.

Jonidan The second division from the bottom of the ranking with 300 wrestlers.

Jonokuchi Means the first step from the bottom. There are 80 wrestlers at this level.

Jungyo An exhibition tour of the provinces.

Juryo The second division from the top, consisting of 26 competitors.

Kachi-koshi A score of 8–7 or more. This means that the wrestler has more wins than losses and will qualify to move up to the next division.

Kanto-sho The fighting spirit prize.

Kawaigatte The roughing-up of new recruits when they join a stable.

Keiko To practice.

Kesho-mawashi A ritual apron made of handwoven silk that hangs down to the ankle and is worn during ceremonies.

Ketaguri A leg sweep technique.

Kimarite General term for sumo techniques.

Komusubi A junior champion who is in the second class. Only two wrestlers at one time can receive this honor.

Kote-nage The forearm throw technique.

Kubi-nage The neck throw technique.

Kyokai Japan's official sumo wrestling association.

Maegashira The senior wrestlers in the top division. They number 1–14, with two wrestlers holding each rank.

Make-koshi A score of 8–7 or more in losses.

Makunouchi The top division. There are 36 contenders in this class.

Makushita The third highest division. This is the second class, with 120 wrestlers.

Masuzeki The ringside seats

Matawari An exercise in which the wrestler does the splits with his legs sideways and his chest and chin resting on the floor in front.

Mawashi The loincloth belt worn by sumo wrestlers. It measures over 10yd in length and is folded lengthwise four or six times, before being wrapped around the waist and then taken through the legs and tied in a knot at the back. Top wrestlers wear silk loincloths, whereas in lower divisions they are made of canvas.

Migi A right-hander.

Moro zashi Occurs when both hands are on the belt.

Moshiai A competition used to eliminate wrestlers during training.

Oicho mage The hairstyle worn by a wrestler in the top division.

Okome A word meaning rice, and which is also the sumo slang word for bonus money earned.

Okuri A dodging technique.

Okuri dashi A carry-out technique.

Oshi dashi The push-out technique.

Oshi taoshi Push-down technique.

Oshi zumo Pushing technique.

Oyakata The elder or senior official of an association.

Ozeki The champion. The term actually translates as "the great barrier", and there are only six wrestlers at this stage at any one time.

Presumo The beginners' section. They have no official ranking.

Rikishi The name given to all ranks of wrestlers.

Sanban Training matches against one opponent.

Sandanme The third division from the bottom. There are 200 wrestlers on the third step.

Sanyaku Three top ranks below yokozuna.

Sekitori The two top division wrestlers.

Sekiwake The junior champion of the first class.

Senshiuraku The last day of the tournament.

Shiko An exercise in which the wrestler lifts one foot high and then stamps it down very hard.

Shittate-nage An inner-arm technique.

Shukun-sho An award for an outstanding performance.

Soto-gake An outer-leg technique.

Sumai The Japanese term for struggle, from which the word sumo originates.

Sumotori The title for sumo who are below the top two divisions.

Tachi-al An initial attack.

Tegata A palm print.

Teppo Open-handed slaps against a wooden pole.

Toshiyori A sumo elder. There are 105 in all.

Tsuki dashi A thrust-out technique.

Tsuki otoshi A thrust-over technique.

Uchi-gake Inner-leg trip technique.

Utchari A technique in which the wrestler throws down his opponent at the edge of the ring.

Uwate-nage An outer-arm throw technique.

Yobidashi The announcer at a basho.

Yokozuna The grand champion, the highest possible ranking.

Yorikiri A force-out technique.

Yori taoshi A force-out-and-down technique.

Yotsu-zumo The name for the grappling techniques.

Yusho The championship tournament.

Zensho yusho A perfect victory score of 15–0.

Kabaddi

Kabaddi originated in India where it is still a very popular game. It is played with two teams of 12 players each, five of them substitutes. The object of the game is to reach the highest score by touching or capturing the opposing team's players, all the while chanting "Kabaddi-Kabaddi". There are varying forms of the game.

AKFI The Amateur Kabbadi Federation of India founded in 1973, it has the right to modify the rules.

Amar A form of Kabaddi where once a player has been touched out he doesn't leave the court. He stays inside, with the team that "touched" him awarded one point. Played to a time limit.

Antis The opposing player or players to the raider.

Baulk line The line that runs down the center of the court and divides the playing area into two.

Canting Each player when entering the opposing team's half of the court must take one breath and chant "Kabaddi-Kabaddi" until out of that breath. If they still remain in the opposition's side of the court when this happens they will be declared out.

Categories Matches are held on the basis of age and weight.

Chu-kit-kit The name for the female version of Kabaddi.

Circle Kaaddi The game is played in a circle.

Court Measures 14yd in length by 11yd in width. The court is divided into two halves. Can be held anywhere and is one of the main reasons that the game is so popular in rural India.

Duration Each game consists of two 20-minute halves with a rest period of five minutes, which is used to change team members. For a women's match, the duration is two 15-minute halves with a five-minute rest period.

Gaminee A form of Kabaddi where there is no revival. Once all the players of a team are declared out the game is over. There is no time limit.

Goongi Kabaddi Not played on a court. Two players wrestle each other.

Hadudu The name for the men's version of Kabaddi.

KFI The Kabaddi Federation of India, which governs the sport. Founded in 1950.

Linesmen Their duties are to record those out in the order of their exit as well as those who are revived.

Lona A bonus of two points awarded if the entire opposing team is out.

Raider The name given to the player who enters the court to try and touch the opposing players and tag them out. Only one raider allowed in at a time.

Referee Always has the final say on any decision. He has the power to warn, award points for and against a team or player, or dismiss a team or player.

Substitutes Five are allowed during the course of a match.

Teams Consist of 12 players with seven allowed on court at any time.

Tiebreaker If the match ends in a tie, then an extra 10 minutes are added to the game. If the game is still drawn after extra time, the first team to gain a point are declared the winners.

Waiting blocks These are placed at either end of the court, 6.5ft away from the end lines. The substitute players sit here until their turn. Once a player is deemed out they also wait here.

Judo

Judo, which means "gentle way", emerged from jiu jitsu during the nineteenth century in Japan, but did not become a competitive sport until after World War II. A match between two fighters lasts until one of them has scored the maximum 10-point ippon or until an allocated time expires, after which the result is determined by judges based on a point-scoring system.

Aiki Word meaning "the harmony of spirit" and referring to a form of self-defence.

Aikido This is the "way" of aiki.

Aite An opponent.

Ao Both vowels are pronounced, as "Ah, oh"; refers to opponents facing up to each other.

Ao-muku-kami-shiho-gatame Term meaning "facing upward upper four quarters"; this is an arm-lock technique.

Ao-muku-yoko-shiho-gatame Term meaning "facing upward side four quarters"; this is an arm-lock technique.

Ashi-guruma A sweeping throw meaning "leg wheel".

Atemiwaza Striking techniques using the body's natural weapons such as the hand, elbow, foot or knee.

Awasette Adding two half-points in competition to make one full point (e.g. a waza-ari awasette ippon is equal to two waza-ari added together to give a win by the maximum ippon score).

Belt The color of a judoka's belt indicates the standard achieved, and ranges from yellow to black or red. Junior judokas start with a white belt and can progress to brown.

Bowing On entering the dojo or mat area, a judoko should perform a standing bow toward the senior instructor. Equally a judoka should bow simultaneously to his/her opponent before and after a randori or shiai.

Breakfall The safe method of falling that all practitioners of judo learn.

Chu-gaeri Forward-rolling breakfalls.

Chui A penalty incurred during a contest that is equivalent to the loss of five points.

Dan A dan is the grade of someone who has earned a black belt. The grade runs from first dan to 10th dan (the highest ever awarded in judo), by which time the judoka will have earned a red belt.

De-ashi-barai Means "foot dash or sweep".

Dojo The training room or hall where judo is practiced.

Dojo rules The ordinary rules of conduct which are adhered to at most clubs around the world. These cover aspects such as personal cleanliness and condition, the judogi, footwear, use of jewelry, leaving the dojo and noise.

Fusen-gachi A default win through nonappearance of an opponent.

Gokyo-no-nagi-waza The original collection of 40 throwing techniques at a judoka's disposal.

Gyaku-juji-jime Means "reverse cross strangle".

Hadake-jime Means "naked strangle".

Hane-goshi A hip throw; means "spring hip".

Hane-makikomi A powerful hip throw; means "spring and winding".

Hansoku-make A win through disqualification.

Harai-goshi A throw; means "sweeping loin".

Harai-makikomi A throw means "sweeping and winding".

Harai-tsurikomi-ashi Means "sweeping drawing ankle".

Hiza-gatame Means "knee arm-lock".

Hiza-guruma A throw; means "knee wheel".

Hon-kami-shiho-gatame It means "basic upper four quarters hold".

Hon-kesa-gatame Means "basic scarf hold"; this is the most widely used hold, and the first that a beginner learns.

Hon-tate-shiho-gatame Means "basic vertical four quarters hold".

Hon-yoko-shiho-gatame Means "basic side four quarters hold".

Ippon Maximum scoring throw or hold worth 10 points.

Ippon-seoi-nage Means "one-arm shoulder throw".

Judoji The tunic and trousers outfit worn by anyone practicing or competing in judo.

Judoka Name given to anyone practicing or competing in judo.

Juji-gatame Means "cross straight arm-lock".

Kansetsu-waza Armlock techniques.

Kata-ha-jime Means "single wing strangle".

Kata-gatame Means "shoulder hold".

Kata-guruma Means "shoulder wheel"; this is a dramatic throw that works best as a surprise move.

Kata-juji-jime Means "half cross strangle".

Kiken-gachi A win through withdrawal of an opponent during competition.

Koka A three-point score.

Koshi-guruma A hip throw that means "hip wheel".

Koshi-jime Means "hip strangle".

Ko-uchi-gari A sweeping move meaning "minor inner reaping".

Kuzure-kami-shiho-gatame Means "broken upper four quarters hold".

Kuzure-kesa-gatame Means "broken scarf hold".

Kuzure-tate-shiho-gatame Means "broken vertical four quarters hold".

Kuzure-yoko-shiho-gatame Means "broken side four quarters hold".

Makura-kesa-gatame Means "pillow scarf hold".

Morote-gari Means "both arms reap"; this is viewed as more of a winning trick than a classic throw.

Morote-jime Means "both hands strangle".

Morote-seoi-nage Means "both hands shoulder throw".

Mune-gatame Means "chest hold".

Nami-juji-jumi Means "normal cross strangle".

Ne-waza Groundwork that is carried out when both competitors are on the ground after a throw or attempted throw. Made up of holds, strangleholds and armlocks. A judoka needs to maintain a hold for 30 seconds to gain the maximum score.

O-goshi A hip throw; means "major hip".

O-guruma A powerful nonsweeping throw; means "major-wheel".

Okuri-ashi-harai Means "side-sweeping ankle throw".

Okuri-eri-jime Means "sliding lapel strangle".

Osae-waza Holding techniques used to immobilize an opponent during groundwork.

O-soto-gari A combination of both sweep and push; means "major outer reaping".

O-uchi-gake Another sweeping move that means "major inner hook".

O-uchi-gari Means "major inner reaping"; this throw involves a combination of sweeping and pushing.

O-soto-guruma Means "major outer

wheel"; this is a very ambitious sweeping throw.

Randori A free practice session.

Reap To displace an opponent's supporting leg.

Rei A bow.

Sacrifice throw A throw in which a Tori allows himself to fall in the process of performing the throw.

Sasae-tsurikomi-ashi Means "propping drawing ankle"; this is a foot throw, although there is no sweep involved.

Seoi-otoshi Means "shoulder drop"; this is a popular throw.

Shiai A judo contest between two judokai.

Shime-waza Strangle techniques.

Shodan The first-dan black belt, which is the ambition of most judokai.

Sode-guruma-jime Means "sleeve wheel strangle".

Sogo-gachi Means "compound win".

Soto-makikomi Means "outer winding", and sees both judokai wind to the mat.

Sumi-gaeshi Means "corner throw", and is referred to as a sacrifice throw.

Supporting leg The leg that supports the judoka's weight and balance.

Sutemi-waza Sacrifice techniques.

Sweep A hook or strike of the leg that removes the uke's balance by displacing his/her supporting leg.

Tachi-rei The standing bow that is carried out by bending at the waist with feet together and a straight back.

Tai-otoshi Means "body drop", one of the best throws for a beginner to learn.

Tani-otoshi Means "valley drop", this is a powerful throw that results in a heavy fall.

Tatami The judo mat upon that all training and contests are carried out.

Tokui waza A judoka's favorite match-winning throw or preferred technique.

Tomoe-nage Means "stomach throw", this is what is referred to as a "sacrifice throw".

Tori The judoka who carries out a throw.

Tsuki-komi-jime Means "thrusting strangle".

Tsuri-goshi Means "lift-up hip"; this is a hip throw.

Tsurikomi-goshi Means lift-pull hip.

Uchi-mata Means "inner thigh"; this is a sweeping throw that generates great power.

Ude-garame Means "arm entanglement".

Ude-gatame Straight arm lock.

Uke The judoka who is thrown.

Ukemi Techniques that teach the judoka how to fall safely.

Uki-goshi Means "floating hip"; this throw employs a rotating action.

Uki-otoshi Means "floating drop"; this is usually used as a counter move.

Uki-waza Means "floating technique"; this "sacrifice throw" requires perfect technique and timing.

Ushiro-kesa-gatame Term that means "reverse scarf hold".

Waki-gatame Means "armpit hold".

Waza-ari Score for a slightly imperfect throw or hold, worth seven points.

Working leg The leg that a judoka uses to perform a throw.

Yama-arashi Means "mountain storm", this is a very fast and ambitious sweeping throw that was not part of the original 40 throws.

Yamei The command to stop training.

Yoko-gake Means "side hook"; a side sacrifice technique because the Tori also goes to the mat landing on his side.

Yudansha A holder of a black belt.

Yuko A five-point score.

Za-rei The kneeling bow that is only performed at the formal opening and closing of a training session.

Jiu Jitsu

Jiu Jitsu is a traditional Japanese martial art that incorporates martial and self-defense strategies. Competitions are divided according to the grade reached by competitors, who compete on a one-to-one basis.

Ajemis Strangle techniques used to gain a submission.

Atemi Body strike techniques.

Bujutsu ryu A traditional form of jiu jitsu that originated in Japan.

Chui A warning by the judge for an infringement of the rules.

Competitions These are divided either by weight or grade.

Corner judge Positioned at the corner of the competition area to assist the senior judge. He uses a red flag and a white flag to signal his decisions. There are four corner judges in all. The two flags correspond to the colored belts of the competitors. When a decision is made relating to a competitor, the judge will hold the corresponding colored flag in the air.

Disqualification Penalty used by the judge or referee for failure to adhere to the rules. Competitors can either be disqualified immediately or barred from future events.

Duration For ne-waza, the time limit is two to three minutes with extra time added if no score has been recorded; either one or two minutes for the gauntlet and V-attack unless a score has been made first; and three minutes for the nage-waza with extra time added for no score at the judge's discretion.

Engagement Begins with both contestants holding on to each other or one gripping the other. Grips are made on the body or limbs and not on the clothes.

Gauntlet An individual demonstration.

Gi The uniform worn by competitors.

Hajime The command given to begin the tournament.

Hakama An ankle-length divided skirt worn by the senior and corner judges.

Hakko ryu A nontraditional form of jiu jitsu that originated in Japan.

Hantei A call made by the senior judge to the corner judges to give their decision.

Hikkiwake Means that a draw has been recorded.

Ippon One full point recorded for a win.

Jiu jitsuka The title given to practitioners of jiu jitsu.

Matte The command given by the senior judge to stop the competition but with the opponents holding their position.

Nage-waza A form of jiu jitsu that means throwing technique. The basic throws are built around hand, leg, shoulder and sacrifice throws.

Ne-waza A form of jiu jitsu that means groundwork. The basic moves are a stranglehold, an armlock or a holddown.

Obi A belt that is colored to indicate the competitor's level of achievement. In nage-waza and ne-waza, the competitors wear a red obi and a white obi, respectively.

Osaekomi To hold or pin down.

Senior judge Takes overall control and responsibility during a tournament. Wears a white gi and black hakama.

Side judge Assists the senior judge.

Timekeeper Official in charge of

ensuring time is kept properly during competition.

Toketa Used by a competitor to signal the fact that a hold-down has been broken.

Tori The defending competitor.

Ukes The attacking competitor.

V-attack The name given to an individual demonstration.

Waza ari A half-point.

Waza ari awazette ippon A second half-point that makes up a full point for a win.

Weight categories For men there are three: under 159lb, 159–187lb and over 187lb. For women there are two: under 132lb, and 132lb and over.

Yame The command used to stop a contest.

Yoi The command used by officials to signal to the contestants that they should be ready.

Yoshi The command given to continue the action.

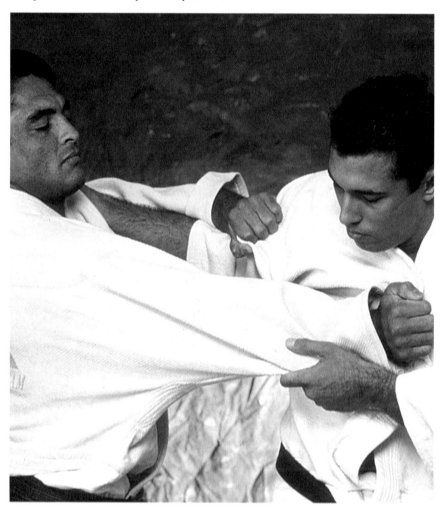

OSAEKOME: Both contestants are performing this maneuver which means to hold your opponent in a firm grip

Karate

Karate is a combat sport that employs a formal method of physical and mental training. All punches, kicks, blows and strikes must be controlled and pulled back before contact to avoid injuries to either contestant.

Arbitrator An official who oversees the operation of the match and the decisions that the referee and judges make when requested. They can express an opinion to the referee if desired. The arbitrator will also direct and supervise the timekeeper.

Bout The term given to the match that takes place between the two contestants. A bout ends when a winner has been declared by the referee.

Deciding bouts If the scores are even between two contestants at the end of a bout, one person is chosen from each team to fight against each other. If the scores are still even at the end of the deciding bout, each team chooses a further representative until a result is obtained.

Disqualification A contestant can be eliminated from the match if they commit repeated fouls after being given a warning by the referee, or if they fail to obey the referee's instructions.

Dress Contestants are expected to wear a white karate-gi. One must wear a red belt on top of the belt and the other a white belt. They must both have an identification sign on their karate-gis. Competitors are allowed to wear a gum shield, boxes or soft shin pads, but protective or safety devices can be used only if permitted by the referee council.

Duration The match lasts for two to three minutes, but it can be extended to five minutes. Any stoppages incurred during the match are not included in the match time.

Encho-sen The term given to an extension of a deciding bout where the two contestants have finished with the same number of points at the end of the bout.

Foul Awarded by the referee against a competitor after they have made a direct attack to the body other than the arms or legs, or have used a dangerous technique or throw.

Hansoku Imposed by the referee after a serious violation has taken place. This results in the opponent's score being raised to a sanbon.

Hansoku-chui Imposed for violations for that a half-point penalty has already been given by the referee in the match.

Ippon A score is awarded to a contestant who has performed according to the following criteria: good form, correct attitude, vigorous application, proper timing, correct distance and perfect finish.

Keikoku A penalty imposed following any minor violations for that a warning has already been given in that bout.

Match area This consists of a flat, square surface without any obstacles. It measures 8.7yd in length.

Penalties If a contestant breaks any of the rules, they will be penalized or warned by the referee. After consultation with the referee panel, the nature of the penalty will be announced by the referee. A warning can be imposed for any kind of minor infractions.

Procedure At the start of a bout the contestants stand facing each other with their toes pointing to the starting line, ready to bow to one another. The referee and judges both take up their positions, and on the referee's call of "shobu sanbon hajime", the match gets under way.

Protests A contestant's team officer can appeal to the arbitrator if they feel that the wrong decision has been made against one of their teammates, or they think a foul or penalty has been committed. The arbitrator will then consult the referee and judge.

Referee The official who controls the match, including starting, suspending and ending the match.

Sanbon This has a value of three ippons, and can be reached by scoring three ippons or by scoring six waza-ari. A contestant can also score this by getting the appropriate combination of the two. When a sanbon has been scored, the referee will shout, "Yame!" and both contestants return to their standing line. The winner is announced and the bout comes to an end.

Scoring Physical contact is not allowed by the contestants, but points can be awarded by using recognized scoring technique on the right scoring area. This entails having the potential to penetrate deep into the opponent's target. A referee with the judge's help will award an ippon or waza-ari.

Shikkaku A term that means disqualification. A contestant is awarded the victory if his opponent commits an act leading to Shikkaku.

Shobu sanbon hajime Called out by the referee at the start of a bout to get the match under way.

Standing line The line behind that the two contestants must stand at the start of a bout, or to that they must return after any points have been scored.

Stoppages The referee can stop the bout for an injury to one of the contestants or to inquire about an incident that may have taken place. Any time lost for a stoppage is not included in the match time.

Temporary halts The referee is entitled to stop the match temporarily if he feels that either of the contestants has committed an infringement, or one of them cannot continue during the bout due to injury or illness.

Tie When the scores are even between the two contestants at the end of the bout, it is a tie.

Timekeeper An official who keeps check on the time during the bout. They will be directed by the arbitrator and signal with a gong or buzzer 30 seconds before the end of the match and when the match finishes.

Waza-ari A half-point is awarded to a contestant for a blow that is almost comparable to that needed to score an ippon.

Winner The winner of the match is the first contestant to score three ippons or six waza-ari, or a combination of the two that equals a sanbon. They can also be declared the winner if the other contestant is disqualified or the referee or judge makes a decision and awards the bout to them.

Yame Called by the referee to stop the bout when a scoring technique is seen by one of the judges. The match is halted and the contestants take up their original positions. The referee will identify the relevant score and award waza-iron or ippon to the appropriate contestant.

Aikido

The name aikido is made up of three Japanese characters meaning harmony, energy and way. There are two different categories of aikido, competitive and noncompetitive, with four different competitions: the kata, that is a formal event; and ninin dori, tanto randori and randori kyoghi, which all are fighting events.

Aiuchi Means mutual striking, when both contestants simultaneously deliver an attacking move.

Area Measures 10yd by 10yd with a smooth surface.

Assistant judges Positioned in opposite corners outside the match area to help judge the contest.

Attention stance A formal stance used by students before beginning training.

Awasette Means "to combine together" adding two half-points together to make one point during competition.

Belt In competition one contestant must wear a red belt and the other a white belt.

Blocking The act of using the body, arm or leg to divert an oncoming attack.

Bokken A wooden sword used by the uke during the ninidori.

Breakfall A way of landing without injury after falling.

Chagi Kicking.

Chudan Japanese for "middle level", a reference to the middle part of the body.

Chudan uke Means "middle level block", and occurs when the defending contestant deflects blows to the middle level area of the body.

Chui Means "warning", and is used by competition officials to alert competitors to mistakes, whether deliberate or accidental.

Chusoki The ball of the foot.

Circular block A circular technique used to block an attack.

Dojo A traditional training hall.

Garami Term meaning "entanglement".

Gi Uniform.

Goshi Japanese term for hip.

Haisoku Japanese term for instep.

Hajime Means "begin", and is used by officials and teachers to begin practice or competing.

Hansoku Used by officials to indicate that a foul has been committed.

Hantei Declares that the judges have come to a decision.

Hara The abdomen.

Hidari The Japanese term for left.

Hiji Describes the elbow.

Hikkiwake Means that a draw has been declared.

Hiza The knee.

Honbu The headquarters of a school or tradition.

Ippon Worth one point in a competition.

Jikan Word meaning time; used to signal when the clock is stopped during a competition.

Jo A stave that is a heavy stick; they can be used in pairs during the ninidori.

Jodan Area upward of the shoulder, neck and head.

Jodan uke An upward block that deflects an attack on the head and shoulders.

Jogai Out of bounds, when a competitor steps out of the competition area.

Joseki The senior judge.

Kakato The heel of the foot.

Kamae The posture taken when practicing.

Kansetsu waza Locking techniques used to immobilize the joints of the attacking competitor.

Kata A prearranged set of movements performed within a two- or three-minute period; it is also the name of the competition.

Kekomi Means "to thrust".

Kihon Means "the basics", and describes the fundamental exercises of the art.

Kime Means "to focus".

Koshi Describes the ball of the foot.

Maai Means the distance between the two competitors.

Meijin Means "expert".

Migi The Japanese term for "right".

Morote uke A double block that involves using both arms.

Motonoichi To return to your original position while competing.

Musubi dachi An informal stance with the heels together and the feet directed outward.

Ninidori A fight involving three competitors.

Randori kyoghi A form of aikido that involves two competitors who freefight.

Renshu Means "to practice".

Senior judge Person responsible for the overall control of a competition.

Shiai jo The place where the competitions are held for a bout of Aikido.

Shimpan The referee.

Shizentai A natural stance that is relaxed yet alert, with one foot slightly ahead of the other.

Shugyo Means "to train intensely".

Soremade Used to signal the end of a round or fight.

Soto uke An outside block with the forearm moving from the middle of the body to the outside to deflect an attack.

Tanto A single-edged knife.

Tanto ippon One point for a knife strike.

Tanto randori A free fight between two competitors with one of them using a knife.

Tatami The Japanese name for a mat.

Teisoku The sole of the foot.

Tori A taker is the contestant who performs a technique on their partner. Taker is a literal translation of the Japanese word "Tori".

Tsuzukete Means "to continue".

Uke Means "to block", and refers to the recipient of the Tori's technique.

Waza Means "technique".

Waza ari A half-point.

Waza ari awazette ippon A second half-point that makes a full point.

Yame matti The signal given to competitors to stop.

Zanshin Posture indicating that a competitor is alert to their opponent's capabilities.

Tae Kwon Do

Tae kwon do originated in Korea. The term is made up of three parts, tae (the foot), kwon (the fist) and do (the way) – the way of foot and fist.

An marki Inner block. The action is taken from the little-finger side of the forearm and is used to smash an incoming technique to the side.

Annun sogi Straddle stance.

An palja sogi Ready stance.

Anuro marki Inward traveling block.

Apcha busigi Front snap kick.

Ap chagi Front kick. When putting this into action, the foot should have the instep fully extended with the toes pulled back. This improves the force of the impact when hitting the target.

Apchook The ball of the foot.

Ap koobi A lunge punch performed by stepping forward with your right foot and then pulling back your left fist while punching with your right. While doing this the palms should be twisted so that the right hand turns the palm down and the left palm faces up.

Ap sogi Short forward stance.

Arae Lower stomach and groin area.

Arae marki Lower block. This technique uses the forearm, which moves in a downward arc and enables the contender to knock the attacking front kick to the side to protect themselves.

Bakuro marki Outward traveling block.

Balbadak The inside edge of the foot.

Bal deung Instep.

Balkal The outside edge of the foot.

Bal twikumchi The heel of the foot.

Bam Joomeok One-knuckle punch.

Bandae dollyo chargi Reverse roundhouse kick. This maneuver uses the sole of the foot with the toes pointing to make contact with the opponent.

Bandal chargi Crescent kick performed using the big-toe side of the foot with the leg almost straight. The power comes from the hips.

Bandal son The reverse knife hand action is made by standing with the hips pointing away from the opponent with the right hand partly extended away from the body, palm up. The competitor then twists his hips and brings the right hand up to strike the opponent in the jaw.

Baro jireugi A reverse punch that is performed by using the opposite arm and leg together so that if the left leg is put forward first then the right hand is the first to move, and vice versa.

Batang son To use the base of the heel to hit an opponent's jaw.

Chagi A kick.

Cha jireugi A thrusting kick using the sole of the foot to push the opponent back. If applied to the chest area, the opposing player will find it a very difficult maneuver to block.

Charyot seogi Attention stance.

Chigi Striking technique.

Chireugi Thrusting technique.

Chojum To focus.

Chookyo marki Head block; using a rising and rotating forearm to deflect the opposing player's punch away from the head.

Choongdan Midsection of the body.

Daebee Position of the guarding hands.

Daeryon Sparring.

Decisions A contestant is deemed to have won by a knockout, a stoppage, a higher score, an opponent being withdrawn or disqualified or a referee's punitive declaration.

Deemyun chargi A flying kick.

Deung joomeuk The back fist used in a circular movement, with the forearm rotating strongly as it straightens out before snapping back.

Dobok The training tunic.

Dollyo chagi A roundhouse kick brings the bent knee in front of the body before kicking the leg into the side of the opponent's head.

Dora A turn.

Dwi chagi A back kick. Performed by turning the hips to the right while lifting the left foot to move diagonally and across, putting all the weight on to the left foot while looking over the right shoulder. The next stage is to kick back with the right foot and make impact.

Gam-jeom A penalty deduction worth one point.

Gup Coloured belt grades.

Hardan marki Lower block.

Hogoo Fighting armor.

Hyung Pattern.

Ilbo daeryon One-step sparring.

Jireugi Striking technique.

Jokdo Little-finger edge of the foot.

Junbi seogi Ready stance.

Kalyeo Means "break", and is used by the referee to keep an attacker from an opponent who has gone down.

Keuman The command to stop, used by the referee to stop each round.

Keysok The command to continue.

Kima seogi Straddle stance.

Knock down A contestant is deemed to be knocked down when any part of their body, apart from the soles of their feet, touches the ground or if the competitor is unable to continue.

Kyong-go A warning penalty. Two will lead to a one-point deduction.

Mit choomuk The hammer fist uses the little-finger edge of the rolled fist as a club. It is first brought up to the ear before striking and then released as the opposing arm is brought backward at the same time.

Momdollyo chagi Spinning back kick.

Momtong marki Midsection block.

Nopunde marki High block.

Olly o chigi Upward traveling elbow strike.

Palkoop chigi Elbow strike.

Parro Return to ready stance.

Permitted area The area on the opponent's body with that a contestant may come into contact when attacking; this comprises the trunk and the face.

Permitted techniques Include using the foot and the fist to deliver hits to the target area.

Pyonson keut The spear hand is performed the same as the knife strike, except that impact is made with the tips of the fingers.

Rounds Contests consist of three rounds of three minutes each, with a break of one minute between each.

Sambo daeryon Three step sparring.

Sandan marki An upward block.

Shijak Means "to start" or "to begin". Used by the referee to start a contest.

Sonnal marki The knife block action uses the edge of the hand to block any punches or strikes from the opposition.

Sudo Knife hand strike. A chopping action using the little-finger edge of the hand to strike the opponent's neck and throat area.

Valid point Scored when a competitor has used a valid movement to strike in the permitted area.

Weight categories There are eight categories altogether. These include fin, fly, bantam, feather, light, welter, middle and heavy.

WTF World Taekwondo Federation, based in Seoul, South Korea.

Yeop chagi Side kick. Performed by standing on one leg while raising the other knee until the heel is in line with the target. The next stage is to thrust the heel out in an upward straight line to hit the target.

Kendo

Kendo is one of the traditional Japanese martial arts and is centuries old. It is fought between two combatants who wear protective clothing and use bamboo swords to fight with.

. . . .

Aiuchi A mutual strike, when both competitors strike at the same time.

Area The fighting area consisting of a smooth, wooden floor and measuring 11yd x 11yd or 12yd by 12yd. The center is marked out by a cross or a circle.

Assistant judges There are two assistant judges positioned inside the area, with one placed forward and the other in the rear. Their job is to control the competitors' conduct, rule on valid techniques and to decide who is the winner.

Bokken A wooden sword that is used for practicing with, as it is less lethal than the shinai.

Budo Means "the martial way", and describes the practicing of martial arts to improve the character rather than for the battlefield.

Bujutsu Describes the fighting arts used by Japanese warriors.

Chief The presiding official who is responsible for the overall control and decisions of the match.

Chudan The middle part of the body.

Chudan no kamae The middle-level guard, that is a basic position.

Chui Means "warning", and is used during competitions.

Dachi Means "position", and describes the posture used during training.

Do The breastplate used to protect the torso. It also means the "way" or "path" in a philosophical context.

Dojo The name given to the "place of way" where the practice of kendo is performed.

Encho hajime A restart for extra time.

The first person to score in extra-time is deemed the winner.

Garami Means "entanglement".

Gedan barai The Japanese word for "downward parry". Describes a forearm deflection against attacks to the lower stomach and groin area.

Hachimaki The toweling headcloth worn by competitors under the men (mask) to keep the sweat out of their eyes.

Hajime Used by the chief judge to alert everyone at the beginning of the match.

Hakama The dividing skirts worn by competitors that reach down to the ankle.

Hansoku The Japanese word for "foul".

Hantei The Japanese word for "decision", that is made by a panel of judges during competition.

Hidari The Japanese word for "left".

Hikiwake Means that a draw has been judged.

Honbu Means "headquarters" – either a martial arts school, or a tradition's main base.

Iaido Means "the way of the sword".

Jikan The word for time, that is used to announce the clock having been stopped during a competition.

Jiu kumite Means "free sparring", used as a training system but with a measure of control.

Jodan Means "upward"; describes the shoulders, neck and head areas.

Jogai Out of bounds; describes stepping out of the competition area.

Kamae Means "stance", the various postures used by competitors.

KENDO: Contestants require protective clothing, including a mask, to take part in the ancient sport

Katsugi The shoulder position; when used, it makes for a shorter and faster movement.

Keikogi The Japanese name for "shirt", that is part of the dress worn when competing.

Kendoka Name given to the fighters.

Kiai The loud shout that the kendoka uses when making an attacking cut to signify his resolve to strike strongly.

Kihon The basics of martial arts practices.

Kiri A cutting action.

Kote Means "wrist"; describes the gauntlets, that are padded gloves worn to protect the competitors.

Line judge Positioned in one of the four corners outside the area.

Maai The distance between two opponents.

Meijin An expert who has taken his skills in martial arts to an art form.

Men The Japanese word for mask, that is a compulsory part of a kendoka's dress when taking part in the sport.

Motonoichi Means to return to your original position when in competition.

Nikomme A restart after one point has been scored.

Renshu To practice.

Shinai Made up of different sections of bamboo that are held together by leather and string. Either one or two shinai can be used by a competitor.

Shobu A restart after each contestant has scored a point.

Shobu ari The end of a match where a victory has occurred.

Tare An apron that is worn as part of the dress of a kendoka.

Tsuki A straight thrust that is used as an attacking measure.

Tsuzukete Term used by match officials to tell competitors to continue.

Yame Called out by the chief judge to end a match. Also means "interruption".

Zanshin An alert posture.

Fencing

Fencing is a traditional sport, based on ancient sword-fighting rituals, that has been likened to a game of chess with muscles. It involves two competitors who contest a bout using a foil, sabre or épée.

Absence of blade Fencers' weapons that are not in contact.

A droite Against the right.

Advancing When the front foot makes a small step forward and the rear foot immediately follows with an equally small or smaller step forward.

Advertissement Warning.

A gauche Against the left.

Aids Other three fingers used to control the sword.

A la coquille On guard.

Allez To fence.

Annule When a hit has been annulled.

Appel The slap of the ball of the front foot on to the floor, that normally occurs when lunging.

Après la parade After the parry has occurred.

Arrêtez To halt the action.

Attack The first extension of the arm that indicates the right of way.

Attaque To attack.

Au bras On the arm.

Au masque On the mask.

Balestra The action of making a short jump before making a lunge.

Barrage A fence-off between competitors who have tied in bout wins.

Beat A sharp hit on the opponent's blade that either deflects or creates a reaction.

Bell The name given to the guard on the foil and épée. See "Guard".

Bent-arm attack The arm is bent when attacking, that leaves the fencer open to counterattack.

Bind A way of removing an attacking blade by making a half circular movement with the tip of the sword when the blades are already in contact.

Bon Good, well done.

Bout A fight between two competing fencers. They normally last for five touches in six minutes.

Breaking ground A forward or backward movement.

Broken time A pause between two movements.

Cadence The rhythm of movement.

Ceding parry When the defensive fencer gives up their sword to the attacking fencer.

Change beat A beat that occurs after the change of engagement.

Change of line Either high to low or inside to outside, and vice versa.

Circular or counter parry Occurs when the tip of the weapon completes a full circular movement without moving forward toward the opponent. It is used as a defensive device to deflect or block.

Class The competitive categories that fencers are put into. The top 10 are always seeded.

Close quarters Being able to engage while still in a phrase.

Closing the line Describes the blocking of an opponent's attack.

Compound attack A method of attack that uses at least two movements that have followed a feint each time.

Compound riposte A riposte that is made up of at least one feint.

Contretemps French expression for countertime.

Coquille The name given to the bell-shaped guard of either the foil or épée.

Corps a corps Body contact such as a clinch that prevents further play.

Coule A straight thrust down an opponent's blade.

Counterattack The action of a defending fencer either stopping a hit directly or by striking back and continuing play.

Counter riposte An attacking motion made after a successful parry of the opposition.

Counter time When the attacking fencer lures the opposition into a counterattack and then carries on the offensive by either blocking or removing the counterattacking blade.

Coupe A maneuver that allows the fencer to cut over and lift the opposition's blade with the tip of their weapon to attack.

Coupe d'arrêt Stopping a thrust.

Coup double A double hit.

Covered The act of closing a line to an attacker.

Croise Using the forte to remove the opposition's blade at the foible and move it down by lowering the wrist and forearm.

Deceive To evade an action by an opponent. Used in attacking or counterattacking.

Dégagez The French term to disengage.

Dérobement Evading an attack on the blade of the defender.

Detachment parry A sharp parry that leaves the blade immediately after deflecting the movement.

Development Another name for the lunge maneuver.

Director The title given to the official who supervises the bout and awards hits. Also known as the president.

Direct thrust A simple, direct attack in the same line of engagement.

Disengage A movement of the blade that passes under the opposition's blade into a different line.

Double A compound attack that deceives a circular or counter parry.

Double touch When both fencers are hit at the same time.

En finale A parry that is played at the last minute.

Engagement When both blades are in contact.

Envelopment Using a circular movement to take the opponent's blade to the original line of engagement done on an opponent's straight arm.

Epée A weapon used to fence. Normally used by more advanced fencers. Weighs 1.7lb and measures 43in in length.

Extending The straightening of the fighting arm toward the target.

False attack Used to test the reaction of the opposition by making a false move.

Feint A deceiving movement that is seen as threatening. Can be made with the foot, the arm or the hand.

Fencing measure The practical distance between the opposing players so that, when making a lunge, they can hit each other.

Fencing time The time taken to make any action of the blade or body, or a mixture of both.

Finger play The deftness of the fingers when making blade movements.

Fleche A running attack that is taken from out of distance. This is a surprise attack.

Fleuret The French term for the foil.

Foible The weakest part of the blade.

Foil One of the weapons used to fence with. Weighs 1.1lb and measures 43in in length.

Forte Describes the strongest part of the blade that is used to parry with.

Froissement A strong attack that is made down the opponent's blade.

Gaining ground The advantage.

Gliding A moderate forward action that is in contact with the opponent's blade.

Ground judges Two judges used to determine hits. They are placed at either end of the court.

Guard The piece of metal on the weapon that protects the hand and can be used to deflect the opponent's blade.

Halte Another term for halt.

High lines The target area placed above the level of the guard. Usually from about the mid-chest upward.

Hit Occurs when the attacking action in a forward movement hits the opponent hard enough to draw blood. A hit can be deemed on or off target.

Indirect An attacking maneuver made by disengaging and moving to end up in the opposite line to the engagement.

In line Occurs when the arm holding the weapon is extended and is threatening the opponent.

In quatata Used by a defending fencer to dodge an attack by side-stepping out of the way of the blade.

Inside lines Placed either high or low on the sixte side.

Insufficient parry Failure to deflect the attacking blade.

Invitation When a fencer opens their line up to attack from their opponent.

Jury The officials who preside over a match.

La belle Describes the deciding touch or sudden death playoff between two fencers who are tied at the end of their bout.

Lateral parry A lateral movement of the arm to redirect the opponent's blade.

Liemente To bind.

Low invitation When a fencer stands with their arm hanging loose from the shoulder, and is therefore not in a position to defend an advancing attack.

Low line Marked from the lower ribs downward.

Lunge The most basic movement used to attack. The fencer takes a step forward with the weapon-wielding arm extended to carry the blade to target.

Mal pare An insufficient parry.

Mesure The French term for distance.

Novice Used to describe a fencer who has not been placed first, second or third in a tournament.

Octave A parry that deflects the opponent's blade to point past the lower back.

One-two A compound attack that is performed by disengaging twice and deceiving two parries.

On guard Used as an instruction by officials to warn the competitors to get ready. If used as an instruction by a teacher, then the students are expected to guard in some way. This position is a balanced one from that you either attack or defend.

Opposition Used to prevent an attack or riposte by holding an opponent's blade.

Outside lines The high and low target areas that are opposite to the arm holding the weapon.

Pare To parry.

Parry A defensive movement used to deflect an opponent's strike with their foible by using their forte.

Pas de touche Means that no touch has occurred.

Passa da sotto A counterattack that moves the body by lowering it under the oncoming blade.

Pas valable The French term for off-target.

Phrase The back and forward movement between the two opponents until somebody is hit.

Piste The French term for path, but meaning the fencing strip. It should be of a flat and even surface made of wood, linoleum, rubber, plastic and metallic mesh. It can either be indoors or outside.

Point in line The arm is extended with the point threatening the target.

Pool Occurs when a group of fencers is brought together to fence each other, with the winners going through to the next round.

Pressing Occurs when a fencer uses the blade to invite an attack by pushing it from one side to the other.

Prêt When the fencer is ready.

Prise de fer To take the blade.

Pronation A position for the sword hand with the knuckles pointing up.

Quarte Used to block the opponent's blade by hitting toward the inside high so that the blade points past the chest or stomach.

Quinte The fifth parry.

Recovering Moving back to guarding and inviting after lunging or extending.

Redoublement A renewal of attack while still on the lunge with at least one blade movement.

Remise Similar to redoublement in which there is a renewal of attack while still on the lunge by replacing the point, but there is no more action of the blade, body or a mixture of both.

Replacement Describes either digging in with the point when the initial attack was flat, or withdrawing the blade and jabbing when the initial attack went past the target.

Reprise An immediate renewal of attack after first returning to guard either forward or backward.

Riposte The attacking action that a fencer will use having successfully parried an attack.

Salle The French term for room or chamber where the fencers practice.

Secondary intentions The first attack would be false, making the opponent perform a parry-riposte, while the real attack would be a parry-riposte or time stroke against the opponent's riposte.

Seconde Used to beat back the opponent's blade by blocking it past the lower back.

Simple An action in one move or count. Refers to parries that are not counters or half-counters, and is also applied to attacks or ripostes.

Simple riposte A direct or indirect movement that only uses a riposte of one blade.

Simultaneous action When both fencers perform movements at the same time, normally when they are close together and are redoubling.

Sixte Aiming the blade to the high outside so as to block the opponent's weapon past the upper back.

Straight thrust A direct and aggressive attack.

Strip Playing area, that measures 2.2yd x 15.3yd.

Supination The hand position with the fingers pointing upwards.

Taking the blade When a fencer takes the blade on an extended arm.

Thrusting The act of extending the arm and threatening the opponent with the tip of the blade.

Touche Describes when a hit has been scored. To score a touche the point must touch the target, that is the trunk of the opponent.

Trompement The French term for deception, that is performed by the attacking fencer.

Uniform The color must be white or of a light color on the torso. A padded jacket must be worn for protection, and gloves are also allowed to be slightly padded. The mask should have a mesh covering and should fit correctly.

7 Target Sports

These are sports that involve a target but not a ball (see Chapter 3: Target Ball Games). Shooting and archery originated as forms of combat but live targets are no longer used in sporting events. Darts may be considered by some to be merely a pub game, but it is the same in principle as archery.

Guns and Ammunition

Air pistol Has a .177mm caliber. Is a compressed air or gas pistol that may only be loaded with one pellet at a time.

Air rifle A form of rifle that uses compressed air or carbon dioxide. Has a caliber of 4.5mm.

Automatic A mechanism that allows a gun to continuously load and fire itself.

Barrel A cylindrical tube placed inside the gun where the round sits.

Calibre The internal diameter of a gun. Also used to describe the diameter a bullet.

Cartridge The ammunition used. There are varying types of cartridge such as black powder, incendiary and tracer cartridges.

Dry firing The release of the cocked trigger mechanism of an unloaded firearm, or the release of the trigger mechanism of an air gun fitted with a device that allows the trigger to operate without releasing the propelling charge.

Free pistol Has a 5.6mm caliber and can only be loaded with one cartridge.

Hangfire Describes the unusually lengthy time between the firing-pin hitting a bullet's percussion cap and the propellant charge catching alight.

Receiver: The main body of a rifle. This is where the barrel is screwed or breached into.

Stock The part of a rifle where the woodwork is found.

Archery

Archery is a target sport consisting of three main types: field, target and crossbow. All of them use a bow and arrows, with the aim of scoring the most points by accurately shooting into the target.

Arrow Missile made of wood, metal or carbon fiber that is fired at the target. Usually weighs less than 1oz, while the length can vary. Consists of a head, nock, fletching and cresting.

Arrow rest The fitting above the arrow shelf. Made of either feather or plastic.

Arrow shelf Placed above the grip on a composite bow, it is marked out by a cutaway.

Back Describes the outer side of the bow.

Bare-bow Also known as instinctive shooting. Classed as shooting in that sighting devices are not allowed to be used.

Belly The term describing the inner side of the bow.

Boss The straw rope that is coiled and placed underneath the stretched and colored target face.

Bow Curved and stringed weapon, with the main body made of wood, metal, glass fiber or carbon fiber. The size and weight can vary.

Bowsight An instrument positioned above the arrow rest that aids the archer in aiming directly at the target. It is adjustable for sighting at any distance.

Brace Means to string the bow.

Bracer The arm guard worn by an archer. It is placed on the inside of the forearm to prevent the arm or clothing from deflecting the bow string.

Butts Describes the field in whch archery occurs or the bales against which the target face is placed in field archery.

Cast The ability of the bow to shoot an arrow quickly and cleanly. It also describes the distance over which it will shoot.

Clout shooting A type of archery in which the target is marked out by a cloth or flag.

Cock feather The feather that is set at right angles to the nock. It may be a different color from that of the other two feathers.

Composite bow A bow that is made up of different materials such as wood, fiberglass and plastic.

Compound bow A bow whose holding weight when at full draw is less than the peak weight with that the arrow is projected.

Cresting The band of color below the fletching on the arrow to aid identification.

Draw weight Describes the effort in pounds needed to draw an arrow to a specified amount. The bows are graded according to their draw weight.

End A specified number of arrows (the usual number being six) shot by archers before the score is taken and the arrows retrieved. A round is broken up into ends.

Face See "Target Face".

Fast A command used by officials to signal to the archers to stop. An abbreviated form of "stand fast".

Field face A paper target fixed to the butts in field archery rounds. The faces on the target are either pictures of animals, or circles with the scoring areas marked out on them. There are three scoring zones, worth three, four or five points.

FITA The Fédération Internationale de Tir à l'Arc, that is the world governing body of target archery.

Fletching The vanes around the nock end of the arrow to keep it on a straight and steady course. The vanes are evenly spaced and number three or four.

Flight archery Its object is to gain the greatest distance possible. There are three classes for this competition standard target bows, flight bows and a freestyle class.

Flight shooting Includes three classes target bows, freestyle and specially designed flight bows. The object of flight shooting is to see who can shoot their arrow the farthest.

Freestyle The most common style for target and field archery. Sighting devices are permitted.

GNAS The Grand National Archery Society, that ensures that the rules are adhered to during competition.

Gold The inner circle of the target, that is yellow in color. Called a spot.

Hanger An arrow that is shot inaccurately at the target and therefore hangs from the face. Shooting will stop until the arrow is removed.

IFAA The International Field Archery Association, that is the world governing body of field archery.

Kisser A mark on the bowstring that comes into contact with the archer's lips when the arrow is fully drawn. This assists the archer in knowing that his draw and alignment are correct.

Lady paramount The title given to the

ARCHERY: Arrows, usually made of carbon fiber, weigh under 1oz and are fired using a bow

female official who presents the prizes.

Let down Means to withdraw your arrow slowly from full draw position without releasing the arrow.

Limb The upper or lower part of the bow, that is thick enough to stop the bow, twisting as it is drawn.

Longbow A self-bow (see below) that is traditionally made of yew.

Loose Occurs when the arrow and the bowstring are released when fully drawn.

Nock Positioned at both ends of the bow and at the end of the arrow where the bowstring is inserted.

Nocking point The correct point on the bowstring where the arrow should be engaged.

Petticoat The part of the target face not covered by the colored scoring rings.

Pile The point of the arrow.

Pin hole The exact center of the target.

Popinjay shooting This version of the sport uses a mast that measures 30yd. Wooden birds are placed on the mast, the object being to displace them. They have different points values and are marked with colored birds to show this. The highest bird is the cock bird worth five points, the hen bird is worth three points with the chicks worth one point.

Quiver The container that keeps the arrows ready for use.

Release aid An instrument that allows the archer to release the bowstring from the fully drawn position without relaxing the fingers.

Riser Also called the handle. The middle part of the bow placed between the limbs.

Round The shooting of a specified number of arrows at specified distances.

Self-bow A bow produced from one piece of material.

Serving An extra piece of thread that is wound around the middle of the bowstring in order to stop it from fraying.

Shaft The body of the arrow between the pile and the nock. Also used to describe the entire arrow.

Sighters Six arrows that are shot at the beginning of a target archery round by each archer. They do not count as part of the round or score.

Spine Relates to the thickness of the arrow. It assesses the weight and flexibility of the arrow, that determines that bow to use.

Spot See "Gold".

Stabilizer Used to balance and stabilize the bow. The extra weights are attached to the bow.

String The cord that gives the bow its tension and is used to fire the arrow toward the target. It is usually made of gut or plastic.

Tab Made from leather, the tab is placed over the fingers on the drawstring hand to protect against the string and aid a smooth release when the arrow is fired.

Target face The canvas that is stretched over the boss. It is marked with five different-colored scoring rings, with the outside ring being painted white and worth one point and the next ring colored black and worth three points. The blue ring is inside of that and worth five points, while red is worth seven points and the center yellow or gold spot is worth a maximum nine points.

Tassel A cloth used to clean the arrows. Usually marked with club colors.

Vane The name given to the feather or thin piece of plastic used to make the fletching.

TARGET ARCHERY

Target archery includes both men and women competitors. They shoot a specified number of rounds. Each round is made up of a certain number of arrows that are shot from specified distances.

Director of shooting The official in charge of all aspects of the competition.

Distance Both men and women shoot from a range of distances. For men they are 98yd, 77yd, 55yd and 33yd. For women they are 77yd, 67yd, 55yd and 33yd.

Field Both men and women compete on the same field, but are separated by a clear lane that measures at least 10m. The field is divided into lanes with two or three targets in each lane.

FITA targets The target face is split into five colored circles with each divided again to make 10 scoring parts altogether. The first outer white part is worth one point, while the inner circle is worth 10 points.

Grand FITA The top 24 men and the top 24 women compete in this competition each year. They both shoot a match of 36 arrows. The rounds get smaller and smaller until there is a winner. They also take part in team competitions.

Long bows These are steadier in the hand and are the most popular type of bow used.

Position Each competitor takes their shots from an unsupported standing position, unless they are disabled.

Scorers Placed beside each target to ensure there is no cheating and that the rules are clearly followed.

Short bows Shoot a faster arrow, as they are less affected by the wind.

Target number Each competitor must wear a clearly marked target number on the back of their shirts.

FIELD ARCHERY

Field archery is divided into two types freestyle and bare-bow. The events are made up of two rounds the hunter's round and the field round.

Duration The hunter's round and the field round take place over two days.

Hunter's round Made up of two units that use 56 arrows each. The faces used are divided into an outer ring, an inner ring and a center spot. The outer ring is worth three points, the inner is worth four points and the spot is worth five points.

Instinctive Also known as bare-bow. This does not allow any artificial forms of aiming.

Range There are two courses, one for each round. Each course is made up of one or two units with 14 targets each.

Scoring The maximum score for a target is 20 points, the maximum score for a round being 560 points.

Targets There are four standard target faces that measure 2ft, 18in, 12in and 6in in diameter.

CROSSBOW ARCHERY

Crossbow archery is divided into two types the match, that is the traditional style; and field, that is the archery style. Match shooting takes place on a purpose-built range, whereas field shooting takes place outside.

MATCH CROSSBOW SHOOTING

Bolts Made from a rounded steel head that has a blunt cylindrical point. The end of the bolt is flightless.

Crossbow Made from composites of glass or carbon fiber for the bow and hardwood for the stocks. Competitors are not allowed to use magnifying lenses.

Match In the individual competitions, contestants can compete in either the 11yd or 33yd matches. In the 11yd, competitors have to shoot a prearranged number of shots within 100 minutes from an unsupported standing position. In the 33yd, competitors shoot in a standing position and a kneeling position with 90 minutes for each part.

Targets These are mechanized and return to the shooter after each shot. The target face is made of paper with an outer ring of black and an inner ring of white.

FIELD CROSSBOW SHOOTING

Bolts Must always be clearly identifiable and identical for the same set. They should all have three fletchings each.

Crossbow field captain The director of shooting, who ensures all the rules are adhered to.

Field crossbows Must be drawn by hand. The maximum weight must be 22lb with a bow tension of 95lb. The bow strings are not allowed to be made of metallic materials.

International rounds Consist of 30 shots from 71yd, 30 shots from 55yd and 30 shots from 38yd. The highest possible score is 900 points.

Targets Made from straw, foam or insulation board, they are placed on wooden stands and the target face is made of laminated paper. The scoring zones are divided into five colored areas: yellow, red, blue, black and white, with scores of 10 for the inner gold down to one for the outer white.

Darts

Contested between any number of players who throw darts at a circular target that is split into segments with different scoring values. There are a number of game variations.

25 ring The ring surrounding the central bull's-eye. It is normally colored green, and scores 25 points.

180 The maximum score that a player can get with three darts; this is achieved by gaining three triple-20 scores. The referee normally shouts this score loudly to emphasize the achievement.

Barrel The key component of a dart that a player holds on to before releasing it toward the dartboard. It is usually made of weighted metal, wood or plastic. It has a torpedo-like shape, that means it is thicker and heavier in the center.

Bull's-eye Otherwise known as bully. This is the only other score a player can finish on apart from a double. It scores 50 points and is the red circle directly in the center of the dartboard.

Cricket A darts game for two teams of equal numbers. The team that wins the toss elects to bat or bowl, and each player then throws one dart in turn and then alternates between the two teams. The team that is batting scores runs for every point they score over a certain number, and the bowling team takes a wicket every time they hit the inner 25 ring, and two wickets for hitting the bull. When five wickets have been taken the teams change roles and the side with the highest score wins the game.

Dartboard The board is made up of numbers ranging from 1 to 20, that are distributed around the board. The numbers are not marked in consecutive order and the divisions and sectors are marked by wires to make it clear in that

sector a dart has landed. The board is always hung so that the number 20 sector is vertically direct above the bull's-eye.

Darts Each player has three darts to throw at the dartboard with the aim of getting the highest score possible. The dart has four basic parts a flight, a shaft, a barrel and a point. A dart should be a maximum of 1.08oz in weight and 12in long.

Double The outer ring running round the dartboard. Each number will have a double mark that is separated by wire. A player will normally have to finish on a double when attempting to win a leg.

Double top The term given when a player has just 40 left to score and will attempt to get the dart in the double-20 slot.

Face of the board The front of the dartboard, that measures 8ft from the oche.

Flight The piece at the top of the dart, usually made of plastic. Most professional dart players will have a flight that has a colorful design and may even have their own name printed on it.

Football A darts game for two players in that each player throws three darts in turn. If a player throws the dart in the "inner bull" they gain control of the ball and can start scoring goals by throwing doubles. They continue to score until their opponent throws a dart into the "inner bull" and then picks up possession of the ball. The first player to score 10 goals wins the game.

Markers Two officials sit on either side

of the dartboard and mark down what each player has scored and then subtract it from the previous score on the scoreboard.

Oche The name given to the point from where the players throw their darts at the board. It is a piece of wood that is fastened to the floor to stop a player from moving over it. If they do step over this line, the referee will call a foul on them.

Referee Also known as the caller, this official calls out a player's score after he has thrown, and makes sure that the markers have recorded it correctly on the scoreboard. When a player is on an out shot, they will tell the player how many they need.

Round the clock A singles game of darts for any number of players. Each player throws three darts in one turn, and after hitting a starting double the aim is to throw a dart into each of the sectors of the board from 1 to 20 in order. The winner is the first player to finish.

Scoreboard Each side's score is recorded on a board after each player has taken their turn to throw three darts. The board is a black-painted or slate board. A marker will record the score in chalk.

Scoring A player's score automatically gets deducted from a starting score of 501. They can score points by throwing their darts toward a designated sector, and are awarded points for the sector number that the dart went into.

Shaft The section between the barrel and the flight, usually made of plastic or metal.

Starting score Most games at professional level start from 501, with the players' scores subtracted each time until one player reaches zero with a double or bull's-eye. Games can also start from 301.

Triple If a player manages to throw one of the darts into the inner treble ring, they can score three times the sector number. Most players will aim for triple 20, that is the highest score possible on the board.

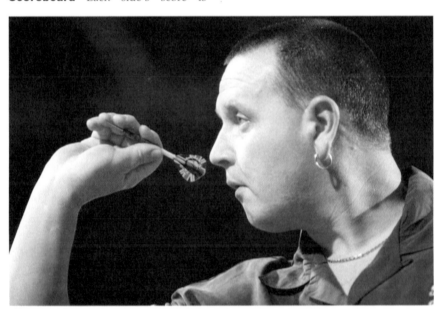

DARTS: The flighted arrows thrown at a dartboard are just 12in long, with a maximum weight of 1.8oz

Shooting

Shooting is a target sport that covers seven different types: rifle, clay, pigeon, skeet, down the line, free pistol and rapid fire shooting. They all use different weapons and ammunition.

··

RIFLE SHOOTING

The sport of rifle shooting is split into three sections air rifle, big-bore and small-bore. These sections depend on the type of rifle used. Additional subdivisions are centered on the type of shooting position used. The three different stances that can be used in rifle shooting are prone, kneeling and standing.

Action The mechanism that is fired on breech-loading and bolt-action rifles.

Aiming off When a competitor makes allowances for the effect of the wind on the bullet when taking aim.

Air rifle Type of rifle that uses compressed air or carbon dioxide. Has a diameter of 0.2in.

Back position A technique undertaken in British and Commonwealth match rifle shooting, performed by first lying on the back with the feet directed toward the target; one knee bent and the front end of the rifle resting on the knee and support head using either the nonfiring hand or a sling.

Backers These plain, white cards are located a certain distance behind each shooter's target and used to determine the origin of the shots, to detect when two shots are fired through the same hole, and to aid the shooter in identifying where his shots have landed.

Backsight A form of apparatus that consists of an eyepiece with a small circular hole for aiming. It is displayed behind the breech and can be moved vertically or horizontally.

Bedding Often referred to as stocking-up. This is an interior device that is used to curb barrel vibration.

Bull The center point of the target, worth the most points. On the UIT scale its value is 10 points and on British and Commonwealth targets it is five.

Canting Allowing the rifle to turn laterally when aiming, with the outcome that the sights are not perfectly vertical when the shot is fired.

Compensation The result of barrel vibration in an upright plane.

Concentric circles The target is divided into nine concentric circles, in that points from one to 10 can be scored, with the central circle scoring 10. If a shot were to hit the borderline separating two scoring zones, the higher value is taken.

Course of fire In a competition a shooter has a set number of shots he can fire, with a time limit in that to fire them. In competition, the course of fire is 40 shots in 90 minutes.

Drag Occurs after a bullet is fired when air turbulence slows it down.

Dummy frame Used for marking in British and Commonwealth full-bore shooting. Replaced by a frame with a colored panel after it is lowered following each shot.

English match A type of UIT competition for small-bore free rifle shooting from the prone stance at 55yd. The course of fire is 60 shots plus 10 or 15 "practise" shots in two hours.

Excess shots Should a competitor fire more than his allocated shots, he is deducted two points for each illegal shot. Should a competitor fire too many shots, he is penalized two points for every extra shot after the first two.

Foresight To help with the shooter's aim, this instrument is placed on the front of the barrel.

Free rifle A category of shooting under UIT rules for modified full-bore and small-bore rifles. The use of aperture sights and aids to holding are permitted. Telescopic and optical sights are prohibited.

Full-bore Rifles must have a maximum diameter of 0.3in. The course of fire for free rifles is 120 shots and an additional 30 sighters in 5 hours 15 minutes; for standard rifles it is 60 shots plus 18 sighters in 2 hours 30 minutes.

Handstop Metal piece attached to the underside of the front of the stock. The handstop supports the nonfiring hand. A handstop is permitted on target and free rifles, but prohibited on service and standard rifles.

Hangfire The unusually lengthy time between the firing pin hitting a bullet's percussion cap and the propellant charge catching alight.

Jump An upward or downward movement of the barrel that ensues from the recoil on firing a rifle.

Kneeling A shooting position in which the shooter can only touch the ground with three parts of his body the toe of the right foot, the right knee and the left foot. For left-handed shooters, the opposite applies.

Magpie Ring of white on a British National Rifle Association target with a scoring zone of three.

Match rifle Shooters can take part in British and Commonwealth competitions providing the rifle used measures a diameter of 0.3in. The shooting is usually from the back position over ranges exceeding 875yd. The course of fire ranges from 7, 10, 15 or 20 shots at 45 seconds per shot. Magnifying or telescopic sights are permitted.

NRA National Rifle Association.

NSRA National Small-bore Rifle Association, founded in 1901.

Prone A shooting position where the shooter lies down facing the target with the elbows supporting the upper part of the body. The arms from hand to elbow must be free of other objects and clear of the ground. Only the shooter's hands, a shoulder or armpit, or a sling can support the rifle.

Receiver The barrel is screwed or breached into the main body of the rifle.

Service rifle A class of shooting for 0.3in-caliber rifles without prohibited alteration or additions, in British and Commonwealth competitions. The blade of the foresight may be undercut, even though sights must be as issued. The course of fire and the range distances are the same as for target rifle. Only in the case of "deliberate shooting" can the use of slings be allowed. On all other occasions, slings and other artificial aids, are not permitted.

Shoulder-to-shoulder Position taken up by shooters at stations in a horizontal line.

Sighters In order to test the accuracy of the zeroing, practise shots, or sighters, are fired.

Sitting Technique frequently used by shooters whereby they sit on their buttocks. Support must not be given to the back when in this position.

Small-bore Shooters who compete with rifles with a maximum diameter of 0.2in. This type of shooting is most commonly practiced by women, and can be undertaken either indoors or outdoors over distances up to 197yd.

Sporting rifle An exercise in that the

rifle used most often is the small-bore. The object is to shoot at moving targets acting as wild game, usually from 50m.

Squadding Term used to describe the stations allotted and time of shooting to competing shooters.

Standard Applies to rifles, either full or small-bore, that comply with the UIT standard rifle stipulations. Allows rifles with aperture sights and bedding. But no holding aids are allowed, with the exception of a sling.

Standing Most commonly used shooting position on both feet with no artificial aids or support.

Station A shooter is allocated a section of a firing range to shoot from.

Stock Part of the rifle where the woodwork is found.

Target rifle A class of shooting for bolt-action 7.62mm or .303in-caliber rifle of customary design, in British and Commonwealth competitions. Slings and handstops are permitted, and backsights may be fitted for horizontal and vertical adjustment. Tubular foresights are added. Shooting consists of 7, 10 or 15 shots plus two sighters at 200–1,000 yards (183–914m), from the prone position.

Three-position Points gained from shooting at the prone, standing and kneeling positions in one competition are combined for a final score.

CLAY PIGEON SHOOTING

Clay pigeon shooting now includes 15 types of competition, all with different positions for the shooting stations and traps. In all types, competitors with shotguns aim at saucer-shaped clay targets freed from traps.

Olympic trench shooting

Ammunition The cartridge loaded must not exceed 2.7in in length and must have a maximum diameter of 0.1in. Black powder, incendiary and tracer cartridges are forbidden.

Birds The name for the clay targets. Shooting continues for a round of 25 birds per competitor.

Dead target Otherwise known as a hit. It is a target that has been properly thrown and shot at, and that has been broken or reduced to dust.

Finals Applies only in international events when the top eight points scorers in the preliminary competition compete in a 10-shot series .

Firing order A ballot decides in which order the squad shoots.

Lost target When the referee judges that the target has not broken in the air.

Misfires When a gun or ammunition fails. A referee can allow up to three repeats of the target as long as it was not the shooter that caused the failure.

No bird Term used to describe a miscalculation in a target's timing. If a shooter has not already fired at the target, a new target is allowed.

Penalties A competitor can be warned, lose a number of targets or even be disqualified if they are judged to be guilty of misconduct.

Referee Official who decides on hits, misses and repeat targets. Referees reserve the right to intervene during the shooting, in the event of poor weather or to mend traps. Competitors must ask permission to change a faulty gun. A referee can decide whether another target is pemitted if the shooter is disturbed or if another competitor has shot at the same target.

Selector system This device enables the path of a station's next target to remain unknown to the shooter; it also randomizes the trap from that the next target is to be released.

Shooting range There are 15 traps and five shooting stations. The traps are divided into five groups, with three facing each section.

Targets These have a height of 1.0-1.1in and weigh 3.5-3.9oz. The target must be in a clearly visible color and must remain identical throughout.

Ties In the case of a tie, additional 25-bird rounds are used to settle the match.

Trap Three traps are grouped together and are designed to fire in different directions to test the reactions of the competitors.

World championships Teams are made up of four shooters from each country. Individual events consist of 200 targets. The first 150 of these determine the best national team.

Weapon 12-bore or smaller shotguns are allowed, as are automatic models.

Skeet Shooting

Ammunition The cartridge must not exceed 2.8in in length. The shot, made of lead or lead alloy, must be spherical and have a maximum diameter of 0.08in. The maximum load of shot is 1oz. The use of black powder, tracer or incendiary cartridges is forbidden.

Cartridges These must be of normal loading. No internal changes are permitted that give special dispersion. Cartridges must be fired only while the target is within shooting bounds. Only one cartridge can be fired at any time.

Doubles targets Even if these appear immediately on the call or three seconds after, targets must always appear at the same time.

Guns Guns that throw broader patterns than trench shooting are used.

High house One of two traphouses. The high house is located on the left of the shooting stations. The target appears at 3.3yd.

Low house This traphouse is situated on the right of the shooting stations. The target emerges at 3.3yd.

Misfires In the event of misfires, only two repeats are permitted in any round.

No bird Allowed for doubles targets only if simultaneously: both barrels fire; the first target was struck; the same shot breaks both targets, although this is allowed only on three occasions; and if the shooter unintentionally hits the second having aimed for the first.

Ready position International rules state the gun must be held in this position on each call until targets appear.

Shooting The squads of six fire in turn from each station. Shooters receive different calls on both singles and doubles from stations 1, 2, 3, 5, 6 and 7. On separate calls, at stations 4 and 8, shooters receive a single target from the high house and likewise from the low house. Each stage comprises 25 targets.

Shooting range There are two traphouses within the eight shooting stations, of which there is the high house and the low house.

Targets Targets must travel between 71yd and 76yd in still air through a central area.

Timer mechanism Following the shooter's call, this device releases the target within a period of 0–3 seconds.

Trap Launches targets at different angles across the shooting area.

Down-the-Line Shooting

Double-rise shooting When two targets are thrown simultaneously.

Innings A competitor's series of shots.

Kill Otherwise known as a hit. Kills are marked on the target that the shot strikes. A first-shot kill gains three points, second-shot earns two points.

No bird Term used to declare that two extra targets are allowed if only one target is thrown or if a target breaks when thrown.

Officials In down-the-line shooting, there is a referee who makes all final decisions, a puller, a scorer and a trapper. There is no jury.

Pull Signal given by the shooter to indicate that he is ready and the targets can be released.

Shooting range There are five stations, each 36in square, all using a single variable-direction trap.

Single-rise shooting One target is thrown with the trap set for it to fall into a defined area. Three points are awarded for a first-shot kill and two points for a second-shot kill.

Trap This apparatus delivers targets at random angles, although within certain defined limits.

FREE PISTOL SHOOTING

In this form of shooting, competitors are permitted 60 shots from a distance of 55yd using hand held pistols. These 60 shots must be fired within the allotted two and a half hours.

Ammunition Bullets made of lead or other soft material and measuring 0.2in in diameter are permitted in free pistol shooting.

Chief range officer The official who can authorize extra time for shots should any competitor have them.

Distance The range at which competitors shoot is 55yd.

Duration of event Competition lasts for two and a half hours, with the event split into two sections (each part lasting one hour, 15 minutes); 30 competition shots must be used.

Miss Term used to describe shots that are fired before the start of shooting time, or after the end, and shots that are not fired at all.

Preparation time Minimum period of 10 minutes in which the competitor may practice. In this time they are allocated firing points and are permitted to undertake dry firing. No shots may be fired during this period.

Rimfire firearm Type of weapon that can only be used if it has been officially approved. It must measure 2.2in (0.22in caliber). Support must not be given to the arm, therefore the grip of the pistol must not be extended. Only one cartridge may be loaded if the pistol is to be used in an event.

Rings The inner ring measures 2in in diameter, while the diameter of each of the other rings is 2in wider than the one inside it. This results in the diameter of the outside ring being 20in.

Scoring zones The scoring ring values are numbered from 1 to 9.

Shooting position The shooter must stand within the firing point free of any support. Only one hand can hold and fire the pistol at the target. No visible items, such as bracelets or wristwatches, may be worn on the hand or arm that is in control of the firearm.

Sighting shots Practice shots fired to test the zeroing on a pistol.

Ten-point zone This zone is not marked with a number and is the highest possible score that can be attained from one shot.

RAPID FIRE PISTOL SHOOTING

Often referred to as silhouette shooting, competitors fire 60 shots at five targets from 27yd. The targets turn simultaneously from a side-on to a face-on position. The target remains exposed for a few seconds, giving the shooter the opportunity to fire.

Ammunition Bullets must be made of lead or a similar soft and even substance.

Butt This component of a pistol must not be lengthened under any circumstances. This would create extra support for the shooter and give an unfair advantage.

Central line of barrel This section of a pistol must, in the orthodox firing stance, pass above the upper part of the hand.

Course of fire The duration of each course in a competition is two series each of eight seconds, two series each of six seconds and two series each of four seconds. There are 60 shots split into two courses of 30.

Demarcation line The line that separates two scoring zones. If a shot strikes the demarcation line, the higher value is recorded.

Distance The line of targets is placed 27yd from the firing line. The targets are parallel with the firing line and comprise revolving silhouettes.

Finals The winner is determined following a final 10-shot series. This applies only in international events and sees the top eight shooters attempting to add to their preliminary score. The shooter with the most points overall wins the competition.

Firearm Only 5.6mm (0.22in caliber) weapons may be used in this form of shooting.

Groups of five Term used to describe the way in which shooters fire at their targets. Competitors fire in this way at various targets that rotate simultaneously.

Height of the barrel This section of the barrel must not exceed 1.6in. This figure includes all of its accessories.

Misfire Occurs if a shot does not leave the weapon. The shooter must then lay his weapon on the table and it is decided whether the failure was caused by a misfire or malfunction. The competitor may be allowed to fire another series of five shots. But even if this series is less than the original series of shots, it is still counted.

Referee Official who decides upon the cause of any misfires. Should it be decided that the failure was not the cause of a misfire or malfunction, then shots fired in that interrupted series are quashed.

Scoring It is possible to score between one and 10 points, with each silhouette separated into 10 sections. The shooter with the highest points total wins the competition.

Shooting position Absolutely no support is allowed in this event and the weapon must be held in one hand, allowing the wrist to operate freely. Until the target faces the shooter, the gun must be pointed downwards at an angle of 45 degrees. The shooter may raise the pistol when the target begins to face. Leather bracelets and any other types of protection are prohibited around the wrist area.

Sighting shots Competitors may fire five practice shots before each course of fire, one at each silhouette.

Targets These come into sight and disappear simultaneously, and are placed 30in apart in groups of five. Shooters have a specified time of 8, 6 or 4 seconds in that to fire at the target. The targets appear at a top speed of 0.4 seconds (0.2 seconds in the Olympics and world championships) and through an angle of 90 degrees. The white edge surrounding each black target has a width of approximately 0.04in. The entire target is split into 10 separate scoring zones.

Ten-point zone The center of this area is always between 32in and 63in above the level of the platform. Competitors invariably aim for this as it is the area from that the most points can be achieved.

Weight The pistol must not exceed 2.8lb in weight, inclusive of all its accessories.

8 Motor Sports

As well as recognized motor sports like Formula One, rallying and motorcycling events, this section also covers powerboat racing and aerobatics (flying). The latter two could have been included under Water Sports or Activity & Adventure Sports, but have more in common with other motorized forms of racing.

Engines and Technology

A-Frame Describes a chassis component that looks like the letter A in shape. Is also known as a wishbone.

Aerofoils Are downthrust aids which are fitted to single-seater racing cars in order to provide negative lift when at high speeds. They are placed on either side of the car and at the back.

Anti-roll bar Is a torsion bar which is mounted transversely from either the front or back axles to the suspension links on the wheels. The purpose of this is to regulate the amount of body roll when cornering.

Carburetar Has the function of converting liquid petrol into a vapor and then to mix it with air to form the very rapid burning charge needed by the engine. The chemically correct composition of the mixture is 15 parts of air to one petrol by mass.

Chassis The frame or skeleton of a car. Its function is to act as a mounting for all the other units and assemblies. The shape will normally be determined by the type of suspension system used.

Engine The function of the engine is to convert the heat energy, contained in the petrol into mechanical energy in the form of turning power to propel the vehicle.

Fuel injection Means of actively pumping fuel into the cylinder at a much faster rate which enables the car to go that little bit faster.

Slicks The name given to the thick treadless tyres used in racing. They have a high level of traction.

Spoiler Another name for an aerofoil.

Suspension system Used to help reduce the amount of shock and vibration transmitted from the road wheels to the chassis and body.

Thermo-probe Used to check the temperature of the tyres.

Tune Means to make sure the engine is at its best to perform with the maximum power and efficiency.

Formula One

Formula One racing has the highest international profile of all motor sports. Drivers race single-seat cars around a track for a set period. The winner is the first to complete two hours or 200 miles of a race, whichever is the shorter.

Aquaplaning Occurs in wet conditions when a layer of water builds up between the tire tread and the track surface, resulting in the tires losing grip and the car going out of control.

Armco The steel crash barriers used on the racetrack.

Backmarker A driver at the back of the field.

Black flag Marked with a number. Signals that the driver with that number must stop at the pit immediately.

Blower Slang term for supercharger.

Blow-up Slang term for a catastrophic engine failure – usually accompanied by clouds of smoke.

Blue flag Indicates to a driver that there is another car close behind; when the flag is being waved, it indicates to the driver that another car is trying to pass him.

BRDC British Racing Drivers' Club, based at Silverstone racing circuit.

Checkered flag Used to signal that the race has ended.

Chicane A safety feature built into a circuit usually consisting of two consecutive sharp bends in opposite directions to slow cars down when approaching a difficult section of the track.

Cockpit The area of the car where the driver sits.

Constructors' Championship This competition is for the whole team rather than one driver.

CSI The Commission Sportive Internationale is a subcommittee of the FIA, which is responsible for the rules of motor racing and draws up the various classes of racing at international level.

Drift Using the throttle to control a four-wheel slide through a corner.

Elapsed time The time taken between two points on the track. Also known as the ET.

FIA The Fédération Internationale de L'Automobile, which is the governing body of world motor-sport racing.

Flat spot Describes the shape of the tire when it has burned away due to a locked tire when braking.

Formula racing Describes single-seater races that conform to FIA-approved specifications on engine capacity, the number of cylinders, the minimum weight without ballasts and other essential requirements.

Full throttle To drive as fast as possible.

Graded drivers The list of drivers drawn up by the FIA on the results of the Formula One World Championship events. This is a select list, and winners from the past five years of this competition are automatically included.

Grand Prix The name given to the Formula One race in each country.

Gravel trap Placed at the corners of the track. Used to slow down a car that has spun out of control.

Green flag Signals that the circuit is now clear of an earlier obstruction.

Grid The area where cars are set into a grid formation in order to start the race.

Hairpin The name given to a sharp corner on the track.

Handling Driving method used when taking a corner.

Jump start Occurs when a driver over-anticipates the change of the starting lights to green and gains an advantage. He incurs a time penalty.

Lap The distance traveled when driving around the circuit once.

Line The path taken by a car through a corner.

Nosecone Attached to the wing and placed at the front of the car. Aids with aerodynamics of the car.

Oversteer When the back of the car has less grip than the front and tries to swing around ahead of the front.

Parc ferme Area of the pit lane where all cars are kept after a race has finished so that they can be checked.

Pit board Used during a race to inform a driver of his position in the race and how many laps he has to go.

Pit-lane speeding Is illegal and all racetracks have speed limits that must be adhered to. For example, the speed limit in Monaco is 44mph.

Pits The area beside the main racetrack where cars can be refueled or worked on while the race continues.

Podium A three-tiered platform where the top three finishers celebrate their performances after the race.

Points The first six cars at the end of the race are awarded points in the order 10–6–4–3–2–1.

Pole position The front place in the starting grid. Awarded to the driver with the best lap time during practice.

Qualifying Timed sessions on the two days preceding the race in that drivers determine their position on the starting grid according to lap times.

Red flag Signals to the drivers that they must all stop racing immediately.

Safety car Used to get the driver or drivers away from the scene of an accident or to move any cars that have stopped on the track.

Silverstone Famous venue where the British Grand Prix is currently held.

Slicks The name given to the thick treadless tires that were once a feature of F1 racing but are not currently used.

Slipstream When a car is closely following another car and is dragged along because of reduced wind resistance caused by the path through the air of the car in front.

Spin To lose control of the car and go into a rotational movement.

Starting flag The national flag of the country that is hosting the race.

Telemetry Device linked between the car and the pit lane. Records speeds, braking speeds and G-forces.

Thermo-probe Used to check the temperature of the tires.

Tire wall A wall of tires, that have been binded together, designed to absorb the impact of cars that hit it after spinning off the track.

Understeer Technical term that describes when a car's front tires do not turn into a corner as well as the rear.

Undertray The bottom back part of the car around that it is built.

Underweight Describes a car that does not meet the minimum weight of the race. Results in disqualification.

Warm-up lap Each car must perform a slow drive around the track just before the race begins.

Wets Deeply grooved tires used for races in the rain.

White flag Signals to the drivers that there is a service car on the track.

World Championship The driver with the most points after the 16 races of the season is World Champion.

Yellow and red striped flag When held still, indicates that there is oil on the track; when waved, indicates that there is oil in the immediate area.

Yellow flag When held still, indicates that there is danger ahead and drivers must not overtake; when waved, drivers must be prepared to stop.

IndyCars

IndyCar racing is the highest level and most popular form of racing in the United States. Cars are similar to those used in Formula One, but the tracks are usually oval-shaped and banked rather than the large flat courses used in Formula One.

Armco Metal barrier that lines most racetracks and is designed to absorb the impact when cars spin off the track.

Backmarker A slower driver at the rear of the field.

Banking The term describing a corner of an oval that is raised on the outside to ensure a large curve. This helps the cars corner faster.

Caution period The period in a race that is run under yellow safety flags. Cars must slow down behind the pace car and not pass.

Checkered flag A flag with alternating black and white squares that signifies the end of the race and is waved first at the winner.

Chicane A track feature consisting of two or more sharp corners close together (and often narrower than the main track).

Dirty air A slang term describing the turbulence which drivers experience when they are following another car, but are not directly in its slipstream.

Downforce Describes the amount of grip a car generates through aerodynamic devices such as wings and ground effect.

Flying lap A lap in that a driver has put in maximum effort and was at the absolute limits.

Ground effect Design feature that channels air under the car and out of a tunnel at the back in order to suck it down on the ground for extra grip.

Hairpin Corner that is very tight and usually doubles back on itself.

Hansford device A small device fit-ted to the rear wing designed to slow the cars down on super speedways.

Flat spot A flat area on a tire that has been caused by a tire skidding after locking up under braking.

Fuel IndyCars use methanol fuel. This is not as combustible as normal fuel, but it does burn with an invisible flame.

Gentlemen, start your engines Phrase used by a celebrity to signify the beginning of the build-up of a race.

High A term to describe a car's position on an oval relative to the banking, either high up or low down.

Indianapolis 500 The most prestigious IndyCar race of the season, traditionally held at the Indianapolis Motor Speedway on Memorial Day weekend.

Kitty litter A slang term for the gravel traps, that are filled with small stones designed to slow cars down quickly.

Lap One complete circuit of a track. A race is made up of a specific number of laps, with the driver who completes the distance quickest being the winner.

Lapping When a driver passes a slower car that is a whole lap behind.

Lean mixture A technical term to describe a setting that makes the engine more economical on fuel. However, this also makes the engine less powerful.

Lockup Describes when a tire stops turning under braking and locks up, thereby skidding.

Low A term to describe a position on an oval relative to the banking, either high up or low down.

Marbles A slang term for the little balls of

rubber that form off the racing line during the race. A car loses grip if it runs over them, as if it were running over marbles.

Outbrake Describes when one driver passes a rival by braking later going into a corner.

Oval A circular track used almost exclusively in the United States. They are high-speed and feature all left-hand or all right-hand bends.

Oversteer When the back of the car has less grip than the front and tries to swing around ahead of the front.

Pace car A road car, usually modified, used during caution periods to keep the cars running at a safe pace.

Pits Area of the track where the cars are worked on and where the team's mechanics are based during the race.

Pit crew The mechanics and engineers who work on the cars and refuel them during a race.

Podium A three-tiered platform where the top three finishers celebrate their performances after the race.

Pole position The leading grid position on the track, claimed by the driver who has set the fastest qualifying time.

Qualifying A session, usually lasting one hour, in that drivers attempt to set the fastest time.

Qualifying tire Super-soft tire that provides maximum grip for a one-off qualifying lap, but that wears out very quickly.

Racing line The quickest route through a corner, that is usually the smoothest and shallowest angle.

Road course Describes the more traditional purpose-built race tracks, like Laguna Seca.

Rolling start The start in an IndyCar race in that the event is begun with the cars already traveling at high speed but in formation.

Roval An oval on which drivers have to brake and change down through the gears. It is a mixture of a road course and an oval, hence "roval".

Set-up Describes the way that the car is built, for example, the suspension and downforce. The technical settings on the car that the driver has chosen in order to try to make the car go faster.

Slicks Tires that feature no grooves to ensure that there is maximum contact with the track, thereby ensuring more grip than grooved tires. They are useless when it's wet.

Slipstream The area of clean air behind a car that is generated by the wings and ground effect. This can be used to advantage by pursuing cars.

Stagger When a tire on one side of the car is bigger than the tire on the other, thereby inducing a permanent turn. This is used exclusively on ovals.

Sticky rubber A compound of tire that is particularly soft so that it grips on to the track. It is less durable than harder rubber.

Straightaway A long straight stretch of track.

Street course Describes a racetrack that has been built on normal roads, such as Long Beach in California.

Super speedway An ultra high-speed oval with very shallow bends where cars can often reach 220mph.

Tire barrier A barrier made up of old tires, to absorb the impact of a crash.

Understeer When a car's front tires do not turn into a corner as well as the rear tires.

Wall A generic term describing the concrete wall that lines the tracks, especially ovals.

Wets A more traditional tire featuring specially cut grooves to channel water away from the treads.

Wings The front and rear airfoils of the cars that are shaped like upside-down airplane wings to generate downforce instead of lift, thus helping the car stick to the track.

Karting

Karts are mini racing cars raced around one of three types of track: permanent, temporary or "round the houses". Competitors are put into one of four classes: cadets, juniors, Class One and Class Four.

Black and white warning board
Flashes a competitor's number to indicate that they will be flagged down if they commit another offense.

Black flag with white number
Indicates to the driver whose number is shown that he must report to the clerk of the course.

Blow-up An engine failure.

Blue flag If held in a stationary position, this indicates that a competitor is following close behind; if the flag is being waved, it indicates that another car is trying to pass.

Brakes Foot-operated, they are either drum or disc. Four-wheel brakes are compulsory for gearbox karts.

Checkered flag Signals the end of a race.

Chicane A feature built into the track with the intention of slowing down the cars before coming to a difficult section of the track. An example is an S-bend.

Classes There are four classes in total cadets, who must be aged between 8 and 12; juniors, who must be aged between 12 and 16, and whose karts must have engines of 100cc and no gearbox; Class One, that is in two sections – the 100 national and the 100 international with no gearbox; Class Four, that is in three sections – the 210 villiers, the 250 international and the 125 international with a manual gearbox.

Closed events Only members of the organizing club are allowed to enter the events.

CSI The Commission Sportive Internationale. This is a subcommittee of the FIA, that controls the rules of motor racing and draws up the various classes at international level.

Dress All karters must wear a crash helmet with a visor or goggles, with a heavy-duty PVC or leather suit and gloves for protection.

Drift A controlled four-wheel slide through a corner, that is performed by using the throttle to balance the effects of the slide.

Drive method All karts must be chain-driven.

Elapsed time The time taken between two points on the track. Also referred to as the ET.

Engine Must be homologated. All engines must have suppressors.

Exhaust systems These must comply with official regulations. Silencers are compulsory.

Farming The slang term for unintentionally leaving the track while racing. Also known as "going to the country".

FIA The Fédération Internationale de L'Automobile, the governing body of world motor sport since 1947.

FTD The fastest time of the day. Also called the best time of the day.

Full throttle The slang term for driving as fast as possible.

Green flag Signals that it is safe to proceed, following removal of a previously notified hazard.

Grid The area of the track where the karts line up in grid position according to their lap times in practice. The karts are staggered so that none is directly behind the one in front.

Handicaps Based on an allowance of time or distance, that is decided by either an assessment of the organizers or a previous timed race.

Homologation When the CSI approves karts as conforming to their requirements for each group.

Lap The distance of one trip round the track.

NAC The National Automobile Club is the governing body of karting and is affiliated with the Federation Internationale de L'Automobile, that is the world governing body of motor sports.

National events May only be entered by competitors who hold a current international kart licence.

National flag A race with a rolling start begins when the flag is raised, while the standing-start race begins when the flag is lowered.

Number plates There are two forms, round and rectangular. The round ones should only be placed on the front and the rear of the kart, while the rectangular ones can be placed on the front, back or sides.

Oversteer When the back of the car has less grip than the front and tries to swing around ahead of the front. If the driver does not take quick corrective action by applying opposite steering lock and/or taking his foot off the throttle, a spin will result.

Permanent A track where the shape can be determined at any time and all protective barriers are in permanent position.

Red flag Signals for all karts to stop immediately.

Restricted events Confined to the club that is organizing and 12 invited clubs.

Rolling start For non-gearbox karts.

The karts move around the course until the signal to start is given.

Round the houses Tracks that use public roads.

Scrutineering All vehicles must be made available to the organizers in order for them to be inspected.

Standing start For karts with a gearbox.

Temporary Any type of track that doesn't use public roads.

Throttle Operated by the foot.

Tires Are pneumatic and measure between 9 and 17in in diameter.

Track There are three types of track,

DRESS: Karters wear a helmet, gloves and leather; all are compulsory for safety reasons

and all must be approved by the NAC.

Understeer When the front of the car has less grip than the rear and tries to plow straight ahead, even when steering lock is applied.

Washout When the driver loses control of the front of the car.

Weight Each karting class has a minimum weight that combines both kart and driver.

White flag Indicates that a service car is on the track.

Yellow flag with red stripes If held still, it signals there is oil on the road; if waved, it signals that oil on the road is imminent.

NASCAR

NASCAR is the National Association for Stock Car Auto Racing which controls the sport in the United States. Stock car racing is performed on an oval track. High speeds and crashes are common. Although the cars look similar to those available to the public, they are in fact highly modified and streamlined for the sport.

Backmarker A slower driver at the rear of the field.

Barge The process of driving another competitor off the track while racing – whether deliberately or accidentally.

Bogged down Making a poor getaway at the start of a race.

Brake balance A device inside the cockpit enabling the driver to adjust how much braking force is applied to the front and rear wheels under braking.

Checkered flag A black and white checkered flag that signifies the end of the race; it is waved first at the winner.

Cockpit The part of the car designed to accommodate the driver.

Curbs A small raised area near the side of the track, usually on the entry and exit of corners, that marks the edge of the track.

Dirty air A slang term describing the turbulence that drivers experience when they are following another car but not in their slipstream.

Double header Two back-to-back races on one day.

Downforce Describes the amount of grip a car generates through aerodynamic devices such as the front splitter and rear spoiler.

Feature race The longer of two touring-car races, that also features a compulsory pit-stop at around the halfway stage.

Flat spot A flat area on a tire that has been caused by a tire skidding after locking up.

Flying lap Describes a lap in which a driver has put in maximum effort and was at the absolute limits.

Gravel trap A gravel area next to the track designed to stop cars that have spun off the track.

Grid The area where the cars line up, usually in two columns, for the start of the race. The fastest qualifier starts at the front, with the slowest at the back.

Handling How a car feels during a lap in terms of grip and cornering ability.

Kitty litter A slang term for the gravel traps, that are filled with small stones to slow cars if they spin off the track.

Lap One complete circuit of a track. A race is made up of a specific number of laps.

Lockup When a tire stops turning under braking and locks up, thereby skidding.

Marbles A slang term for the little balls of rubber that form near the racing line during the race. A car loses grip if it runs over them, and it becomes like driving on marbles.

Outbrake When one driver passes another by braking later going into a corner.

Oversteer When the back of the car has less grip than the front and tries to swing around ahead of the front. If the driver does not take quick corrective action by applying opposite steering lock and/or taking his foot off the throttle, a spin will result.

Pits The area of the track where the

cars are worked on and where the team's mechanics are based.

Podium A three-tiered platform where the top three finishers celebrate their performances after the race. The winner is placed centrally and higher than the second- and third-place drivers.

Pole position The leading grid position on the track that is claimed by the driver who has set the fastest qualifying time.

Privateer A competitor who pays for his own racing team, usually without backing or funding from a major car manufacturer.

Qualifying A session, usually of one hour's duration, where drivers attempt to set the fastest time. The quickest drivers start from the front of the grid.

Racing line The quickest route through a corner, usually the smoothest and shallowest angle.

Ride height A measurement of the height between the floor and the bottom of the car. Every competitor's car must conform to this, and they will face exclusion if it does not.

Rumble strip A strip of concrete added to the end of curbs that is designed to vibrate any wheel (and in doing so make a noise) that runs over them. This warns drivers they are near the edge of the track.

Safety car A road car (usually modified) used during caution periods to keep the cars running at a safe pace.

Safety car period Describes the period in a race that is run under yellow safety flags. Cars must slow down behind the pace car and not pass.

Skid When a car's wheel locks up and slides on the track.

Slick A tire with no grooves. This ensures that there is maximum contact with the track, thereby ensuring more grip than grooved tires. It is useless in wet conditions.

Slipstream The area of clean air behind a car that is generated by the rear spoiler. Pursuing drivers can use it to get a "draft" (a tow).

Split A term describing a section of the track where lap times are taken so that comparisons can be made between drivers.

Splitter An aerodynamic device fitted to the front of the car that generates downforce and therefore grip.

Spoiler An inverted airfoil-shaped device fitted to the rear of the car that generates downforce and therefore grip.

Sprint race The term for the shorter event in a touring car race, that usually sees drivers sprinting to the finish with no pit stops.

Sticky rubber A compound of tire that is particularly soft so that it grips on to the track.

Swapping paint A slang term for two cars bumping into each other while jockeying for position.

Tap Describes the process of lightly hitting a rival's car with the front of yours. Cars can be tapped into spins.

Tin-top A slang term for race cars that feature a roof and doors, as opposed to single-seater cars like those seen in Formula One.

Tire wall A wall of tires bound together, designed to absorb the impact of any cars that spin off the track.

Traffic Describes a situation when a competitor is being held up by back-markers and finds it difficult to pass.

Touring car A modified race version of a normal mass produced road car.

Understeer When the front of the car has less grip than the rear and tries to plow straight on, however much steering lock is applied.

Wets More traditional tires featuring specially cut grooves to channel water in the event of a wet track.

Works team A team funded and backed by an official car manufacturer.

Drag Racing

Drag racing is carried out on a straight track called a strip. Each race has two competitors and they can reach speeds of over 200mph. There are different classes of cars (dragsters). This is one of the most spectacular motor sports.

Airfoil A downthrust aid fitted to give negative lift when driving at high speeds. An airfoil is positioned on each side of the car at the front end and up high at the rear of the car.

Antiroll bar A torsion bar mounted transversely from either the front or rear axles to the suspension links on the wheels. This aids the driver by regulating the amount of body roll when cornering.

A/S Denotes a class-A car in the stock category.

A/SA Denotes a class-A car with automatic transmission.

Blower The slang term for a supercharger.

Blow-up Slang term for engine failure.

Capacity The measurement in either cubic centimetres (cc) or inches (cu.in.) of the cylinders through which the pistons move.

Christmas tree The name given to the lighting system used to start the race. It has five yellow lights that flash at half-second intervals, leading to a green sixth light that will signal the start of the race. There is a red seventh light, that will come on if a car advances too early. If this happens, the driver is automatically disqualified from the race.

Classes These are decided by the vehicles' mode of construction – such as whether they are modified production models or specially designed, what state of tune their engines are in and the kind of fuel they use.

CSI The Commission Sportive Inter-

nationale, a subcommittee of the FIA.

Dragster A hot-rod racer.

Dress Drivers must wear fireproof clothing, a face mask, protective gloves and a crash helmet.

Elapsed time Also known as ET. The time taken between two points, for example, the start and finish of a strip.

Eliminator The name of the long narrow-chassis dragsters with bicycle wheels at the front. They can be fueled by nitromethane or gasoline.

FIA The Fédération Internationale de L'Automobile, which has been the governing body of world motor sport since 1947. It controls the rules of motor racing and draws up the classes for racing at international level.

FTD The fastest time of the day.

Full throttle Driving as fast as possible.

Funny cars Dragsters that have been made with plastic or fiberglass bodies and are powered by modified and supercharged engines.

Homologation Confirms that the CSI has recognized that a car conforms to its requirements for that particular group.

Limit The fastest speed possible once the driver has taken into consideration the conditions of the car, the track and the weather.

Monocoque A method of construction that uses a single-shell frame instead of a chassis or a multi-tubular spaceframe.

NHRA The National Hot Rod Association, that was the originating governing body of drag racing.

Parachutes Used by the fuel dragsters

PARACHUTES: Used as a safety device to help cars slow down after reaching speeeds of up to 200mph

to help them to slow down. There are normally two parachutes at the back of each car.

Runways Used to race on when there are no strips.

Shutdown area An added section of the strip that is used by the drivers for slowing down and stopping once they have cleared the finish line.

Slicks The thick, treadless tires used on race cars. They have a high level of grip.

Slingshots Another name for the fuel dragsters.

Spaceframe A type of multi-tubular chassis construction.

Spoiler Another name for an airfoil.

Squirt A short burst of speed.

Strip The name given to a drag-racing track. It must measure 440yd long and 50yd wide.

Supercharger A mechanical device that boosts the fuel/air mixture into the combustion chamber, resulting in an increase in power.

Ten-tenths Driving on the limit.

Thermo-probe A device used for checking the temperature of tires.

Ton The slang term for 100mph.

Turbocharger Type of supercharger.

Unblown Describes a car without a supercharger or turbocharger.

Stock Car Racing

Stock car racing is a fast and exciting sport that takes place on a speedway. The American and English versions differ in the types of vehicle used.

Aquaplaning Occurs when a car's tires do not grip the surface of a wet road.

Backmarker A driver at the back of the field who is likely to be lapped.

Black flag Held up with the driver's number on it to let him know that he must stop racing and go into the pits.

Blow-up Slang for engine failure.

Blue flag If held still, the flag indicates that a driver is very close behind; if it is being waved, the flag indicates that the driver behind wants to overtake.

Checkered flag Colored black and white in alternate squares, and waved to indicate that the race is over.

CSI The Commission Sportive Internationale. A subcommittee of the FIA, it is responsible for making sure that the rules are adhered to.

Daytona Venue in Florida, most famous for stock car races. They were originally held on the beach before moving onto the speedway track in 1959.

Drift A controlled four-wheel slide through a corner. The driver uses the throttle to balance the effects of the slide.

FIA The Fédération Internationale de L'Automobile, that is the governing body for world motor sports.

FTD The fastest time of the day recorded in all the races.

Full throttle To drive as quickly as possible.

Grand National cars Includes Fords, Plymouths, Dodges, Chevrolets and Mercurys.

Grand American Includes Mustangs, Challengers and Firebirds.

Green flag Indicates that the circuit has been cleared of an earlier obstruction.

Homologation Describes the fact that the CSI has recognized a car as conforming to its requirements.

Lap The distance around the track.

Line The path that a car takes when going through a corner.

NASCAR The National Association for Stock Car Auto Racing, that controls the sport in the United States.

Oversteer When the back of the car has less grip than the front and tries to swing around ahead of the front. If the driver does not take quick corrective action by applying opposite steering lock and/or taking his foot off the throttle, a spin will result.

Pit board Used to display to the drivers what their position is, how many laps they have remaining and their general standing in relation to the other drivers.

Pits The area alongside the track where cars can stop and refuel or be repaired during the race.

Red flag Indicates that all cars must stop immediately.

Slicks The name given to the thick, treadless tires used on racing cars because they have a higher level of traction.

Slingshot A tactical move in which a driver moves out of the slipstream of the car in front and "slings" past the driver in front with the power he had reserved by being dragged along.

Slipstreaming When a car drives very close to the car in front. As a result of reduced wind resistance, the car behind gets dragged along.

Speedway The name given to the race-track. It is oval in shape and the cars race counter clockwise.

Spin When the driver loses control of the car and it revolves around its axis.

Starting flag The national flag of the country where the race is being staged.

Ton The slang term for 100mph.

Tuning Preparing an engine so it performs at its best.

Understeer When the front tires lose their traction before the rears wheels and therefore do not respond fully to the steering.

USAC The United States Auto Club, that organizes championship racing such as the Indianapolis 500.

Washout Occurs when a driver loses control of the front end of his car.

White flag Indicates that there is a service car on the track, such as an ambulance.

Yellow and red flag Indicates that there is oil on the track.

Yellow flag Indicates that there is grave danger ahead.

Rally Driving

Rally drivers use saloon cars to compete over public roads on a route that is split into a number of stages. Each stage is timed, and the overall winner is the driver who completes all the stages in the quickest time. The drivers are helped by a navigator in the passenger seat.

Blow-up Occurs when the engine fails.

BTD The best time of the day.

Drift Occurs when a four-wheeled vehicle slides through a corner using the throttle to control the effects of the slide.

FIA The Fédération Internationale de L'Automobile, the world governing body for motor sports since its inception in 1947.

Factory support teams Provide different tires and change the wheels when needed. They are very expensive to hire.

Forest rally A rally in which the majority of the special stages are run on forest roads.

Full throttle To drive as quickly as possible.

Homologation When the CSI recognizes that a car in one of the authorized FIA categories conforms to its requirements for that group.

Intercom A microphone and earphone attachment connected to the helmets of both the driver and the navigator so that they can communicate effectively above the considerable engine noise.

International RAC Rally This race uses many sections of the Forestry Commission roads instead of public roads or private circuits.

FOREST RALLY: Just one of the stages of a rally, where drivers race on forest or countryside roads

Limit The quickest possible speed without losing control of the car. It takes into account the car, the track and the weather conditions.

Navigator The codriver who will steer the course and warn the driver of any hazards or dangerous terrain.

Oversteer When the back of the car has less grip than the front and tries to swing around ahead of the front. If the driver does not take quick corrective action by applying opposite steering lock and/or taking his foot off the throttle, a spin will result.

Pace notes Notes used by a rally crew so that the navigator can inform the driver as to the surfaces, gradients, crests and curves on the course and at what speeds the corners can be taken. Added to this list are the distances needed to be driven.

RAC The Royal Automobile Club, that is the controlling body of motor racing in Britain.

Repairs If a car breaks down in between stages during a race, it can be repaired without penalty to the driver, but if it happens on a stage, then the driver has the time it takes to repair the car added to his time slot.

Road racing Races on public roads closed for the duration of the race.

Selective Occurs when a section of a public road that hasn't been closed off is used to race on. The competitors must reach a certain target time.

Set-up The preparation of the tires, suspension and steering to gain the best roadholding on a road circuit.

Shunt The slang term for an accident.

Slicks Thick, treadless tires that have a high level of traction up to a certain point.

Special stage A private or public road that has been closed off, but wherever possible is over rough terrain. This section of the rally route is timed to the second, and penalties are gained for not meeting the target time.

Ten-tenths Driving on the limit.

Thermo-probe Used to check the temperature of the tires.

Ton The slang term for 100mph.

Tuning Making sure the engine is at its best to perform with the maximum power and efficiency.

Understeer Occurs when a car's front tires lose traction before the rear wheels and therefore fail to respond fully to the steering.

Washout When a driver loses control of the front of the car.

Yump When a car goes over a bump and consequently can become airborne.

Motorcycling

Motorcycle racing is similar to motorcar racing in that both events are held on tracks or roads, with the winner being the rider with the fastest time. Competitors race at high speeds with a high element of danger.

Back protector A foam-based block that is encased in impact-resistant plastic and fitted on to a driver's back underneath his leathers. It provides protection in case the rider is thrown off the bike and on to his back.

Bank A raised bank of earth or mud that is often used as a safety barrier in motorcycle racing, although it is usually protected by straw bales.

Bogged down The term riders use to describe making a poor getaway at the start of a race.

Checkered flag A black and white checkered flag that signifies the end of the race and is waved first at the winner.

Chicanes Two consecutive right-hand corners, in opposite directions, that are designed to slow the bikes down.

Curbs A small raised area near the side of the track, usually on the entry and exit of corners, marking the edge of the track.

Flat spot A flat area on a tire that has been caused by a tire skidding after locking up the brakes.

Flying lap A term to describe a lap in which a rider has put in maximum effort or was at the absolute limit.

Gravel trap A gravel area next to the track designed to stop bikes that have crashed off the track.

Grid The area where the bikes link up, usually in five or six columns, for the start of the race. The fastest qualifier starts at the front, with the slowest at the back.

Hairpin A very tight corner that usually doubles back on itself.

Handling The term describing how a bike feels during a lap. A well set up bike will handle better than one that is badly set up.

Kitty litter A slang term for the gravel traps, that are filled with small stones to slow down bikes if they crash off the track.

Lap The term describing a complete circuit of a track. A race is made up of a specific number of laps, with the rider who completes the distance quickest declared the winner.

Leathers The leather overalls that riders wear as protection during the races. They are fitted with extra padding on the knees and elbows in case of accidents and to help when cornering.

Lock-up The term to describe when a tire stops turning under braking and locks up, thereby skidding.

Outbrake The term to describe when one rider overtakes a rival by braking later going into a corner.

Oversteer When the back of the bike has less grip than the front and tries to swing around ahead of the front.

Pits The area of the track where the bikes are worked on and where the team's mechanics are based during the race.

Pole position The leading grid position on the track that is claimed by the rider who has set the best time in qualifying.

Qualifying A session, usually of one hour's duration, where riders attempt to set the fastest time. The quickest riders start from the front of the grid.

Road racing Bike races that take place on closed circuits as opposed to dirt tracks.

Set-up The term to describe the technical settings on the bike that the rider has chosen to make it go faster.

Shunt A slang term for an accident or crash.

Skid When a bike's wheel locks up and slides on the track.

Tank slapper When a rider skids his bike and it slides to the left and then the right, as though the back of the bike was being hit from different directions.

Tire wall A wall of tires bound together, designed to absorb the impact of a bike that has spun off the track.

Traffic When a leading rider encounters a number of other bikes close together – usually backmarkers – and is finding it difficult to pass them.

Oversteer When the front of the bike has less grip than the rear and tries to plow straight ahead.

Wheelie When a rider applies the power too quickly and the front wheel lifts in the air. Riders often do this deliberately as a way of celebrating victory.

TRIALS

Motorcycle trials involves two different events: time trials and observation trials. Both emphasize the riders' skills in handling their bikes. The course consists of surfaced roads and rough terrain.

Capacity The measurement in cubic centimeters of the cylinders through whichthe pistons move. It is used as a means of determining that class a rider races in.

Clean When a rider has not incurred any penalties on his run.

Course Consists of a mixture of surfaced roads and rough terrain. The entire course is marked out and the riders must stay within its perimeter.

Dab A one-point penalty action. Occurs when the rider touches the ground with any part of his body, normally the foot.

Enduro A form of time trial.

FIM The Fédération Internationale Motocycliste, which is the governing body of world motorcycle sport.

Footing A three-point penalty action for touching the ground with any part of the body twice or more.

Four-stroke A type of engine in which every fourth stroke of the piston produces power.

Gearbox Usually has four or five gears.

ISDT The International Six Day Trials are mainly a team event but individual riders can win gold, silver or bronze medals. It is the equivalent of the Olympic Games for motorcycle sport.

J.R. Alexander Challenge Trophy The most important race on the observational trials calendar.

Leathers The one- or two-piece protective clothing made of leather that is worn by the riders.

Lights Must be permanent. The riders are not allowed to use flashlights.

Marshals The officials in charge of ensuring that the rules laid down by the governing body are adhered to during a race.

Number plate Must be placed at the back of the motorcycle.

Observed sections The obstacles placed on the course such as tree roots, stream beds, rocks and mud.

Outfit The name given to a motorcycle and sidecar combination.

Two-stroke A type of engine in which every second stroke of the piston produces power.

Speedway

Speedway racing is a highly specialized form of motorcycle sport that uses custom-made bikes with no brakes. They race on an oval track and often travel at speeds of up to 62mph.

BROADSIDING: The dynamic method of cornering that makes the sport of speedway quickly recognizable

Broadsiding The method of cornering used by the riders. They use their left leg and foot as a pivot. This technique is also known as power sliding.

Capacity The measurement in cubic centimeters (cc) of the cylinders through that the pistons move.

Cinder/shale surface Loosely covers the surface of a speedway track. It is vital to the sliding cornering action, because when dampened it provides the right consistency to make this action most effective.

Diamond Describes the main frame of the bike, that is diamond-shaped.

Dress Consists of padding worn under the leathers with a helmet, goggles or a visor, a face mask, gloves and steel-shod boots.

Engine The size of the engine is not allowed to exceed 500cc.

FIM The Fédération Internationale Motocycliste, which is the governing body of world motorcycling sport. It was founded in 1947.

Four-stroke Type of engine in which every fourth stroke of the piston provides power.

Fuel The fuel used for speedway bikes is methanol.

Green lights There are two, one placed in front of the starting gate and one placed behind the starting line. They are used to signal to the starting marshal and the riders that they are under starter's orders.

Greyhound track Speedway races are

staged on greyhound tracks when there are no proper tracks available. This is very much the case in Britain, where only two purpose-built speedway tracks are available.

Grid The starting positions of the riders. They are positioned according to a ballot drawn before the race. A rider will be excluded from the race if the wheel of his bike moves outside the grid before the race has begun.

Individual World Championships The most important and prestigious of speedway races. It gives the winner status and also the highest amount of prize money.

Laps There are generally four laps in each race. They are raced in a counter-clockwise direction. The track measures 383yd long.

League programme Held in Britain, it consists of two divisions, with 19 teams in the first and 17 teams in the second.

Leathers Worn tight and either in one or two pieces to protect the riders. If entered into a team race, the riders will wear distinctive colored uniforms. If entered into an individual race, the rider can wear his own leathers with a number on the back.

Pits Where the riders stay while they are not racing, and where they attend to their machines. Only riders, mechanics and officials are allowed into these areas.

Points The winner of the race is awarded three points, the second-place rider two points and the third-place rider one point. The last rider is not awarded any points.

Power sliding See "Broadsiding".

Red lights There are six in total around the track. Their main purpose is to signal to the riders that the referee has decided to stop the race for safety reasons.

Referee The official in overall charge of the race. He watches from a specially made box that is placed in line with the starting line. He is linked to all of the other officials on the track.

SCB The Speedway Controlling Board in Britain, which licenses tracks and racers.

Scrutineering Performed on each bike before the start of a race to ensure that they conform to the rules and safety regulations. The rider of any machine that violates the rules and regulations will automatically be disqualified from the race.

Starting marshal The official responsible for ensuring that the race gets off to a good start without any infringements occurring.

Tapes Used at the start of a race. The tape is stretched across the track, and the riders must stay behind it until the race begins.

Two-stroke Type of engine in which every second stroke of the piston produces power.

World Team Cup Has been held since 1960. Each team represents their own country and consists of four riders, plus a reserve rider.

Motocross

Motorcross races are held on cross-country courses that encompass rough terrain. Most of the races are held for solo drivers, although sidecar races are growing in popularity, especially in Europe.

Bank A raised bank of earth or mud that often is used as a safety barrier in motocross racing, although it is usually protected by straw bales.

Bogged down The term riders use to describe making a poor getaway at the start of a race.

Checkered flag The black and white checkered flag that signifies the end of the race and is waved first at the winning rider as he crosses the finish line.

Chicane Two consecutive right-hand corners, in opposite directions, designed to slow the bikes down.

Flying lap A lap in which a rider has put in maximum effort and was at the absolute limits.

Hairpin A tight corner that usually doubles back on itself and tests the rider's control and reflexes.

Handling The term describing how a bike feels during a lap. A well set up bike will handle better than one with a bad set up.

Lap The term describing one complete circuit of a track. A race is made up of a specific number of laps, with the rider who completes the distance quickest being declared the winner.

Lockup Occurs when a tire stops turning under braking and locks up, thereby skidding.

Marshals The track workers who look after safety at the track, wave warning flags and attend to riders in the event of a crash.

Outbrake To pass a rival by braking later going into a corner.

Oversteer When the front of the bike has less grip than the rear and tries to swing around ahead of the front.

Pits The area of the track in which the bikes are worked on and where the teams, mechanics are based during the race.

Podium A three-tiered platform where the top three finishers celebrate their performances after the race. The winner is placed centrally and higher than the second- and third-place riders.

Pole position The leading grid position on the track that is claimed by the rider who has set the best time in qualifying.

Qualifying A session, usually of one hour's duration, in which riders attempt to set the fastest time. The quickest riders in the qualifying section start from the best position at the starting gate.

Set-up The term describing the technical settings of the bike that the rider has chosen to make it go faster.

Shunt A slang term describing an accident or crash.

Skid When a bike's wheels lock up and slide.

Starting gate The gate where the riders all line up alongside each other for the start of the race. The event starts when the gate is dropped.

Tank slapper An incident on the track when a rider skids his bike and it slides to the left and then the right, as though the back of the bike were being hit from different directions, before the rider can correct it.

Tire wall A wall of tires, which have

WHEELIE: The spectacular stunt of riding a bike on its back wheel while the front wheel stays in the air

been bound together, designed to absorb the impact of bikes that hit it after spinning off the track.

Traffic A situation in which a rider encounters a group of other bikes, usually backmarkers, and is finding it difficult to get past.

Understeer When a bike's front tires do not turn into a corner as well as the rear tires do.

Waiting zone The area where the riders (up to 50) must wait before being called up before the start of the race.

Wheelie When a rider throttles up quickly and the front wheel lifts in the air. Riders often do this deliberately as a celebratory maneuver at the end of a race.

Yumps A slang term to describe the big jumps that are a feature of motocross racing.

Rallycross

Rallycross racing is performed on a track that combines rough surfaces with tarmac. Heats are held with between four to eight cars over three laps of the course. The fastest drivers go on to the finals, where the first car over the finish line is deemed the winner.

Armco barrier A purpose-built metal barrier erected at the side of the track to absorb the impact of cars hitting it after spinning off.

Barge A term used to describe the process of driving, deliberately or otherwise, another competitor off the track while racing.

Black flag Displays the number of the driver who is being asked to leave the track.

Blow-up Slang term for engine failure.

Blue flag When held still, the flag indicates that another driver is close behind; when it is being waved, the flag indicates that another driver is trying to pass.

Bogged down The term drivers use to describe making a poor getaway at the start of a race.

Classes The cars are divided into different classes such as the front wheel drive saloon, the front engined rear-wheel drive saloon, the rear-engined saloon, the sports car and special.

CSI The Commission Sportive Internationale is a subcommittee of the FIA, and is responsible for controlling the rules and drawing up the various classes for international competition.

Curbs A small raised area near the side of the track, usually on the entry and exit of corners, marking the edge of the track.

Dirt The generic term for the gravel or mud that rallycross courses often comprise.

Downforce The term to describe the amount of grip a rallycross car generates through aerodynamic devices such as a rear spoiler.

Flatspot A flat area on a tire that has been caused by a tire skidding after locking up.

Flying lap A lap in which a driver has put in maximum effort and was at the absolute limits.

FTD The fastest time of the day.

Full throttle To drive as quickly as possible.

Gravel trap An area next to the side of the track filled with small stones. It is designed to quickly stop cars that have spun off the track.

Green flag Signals that the track has been cleared of an earlier danger.

Grid The area where the cars line up, usually in two columns, for the start of the race. The fastest qualifier starts at the front, with the slowest at the back.

Hairpin A tight corner that usually doubles back on itself.

Handicap Any competitor driving a four-wheel-drive vehicle will be given a time handicap of five seconds because of their greater tractional advantage over other vehicles.

Handling Describes how a car feels during a lap. A well set up car will handle better than one with a bad set up.

Heats Rallycross events usually are made up of a number of qualifying heats, with the winners from each one going through to a grand final to decide the overall winner.

Homologation Describes the recognition shown by the CSI that cars conform to the guidelines set down by the FIA.

Jump start Occurs when a car drives over the starting line before the starting signal has been given, resulting in a time penalty.

Lock up The term describing when a tire stops turning under braking and locks up, thereby skidding.

Outbrake When one driver passes a rival by braking later going into a corner.

Overalls The safety clothes that the drivers wear in the car. They are fireproof and often adorned with sponsorship logos.

Oversteer When the back of the car has less grip than the front and tries to swing around ahead of the front. If the driver does not take quick corrective action by applying opposite steering lock and/or taking his foot off the throttle, a spin will result.

Paddock The area in which the cars are kept and seen to before the race begins.

Pits Area of the track where the cars are worked on, and where the teams, mechanics are based during the race.

Pole position The leading grid position on the track, claimed by the driver who has performed best in the heats.

RAC The Royal Automobile Club of Great Britain.

Red flag Indicates that all cars must stop at once.

Roll cage A strong metal frame built into rallycross cars to ensure the roof does not collapse if the car rolls over.

Set up The term to describe the technical settings on the car that the driver has chosen to make the car go faster.

Skid When a car's wheels lock up and slide on the track surface.

Slicks The thick, treadless tires used on racing cars. They have a high level of traction in dry conditions and when they have reached their correct operating temperature.

Spin Describes when the driver loses control of his car and it goes into a spin.

Starting flag The national flag of the country hosting the race.

Tank slapper An incident on the track when a driver skids his car and it slides to the left and then the right, as though the back of the car were being hit from different directions.

Tap A motor racing term describing the process of lightly hitting a rival's car with the front of yours. Cars can be tapped into spins.

Thermo-probe An instrument used to measure the temperature of the tires.

Tin top A slang term for race cars that feature a roof and doors, as opposed to single-seater cars like those seen in Formula One.

Tire wall A wall of tires, bound together, to absorb the impact of cars that hit it after spinning off the track.

Ton The slang term for 100mph.

Tune To prepare an engine to perform its best.

Traffic When a competitor encounters a cluster of rival cars, usually backmarkers, and finds it difficult to pass.

Understeer When a car's front tires do not turn into a corner as well as the rear tires.

Washout When the driver loses control of the front end of the car.

White flag Signals that a service car/ambulance is on the course.

Yellow and red flag Indicates to drivers that there is oil on the track.

Yellow flag Signals grave danger ahead.

Yump Describes a bump on the track that can make a fast-moving car become airborne.

Powerboat Racing

Powerboat racing is divided into two main categories: racing on inland water and offshore racing at sea. The boats are divided into a number of classes according to size.

Black flag Always shown with a number indicating that boat must withdraw from the race.

Buoy Floating markers that are used to map the course of the race.

Checkered flag Always colored black and white. Indicates that the race is now finished.

Classification There are six classes that can be entered: Class One offshore; Class Three offshore; on class circuit, the hydroplane, the class four offshore and the national class cruiser.

Eligibility All boats must comply with the class rules as laid down by the official governing body, the UIM.

Events Are divided into international, national and club events.

Hydrofoil The design of the boat that makes it possible to hydroplane. The hull of the boat is V-shaped or rounded at the bow and flat near the stern where the boat is cut away square.

Hydroplaning When the boat comes partially out of the water and skims the surface.

Lap scoring Uses four officials. As the boats pass through the start and finish lines, the numbers of each boat are recorded by the lap scorer.

License Competitors must be issued with a license that is validated by the governing body of powerboat racing. They must also obtain third-party insurance issued by the same authority.

Life jackets Must be worn by all con-

HYDROPLANING: Event in which the boat must skim the surface of the water to gain higher speeds

testants as part of the safety regulations.

NPRA The National Powerboat Racing Authority that issues licenses for competitors to enter international races.

Offshore This category is raced offshore and includes both long-distance racing and basic offshore racing for smaller boats.

Points For races with two or more heats, a points system is used. There are 20 boats, with the first gaining 400 points, the second gaining 300 points, 225 points for third and 169 points for fourth, down to one point for the 20th boat.

Records For world and national records to be recognized, they need to correspond with the rules drawn up by the UIM. Anybody attempting to break a record must notify the national authority within at least four weeks.

Red flag Alerts the competitors that the race has been stopped.

Rescue craft Must be available in all races. They must carry signal flags, a fire extinguisher, ropes, a boat hook, first-aid equipment and two staff that are exceptional swimmers. On shore, an ambulance must be in attendance.

Scrutineering Occurs before a race. The officiating body must check that the boats conform to the rules and are safe for competitors to race in.

Sportsboat This category is raced on inland water and is usually divided into heats. There is another division of sportsboat racing called hydroplane racing.

UIM The Union International Motonautique, that is the international governing body for powerboat racing based in Monaco.

Yellow flag If held still, the flag signals to competitors to use caution because of a hazard ahead; if it is being waved, it warns the competitors of extreme danger ahead.

Aerobatics

Competitive aerobatics is a skillful and challenging sport that tests both the pilot and the aircraft. The competitions combine both compulsory and free sequences, the winner being the competitor with the highest score. The aircraft used are single-engine light planes, but in international and world competitions, piston-engine planes must be used.

PERFORMANCE ZONE: Measures 1,093yd by 1,093yd and competitors are penalized if they go beyond it

Briefing All competitors are briefed every day throughout a competition, and everyone involved must attend.

FAI The Fédération Aeronautique Internationale, that picks the jury for the World Championships.

Height During international and world championships, the height specifications are no lower than 328ft and no higher than 3280ft. In competitions where the standards are lower, the specifications are between 948ft and 1640ft.

Horizontal eight An inside loop and an outside loop flown in a horizontal position.

Horizontal slow roll While flying in a straight line, the pilot slowly rolls his aircraft over while continually flying horizontal.

Inverted flight Also called a negative flight. The plane flies upside down in a continuous straight line.

Jury For the World Championships, there are seven judges from differing countries who are selected by the FAI and a chief judge who has no vote. Assistants to the judges and four positioning judges who are placed at each corner of the performing zone also help officiate.

Linesmen Their job is to help measure the edges of the flight zone with special instruments supplied.

Penalties These are given for flying over the time limit, flying too high or low, or for flying outside of the performance zone. Pilots are also penalized for interrupting their sequence to reprogram or for climbing to regain height.

Performance zone The competition area marked out on the ground. It must measure 1093ft by 1093ft. If the aircraft flies outside the area, the pilot will be disqualified.

Program one A compulsory sequence known to the pilots in advance. It includes both normal flight and inverted flight, which must be carried out in the correct order as specified.

Program two The free program where the pilot has to perform 18 figures of his choosing.

Program three The unknown compulsory program which involves at least 15 figures and is arranged into order by the jury.

Program four The freestyle program which lasts for four minutes. The pilot is allowed to perform as many figures as he wants within that time.

Replacements An aircraft may be replaced at any point during the contest. If an aircraft is damaged during a flight, the contestant may fly again if the jury agrees.

Rolling circle with horizontal rolls The plane flies in a horizontal circle while rolling on itself four times.

Scoring The freestyle program is judged on its entirety, whereas the other three program are marked on each figure displayed.

Sequences The standard competition is made up of three or more sequences, that each incorporate 15–30 individual maneuvers. The first sequence is preset; the second is made up of figures that the pilot sees only 24 hours before the start of the contest; and the third sequence has the pilot choose his own maneuvers in order to display his mastery of his aircraft.

Spin Occurs with the aircraft flying downward while flying around an imaginary pole.

Stall turn Also known as a "hammer head". The aircraft flies straight up until it is almost stationary, then immediately turns on itself and flies down.

Tail slide Also called a whip stall. The aircraft flies in a small upright curve to continue straight up before flying back down to half of the distance before straightening up and flying vertically forward and down.

Teams For the World Championships, no more than five pilots are allowed. The team can be made up of both men and women. Competitors are also allowed to enter individually.

Time limit Each competitor is given 15 minutes for the first three programs and four minutes for the fourth.

Training flights Competitors are allowed 15 minutes to familiarize themselves with the local conditions of the performance zone.

Vertical eight This figure is an inside loop and an outside loop that make the figure eight.

Vertical half-roll Occurs when the aircraft comes in from the left and flies directly up and around before flying down and to the left.

World Championships Are made up of three programs, a known compulsory program, a free program and an unknown compulsory program. Each program has a draw to decide the starting order of the competitors.

Weather conditions In relation to the World Championships, the cloud base must be at least 164ft above the maximum height at which the aircraft are allowed to fly, with visibility of at least 5500yd.

9 Water Sports

The common thread running through these sports is that they all take place in or on water, either in some form of floating vessel (rowing, canoeing or yachting) or with the competitor immersed in water (swimming or diving). Synchronized swimming has close links with gymnastics, but is officially classified as a swimming event.

Sports Locker

Belt Used in weightlifting to support the back but is not compulsory. Can measure 4.7in at the widest point.

Boxing gloves Made of leather and padded, must be worn by both amateur and professional boxers. Usually weigh 8–10oz.

Caps Worn in swimming events to hold the hair in place and aid streamlining.

Fire-resistant clothing Worn by drivers who compete in motoring events.

Goggles Worn in swimming events to protect the eyes and help with vision underneath the water. Also worn in skiing events to protect the eyes.

Gumshield Worn by boxers to protect their gums and teeth in the ring. Also worn in other contact sports, such as karate and rugby.

Hachimaki A toweling headcloth that is worn underneath a wire mask when competing in kendo.

Hakama Is an ankle-length skirt that has a split to allow for movement. Worn by Kendo competitors.

Headband Worn in many sports to keep hair back and sweat from the eyes. They can also be worn by rugby players to prevent injury to their ears.

Headguard Worn in many sports to protect the face and head. Used by amateur boxers, American footballers, lacrosse players, hockey goalkeepers and ice hockey players, baseball catchers, and many others.

Helmet Worn for safety reasons in many sports, including cricket, cycling, horse events, and adventure or motor sports.

Judogi Trouser and jacket combination worn by judo, karate, jiu jitsu and aikido competitors. Colored white or off-white and tied with a colored belt.

Leathers Worn by motorcyclists because they are tough and give some protection in the event of a crash.

Leotard Worn by both men and women for gymnastic events. A one piece outfit that enables competitors to not only feel comfortable but also allows flexibility.

Life-jackets Worn for safety reasons in most aquatic events such as sailing, canoeing and powerboating.

Wet suit Worn for warmth in many aquatic sports such as surfing, windsurfing and diving.

Whites All-white clothing worn by competitors who play cricket, bowls, croquet, court handball, tennis and paddleball.

Canoeing

Canoeing is divided into two main events, sprint racing and slalom events. Sprint racing is held for one-man, two-man and four-man kayak and Canadian canoe events. Slalom racing is held in individual and team events for one-man kayaks for both men and women, and one-man and two-man Canadian canoe events for men only.

Aft The area of the canoe between amidships and the stern.

Amidships The center of the canoe at an equal distance between the stern and the stem.

Back-paddling Used either to stop the canoe or to travel backward.

Bilge The section of the canoe hull under the water.

Blade The broad end of the paddle that is used to propel the canoe.

Bottom board The loose board which can be removed from the hull. It is designed to take the canoeist's weight so they can sit on it.

Bow The forward part of the canoe.

Bowman The paddler who sits nearest to the bow.

Bow rudder A paddling stroke used to turn the bow toward the side on that the bowman is paddling.

Bow stroke Used in Canadian canoes. The canoeist starts their stroke at a 45-degree angle with the hand on the shaft pulling directly back, while the hand on the grip pushes forward from the shoulder, moving in a straight direction by pushing out at the end of the stroke.

Brace A stroke used by the paddler to stop the canoe from capsizing. This is done by leaning onto the paddle.

Breakout A canoe stroke used for getting out of the mainstream.

Buoyancy Aids placed at the bow and the stern to stop the canoe from sinking.

C The initial used to signify that a canoe in competition is Canadian. A figure shown next to this letter indicates the number of crew on board.

Canadian A type of rudderless canoe. The paddler uses a single-blade paddle.

Chute A narrow, clear path through rapids.

Coaming Also known as the washboard. This is a raised board that is placed around the cockpit to stop water from washing into the hull.

Cockpit The space in a decked canoe in which the paddler sits.

Deck The top covering of a closed canoe.

Deep water rescue Using another canoe or canoes to help a capsized paddler or paddlers.

Down river racing See "Wild Water Racing".

Draw stroke Used to move the canoe sideways with the paddle.

Drip rings Placed on the neck of a double-sided paddle to stop water from running down the loom and onto the paddler.

Eddy A part of the river. Occurs when part of the current runs against the normal flow because of the contours of the water bank or bed. Can also be made artificially.

Eskimo kayak A decked canoe with a small cockpit and an upswept stem.

Eskimo roll A full 360-degree turn through the water.

Ferry glide When a canoeist uses the current to cross a river at right angles by setting the canoe diagonally to the flow.

Fish form A hull shape in which the largest beam is forward of amidships.

Freeboard The area from the waterline to the upper edges of the hull where the canoe is loaded.

Free gate A slalom gate that is marked with black and white rings.

Gate The name given to a slalom obstacle. It consists of two poles that the canoe must move through cleanly without gaining penalties. The port side pole is red and white, and the starboard pole is green and white.

Gunwale The name given to the upper edges of the hull.

Haystack A standing wave that is topped with white water.

J-stroke A steering action that comes at the end of each stroke. Used by single-blade paddlers.

K Used to signify that a kayak is in competition.

Kayak A canoe similar to the Eskimo style. The paddle used has a double blade and the canoeist sits in a covered cockpit.

Keelson An internal part of the canoe that runs lengthwise along the keel.

Leeboards Boards that are set down in the water at the sides of a sailing canoe to stop it from drifting sideways.

Line-down To lead the canoe through obstacle-strewn water with a painter.

Long-distance racing Usually takes place on rivers, lakes and open water. Competitive racing over varying lengths and conditions.

Loom The shaft of the paddle that reaches as far as the blade.

Modified Sweden form Also known as symmetrical form. Describes the hull shape in which the maximum beam is amidships.

Number plates Have a black foreground with yellow lettering. All competition canoes must have them clearly visible, with kayaks placing them on the afterdeck and Canadian canoes placing them on the foredeck.

Open water The sea or a river estuary.

Paddles Made of wood or fiberglass, they are specially designed for speed and lightness. Kayak paddles have two blades whereas Canadian paddles have only one.

Painter The rope attached to the bow or stern.

Pawlata Performed when the canoeist uses an Eskimo roll to right the canoe, while all the time leaning forward.

Pry over The paddle is pried away from the side of the boat in order to move the canoe sideways. Used on Canadian canoes.

Recovery The stroke used during an Eskimo roll to bring the boat back into the correct position. Also describes the period from the completion of one paddle stroke to the beginning of the next.

Rib The part of the frame that runs at right angles from the keel to the gunwale.

Riffle The name given to a small, shallow rapid.

Run off Additional water in a river due to heavy rain or thawed snow.

Screw An Eskimo roll performed with the hands kept in an ordinary paddling position.

Sculling A movement of the blade used to move a canoe sideways, and used by a canoeist to support himself in a near-capsize position.

Slalom A fast-water competition in which competitors must negotiate their way around a course of gates and natural obstacles over two timed runs.

Spooned blade A blade shaped like a spoon used to gain a better pull through the water.

Spray cover A waterproof apron fitted around the coaming and the canoeist's waist to stop water from entering the canoe.

WILD WATER RACING: It is vital for the canoeist to have great upper body strength as the water on the course can be fast and furious

Sprint A racing event performed on still and flat water.

Stem The pillar placed at the front edge of the hull.

Stern The rear end of the canoe.

Steyr A maneuver to put the canoe back in position by using an Eskimo roll. The canoeist leans back throughout the action.

Stopper Also known as a hydraulic jump. Describes a wave that is large enough to capsize a canoe. Found in rapids.

Straight stroke The most basic stroke involving the canoeist paddling from side to side of the canoe to move the boat forward in a straight line.

Swedish form See "Modified Sweden form".

Sweep A stroke performed to move the canoe to starboard or port.

Telemark A stroke performed by extending the paddle out to one side and leaning in on it to effect a sharp turn.

Tiller bar Foot control for a rudder.

Trim The level at which a canoe rides in the water.

White water Also known as wild water. Occurs where fast water flows over rocks or obstacles, creating a white foam.

Wild water racing Performed over one timed run, the canoeist moves over fast-moving water with natural and man-made obstacles along the way.

Yaw To go off course by swinging from side to side.

Yoke Placed on a rudder to which control lines are attached.

Canoe Polo

Canoe polo is contested by two teams of five players each. Using polo kayaks, the competitors' objective is to score as many goals as possible against the opposing team.

Ball Must have a circumference of 27in-28in and a mass of 14in-17.5oz..

Corner throw Type of throw that, under the referee's orders, must be taken from the corner of where has been decided.

Dress Players must wear safety helmets and life jackets. The same color of kayak must be used by team members. Each player displays a number on his body and helmet.

Duration A match consists of two 10-minute periods, with a three-minute halftime period. Extra time consists of two periods of three minutes each.

Fouls Dangerous use of the paddle, holding, illegal possession, illegal tackles, obstruction and unsportsmanlike behavior.

Free throw The ball may not be thrown directly at the goal.

Goal A shot that has passed through the plane of the front of the goal frame. Following a goal, the team that conceded it restarts the game with a throw from the center of the playing area. All players must start in their own half.

Goal-line throw Throw that can be taken anywhere along the goal line.

Hand tackle Performed when a player pushes an opponent's side or arm with an open hand. The player being tackled must have sole possession of the ball.

Kayak tackle A tackle performed by a player with his kayak pushing an opponent's kayak. Under no circumstances can contact be made with the tackled player's body while this tackle is being made. The player being tackled must be in competition for the ball and be within 3.3yd of it.

Kayaks A kayak must measure 2.2yd-3.3yd in length and of 20in-24in. in width.

Officials A first referee, a second referee (umpire), a timekeeper, scorekeeper, two goal linesmen and a scrutineer.

Open-framed goals Placed over the center of each goal line.

Out of play When the ball crosses the sideline or touches the vertical plane of the goal line. The team not last to touch the ball with their paddle, kayak or person is awarded the throw by the referee.

Paddles Each player has one double-bladed paddle, measuring no more than 20inx10in in plan. No part of the edge can be less than 1.2in radius in plan. Paddles must not have any sharp or hazardous characteristics.

Penalties These include: a free shot, a free throw, a goal penalty, sending a player off for two minutes, sending a player off for the rest of the game and reporting an offending player to the National Federation Canoe Polo Committee.

Playing area The area that the match is played in must be rectangular and have, where possible, a length-to-width ratio of 3:2. The depth of the water should be at least 90cm.

Possession A player must not hold on to the ball for more than five seconds.

Sideline throw Awarded by the referee when the ball crosses over the side-line and out of play. The side-line throw must not result in the ball being thrown in the direction of attack.

Substitution This is permitted at any stage of a canoe polo match.

Teams Each squad comprises eight players, with only five allowed on the playing area at any one time.

Rowing

Rowing is a traditional sport that is divided into two basic types of competition: regattas and head-of-the-river races. The regatta is decided by knockout, with a final being held to determine the winning crew. Head-of-the-river races are decided by the crew that achieves the fastest time over the course.

Alignment All boats must be aligned with the starting line before the start of a race.

Backstops The farthest point to that the slide (seat) can move in the direction of the bows.

Best boat A light racing boat with a smooth skin.

Blade The name given to the wide end of the oar that goes into the water. It is normally painted in club colors for easy identification. In international events, the blades must be painted in the national colors.

Boat Race The world-famous annual race between Oxford and Cambridge Universities. The race class is eights, and the race is always held on the River Thames between Putney Bridge and Mortlake in London.

Bow The oarsman positioned nearest to the bowside or front of the boat.

Bowside Starboard side of the boat.

Breakages If a breakage of equipment occurs, then a race may be stopped and rerowed, provided it happened within 109yd of the start – unless the breakage is due to a collision or an accident caused by an outside force.

Bumps A traditional form of racing where the competing boats must try to bump the boat in front in order to knock it out so that they can move up a place in line for the following day's racing. Originated on waters where there was not enough space for the boats to race side by side.

Button Describes the movable collar fitted to the shaft of the oar so that it does not slip through the rowlock.

Canvas A margin of victory just by the length of the bow or stern section of the boat.

Card Each boat must have a numbered card attached to its bow.

Catching a crab To feather the blade before the end of the stroke. When this happens, the water catches the oar and the momentum of the boat is disturbed, that makes it awkward for the oarsmen.

Clinker A way of building a hull with overlapping planks laid both fore and aft.

Coastal rowing A popular branch of the sport in which crews race along the coast.

Countdown start An alternative starting method used. The starter counts down from five and then gives the normal starting commands.

Cox The person who steers the boat, and the only crew member who does not actually row. He or she also calls out the number of strokes rowed per minute.

Crews Can be made up of two, four or eight oarsmen and one, two or four scullers.

Curve The more curve on a blade, the easier and more effective the stroke, as the water is caught more efficiently at the beginning of the stroke.

Disqualification When a crew is barred from competing further in the regatta due to a blatant disregard of the rules.

EIGHT: The longest boat used in competition. Made famous in the annual Oxford-Cambridge boat race

Double A boat that contains only two scullers.

Eight The fastest and longest of rowing boats. It contains eight oarsmen and a cox. It measures 53ft-59ft in length.

Elite class The highest class of rowing. To be eligible, the oarsmen must have won six races as seniors.

Exclusion Occurs when a crew is disqualified from one race but not the whole event.

False start Occurs when a crew's bow crosses the starting line before the starting signal has been given. The race will be recalled with the crew being warned. If a crew commits two false starts, it will be disqualified from the race.

Feather Describes turning the blade flat and parallel to the water between each stroke. This lessens the wind resistance and stops the oar from hitting the water after the recovery.

Fin Placed near the stern and under the hull of the boat. Made of metal, it aids stability and steering.

FISA The Fédération Internationale des Sociétés d'Aviron, which is the governing body of rowing.

Fours An event for a four-oared boat. It can be entered with or without a cox.

Frontstops Describes the farthest distance the slide can move in the direction of the stern.

Gate The device on the rowlock that can be unscrewed and removed to allow the oar to be inserted or taken out.

Head of the river A rowing event in which competitors are individually timed, with the quickest crew being the winner. It is also used to describe the winners in the bumps.

Head race Competing crews who race on a course at different times are pitted against each other, with their finishing times determining their placings.

Head rest Used by the cox of a coxed pair or coxed four. The cox lies down in the bow with his head resting on the cushion. This reduces wind resistance and drag in the stern of the boat.

Henley The Royal Regatta course measuring 1.5 miles in length. One of the most famous regatta courses in the world.

Inboard The part of the oar that stretches from the handle to the button.

Jury Consists of the chief referee and four other officials who adjudicate on any protests.

Lightweight category Each rower must weigh no less than 154lb and no more than 158lb.

Macon blade Another name for the spade blade.

Novice An oarsperson who has never won an open event at a regatta.

Oar A sweep oar must be at least 0.2in thick measuring 0.1in from the blade's tip, and a scull oar must be at least 0.1in thick measuring 0.07 from the tip. All oars are hollow for maximum lightness.

Oarsman One of the crew who uses an oar in order to propel the boat.

Olympic categories Include coxed fours, double sculls, coxless pairs, single sculls, coxed pairs, coxless fours, quadruple sculls and eights. Events are always rowed in this order.

Outboard The part of the oar stretching from the button to the tip of the blade.

Paddling The pressure applied by the rower or sculler combined with the rate of striking. Classed as full pressure, half pressure or light paddling.

Pairs An event for two-oared boats either with or without a cox.

Petit finale The race that decides the 7th–12th positions in an international regatta or FISA Championship.

Pinch the boat Means that the pressure applied goes inward rather than outward because the stroke is started at a steep angle.

Pivoting shoe The means by which an oarsman steers a boat when there is no cox. The pivoting shoe is attached to the rudderlines.

Plastic ball Placed on the bow, it must measure 1.6in in diameter. It is used to aid visibility and protect against injury.

Processional races The boats start at set intervals, with the crew that achieves the fastest time being declared the winner.

Puddle The swirl of the water left by the blade after a stroke.

Quadruple scull A sculling boat manned by four scullers with or without a cox.

Rake The angle of inclination on the stretcher.

Rate of striking The number of strokes rowed per minute.

Recovery The period of time between the end of one stroke and the beginning of another.

Red flag Used to signal the start of the race. It is also used before the start of a race to signal that alignment has been lost.

Regatta The term used to describe a racing event in which a combination of events is treated as one unit.

Repechage A system allowing the losing teams of a heat to race again and get the chance to go through to the finals, thus ensuring that the best crews get to compete.

Reprimand An informal caution.

Restricted four A boat which has an outside keel.

Rigger The outrigger, which extends from the side of the boat and supports the rowlock.

Rigging Describes the way in that the riggers and stretchers are set.

Rower Another term for an oarsman.

Rowlock Also called a swivel, it supports the oar. It pivots from a vertical pin attached to the end of the outrigger, and has a latch or gate that can be unscrewed and lifted so that the oar may be removed.

Rudder Made of either wood or metal, and used to steer the boat.

Sculler A person who rows with two sculls.

Sculls Smaller and lighter than normal oars, with smaller blades.

Shell A racing boat with a smooth exterior. It does not have an outside keel.

Shoot the slide When an oarsman drives with his legs before the blade takes the water. This dissipates the power of the leg drive.

Skiff A heavy clinker-built boat that is moved by sculls.

Skill categories Broken up into intermediate, senior and elite.

Sky To lift the oar too high above the water before starting a stroke.

Slice To put the blade into the water too deeply before taking a stroke.

Slide The seat on which the oarsman sits. It gets its name because it allows the rower to slide along and gain more momentum in his stroke.

Spade blade The shorter, wider blade that is normally used.

Spread Also known as the thwartship distance. Occurs when the gearing of the stroke is modified by changing the position of the rowlock in relation to the center of the boat.

Squared Describes the position of the blade as it moves through the water.

Stakeboat A moored boat from which the stern of the boat is held to keep it in position until the race begins.

Starting area Encompasses the first 109yd of the course. Once the crews row out of this area, they may not protest that the start is unfair.

Station Describes the lane of the course allocated to each boat in that they race.

Stays The metal tubes that form the rigger.

Stretcher Area of the boat in which the oarsman rests his feet. He pushes against this when making a stroke.

Stroke The oarsman who sits in the stern seat. He is responsible for setting the rate and rhythm for the crew to follow.

Strokeside The port side of the boat where the stroke's oar is normally positioned.

Substitutes Permitted for up to half the crew and the coxswain until one hour before the first race – or later, if a crew member has a serious illness. No substitutes are permitted in single sculling events.

Sweep An event in which each rower uses a single oar.

Swivel A rowlock that moves from a vertical pin that is joined to the outer end of the rigger.

Tiebreaker If this occurs in a final, the crews will have to rerow after a rest period. In some cases, a tie is awarded without a rerow.

Tub A wide, heavy boat used to teach rowing to beginners.

Warning If a crew receives two warnings during a race, it will be disqualified.

Washing-down To deliberately place your boat in front of another, causing the other crew to row in its wake or puddles.

Wash out To remove the blade slightly from the water before the stroke is finished.

Watermanship Refers to a rower's skills of handling and balancing both boat and oars.

Weight restrictions Coxes must weigh at least 110lb. Any cox who weighs less than this must make up the weight and place it in the boat with him.

White flag Used to signal that alignment has been secured. It is held up until the start of the race.

Dragon Boat Racing

Dragon boat racing is a team event in which competitors use Oriental-style boats, with dragon heads on the front. Each boat has a drummer to beat out a rhythm and keep the crew in unison when paddling. The winning team is the first to pass the finish line.

BDA The British Dragon Boat Racing Association, which is the official governing body for the sport in the United Kingdom.

Black flagged Occurs when a race official raises a black flag to warn a crew or a crew member that their behavior is unacceptable.

Bracing the boat Describes a team leaning out slightly over the side of the boat and pressing their paddle blades flat on the water at arm's length in order to steady the boat when sideways to the wind.

Buoys There should be a minimum of four, two at the outside of the start and two at the finishing posts. Extra buoys can be used to mark out the lanes along the course.

Course This must have calm waters with a width capacity for at least two boats. The minimum length required is 273yd.

Crew Up to 22 members per boat, with 10 members on each side. In addition to the crew, there is a steerer and a drummer.

Crew list Must be handed in before the beginning of the race, and must list the crew officials, the actual crew (by name) and confirm that all the crew members are able to swim.

Divisions The sport is divided into two divisions, the Premier and the Standard. The maximum number of teams in a division is 18.

Dragon boats Measuring 39ft in length, they are constructed of fiberglass fiber. They have wooden gunwhales and seats. The boat has a dragon's head at the front and tail at the rear, with a fitted drum for racing.

DRAGON BOATS: Made of fiberglass with carvings of a dragon's head and tail at either end of the boat

Drummer The drummer sits in the boat and drums to keep the crew in unison while paddling.

Embarking area All boats must assemble here before the start of a race and at the end of a race. Once a crew has crossed the finish line, it must paddle back to the embarking area within three minutes.

False start Occurs when a crew moves off between the commands, "Attention" and "Go". If a crew performs two false starts, it will be disqualified from the race.

First past the post The way in which a race is decided, although runners-up also get a chance to go through to the next round.

International races These are established in more than 30 countries, including the Far East, Australia, New Zealand, Canada, South Africa, America and Europe.

Long-distance races These are held over distances between 0.6 miles and 12 miles.

Penalty points Up to four points can be awarded against a contestant or crew for using verbal abuse against a race official.

Points scoring Each crew is awarded points on a sliding-scale basis that depend on their finishing position in each event.

Race conduct All boats must race in a straight line and keep within their allotted lanes from the start to the finish of the race. Steerers must ensure that the other boats' paddles are at least 3.3yd away.

Racing class Consists of open crews (men and women), mixed with a minimum of eight women, youth and juniors.

Racing paddle This is divided into three sections: the blade, shaft and handle. The shaft must be straight and the blade's surface must be smooth. The minimum length should be 41in with a maximum length of 51in. The blade should measure 7in in width.

Safety boats These are compulsory when a competition is in progress as a safety measure in case of a boat capsizing, etc.

Scratch class Held for nonmembers and members who have not qualified for the national league.

Sighting posts Placed on the bank to mark the start and finish lines. The judge timekeeper needs to have a line of sight across the finish line in order to see the sighting posts clearly.

Starting area The first 55yd of the race.

Starting position The foremost part of each boat must be on the starting line with all the boats aligned.

Starts All crew members must be in their boats and in the start area at least five minutes before the starting signal.

Steerer Steers the boat with a steering oar.

Turns Must be made in a counterclockwise direction when racing in lanes. The buoy must pass on the left-hand side of the boat.

Windsurfing

Windsurfing has developed only in the last 20 years, but has become technically advanced during this period. The race takes place between a set number of competitors (depending on the competition) on water using a board and sail to move across the water. The winner is the first competitor to cross the finish line.

All-around Describes a board or sail that is suitable for all-around use – meaning both light and strong winds or different sea conditions.

Batten A piece of flexible fiberglass that slots into a "pocket" in the sail creating an efficient aerodynamic shape. A full-length batten extends across the sail.

Beach start A racer steps onto the board in shallow water with the rig already in the sailing position. The rig does not have to be raised from the water using this technique.

Bearing away Steering the board away from the wind.

Beating To sail as close as possible to the direction in that the wind blows.

Board Any board can be used during a race, except for the Olympic Games where the IMCO (International Mistral Class Organization) is chosen for use by the competitors. There are also one-design races in that every sailor races on the same equipment provided by one manufacturer.

Boom A curved alloy tube that is covered with rubber and is held to control the sail.

Bottom turn A high-speed turn performed by a racer on the bottom of a wave, which takes them up the same wave, enabling them to continue their ride in.

Center of effort An imaginary central point in the sail through which the power of the sail acts.

Center of lateral resistance Main point from that the board will resist sideways drift, and about that it turns.

Cheese roll An aerial maneuver that involves spinning the board and sailing horizontally through 360 degrees in midair.

Cleat Small fitting that secures the control lines of the rig.

Clew Back corner of the sail that is fitted on to the end of the boom.

Cringle The metal eyelet at the tack and clew of the sail through which the downhaul and outhaul ropes are threaded.

Cutback A maneuver used to head back down from the top of a wave.

Daggerboard A large fin that provides stability to the board and stops it from slipping sideways.

Donkey kick Kicking the board out sideways at the top of a jump.

Expression session Contest in which all the competitors are on the water at the same time (normally for 30 minutes). The most radical maneuver wins the competition.

Eye of the wind The precise direction from which the wind is blowing.

Fin Small piece of plastic or fiberglass protruding at the tail of the board to keep it sailing in a straight line.

Foot Bottom edge of the sail.

Footsteering A racer uses the weight of their feet to steer the board in strong winds with the daggerboard up.

Footstraps A racer puts their feet into

straps at the back of the board when sailing quickly in stronger winds.

Freestyle Specialist section whereby each competitor finds as many different ways of sailing the board as possible.

Gnarly Expression used to describe difficult conditions.

Heading up Steering toward the wind.

Heat Term used to describe the actual race through a course. In the slalom racing events, there are a total of 34 heats that need to be completed in order to finish a full slalom round of 64 racers.

Imaginary line At the start of a race, all the racers line up together, but they must stay behind an imaginary line that is set in front of all the racers. This is a transit between the start boat and the outer marker.

Jibe A racer turns the board around by steering away from the wind and letting the sail move over the front of the board.

Jumps In the wave performance, racers are judged on the number of jumps they make during the contest. A jump entails the rider jumping as high as possible off the top of a wave.

Leeway Describes the amount by which a board slips sideways.

Lollipop To jump while riding down the face of a wave.

Man-on-man The term relates to the wave-performance contest in which one racer comes up against another. The winner progresses to the next round.

Nose Front end of the board.

Offshore wind Wind blowing away from the shore.

Plane A board sailing at speed, when it rises up and travels across the water surface rather than pushing the water aside and sailing through it.

Rail The side of the board.

Railride A move used by a windsurfer in the freestyle competition. The sailor rides the board on its rail.

Restart A race can start again if one of the racers crosses the start line before the starting signal has been given.

Rig Collective name given for the mast, boom and sail when assembled.

Shoulder The unbroken part of a breaking wave.

Slalom racing A knockout contest that runs in heats of 8–10 racers at one time around a set course. The first four or five racers to cross the finish line progress to the next round and continue until they reach the final. For a full slalom, there needs to be a total of 32 heats, which entails 64 racers.

Start There is a sequence of a six-minute, three-minute and then a one-minute warning at the start of a race.

Table top An aerial maneuver in which the board is kicked up above the sailor at the apex of the jump.

Tail Back end of the board.

Uphaul Thick piece of rope used to raise the rig from the water.

Water start Advanced maneuver that is performed in stronger winds. The sailor lets the sail pull him onto the board from a position in the water.

Wave performance A competition that demands a high degree of skill from the racer and is classified as the most entertaining competition. The racer to score the most points progresses to the next round.

Wetted area The area of the board's bottom that is in contact with the water. The drier the area, the faster the board will go.

Windshift The change in the wind's direction, that can be either sudden or gradual. This becomes an important part of the tactics on upwind legs of the race as competitors reach higher standards.

Wipeout To take a major fall off the board.

Surfing

Surfers ride waves on a shaped board designed for optimum speed and stability in water. In competition, surfers are required to ride several waves, with each performance being scored separately.

Angle off Means to gradually descend the face of the wave toward the left or right.

Ankle strap Secures the leash of the surfboard to the ankle.

Backhand turn Either a natural rider's turn to the left or a goofy footer's turn to the right.

Backside To ride with one's back to the wave.

Backwash Describes a wave that reflects back to sea.

Belly A convex bottom contour.

Catch a wave To ride a breaking wave.

Chine rails Rails that are faceted or bevelled rather than rounded.

Close-out A wave that breaks all at once.

Concave A concave bottom contour.

Crest The highest point of a wave before it breaks.

Curl The curve that forms as the top of the wave breaks.

Deck The top of the surfboard.

Drop in To ride off on a wave and then slide down its face.

East swell A swell that comes in from the east.

Easterly wind Wind that blows from the east.

Ebb Term to describe a high tide changing to low tide.

Fetch The area of water the wind has to act upon in the creation of waves.

Fin box The plastic channel into which the fin slides.

Fins Placed on the bottom of a board to help give it balance.

Flood A low tide changing to high tide.

Frontside To face the wave while riding.

Glassy A wave that is smooth in appearance and texture because the water has not been disturbed by the wind.

Goofyfoot A surfer who rides with his right foot forward.

Hard rail A rail with more of a corner.

Impact zone The area in which the wave first breaks.

Juice Used to describe the power of a wave.

Kick Rocker of the nose area.

Kick-out When a surfer steps off the back of his board into a wave in order to try not to lose it in a wipeout.

Leash The cord that ties the surfer to his board.

Left A wave that breaks from left to right as viewed from the shore.

Lip That part of the wave that comes over first when the wave breaks.

Locals The name given to surfers who live in a certain area or who surf an area the most.

Lull The period between sets when the waves are small or nonexistent.

North swell A swell that moves from north to south.

Northerly wind A wind that blows from north to south.

Nose The front third of a surfboard.

Nose ride Standing and riding on the nose.

Offshore A wind that blows from the land toward the sea.

Onshore A wind that blows in from the sea toward the land.

Outside An area beyond which most set

waves are breaking.

Peak The crest or the first part of the wave to break.

Pearling When the nose of the board catches in the water.

Planing surface A surface that skims on top of the water; the bottom of the board.

Prone out Where a surfer straightens out in front of a wave and lies down on his board.

Quiver A set of surfboards that will accommodate varying conditions.

Rail The outside edge of a surfboard.

Rail radii The curve that joins the top and bottom of the surfboard.

Rail saver A nylon strap used to prevent the leash from tearing into the rail.

Regular foot When a surfer rides the board with their left foot forward and right foot back.

Right A wave that breaks right to left as viewed from the shore.

Rip The current that runs from the shore back out to sea as the water that has come in with the breaking waves escapes. Also describes radical surfing.

Screw foot To ride a surfboard with the right foot forward and left foot back.

Sets The largest waves on a given day.

Shoulder The part of a wave that hasn't broken.

REGULAR FOOT: Surfer riding left foot forward

Skeg The fin of the surfboard.

Soup The white water or foam of a broken wave.

South swell A swell moving from south to north.

Southerly wind Wind that blows from south to north.

Speed bead A resin ridge near the rail on the bottom of the board. Used to direct water flow and increase speed.

Straighten off To straighten out in front of the whitewater to escape the wave.

Surfboard Made to a surfer's specifications according to height, weight and experience. Novice surfers usually use a board with one fin, whereas experienced surfers use a three-fin board.

Surf cord A leash that attaches the surfer to the surfboard.

Surfer's ear A condition that affects surfers in which a bony growth closes the ear canal.

Swell Waves created by a common storm system.

Switch-stance Technique used by a surfer who can ride with either his left or right foot forward.

Tail The back third of a surfboard.

Trim Orienting yourself on the surfboard so it can go as fast as possible.

Trough The bottom of a wave.

Tube The tunnel inside a breaking wave.

V Flat-angled bottom contour, not curved.

West swell A swell that moves from west to east.

Westerly wind A wind that blows from west to east.

Wet suit Made of neoprene rubber, it is a one-piece suit that allows a thin layer of water inside, that is warmed by body heat and keeps the surfer warm.

White water The foam created from a breaking wave.

Wipeout To fall off the board.

Yachting

Yachting competitions are held on specially marked off courses or offshore. There are many different classes of yacht, most of them using only sail power.

Aback When the wind is on the wrong side of the sail.

Abaft Nearer the stern than a person or piece of equipment.

Abeam On the beam, that is at right angles to the boat's center-line.

Admiral's Cup An international race for teams of three Class One offshore yachts per country. It is held every two years.

America's Cup An international challenge race in which the winner is decided over nine races held every four years.

Apparent wind The wind felt by a moving boat. It is a combination of the true wind and the boat's speed through the air.

Back Slowing down the boat or turning the boat away from the wind by trimming the sails to windward.

Backing When the wind changes in a counter clockwise direction around the compass.

Backstay The rigging that stops the mast from moving forward. It stretches from the top of the mast to the stern.

Balanced lug A rig where the boom and gaff are on the leeward side of the mast.

Ballast Extra weight added to the yacht to improve its stability and to act as a counterbalance against the effects of the wind on the sails.

Bar Formed by the natural movement of the tide or current. It is often found across the mouth of a river, that makes the water levels very shallow at that point.

Batten A thin strip of wood or plastic positioned across the leech, which helps control the tautness of the sail.

Batten down To secure all hatches, portholes and loose equipment on board during stormy conditions.

Beam The widest part of a craft.

Beam reach To set sail with the wind at right angles to the line of the yacht from bow to stern.

Bear away A fall in wind strength.

Bear down on To move toward a certain object or area.

Beat To sail to windward on alternate tacks on the upwind leg of a race.

Belay Securing a rope around a cleat in figure-of-eight turns.

Bending sails To secure sails to their spars.

Bermudan The most common rig used. It sets a high triangular mainsail with the luff parallel to the mast and the foot attached to the main boom.

Bilge The curve of the hull from the topsides to the bottom of the boat.

Bilge keel A fin that is attached to the bilges to gain extra stability.

Blue Peter The flag hoisted five minutes before the start of a race. It is blue in color with a white rectangle in the center.

Bolt rope Gives added strength to a sail by sewing a rope along the edge of it.

Boom The spar positioned at a right angle to the mast in order to hold the foot of the sail along its length.

Bow The forward end of a craft.

Bowsprit The spar leaning forward of the bows in order to set either an extra or bigger foresail.

Bring up To stop or come up to anchor.

Burgee A flag that indicates the club a yachtsman belongs to. It is either a small triangular flag or a swallow-tail flag.

Cat rig The rig used to hold only one sail, the mainsail.

Catamaran A twin-hulled yacht that has its two hulls held together parallel to each other by a bridge deck.

Center-board A flat piece of wood or metal placed through a slot on the center line of the hull to enable the yacht to steer a course close to the wind.

Cleat A T-shaped fitting used to secure ropes to.

Clew The lower aft corner of a sail where the leech meets the foot.

Close hauled To sail as close to the wind as possible.

Committee boat A boat staffed by the race officers and placed so that they can control the races. It is sometimes used to form one end of the starting line.

Cutter rig A yacht that has two or more foresails as well as the mainsail.

Draft The measurement of the hull from the waterline to the lowest part of the keel. It determines the amount of water needed to sail the boat.

Draw Describes the sails when filled with wind.

Drop keel Also known as the center-board or center-plate.

Ease sheets To let out the sheets, or to alter the course away from the wind.

Eye of the wind The direction from that the wind blows.

Fall The section of the halyard where the crew member pulls.

Fathom The nautical measurement of depth equal to 6ft. Also used as a measurement for lengths of rope.

Feather the rig The action of slowing the yacht down while still staying in control of the boat.

Flake To stash a rope in a serpentine fashion so that it can be let out easily.

Foot The lower edge of the sail.

Foresail Any sail that is positioned ahead of the main mast.

Forestay The rigging positioned from the front of the mast to the bow.

Free Describes the wind when it is blowing from the beam or abaft.

Freeboard The hull positioned above the waterline.

Gaff A spar that is placed at the top of a four-cornered sail.

Genoa A large jib (headsail) that reaches aft of the mast to overlap the mainsail.

Go about Sailing from one tack to the other, making the bows pass through the eye of the wind so that it blows on the opposite side of the sails.

Gooseneck The fitting that joins the spar to the mast.

Gunter rig A rig that sets a triangular mainsail with the upper part of the leading edge of a sail that is attached to a vertical yard.

Guy A piece of wire or rope that holds a spar in place.

Halyard The rope or wire used to hoist and lower flags, sails or spars.

Handicap The time allowance given to yachts whose rating is very low when not at racing level.

Hank The clip that holds the leading edge of a sail to a stay.

Harden in To haul in the sheets.

Head The top corner of a triangular sail or the top side of a gaff sail.

Headsail A sail set in front of the mast.

Head up When the course is changed toward the wind.

Heave to By keeping the bow head onto the wind or sea, the yacht can be brought to a stop.

Helm A piece of equipment attached to the rudder in order to steer the yacht. It is normally either a tiller or a wheel.

Helm down When the tiller is put into a leeward direction so that the bow turns to windward.

Helmsman The crew member who steers the yacht with the helm.

In irons When a yacht is stopped head to wind and becomes unsteerable.

IYRU The International Yacht Racing Union, which is in charge of governing world yachting.

Jib Also known as the leading headsail.

Jibe Changing course away from the wind when sailing downwind.

Jury rig A temporary rigging made if the standard rig is broken.

Kedge To move a boat by pulling on the anchor rope, hauling up the anchor, re-anchoring and then repeating the maneuvers again.

Keel boat A yacht with ballast added to the bottom of the hull.

Kicking strap A wire or rope attached from the foot of the mast to the boom, which stops the boom from rising when the sheets are eased.

Knot A nautical mile, that measures 1.1 mile.

Lee bowing Occurs by sailing across a tidal stream with the current flowing against the lee bow.

Lee helm A yacht that has a tendency to turn its bow away from the wind.

Leech The aft edge of a sail.

Lee shore The shore on which the wind is blowing.

Leeward The side of the yacht opposite to which on that the wind is blowing.

Leeway The sideways movement of a boat to leeward when in motion.

Leg The stretch of water between two racing marks.

LOA Abbreviation for "length overall", describing the extreme measurement of the hull from stem to stern.

Luff The leading edge of a sail.

Luffing To slow a boat down or to take the pressure out of the sails to allow the crew to haul in sheets.

Lugrig A rig used to set a lugsail.

Lugsail A four-sided sail, most of which extends forward past the mast.

BERMUDAN CAT RIG: Specifically for one man races, often used, with a high triangular mainsail

Mainsail The principal sail, joined to the main mast.

Mare's tails Describes white feathered clouds that foretell an increase in the force of the wind.

Mark Buoys, posts or other markers that are used to mark off the racing course. They must be round on the specified side.

Mast A vertical spar from that the sails are set.

Miss stays Occurs when the helmsman of a boat falls short of moving the vessel on to a new tack and it reverts to the original one.

Mizzen A mast smaller in size than the main mast and set aft of it.

Multihull A yacht with more than one hull, such as a catamaran or a trimaran.

Neaped When a boat runs aground during the spring tides and does not have enough water on the next tide to move off.

Neaps Tides that have the smallest range of rise and fall.

Obstruction to sea room When other vessels or objects block a yacht and force it to alter its course in order to avoid a collision.

Off the wind When a vessel is not close hauled.

Overlap When the bow of a yacht moves ahead of the stern of another.

Pay off When a yacht turns the bow away from the wind in order to fill her sails.

Peak The upper aft corner of a four-sided sail.

Pinching When a yacht sails too close to the wind, leaving the sails unable to draw properly.

Planing Describes skimming over the water instead of going through it.

Points The points of the compass. In all there are 32.

Pooped When a boats runs before a stormy sea when a wave breaks over its stern.

Port The left-hand side of a craft.

Port tack To sail with the wind coming in from the port side.

Rake The angle of a boat's mast off its vertical line.

Reefing Describes reducing the sail area. Happens because the wind force suddenly increases.

Rig The setup of the sails, masts and spars on a yacht. A yacht is defined by its rig when put into classes for competition.

Rigging Describes the standing and running ropes aboard a yacht.

Roach The curved edge of the leech.

Running Describes a boat sailing downwind.

Running rigging The halyards and the sheets.

Sheets The ropes used to trim the sails.

Shrouds The rigging wires that run from the mast to the side of the boat.

Sloop A yacht that is rigged to set one foresail as well as the mainsail.

Spar A solid or hollow piece of wood or metal on that a sail is set. It may be a boom, a gaff or a mast.

Spinnaker A three-sided sail that is cut very full and positioned past the mast in order to increase speed when running or broad reaching.

Spritsail A four-sided sail that is almost rectangular in shape.

Standing rigging The stays and shrouds that keep the mast in place.

Starboard Right-hand side of a boat.

Starboard tack When a yacht sails with the wind coming in from the starboard side.

Stays The wires that run from the top of the mast to fore and aft of the yacht and brace the mast.

Step The point at that the bottom of the mast is secured.

Tabernacle The box where the mast is pinned and secured. It projects over the deck.

Tack The bottom forward corner of a sail where the luff and foot join.

Tier The band of canvas that attaches the mainsail to the boom when lowered.

Tiller The lever placed on top of the head of the rudder and held by the helmsman in order to steer the yacht.

Topsides The side of the hull above the waterline.

Transom The name of the flat board forming the stern of a yacht.

Trapeze A wire and harness used by a crew member so that they are able to go outside of the boat in heavy weather and balance it.

Trimming Adjusting the sails with the sheets to fill or empty them of wind as needed.

Unbend To move a sail away from its spar.

Veering The wind changing direction clockwise around the compass.

Wear To alter course while the vessel's stern is into the wind.

Weather helm Describes a boat whose bow turns into the wind.

Windward The side of the boat on to that the wind blows.

Yacht Originates from the Dutch term "ship for chasing".

Yard A spar slung from a mast on that a sail is hung.

Yaw When the boat goes off course due to bad steering or wrongly trimmed sails.

Swimming

Swimming competitions are held in four major categories: freestyle, breaststroke, butterfly and backstroke, over a variety of distances. They include both individual and team events.

Action Any movement of the limbs in swimming.

Aerobic An energy system used when exercising, especially for endurance work, to supply energy over a long period of time. Needs a good supply of oxygen.

Aids Any object, usually buoyant, that helps swimmers to get used to moving around in the water or to help practice arm or leg movements.

Anaerobic An energy system used when exercising, especially for sprinting, as it supplies a limited amount of energy quickly. It does not use atmospheric oxygen.

Alternate stokes Describes back- and front-crawl strokes (see individual entries for more detail).

Aquatic The skilled control of breathing while the head is partially or completely submerged under water.

Arm-up start Similar to the track start, but the arm opposite the forward foot is swung back and held up high in the air while the other hand grips the front of the starting block.

Back-paddle Swimming on the back with the legs making a crawl-like kick and the arms remaining by the side, with the hands making propeller-type movements.

Backstroke Method of swimming in which the swimmer lies on their back and propels themselves forward by using a windmill maneuver with the arms, while the feet perform a flutter kick. It is the only stroke in which competitors start in the water. This stroke is the third-fastest of the four racing styles.

Ballistic A fast flinging action of the arms in recovery.

Bent arm The most effective way of using the arms in all swimming strokes.

Biathlon Competitive event that combines running and swimming.

Bilateral Breathing to alternate sides every third arm stroke.

Bow wave A wall of water in front of the head created by the swimmer moving quickly.

Breaststroke Method of swimming in which the arms pull back simultaneously with a circular motion and are pushed forward together from under the chest, the legs are drawn up together with the feet turned out and kick out and back. The arms and legs remain underneath the water at all times. This is the slowest of the four racing styles.

Broken swim A race swam over the actual race distance at racing speed with short rest breaks at intervals.

Buoyancy Determined by three factors: lean body mass (muscles and bones etc.), body fat and the air in the lungs, that affect a swimmer's flotation in the water.

Butterfly Method of swimming in which the arms and legs move simultaneously. The arms pull back and recover above the water to the starting position. The legs kick in a simultaneous vertical dolphin movement. It is the second-fastest stroke.

Catch point The point at which the hands begin to exert pressure on the water during a stroke.

Catch up Also known as sliding or

BUTTERFLY: The second-fastest swimming stroke, with arms and legs moving simultaneously

overlap. Occurs when the swimmer uses a crawl stroke where one arm waits just before the catch point for the other arm to join it.

Cross-over kick Kick in which one leg kicks across the other.

Disqualification Occurs if a competitor impedes or obstructs the progress of another swimmer, appears late at the starting blocks, fails to follow instructions, walks on the floor of the pool (except in a freestyle event), uses aids to get ahead, finishes in a lane other than their own or uses foul language.

Dog paddle Describes swimming on the front while using an alternating crawl leg kick and arm action with an underwater recovery.

Dolphin kick A flexible vertical leg kick where both the legs and lower trunk move through the water with an action resembling a dolphin.

Dorsi-flexed Means that the toes are pulled up toward the shins.

Drag Resistance in the water.

Drill Exercises performed to improve technique.

Elbow leading An arm action that sees the forearm slipping inefficiently back through the water.

Endurance The ability to keep exerting force against a resistance.

Entry The point at which the hand enters the water for its underwater stroke.

Explosive breathing Breathing technique in which air is blown out quickly and forcefully before a new breath is taken.

Extension The opening of a joint in a limb.

False start Occurs when a competitor starts before the starting signal is given. One false start is allowed, but a second incurs automatic disqualification.

False-start rope A rope used to stop swimmers if the starter decides that a race has started without his consent.

Fast pool Describes a pool specifically built to use deep water, effective lane lines and wave-restraining gutters, all of which can help produce faster times.

FINA The Fédération Internationale de

Natation Amateur, which is the world governing body for swimming.

Finals The final race of an event that decides the overall winner. The fastest swimmers from the heats go on to the final race.

Flags Lined across the pool to warn backstroke swimmers that the turn is imminent. They should be placed 5.5yd from the end of the pool.

Flight The part of the dive that occurs in the air.

Flutter kick A vertical leg kick where the legs move alternately.

Flyer An outgoing relay swimmer who leaves the starting block before the incoming swimmer touches base. This results in immediate disqualification.

Freestyle Any stroke may be used for this event, although generally competitors use the front crawl because this is the fastest of the four racing styles.

Freestyle relays A swimming race in that four swimmers each swim a leg or section using any stroke.

Front crawl Starting from the prone position, the swimmer then pulls the arms alternately down and back under the body and recovers above water while the legs perform the flutter kick.

Glide A streamlined, arrow-like position as the body moves through the water with no arm or leg action. Can be performed on the water's surface or below it, and on the front or back.

Grab start The swimmer starts by grabbing the starting block and placing the hands either between or outside the feet, pulling on the block to then over-balance into the water, therefore achieving a faster start.

Heats The preliminary rounds to the finals where competitors line up either at random, by seeding or by grading.

High elbow A form of arm recovery in the front crawl with the arm close to the head and the elbow well flexed. It also describes a technique used in all strokes in which the arms are flexed, with the forearm pointing down when level with the shoulders.

High-lift style A style of breaststroke used to increase speed.

Hungarian repetitions A training technique using both long and short distances with regular intervals.

Hypothermia The loss of heat from the core of the body.

Hypoxic training A technique used by swimmers to improve their tolerance of oxygen debt. This is done by swimming short distances without breathing.

Inertia A resistance to movement.

Interval training Swimming a series of repeats with a controlled rest in between.

Intoeing When the feet are turned inward to give greater extension, making the foot a more effective paddle.

Keyhole pull The shape of the butterfly pull when seen from below. The hands enter in front of the shoulders and pull out and down and then together, until they almost touch under the stomach, before pushing back and slightly out.

Kick Part of a stroke in which the legs and feet are used.

Kickboard A rectangular-shaped float used when practicing leg movements. Made of polystyrene, it is also known as kick float.

Lanes Each competitor is given their own lane to swim in. They are numbered from the right-hand side facing the course, and should be 7ft wide.

Leg The distance swam by one member of the relay team.

Leisure pool A swimming pool specifically designed for leisure activities.

Lifesaving To learn how to save a person in difficulty in the water, and the practice of resuscitation.

Long course Refers to events held in

a 55yd pool.

Long-distance swimming Any type of open-water swimming such as lake, river or sea events. One of the most famous events is the swimming of the English Channel.

Medley events In individual events, competitors swim a sequence of butterfly, backstroke, breaststroke and freestyle. In the relay events, competitors swim a sequence of backstroke, breaststroke, butterfly and freestyle.

Meet The name given to a gathering of swimmers from more than one organization to compete against each other.

Negative split Swimming the second half of a race faster than the first half.

Olympic pool A 55yd pool that is divided into eight lanes.

Over-center entry Occurs during the front and back crawl. Describes the swimmer reaching across the centerline of their body when their hand enters the water.

Oxygen debt The amount of oxygen needed to return the body to normal.

Physiology The study of how the body functions.

Pitch The angle at which the hands and feet move through the water.

Placing judges Adjudicate on the order in which swimmers finish a race.

Plantar-flexion The pointing of the feet and toes when swimming.

Prone Describes a swimmer lying flat on their front.

Propulsion Movement through the water as a result of leg or arm action.

Pull Part of the stroke performed by the arms.

Pullbuoy A float held between the legs when practicing arm movements.

Pulling Training technique in which only the arms are used.

Push-and-glide position The swimmer's body is fully extended to become as streamlined as possible. The movement is used to push off from the poolside to glide through the water.

Recorder Keeps a complete record of race results.

Recovery Movements that return the limb to its original position.

Reducing swims The swimmer's pace is gradually increased over the repetition swims, with the swimmer approaching his best time on the last swim.

Relays Consists of four competitors per team who swim in sequence.

Resistance The way in which water acts against the solid mass of a swimmer's body and slows down their progress.

Screw kick An ineffective breast-stroke leg action.

Sculling Using small hand movements to aid propulsion with the change in pitch.

Semifinal The second round of eliminator races between heats.

Short course Refers to events held in 27yd pools.

Sidestroke Describes swimming to the side. Originated from breast stroke.

Simultaneous strokes Describes both the breast-stroke and the butterfly.

Sitting dive The swimmer sits on the edge of the pool with their feet placed on the rail. The knees are kept together and the back is rounded so that the head is pointed toward the water, with the arms pressed against the ears and one hand on top of the other.

Slow pool A pool that is not conducive to swimmers achieving a fast time.

Spearhead principle The arrangement of swimmers in finals. They are placed in accordance with their heat time so that the fastest swimmers are in the center of the pool with the slowest being in the outside lanes.

Splits Intermediate times taken during a race.

Sprint training A swimmer has to swim as fast as possible over a distance of 5yd-25yd.

S-pull A backstroke arm action. The arm makes the shape of an S in the water.

Standing dive Both feet grip the edge of the pool standing hip-width apart. The body is bent at the knees and hip, with the upper body, head and arms curved and pointing at the water.

Start Backstroke competitors start in the water, whereas all other competitors begin from starting blocks.

Starter Ensures that each swimmer is in the correct lane and is in control until the race begins. They use the command "on your marks" to start the race.

Starting block The raised platform from which a swimmer starts their race. It has a non-slip surface.

Straight arm When the arm is held straight, it produces less propulsion and is therefore less effective than using a bent arm stroke, that uses a shorter lever and results in a faster action.

Stroke cycle One complete arm and leg action in any stroke.

Stroke judges Ensure that each competitor's strokes adhere to the rules.

Sweep The movement pattern of the hand through the water in order to achieve propulsion.

Time control swim A training method. Floats are positioned every 5.5yd down each side of the pool, with the swimmers opposite the floats. They then swim for a set time, with the distance achieved being noted. After a rest period they repeat this while trying to better the distance in the same time.

Timed final Competitions in which heats are swam, with the final placements being determined by times recorded in the heats.

Timing system The electronic equipment used during major competitions to operate the starting Klaxon for each lane, the finishing touch pads, and the automatic readout of finishing times and positions of the competitors.

Touch Each competitor must touch the end of the pool at a turn and at the finish in order for the race to be valid.

Track start One foot is placed over the edge of the starting block, with the other placed behind. Both hands grip the front edge of the block, with the head facing down.

Transition The period of time for which the swimmer is underwater during a start or turn.

Treading water A way of staying afloat in the water. The legs are kept vertical and perform a breaststroke kick; the arms scull close to the surface.

Tumble turn Fast way of turning at the pool wall by performing a forward roll.

Turn To change direction at the end of the pool to start another length.

Undulation The unavoidable but controllable movements of the head, trunk and legs in butterfly. Caused by the overwater arm recovery.

Wedge kick A breaststroke leg action that is wider than a whip kick.

Whip kick The name given to the breaststroke leg action. The hips are held in a high position while the feet move in a circular motion to full extension, accelerating throughout. The heels are placed close to the seat.

Wide entry Used in both front crawl and back crawl. Caused by the hand entering the water outside the line of its own shoulder.

Wind-up start A start used in relay exchanges in that momentum is built up by circling the arms.

Synchronized Swimming

Competitors are judged on their performance of set swimming movements performed to a musical accompaniment. They perform compulsory figures and swimming routines. There are polos, duets and team routines.

TEAM COMPETITION: In the synchronized team event, teams of up to eight swimmers perform to music

Arm action Used by a swimmer for expression and to maintain as much height as possible.

Back crawl A swimmer will lie with their back in the water, with the head raised and looking up. The arm moves in a straight clockwise direction, with the legs having an alternating flutter-kick working in the vertical plane.

Back layout A swimmer lies horizontally on their back in the water. The toes, thighs, hips and face will all be near the water surface. The body is stationary.

Back-pike position This movement is a closed-pike position. The swimmer's body is bent sharply at the hips and the trunk is straight. Legs are kept close together and the aim is to keep the position as compact as possible.

Bent-arm back crawl As the swimmer's arm leaves the water, it is bent during recovery with a high elbow.

Bent-arm front crawl When a swimmer's arm leaves the water, it can be bent and then shows a high elbow in recovery. The arm underwater then sculls to balance.

Bent-knee position The body can be in a front, back or side layout. One foot is raised above the other leg until the big toe of the bent leg is above the knee of the extended leg.

Body position A swimmer's body is tucked with the hips underneath the water. The head is raised and steady with the eyes looking directly forward. The facial expression is cheerful.

Breaststroke A movement a swimmer uses that entails their head being held high and steady with the legs providing a wedge kick, that bends and drives the swimmer through the water.

Compact tuck position A movement used during back-and-forward rotation. From the back layout position, a swimmer tucks their knees into the chest, with the legs pushed close together and feet wrapped around the bottom.

Double ballet-leg position A swimmer takes up the flamingo position. Both legs should then be pressed together with their toes pointed and in line with their thighs.

Double-circle routine A surface routine for 12 swimmers, using a double-circle formation. Beats of the music will be counted by the swimmer.

Duet Two swimmers perform a routine to music. Their average compulsory figures are added to the technical merit and artistic-impression marks for the final total.

Egg beater kick This is frequently used by a swimmer instead of the front-crawl flutter kick. It involves an alternate downward pressure that is continuous, and the body is able to travel more smoothly with stability. It is possible to gain a lot of height with this kick and change direction if the swimmer wishes to do so in their routine.

Figure competition All competitors perform the same four FINA (Federation Internationale de Natation Amateur) figures before the same judges. Each figure is specified and require to be practiced for a long time. These figures include two compulsory figures, and the referee of the event will draw one group of two figures prior to the event. Each figure has a degree of difficulty attached to it to show the difference between the four figures to be performed. Each judge gives a mark out of 10 (marked in tenths).

Flamingo position A swimmer takes up the single ballet-leg position. The horizontal leg is taken along the surface and then pressed to the chest. At all times during this position, the knee and foot of the bent leg will remain at the water surface. The swimmer's head will rest in the water with their head looking up.

Flat scull A supporting scull employed when the body is held stationary.

Front layout The swimmer's body faces down onto the water with the heels, head and hips all at the surface. The face can be in the water or out of it.

Front pike position A swimmer takes up the front layout position and then bends their body at the hips to form a 90-degree angle. Their legs are straight together with their toes pointed.

Hybrid strokes All swimmers will learn to use more imaginative variations to the standard strokes, each one to different pieces of music.

Inverted-vertical position The body is extended in a vertical line, with the legs and feet above the surface of the water. The whole body should be straight, with the head, body, hips and legs in line. The head will be in line with the body underneath the water.

Judging figures Each figure is judged on whether it is performed high, controlled and in uniform motion with each section clearly defined. There may be one, two, three or four panels of judges, with each panel containing five or seven judges.

Leg action A swimmer will incline their body to a sufficient degree to produce an efficient leg kick. This propels the body and keeps it up.

Officials FINA (the world governing body of swimming) rules state that there must be a referee, an assistant referee, 5–7 judges for figures, 5–7 judges for technical merit, 5–7 judges for artistic impression, a chief scorer and three additional scorers.

Penalties Should a swimmer perform an incorrect figure, a two-point penalty is given. During routines, swimmers are penalized if the deck work is more than 10 seconds and the routine is over the permitted time. For solos, the permitted time is 3min 30sec.; duets, 4min.; teams, 5min.

Pool The pool area should be at least 13yd in length and width. The depth of water for competition and figure work needs to be 10ft, and for routines it has to be 6.5ft. The water has to be clear enough for the bottom of the pool to be visible.

Reverse scull A propelling scull movement used for traveling feet first. The body position is the same as that for a standard scull, but the arms are held straight by the side and the figure-eight movement is used with the pressure going toward the head.

Routine competition A competition may consist of a minimum of two sections: figures, technical and free routines. There are three events: solo, duet and teams. When a figure section is included, each swimmer's score is carried forward to the free routine section. In technical and free routines, the scores are added together. A team may consist of at least four and not more than eight swimmers. For each swimmer less than eight, a half-point deduction is made during routines.

Scoring figures Each figure or routine performance is marked with scores from zero to 10 with half-point increases by each judge.

Side layout The body should start off in the back layout with the arms stretched out. The body then rotates to the side on which the swimmer wishes to lie. It can be arched or extended depending on the figure they are about to perform.

Single ballet-leg position A swimmer starts off in a back layout. One leg takes up the bent-knee position and is straightened until it becomes vertical. Their hips, knees and toes should all be in a straight line. When the leg is returned to the bent-knee position, the thigh must remain vertical.

Standard scull A propeling scull movement used for traveling headfirst. The swimmer begins in a back layout with the body extended and the face, hips, knees and toes at the surface. The arms are held at the side with straight elbows, with the wrists hyperextended. The hands make a figure-eight movement.

Straight-arm back crawl As the swimmer's arm leaves the water, it is held straight and firm with the thumb clearing the water first. When the extended arm reaches the vertical, it is rotated so that it goes into the water before the head.

Straight-arm front crawl The swimmer's extended arm leaves the water with thumb up. The body is pushed onto the side and the arm re-enters the water with their thumb first.

Tap-tap back crawl As an example, the right arm of a swimmer leaving the water is held straight and firmly with the thumb clearing the water first. The arm moves across the body with the palm face down.

Team At least four and not more than eight swimmers performing a routine to music at the same time.

Tub position Starting in the backward position, the swimmer rests their knees, lower legs and feet on the surface of the water until their thighs are vertical and above their hips. They then lower into the water as the knees bend.

Diving

Diving is a specialized sport and requires its competitors to combine agility and strength with balance and coordination. There are two main categories: the springboard and the high board.

Arm stand Performed only on the highboard. The diver starts off in a handstand position at the end of the board.

Back dive The diver starts the dive with their back to the pool, and lands in the water backward.

SPRINGBOARD DIVING: Diving from a flexed and springy board, giving the diver extra height

Back fall in The diver stands on the balls of the feet at the end of the board with the arms raised above the head, hands together while looking straight ahead. Then they overbalance slowly, reaching back with the head and arms. The head should be kept slightly back,

with the arch in the upper back and the arms closed ready for entry.

Back jump straight The diver enters the water backward with the feet entering the water first and the hands touching the thighs.

Back jump tucked The diver enters the water backward with the knees held up to the chest in a tight tucked position with the head held upright, before extending the legs downward and having the body fully straight on entry into the water.

Back somersault tucked The diver gets a good spring on takeoff, reaching up with his arms. The body moves into an upward backward reach before going into a tuck. The diver brings his knees up to his chest and grips his shins. The elbows are tucked into the sides before entering the water feet first.

Backward dive straight Reaching up with the hands while keeping the head and shoulders forward until the peak of the dive. The body should be kept straight during flight. The next stage is for the head to move slowly back with the arms pulled back to enter the water first.

Belly flop An incorrect dive where the diver's body smacks down flat on to the water. Normally caused by too high a head position during the flight.

Break-out When a diver changes his position during flight from a tuck or pike to the straight entry position.

Crouch dive The diver gets into a crouched position and curls the toes of the front foot around the edge of the pool with the other foot placed slightly behind to gain stability. The arms and hands are pointed at the entry point with the head tucked in. The diver then pushes off from the feet, straightening at the knees to dive in.

Dive groups There are six official groups of dives: forward, backward, reverse, inward, twist and arm stand.

Diving list Tells the divers what dives are required of them in a competition.

Draw Used by the judges to decide who will go in what order for the competitions.

Entries Each diver must hand their list of dives to the secretary before the competition starts. If they do not perform the dives listed, they will be penalized.

Entry The moment when the diver enters the water after flight. Also the manner and shape of the body as it enters the water.

Failed dive A dive performed that the referee is sure was not listed in the entry list.

Flight The moment between takeoff and entry into the water when the diver is in the air.

Forward dive A dive in that the diver stands facing the water on take-off and enters the water facing forward.

Forward dive piked The arms are raised up and the legs are straightened. They are then drawn forward to move the body into a piked position with the hands touching the toes. Holding this position until the trunk rotates bringing the upper body near vertical, they then open out with the legs lifting and the arms moving forward to a point above the head for entry.

Forward dive tucked At the peak of the dive, the knees are raised into a tuck position. The body then rotates as the head drops with the body stretching and the arms above the head to enter the water.

Forward jump piked The arms reach forward and up with the legs together being raised into the pike position. The arms then reach down with the hands touching pointed toes before the body straightens out for entry, with the feet going into the water first.

Forward jump straight On take-off, the arms lift forward and upward. The head should be upright with the body vertical. After the peak of the jump, the arms sweep sideways and down to the thighs for a feet-first entry.

Forward jump full twist A progression to a full twist dive, that can be either to the left or right. One arm reaches with the shoulder pulling backward and dropping behind the head with the other arm swinging across the body in the direction of the twist. When one twist has been completed, the arms are moved sideways to check the twist before entry into the water.

Forward jump tucked The body is fully extended before the knees are raised to the chest in a tucked position. This position is held momentarily before the feet are shot down for a vertical entry with the hands positioned at the sides.

Forward one-and-a-half somersault piked The diver reaches up with the hands while lifting the hips into a tight pike. He then performs a one-and-a-quarter somersault before lifting the head and shoulders toward the point of entry.

Forward one-and-a-half somersault tucked The diver pushes vertically up and reaches high up with the arms while lifting the hips. The heels are then brought up and back toward the seat, with the arms, head and shoulders pressed into a tucked position with the arms holding the shins. This is held for one-and-a-quarter turns before opening out with the legs extending and pressing backward with the arms reaching for a stretched entry.

Free A dive that involves using a straight, pike or tuck body position when performing a twisting dive.

Highboard diving Also known as platform or tower diving. Competitors dive from a rigid platform positioned 16ft, 23ft or 33ft high.

Hurdle An upward jump on one foot taken before the final two-footed jump in running for a dive.

Inward dive The dive is started with the competitor facing backward towards the board, but the diver turns in the air and enters the water facing away from the board.

Inward dive piked On leaving the board, the diver jumps up and back while rotating forward with the hips up above the shoulders. The arms move forward and down to touch the toes before moving into a vertical figure with the hands going into the water first.

Inward dive tucked Pushing high, the shoulders and hips are kept over the board until the upward drive. The legs are then lifted with the knees forward into a tuck. The diver then stretches the body for entry when a half-somersault is completed.

Isander The original name for the reverse dive. Named after its Swedish creator.

Judges Up to seven judges can sit on the panel. After each dive, the referee will signal to the judges to hold up their scores. The maximum score for each dive is 10 points.

Lunge dive The diver starts off in the split stance with the front knee slightly bent, the toes gripping the edge of the pool and the body leaning forward from the hips. The back leg should be straight, with the push made off the front leg.

Mollberg The original name for the reverse somersault dive. Named after its Swedish creator.

Notification of dives Each competitor must hand in their complete statement of the dives they have selected at least 24 hours before the start.

Pike The body position used in somersaults. The diver bends his body at the hips while keeping his knees straight.

Plummet line A vertical line that extends through the center point of the front edge of the diving springboard or platform. Used as a basic measuring point of reference.

Plunge dive The diver stands with his feet slightly apart, his toes gripping the edge, his knees slightly bent and his body in a horizontal position. The diver pushes off with the legs.

Points system Completely failed, zero points; unsatisfactory 0.5–2 points; deficient, 2.5–4.5 points; satisfactory, 5–6 points; good, 6.5–8 points; and very good, 8.5–10 points.

Preliminaries The first round or series of dives in a competition.

Required A specific dive that each contestant is required to perform.

Reverse dive This dive is started with the diver facing forward, but is ended by entry into the water in a backward position by pulling the feet forward and upward.

Saving Describes underwater maneuvers performed by the divers in order to allow them to either attain or maintain the correct entry position.

Scratches Means that a diver has decided to withdraw from a competition.

Secretary The official in charge of recording the marks awarded by the judges. He/she works out the scores for each dive and diver.

Sitting dive The swimmer sits on the edge of the pool with their feet placed on the rail. The knees are kept together and the back is rounded so that the head is pointed at the water, with the arms pressed against the ears and one hand on top of the other.

Somersault Requires the diver to rotate their body around its center of gravity. They can use the straight, piked or tucked positions.

Springboard Measures 20in in width and 16ft in length, and is set at 3.3ft or 3.3yd above the surface of the water. It is made of flexible material with a non-skid surface.

Standing dive Both feet grip the edge of the pool standing hip-width apart. The body is bent at the knees and hip, with the upper body, head and arms curved and pointing at the water.

Straight Body position used during a dive. The body and legs must be kept completely straight.

Swallow dive Describes a forward dive with the arms held out to the side until entry into the water.

Takeoff The point at which a diver leaves the board, block or side to dive into the water.

Tariff Describes the established figure from that the judges' marks are multiplied to gain the total score for a specific dive. Can also be described as the degree of difficulty for each dive.

Trampoline Used by divers for practicing routines.

Tuck Body position used by a diver during a somersault. The diver brings his knees up to his chest and holds them in place with his hands.

Twist Describes a sideways rotation around the body's longitudinal axis.

SWALLOW DIVE: Diver faces forwards with their hands held out straight to the side of the body until entry into water

Scuba Diving

Scuba diving involves diving to depths of up to 50m using breathing apparatus. It is an exciting sport with a strong emphasis on safety. Skin diving, without any breathing apparatus, explores shallow waters.

A-clamp Screw fitting that connects the regulator to the pillar valve.

A-flag International signal that indicates that a diver is down. Must always be flown by the cover boat, but can also be placed on the surface marker buoy.

Alveoli The air sacs in the lungs where gaseous exchange takes place.

Anoxia A total lack of oxygen.

Assisted ascent Describes an ascent where two divers share one Aqua-Lung.

Atmospheric pressure Force exerted by air at sea level, measured in atmospheres (atm) or bars.

Bends Colloquial name for decompression illness. So called because bending the affected limb relieves the pain.

Bezel The adjustable ring on a watch or compass used to set time or bearing.

Bottom time The time lapse between the start of descent and start of ascent.

Breath hold dive To dive without any breathing apparatus. Also known as skin diving or snorkeling.

Buddy The name given to a companion diver.

Buoyant ascent Ascent made with extra buoyancy gained from a buoyancy compensator or dry-suit inflation, or even through ditching a weight belt.

Buoyancy compensator Also known as a stabilizer jacket. A buoyancy jacket that can be inflated (and deflated) with air from the scuba unit in order to adjust neutral buoyancy.

Buoyancy trim Adjusting buoyancy with weights to achieve neutral buoyancy at the start of a dive.

Compressed air Describes breathing gas used by the majority of scuba divers. It is ordinary air compressed to high pressure, and is made up of 79 percent nitrogen and 21 percent oxygen.

Cracking Opening the cylinder tap or pillar valve carefully to allow a short burst of air to escape.

Cylinder A pressure vessel used to contain the diver's breathing gas. The compressed air is usually made up of nitrox or a mixture of other gases.

Dead air space The air space in the respiratory system that takes no part in gaseous exchange. These are the trachea, nasal passages and pharynx.

Decompression illness A diving disorder that is caused by bubbles of nitrogen forming in body tissues and the bloodstream. Also known as the bends.

Decompression stop A planned pause in the final stages of descent from a dive. Performed by pausing close to the surface to ensure the elimination of any excess nitrogen and therefore stop decompression sickness.

Decompression tables Used to allow divers to calculate safe depths, times and rates of ascent during a dive.

Depth gauge Used to measure and indicate ambient depths.

Ditching Means to abandon equipment and/or the weight belt to gain buoyancy.

Drift diving Diving when the tidal stream or current carries the diver along underwater.

Dump valve A valve placed on the buoyancy compensator that rapidly releases air to stop an uncontrolled descent.

Ear clearing A technique of balancing pressure on the ear drum by forcing air up the eustachian tube to the inside of the eardrum. Can be achieved by holding the nose and blowing gently against the pressure.

Expired Air Resuscitation (EAR) An emergency method used to restart breathing. Performed by either using the mouth-to-mouth or mouth-to-nose procedure. Also known as artificial ventilation (AV).

First stage The part of the regulator that attaches to the cylinder. It reduces the pressure of air from the cylinder before it is set to the second stage.

Free ascent An emergency procedure used to return to the surface. The diver swims or floats to the surface while breathing all the way up.

Freeboard Describes the height of the boat's side above the surface of the sea.

Gunwale Upper edge of a boat's side.

Hard-hat divers The traditional and old-fashioned image of the diver who wears a bulbous helmet.

Hydrostatic pressure Ambient water pressure at any point. Increases with descent and decreases with ascent.

Log book Used to keep both a personal record of diving qualifications and dives performed.

Negative buoyancy Means that you are heavier than the water you displace and will therefore sink.

Neutral buoyancy Describes the state where a diver neither sinks nor floats but maintains the same position.

Nitrox Air to that extra oxygen has been added, for example, 32 percent oxygen and 68 percent nitrogen. The use of nitrox delays the threshold of DCI (decompression illness).

No-stop dive A dive where the depth and the length of time of the dive means that no stops for stage decompression are needed during ascent.

Octopus rig A spare second stage that, when attached to your regulator first stage, can be used by another diver.

O-ring The washer in the pillar valve that forms an airtight seal for the regulator.

Positive buoyancy Means that you are lighter than the water you displace and will therefore float.

Purge valve A button on the second-stage unit. Pressing will induce a continuous flow of air to clear water from the mouthpiece.

Recompression chamber (RCC) Used to recompress a diver and then slowly decompress them back to atmospheric pressure at a controlled rate. Used to treat decompression illness and other pressure-related injuries.

SCUBA Self-Contained Underwater Breathing Apparatus comprises an air cylinder, buoyancy compensator, regulator and contents gauge.

Second stage Describes the part of the regulator including the mouthpiece, the purge valve and the exhaust valve.

Skin diving To dive without any breathing equipment.

Staged decompression Stopping at set depths and times in the final stages of ascent to allow excess nitrogen to escape from the body.

Surface marker buoy A buoy trailed by a diver to show the surface party their approximate underwater location.

Tender A surface diving assistant linked to the diver by a lifeline.

Venting Deliberate release of air from a dry suit or a buoyancy compensator.

Weight belt Used to carry weights. Needed to achieve neutral buoyancy.

Wet suit Diving suit that traps a film of water at body temperature

Water Polo

Water polo can be described as a form of water handball. It is a team sport played by both sexes that demands that its participants are not only excellent swimmers with good mobility in the water but are able to shoot and catch, preferably with either hand.

Advantage Used to keep the pace of the game going. At the referee's discretion the game can be continued if he feels that to stop it would be disadvantageous to the nonoffending team.

Ball Must be round in shape, fully inflated and completely waterproof. Its circumference must be between 27in-28in for men and between 25in-26in for women with a weight between 14oz and 16oz.

Bat shot Also known as a knuckle shot. Occurs when the ball is flicked into the air with one hand and batted with the open hand or knuckled with the hand partially closed.

Brutaiity Deemed to be a major foul. Occurs when a player deliberately kicks or strikes an opposing player or official.

Caps Caps with malleable ear protectors are worn by players for identification purposes. The goalkeeper wears a red hat with the number 1 marked on it, the other players wear either blue, white or team colored hats with the numbers 2–13 marked on them.

Corner Occurs when the ball goes out of play over the goal line. An attacking team member is given a free throw when a defending player was the last to touch the ball before it went out of play. Is taken from the 2.2yd line.

Deep water Water 6ft deep or more. All major domestic, national and international tournaments are played in deep water.

Disallowed A goal is disallowed if the ball has been punched, scored direct from a free throw within 8yd of the goal, or has not been played by two players after the start or a restart of the game.

Dry pass A pass made so that the ball can be caught.

Extra man Occurs when the opposing team has a member excluded. The other team is then said to have an extra man.

Extra time A match will go into extra time when the game has finished and the scores are even. After a five-minute interval, play is resumed with two three-minute periods of play with a one- minute break in between.

Field goal A goal scored from open play rather than from a penalty or direct from a free throw 8yd from the goal line.

Free throw Awarded to the nonoffending team for a foul against them. The player nearest to the place where the foul was committed will take the free throw unless it was committed in the 2.2yd area. Goals scored from a free throw within 8yd of the goal are invalid.

Goal A goal is scored once the ball has fully crossed the goal line between the uprights and gone under the crossbar.

Goal judges There are two, and each is positioned at either end of the pool level with the goal line.

Goalkeeper The goalkeeper's job is to protect the goal area. He is the only player allowed to punch the ball or touch it with two hands.

Half-screw Either a backhand pass or a shot that moves the ball sideways from the player.

Hole Area in front of the goal.

Major fouls If a player is deemed to have committed a major foul, he/she will be excluded for 20 seconds of play and awarded a personal foul.

Neutral throw Taken by the referee to restart the game after a stoppage has occurred for a sick or injured player, when a foul has been committed and the referee cannot tell who caused it, or for any other reason that unfairly gives advantage to one team.

Ordinary fouls Minor infringements of the rules. Are punishable by a free throw being awarded to the opposing team.

Penalty throw Occurs from any point along the 4yd line. Awarded to the team that had a foul incurred against it.

Personal foul Recorded against a player for committing a major foul or giving away a penalty. On receiving a third personal foul, the player is thrown out of the game.

Pool For men's International's and major competitions, the pool measures 22yd in width by 33yd in length with a minimum depth of 6ft. The goal line and halfway line are marked in white, the 2.2yd line in red, the 4yd line in yellow and the 8yd line in green. For women, the pool is 19yd in width by 27yd in length.

Possession A team that has possession of the ball. Possession can only be held for 35 seconds without shooting at goal before a foul is awarded.

Punching Describes hitting the ball with a closed fist. It is illegal for any player other than the goalkeeper to punch the ball.

Push shot A pass made by picking up the ball and moving it by straightening the arm.

Screw A backhand shot that moves the ball directly behind the thrower.

Secretary The official in charge of keeping a record of the score and personal fouls given to the players.

Sling shot Occurs by throwing the ball with a straight horizontal arm. Normally started with the player's back facing the goal.

Standing Means that a player is resting one or both feet on the floor of the pool. This is not allowed and is penalized by an ordinary foul.

Substitutes Each team is allowed a maximum of six substitutes. A player excluded for three personal faults is allowed to be substituted.

Sudden death The term used to describe the third period of play after extra time when the scores are still level. Play will continue until the first team scores. They are then deemed to have won the match.

Swim-up Occurs when the game starts or is restarted. Usually with a player from each team swimming up to the halfway line where the referee puts the ball into play.

Teams Each team is allowed 13 players with only seven in the water.

Timekeeper In charge of keeping the time, signaling the end of play, 35 second possessions and 20-second exclusions. It is usual for an assistant to be provided.

Timeout Each team is entitled to timeouts of one minute during the game. These are called by the coach.

Time period Overall the game lasts for 20 minutes split into four five-minute intervals with a two-minute break in between.

Walking Is illegal unless performed by the goalkeeper. Punishable by an ordinary foul.

Wet pass Describes a pass made on the water and not in the air.

Water Skiing

Water skiing involves a skier being attached to a boat by a towrope and being pulled along the water's surface at great speeds. In competition, it is divided into three sections: slalom, trickriding and jumping – all of which take great skill and precision.

Bad gate A bad start on the slalom course by taking the wrong line through the gate.

Balk When a skier refuses to take a jump in a contest.

Bananas Another name for trick skis. They are much shorter than regulation skis and have no directional fins.

Banking A way of going through the air after jumping. The body is more horizontal than upright, with the skis extending out to the left-hand side while still pointing in the correct direction.

Barefoot To plane on the water without skis.

Beachie A barefoot start from the beach.

Binding Made of rubber and designed to keep the toe and or heel in position on the skis.

Cut To shorten the tow rope during slalom. Made from the boat, the reductions total three in all and are called the first, second and third cuts.

Deepie A barefoot start in deep water.

Deepwater start Starts with the skier in a crouched position in the water with the skis pointing out of the water and in line with the boat. As the boat moves off, the skis rise to the surface.

Dock start The skier sits on the dock with the front of the skis pointing out of the water. As the boat moves off, the skier is launched on to the surface

Early buoy Describes taking a good line around the first slalom buoys, that means making a good start to the pass.

Figure skating Another term for trick skiing.

Flying beachie A barefoot start from dry land. The skier runs to the edge of the water and launches himself into the air, landing back in the water into a deepie.

Gassing Occurs just before the skier takes his jump on the ramp. The boat needs to gain more power to compensate for the sudden drag of the skier pulling on the tow-rope in order to make his cut.

Gate Positioned at each end of the slalom course. The boat and the skier must both pass through it.

Handle throw When a skier refuses to enter a course by throwing their handle in the air before reaching the entry point.

Helicopter A 360-degree turn either off the ramp or off the wake.

Hooking When a skier's ski turns in too far as he rounds a buoy, so that it looks as though he is backing up on himself.

Hot-dogging Performing spectacular tricks such as somersaults or helicopters.

Jumping One of the three main competition events. The skier has to jump from a ramp and back onto the water.

Jump skis Longer and wider than regulation skis, with wooden or alloy fins.

Line-off The American term for making a cut.

Observer The person who sits in the boat and faces the skier so that they can interpret the skier's signals to the driver as well as making sure they are safe.

Parasailing A form of the sport in which a parachutist is kept in the air by being towed by a boat. His chute is open from the start and he takes off from the land but comes down in the sea.

Pass One length of a slalom course or tricks course.

Pylon A towrope hitch, placed more amidships than the transom hitch. It is normally made of a metal pyramid and should be placed high enough for the towrope to clear an outboard motor.

Racing A form of water skiing in which competitors race against each other over set distances.

Rope on neck A barefoot trick in which the skier places the long V-handle over his neck, and skis with his arms extended.

Rope on teeth A barefoot trick in which the skier holds the handle between his teeth while in motion.

Salute Occurs when the skier lifts one ski clear of the water and holds it straight ahead at a steep angle.

Scooter start A way of starting used by monoskiers. The skier moves from the shore on to the water, propelling himself along with one leg in a scooting action as the boat moves along.

Sideslide A trick maneuver that is performed with the ski or skis at right-angles to the line of advance.

Skis Must be no wider than 30 percent of their length. They include jump, slalom and trick skis.

Slalom One of the main competition events. The skier zigzags through a course marked out by six buoys, and must enter and leave the course through the gates.

Slalom skis They have a tapered tail and a deeper fin than regulation skis.

Speed For jumping events, the boat may travel up to 57km/h for men and 51km/h for women. For slalom events, the boat may travel up at to speeds decided by the judge. For trickriding, the skier is free to choose their own.

Step-over turn A trick movement performed on one or two skis. The skier lifts his free leg or one ski over the tow-rope while making a 180-degree turn.

Surface tricks Describes tricks that are performed on the water as opposed to on the wake of the boat.

Toe-hold slide A one-skied trick maneuver with the skier placing his foot into the toe strap.

Toe release Device used to release the towrope from the boat when a skier falls down performing a toe-hold trick.

Toe strap The special fitting placed within the handle of the two ropes and used in tricks.

Transom hitch A connection for the towrope at the back of the boat.

Trick-skiing One of the three main competition events. The skier uses specially made skis and performs as many tricks as possible within two 20-second periods.

Tumble turn A barefoot trick where the skier rolls forward over one shoulder on to his back and, once there, twists forward back into his original upright position.

Turns Maneuver used in trickskiing. There are two main turns: the 180-degree front-to-back turn followed by a back-to-front turn through the same angle, and the 360-degree complete turn made without any pause while transferring the handle from one hand to the other.

Two-ski slide A side slide performed on two skis.

Wake Disturbed water behind the boat.

Wake tricks Tricks performed on the wake from the tow-boat.

Wax Coated over the jumping ramp and kept wet at all times so that the ramp is as slippery as possible.

10

Winter Sports

Winter sports all originated in cold, wintry weather, usually on snow or ice, but many of them can now be performed throughout the year in carefully regulated conditions. Ice hockey and figure skating, for example, played all year round at indoor stadiums.

Weather Forecast

Adiabatic A change in temperature of a mass of air caused by changes in pressure without any gain or loss of heat from its surroundings.

Atmosphere Describes the air which is made up of a mixture of nitrogen, oxygen, carbon dioxide and small amounts of other gases and water vapor.

Backing Wind changing in an counter -clockwise direction, i.e. from west to south.

Blue thermal Rising bubble of air with no attendant cloud.

Chop Small wind-blown waves.

Cirrus Clouds that are wispy streaks of high level clouds that are made of ice crystals.

Cornice An overhanging ridge of snow.

Crust: Describes snow that has melted and refrozen, or is wind-blown, and has a hard, crusted surface.

Cumulus Small, separate, fluffy cloud which often forms at the top of a thermal.

Ebb Describes a tide that is going from high to low.

Glassy A smooth, calm water surface with no presence of wind.

Gust A sudden increase in wind.

Latitude The distance measured North or South of the Equator, measured in degrees, taking the latitude of the Equator as 0 degrees.

Meteorology The study of the weather, a very important tool that needs to be learnt when performing certain sports, such as ballooning, paragliding and mountaineering.

Offshore wind A wind that blows away from the shore.

Powder Fine, light, dry, new snow.

Precipitation Describes water falling from the sky in solid or liquid form such as snow, rain or hail.

Soup Wet, heavy snow found in warm conditions.

Stratus Clouds that are made of thick sheets of water drops at a low level. Usually bring drizzle with them in winter.

Swell Waves caused by a common storm system.

Thermal A rising bubble of warm air. Thermals are formed when the lower parts of the atmosphere are warmer than the upper parts, usually caused by the sun warming the ground.

Veering Wind changing in a clockwise direction, i.e. from south to west.

Weather elements Include the temperature, humidity, pressure of the air, winds, clouds, snow and rain.

Bobsled

Teams of between two and four men or two women compete on a specially built course consisting of a twisting downhill run in a narrow channel of ice. They aim to complete the course as rapidly as possible by taking the best line on the banked bends and maximizing their speed on the straightaways.

FOUR-MAN: A four-man bobsled team can gain extra speed because of the collective push at the start

Bob All members of the team lean backward at an extreme angle then snap forward in unison. Traditionally this was believed to provide a bobsled's acceleration.

Bobsled They are made of steel and composite material. The driver is able to steer his bob by pulling on ropes which are connected to a front axle. The maximum weight for a two-man bob is 858lb for a two-woman bob 814lb and for a four-man bob 1386lb.

Brakeman The person who sits at the back of the bob, whose role is to slow the bob down at certain stages throughout the course in order to stop the bob from crashing into the sidewall. They slow the bob down by using a harrow-

type brake. They also provide the initial impetus at the start before climbing into the bob.

Braking straight An area after the finish clock used by the brakeman to slow the bob down before it comes to a halt at the finishing exit.

Buzzer Used to signal to the driver at the start of the race that he is clear to get under way.

Control stations Situated at various locations around the course. They are used to monitor the position of the bobsleds and to ensure that the run is kept clear before each heat. They are connected by telephone and radio to the main control building.

Cornering The term used to describe a

bobsled that is driving around the bends of a course. The driver uses a special technique to drive around the bends and still sustain a high speed without crashing.

Course A course must have at least 14 banked curves with walls high enough to keep the bobs in the track. This will prevent a serious crash from occurring. It has to be at least 1312yd in length.

Disqualification A team can be disqualified if it fails to start on time, or finishes the heat minus a team member. It can also be disqualified if it violates any of the FIBT rules.

Dress A rider must wear a full-face crash helmet for safety reasons.

Driver The person in control of the bobsled who steers it around the course by using steering ropes attached to the front axle.

FIBT The Federation International Bobsleigh and Tobogganing. They control the allocation of competitions to tracks and judge all the events, as well as being in charge of the rules.

Finish clock A clock situated at the finish line to inform the drivers and spectators of the time for their run. It is electronically controlled.

Four-man A team of four men racing together in the same bobsled during a run. The main difference between a four-man and a two-man sled is that there are two side pushers in addition to the brakeman and driver, which will make the sled go faster because of the extra weight, and also give them a faster start.

Green light When a green light is signaled, a team is clear to begin its run down the course. It then has one minute in which to start.

Harrow-type brake A kind of brake used by the brakeman to slow the bob down by digging into the ice.

Heat The term used to describe a fully completed course by a team.

Race officials Appointed by the FIBT and consisting of a jury, president, a minimum of two jury members and a technical jury. Their role is to ensure that the competitors operate under the FIBT rules.

Red light At the start of a run, the red light is signaled to stop the team from beginning its heat. Only when the red light changes to green and the buzzer is sounded can it begin.

Run Describes the course, but is also known as a heat. This refers to a successful completed run around the course.

Side pushers Refers to competitors who participate only in a four-man bobsled. They add extra weight to the sled and help it move faster at the start.

Start The sleds are lined up in the correct running order with the start area kept fully clear. Once the red light turns to green and the buzzer is heard, the first team has one minute in which to start.

Start area The area from which the teams are allowed to build up momentum before they begin their run and move past the starting clock. It is at least 16ydlong and is marked by a piece of wood.

Start block Made of wood and frozen into the ice to assist the driver with the initial push. The distance between the block and the start of the run is 16ydwith a decline of 2 percent.

Tie Occurs when the times are exactly the same for more than one team at the end of a run. In the event of this occurring, joint places are allocated.

Timing points Placed at certain points along the track giving the start, intermediate and finish times. They indicate the progress of the sleds, and can be used by drivers and their coaches to evaluate how they are faring during each run. They are electronically controlled.

Two-man A two-man or woman team in a bobsled. One person is the driver, and the other takes the role of brakeman.

Luge

The luge is contested in toboggans down a purpose-built ice track, and is similar to bobsled racing. Competitors make four runs, and there are individual events for men and women. The winner is the competitor with the best aggregate time. The main difference between the luge and bobsled is that the courses are usually more twisting and tortuous.

Competitions Main competitions are Olympic Games, World Cup, World Championships and the European Championships.

Competitors Must be amateur, and members of an association affiliated to the Federation Internationale de Luge.

Course Every course is artificial and has a concrete structure featuring a left-hand bend, right-hand bend, hairpin, S-bend and labyrinth as well as straight sections and a starting ramp provided. For men's singles the course length should be 1093yd-1366yd, for women's singles it should be 874yd-1148yd..

Dress Competitors must wear aerodynamic speed suits and boots. Crash helmets are compulsory, and further protective clothing is recommended.

Duration The race varies according to the type of tournament. In the Olympic Games, it comprises four runs for singles and two runs for doubles. World Cup events consist of three runs for singles and two for doubles, while in the World Championships there are two runs for all categories and a team event.

Offense Competitors can be penalized for any offense violating the rules. This can vary from failing to wear a crash helmet to acting in a dangerous manner during training or a race.

Officials The race director, starting and finishing officials, timekeepers and a course supervisor. A three-member jury is responsible for overall control.

Start Competitors have to sit down at the start for all the events. The starting order is decided by lot, and varies over the four runs to ensure that the conditions for all competitors are equal.

Starting area The area from which the competitors begin their run. There should be two starting points so that all classes or events reach a common finish line. The positions should have a horizontal iced surface where the competitors can seat themselves on their toboggans.

Steering The competitor lies flat, with their body from the waist facing up over the back of the toboggan. They will put slight pressure from their shoulders, hands and feet on the respective parts of the sled and transmit steering force through the bridges and runners to the steels.

Substitution A competitor can be replaced by a reserve rider. This can only happen if a team member is injured during training. A substitution is not allowed once a race is in progress.

Timing Electronic timing is used, accurate to 1/1,000th of a second.

Toboggan The vehicle in which a racer rides. It has two steel runners bolted to wooden runners that curve up the front. Toboggans must not exceed 48lb for an individual toboggan and 55lb for a doubles toboggan.

Training Competitors must practice their run before competing. Single competitors are expected to make five training runs, doubles at least three.

Skibob Racing

Skibob racing incorporates downhill, Super G, giant slalom, slalom and parallel slalom events. Competitors ride a skibob (that is like a low bike on skis instead of wheels). The winners of all types of competition are those who finish the course in the fastest time.

Disqualification Applied to competitors for accepting outside help, failing to make way for another competitor, failing to cross gates, taking a shortcut, not observing safety regulations or not crossing the finish line.

Dress Crash helmets, ski boots, foot skis, a starting number and goggles must be worn for safety reasons.

Downhill course Must be long enough for the best competitor to finish within two minutes. The altitude difference for a downhill course is a minimum of 765yd and a maximum of 1093yd for men and 437yd-756yd for women.

Downhill start Each competitor starts at 60-second intervals, with the starting command of "Attention" given 10 seconds before.

FISB The Fédération Internationale de Skibob, international governing body.

Foot skis Each competitor wears small skis on their feet that must measure between 20in and 22in in length.

Giant slalom course This course is longer than the slalom, with gates placed farther apart. Competitors select their own line between gates. The altitude distance between start and finish is 437yd The course is least 22yd wide.

Nonstop training Each competitor must test-run the course at least once during official training.

Officials Include a race director, FISB judge, chief judge, start and finish judges, gate judges, a course chief, course tracer, chief timekeeper, starter, umpire and various assistants.

Official training An integral part of the training that must last for at least one day.

Parallel slalom course Two courses are positioned side by side. The altitude difference between the start and finish is between 88yd and 109yd. The flags indicate the curves along the course.

Rectangular flags Used for downhill, giant slalom and super-G events. The flags are red or blue, and placed on vertical poles alternately along the course.

Skibobs Single-track vehicles steered by handlebars at the front. The front and back are connected to two skis.

Slalom course The altitude difference between start and finish is 219yd. There must be between 50 and 75 gates placed at least 6ft above ground along the course, with all gates being numbered.

Slalom result The competitor with the fastest aggregate time is the winner.

Super-G course This should have large to medium turns with gates 6.5yd-9yd apart. The altitude difference between start and finish is 437yd for men and 328yd for women. The gates must not be positioned just along the line of descent.

Triangular flags Used for slalom and parallel slalom events. The flags are red or blue on vertical poles. For the slalom events, the flags are placed alternately by color. For the parallel slalom events, the flags are placed red for the left-hand course and blue for the right.

Wooded terrain Used as part of a downhill course. Must be 22yd wide.

Skiing

Skiing is divided into three categories: Alpine, Nordic and freestyle. Alpine includes downhill, slalom, giant slalom, super-G races and the Alpine combined event. Nordic skiing includes cross-country, ski jumping and the Nordic combined event. Freestyle includes aerials, mogul skiing and ballet.

Abfahrt The German term for a downhill ski run. Usually over two or three miles for men, and one to one and a half miles for women.

Abonnement Season ticket for lifts and lessons.

Alm A mountain pasture.

Angulation A bending of the body at the hips while simultaneously rotating the legs and inclining inward to allow pressure to be applied to the inside edge of the outer or lower foot and ski.

Anticipation Method of turning or twisting the upper body with the help of a ski pole planted in the anticipated direction of a turn before starting the turn.

Antifriction pad Placed behind the toe piece of binding to ensure the prompt release of the boot.

Artificial skiing Another name for dry skiing.

Avalanche cord A brightly colored cord tied to a skier performing in dangerous terrain as a safety device in case of an avalanche. The cord will float to the surface of the snow, helping rescuers find the skier.

Banking To lean your body into a turn.

Basket A plastic disc that sits above the tip of the ski pole in order to stop the pole from sinking too far into the snow. Also describes a basic cage lift with no seats.

Bending turning A parallel turn made by bending the knees before banking your knees into the turn.

Bindings The device that attaches the bottom of the ski boot to the ski.

Bird nesting Off-trail skiing through trees.

Black run A difficult, steep marked run used by advanced skiers.

Blood wagon The slang term for the sledge used to carry injured skiers.

Blue run Run marked for intermediate skiers.

Boots Must support the ankles fully. They have specially constructed soles that fit onto the skis and are fastened with clamps or binding.

Bottleneck A narrow part of the trail where the terrain does not leave much room for more than one skier.

Bubble A gondola-style lift.

Bullfighter turn Skis should be placed across the slope with the poles planted downhill from the skis. The uphill tail should be placed out by 45 degrees pivoting the ski about its tip. The downhill ski should be placed into the fall line tail to tail with the uphill ski. The last stage is to bring the uphill ski into the fall line to position into a snowplow facing downhill.

Button A one-person drag lift that uses a supporting disc instead of a bar.

Cable car An enclosed carriage that carries skiers up the mountainside.

Camber The arc in the ski that ensures that the skier's weight is spread along the whole of ski and not just the middle of it.

Canting A method of adjusting ski boots so you remain flat on your skis.

Carved turn Occurs when a skier

turns and the whole edge of the ski passes through a single groove in the snow.

Chair lift A seat that carries a skier up a mountain while enabling them to keep their skis on.

Chattering The noise made by skis when traveling at fast speeds over hard snow.

Chill factor Describes the apparently cooler temperature due to the cooling effect of the wind.

Climbers Also known as creepers. Attached to the bottom of the skis, they help prevent backslide when a skier is ascending.

Combi skis In terms of flexibility, they are in between hard and soft skis, and are used for moving in icy conditions or deep snow.

Comma A skiing position with the skier leaning his upper body slightly away from the slope, with his hips curved toward it.

Committee The board of officials used to ensure that everything is set up correctly for a competition.

Compound skis Skis made up of a number of different materials, with each material used to impart a specific benefit.

Compression The movement of absorbing a bump by flexing the knees and thighs. It is a vital part of the jet and kangaroo turns.

Cornice Overhanging ridge of snow.

Corn snow See "Sugar snow".

Couloir A steep, narrow descent.

Counter rotation In that a skier will twist his upper body in a different direction from the turn.

Crevice A crack in glacier ice that is often covered in snow.

Crud See "Crust".

Crust Snow that has melted and refrozen and therefore has a hard, crusted surface.

Double pole push The skier places both poles in front of his body and uses them to push off while sliding the skis forward.

Downhill turn A turn made in and out of the fall line while moving downhill.

Drag lift Describes a lift that pulls the skier up the slope.

Edge change To transfer the pressure from the edge of one ski to another.

Edges The metal strips running along each side of the ski. Their function is not only to protect the skis but to aid in gripping the snow when pressure is placed on them.

Edging To tilt on to the metal edge of the skis.

Egg position Occurs when the skier crouches down and places his head lower than his back with his elbows held close to his body to lessen the wind resistance.

Fall line The most direct line of descent down a slope.

Fergie A double side kick.

FIS The Fédération Internationale de Ski, that is the world governing body of skiing.

Flat ski A ski that is not edged.

Flofit A padded inner boot that adapts to the contours of the foot.

Flying kilometer/mile A straight downhill course used for speed competitions.

Fohn A warm wind that causes the snow to melt.

Forerunners Noncompetitors who ski down or across a course to check the conditions and mark a course through the gates before the race begins.

Funicular A tracked railway used for steep slopes.

Gaiters Waterproof cuffs worn around the bottom of ski pants and at the top of ski boots.

Gate Marked by two poles with colored flags on top of which slalom skiers must pass through.

Glacier An ice mass often used for summer skiing.

Grass skiing A summer sport where skiers perform on grass. They use caterpillar-track skis.

Green run A marked course used for beginner skiers.

Gun barrel A natural gully with steeply banked sides where skiers are able to ski.

Herringbone A method of climbing small-scale slopes by facing uphill with the tails of the skis placed together, the tips apart and the poles behind.

Hard skis Skis that are stiff when flexed. Used for skiing on icy surfaces.

Heli-skiing Skiing using helicopters as transport.

Hockey stop A method of stopping from a downhill run. The skier will flex their knees while bringing them around to face the fall line. This ensures that their weight is brought down hard onto the skis, forcing them to stop.

Inner ski Describes the ski that is on the inside of a turning circle.

Jet turns A parallel turn where a bump is taken in compression and as the feet reach the top of the bump, the feet and legs are thrust forward around and down, finishing the turn on the valley side of the bump.

Jump turn A turn performed with both skis lifted clear of the snow.

Jury Used for each competition to adjudicate on protests, disputes and other problems.

Kick turn A stationary turn through 180 degrees. One ski is lifted into a vertical position and pivoted around its tail to face in the opposite direction. The other ski is then lifted around parallel to the first ski.

Lower ski The lower of the two skis when crossing the fall line.

Mono-skiing Performed on one wide ski.

Motorway A broad, easy trail.

Nursery slope A gentle slope used for beginners to practice on.

Off-trail Natural snow that has not been flattened down like the snow on trail.

Outer ski The ski on the outside of a turning circle.

Outrun The flat terrain on that a skier lands and stops after a ski jump.

Parablock A block placed on the tip of the ski to stop the skis from crossing. Used mainly for beginners and for practicing the jet turn.

Parallel turn A turn performed with both skis parallel.

Passing Always assume that the skier you wish to pass has not seen you. The responsibility during this maneuver is always with the skier who is passing.

Pedalling To bend one leg while straightening the other leg, resulting in a transfer of weight.

Penalties Incurred for not complying with the rules laid down by the governing body. Offenses include receiving unauthorized assistance, not following the correct course or not giving way to a passing skier at the first request.

Pole planting Poles are placed in the snow to aid with turning control when parallel skiing.

Poles Made of steel, aluminium tubing or graphite, they are used for balance, to aid in climbing and to gain momen-

EDGING: When the skier tilts onto the metal edges, giving them a better grip on the snow

tum at starts and turns. The length varies with the height of the skier. The handles are made of plastic and may have may adjustable straps.

Poma lift See "Drag Lift".

Porridge Sticky, lumpy snow.

Powder Light, dry snow usually found on the higher slopes.

Pre-jumping A short, low jump used to clear a slope edge and avoid being thrown into the air.

Ratrac The name of the machine used to pack the snow tightly on the trails.

Reverse shoulder skiing See "Counterrotation".

Ruade To jump slightly before a parallel turn. Used to help the skier unweight.

Rut A dent made in the snow by skis running constantly down the same line or track.

Safety strap A small strap that connects the skier to his skis and stops the skis from running away if they come loose.

Salopettes Dungaree-style pants that are waterproof.

Schussboomer The name given to a skier who skis wildly or at speeds beyond their control.

Schussing Skiing straight down the fall line with the skis parallel.

Scissors The movement of one ski to turn into a scissors shape.

Short swing A series of rhythmic linked turns performed on a downhill run that enables the skier to take the slope at a steeper angle.

Shovel The upturn at the tip of the ski.

Sidecut The waisted shape of a ski.

Sideslip A controlled sideways slide down a slope.

Sidestep A method of climbing sideways uphill by stepping up one ski at a time and edging it into the slope.

Skating Involves stepping one ski at an angle and pushing off from it. It is used to increase speed, and can be done with one or both skis.

Ski bum An American slang term for a skiing enthusiast who works his way on the ski resorts for free skiing time.

Skidding Occurs when skis are turned at an angle to the direction of travel and momentum.

Skins Strong material strips that are placed on the bottom of the skis by straps, buckles or clips. They enable the skier to climb almost any slope unaided and keep them from sliding backward.

Skis Made of synthetic materials. The weight and length of the skis depends on the height of the competitor and which event they are performing in. Downhill skis are shorter and heavier, slalom skis are shorter and easier to turn, whereas cross-country skis are narrow and light with a toe fastening that allows for greater freedom of movement for the heels.

Ski stopper A small spring-loaded break on a binding that, when released, digs into the snow to stop the ski from sliding downhill.

Snowblindness Occurs when a skier does not wear sunglasses or goggles, and is caused by strong glare from the sun at high altitudes. Usually temporary, but can lead to permanent eye damage.

Snow cement A compound used to harden snow surfaces.

Snowmaking Occurs in places where natural snow is in limited supply. The artificial snow is made from a mixture of compressed air and water. It is sprayed from guns to give it the correct consistency.

Snowplow Skiing technique used to control speed. The skier glides with his skis opened in a V-shape with the tips together and tails apart and the greatest pressure on the inside edges.

Snowplow turn Made in the snowplow position by putting more pressure on the outside ski.

Soft ski Used for skiing in deep or powder snow. So called because they bend easily when flexed.

Soup Wet, heavy snow found in warmer conditions.

Star turn First plant the poles out of the way and step one tail out 20 degrees keeping the tip down. The next stage is to transfer the body weight onto the repositioned ski and lift the other one, bringing both skis parallel together ready to take the next step.

Stemming To ski with one ski at an angle to the other. Also known as half a snowplow.

Step-in heel binding Describes a safety binding that shuts automatically when the boot is inserted.

Stick Another name for a ski pole.

Stop swing Involves coming to a stop with the skis parallel, swinging them around at right angles to the fall line.

Straight running Downhill skiing in a straight line with the skis parallel and the knees slightly bent.

Sugar snow Granular snow that quickly turns to slush in warmer weather.

Swing A high-speed turn made with the skis parallel.

Tail The squared end of a ski.

Tail hopping The skier hops to lift the tails of the skis off the ground while flexing his knees into a crouching position.

T-bar See "Drag lift".

Thin snow cover Anything less than 4.7in could create difficulties.

Tip The upturned front end of a ski.

Tracking Describes the skis' ability to maintain line and direction.

Trails Ski runs that are beaten into a smooth surface by machines. All runs are graded according to difficulty and are marked by differing colors; green is the easiest, progressing to blue and red to black, that is the most difficult.

Tramlines Describes ruts in the snow.

Transponder A transmitter that is tuned in to the local rescue services frequency and worn for safety reasons in case of an avalanche.

Traversing Means to ski across the fall lines. The skier gets into the comma position and puts most of his weight on the lower ski while facing downhill.

Unweighted ski A ski that has little or no weight.

Unweighting The method of momentarily reducing the body weight on the skis before taking a turn. Can be done by either quickly straightening up the body or suddenly bending low.

Uphill turn Used for stopping and braking. Involves a turn away from the fall line in an uphill direction.

Upper ski Describes the higher ski when going over the fall line.

Wall A steep, wide descent.

Wax Substance applied to the skis in order to improve their performance.

Wedeln Translated from the German, it means "tail wag". It is an elegant version of the short swing.

Whiteout Weather conditions that reduce visibility to almost nothing.

Windslab A surface crust of snow formed by wind action.

FREESTYLE SKIING

Acrobatics Also known as upright aerials, they are freestyle stunts performed in midair with the skier remaining upright as opposed to somersaulting, etc.

Aerials Any freestyle stunt performed in midair from a jump.

Back flop Occurs when the skier sits back and then lies back on his skis while still moving.

Back scratcher An aerial maneuver in which the ski tails are brought up behind the skier to touch his back with the tips of the skis pointing downward.

Backward snowplow When the herringbone position is taken up and the skier then moves backward down the slope. By linking this to the snowplow and the snowplow turn, a set of spins through 360 degrees may be performed.

Ballet skiing Skiing to music through a series of links and turns. This is one of the three freestyle disciplines.

Butterfly See "Spinners".

Charleston ski dance A ski dance that is performed by using a steady, constant rhythm. As one ski tail swings down, the other ski tail swings up.

Crossover turns A ballet maneuver in which the skier lifts one ski over the other.

Daffy An aerial stunt in which the skier takes a jump and, while in midair, points one ski forward and up and the other ski backward and down, bringing them together before landing. Also known as a mule kick.

Double helicopter An aerial turn performed twice through 360 degrees.

Doughnut Used in both ballet and mogul events, it is a 360-degree turn performed with one buttock as the pivot.

Floater A ramp built for aerial competitions. Also used for upright jumps.

Helicopter A 360-degree turn performed midair with the body vertical.

Hotdog skiing Another name for freestyle skiing. Hotdogging is the American slang term for a spectacular maneuver.

Inverted tricks Describes maneuvers involving rotations around the horizontal axis while in flight.

Iron cross An aerial stunt in which the skier brings up both skis behind him in midair to form a cross.

Kicker Specially-built jumps used for taking off in aerial maneuvers.

Killer-kick Describes a kick turn in a sitting position at high speeds.

Layouts Describes various aerial somersaults with the hands in a swallow position.

Leg breaker A ballet maneuver where the skier lifts one ski and places the tail near the tail of the other ski, transferring his weight on to it.

Moebius An aerial front layout with a full twist.

Mogul A hillock or bump on a trail created by a number of skiers who have used the same point at which to turn.

Mogul field A slope covered in bumps. Found on trails that are too steep for a machine to get onto.

Mogul run One of the three freestyle events in that competitors are judged on the stunts performed and their use of aggression, speed and control.

Mule kick A back scratcher performed to the side of the body.

Outrigger turn A ballet turn in which the skier crouches down and puts all his weight on the inner ski, with the outer ski extended to the side off the ground.

Royal Christie A ballet turn performed on the downhill ski with the other leg being extended behind the skier.

Shoulder roll A ballet maneuver in which the skier performs a forward head roll.

Side kick An aerial maneuver in which the skier moves both skis while either parallel or crossed to one side in midair after a jump.

Somersault Used in aerial skiing, it is one of the most basic maneuvers performed.

Spinners A ballet maneuver that involves a 360-degree turn in contact with the snow.

Spread eagle Aerial jump in which the skier spreads his arms and legs wide.

Tip roll A 360-degree ballet turn in

which the skier lifts himself onto his ski tips while being supported by his poles, and swings right around.

Tip stand When the skier stands on the tips of his skis with the heels crossed behind his back while supporting himself in front on his poles.

Tornado A ballet maneuver that uses a number of different linked jump-overs. The uphill ski is lifted and is jumped over the downhill ski with the weight of the body being supported by the poles.

Twister An upright aerial with a combination turn.

Window frame A 180-degree turn that resembles the tip roll. The skier goes through his poles and twists around to face in the opposite direction.

Wellen A technique used when skiing and turning around moguls.

Wongbanger A ballet maneuver involving a sharp up-and-forward projection of the body, with the ski tips of the vertically placed skis in contact with the snow. Named after Wayne Wong.

ALPINE SKIING

Allais chicane A four-gate combination named after Emil Allais.

Carving Method in which the upper ski is severely edged inward at the entrance to a turn, with the skier's weight placed well forward on that ski. This maneuver flattens the arch of the ski and allows the curve formed by the tip and the waisting of the inner edge to track along its natural radius.

Citadin A class of Alpine ski racing restricted to part-time skiers who are not resident in an Alpine region.

Closed gate A single gate set vertically in the fall line that has to be approached at an angle.

Combination gates Gates that can be put into combinations of pairs, triplets or groups of four or more.

Combined event Event in which skiers are placed according to their results in the downhill, slalom and giant slalom.

Diagonal side step A combination of the two-phase and the sidestep, stepping uphill and forward at the same time.

Flush Describes two or more pairs of flags set in a straight line, either in the fall line or at an angle. This is the most common form of gate used.

Gate A set of two poles with flags on top that slalom skiers must pass through on their way down the course. They are colored alternately red and blue.

Nastar A weekly standardized slalom race held in American ski resorts.

Offset hairpin A pair of gates that have either a steeply angled turn or an almost direct passage according to the following gates.

Open gate See "Gate".

Seelos A three-gate combination named after the Austrian gold medalist Anton Seelos.

Two-phase walk Performed on flat terrain, the skier uses alternate ski sticks for support steps forward and walks as normally as possible with the right arm and left leg forward, the left arm and right leg forward.

NORDIC SKIING

Angulation Arcing the body at the hip, knee and ankle joints to achieve a higher degree of ski edge.

Arresting Stopping a slide down a steep slope by using the ski poles as a brake. Taking the hands out of the ski straps and holding the poles across the chest while forcing the bottom two inches of the sticks into the snow. This results in the upper body weight bearing down on the poles. Although it might not completely stop the descent, it will certainly slow it down.

Cross-country turn Occurs when the skier shifts his weight from his outer ski and then pushes out and away as his weight transfers on to the inner ski.

Christi turn A skiing turn with a skidding phase.

Diagonal stride A basic maneuver in which the right arm is moved forward with the left leg and vice versa, creating a kick-and-glide movement.

Double poling Describes the skier putting his skis together and placing his poles in front, pulling himself through the poles to propel himself forward.

Glide zones The front and back sections on the base of cross-country skis. They allow the skis to glide forward when standing with equal weight on both skis.

Grip zone The central section on the base of cross-country skis. This allows the skis to grip the snow when most of the body weight is on one ski.

Herringbone Moving forward on cross-country skis in a stepping mode with the ski tips farther apart than the tails, forming a herringbone pattern in the snow.

Inclination Leaning of the body in the direction of the turn to engage ski edges and resist centrifugal forces from the turn.

Kick and glide See "Diagonal Stride".

Kick turn A way of turning to the opposite direction of travel by kicking one ski to a 180-degree position followed by the other ski.

Klister A soft wax applied to the grip zone of cross-country skis. It aids in gripping the snow and preventing the skis from sliding backward.

Langlauf The German name for cross-country skiing.

Loipe A marked trail for Nordic skiers.

Marathon A long-distance cross-country race. In America it is called citizen racing, because anyone can enter.

Parallel skiing Skiing with the skis parallel. Skis can be either together or apart.

Rottefella binding The Norwegian name for a toe clamp used for the lighter models of cross-country skis. Also known as rat-trap bindings.

Skating Propelling the body forward by using one ski as a platform and the other ski as the sliding ski in a manner like a skater.

Skinny skis Another name for cross-country skis.

Side step Moving laterally in small steps on cross-country skis.

Straight run Travelling straight down a hill with the skis paralel and the body on the skis in balance.

Telemark A cross-country turn. The outside ski is moved forward until the boot is next to the tip of the inside ski. The skier lowers himself down, bending his inside knee low as the outside ski steers the turn.

Tour racing Also known as citizens racing.

Trail marking signs Used along the trail to let skiers know in what direction they are traveling and the distance they have covered.

Wedge turn Also called the snowplow turn. It is an elementary turn with the skis in a wedge position where the tips of the skis are closer than the tails.

Biathlon

Biathlon is a winter sport that incorporates both cross-country skiing and rifle shooting. Competitors use small-bore rifles. The biathlon includes both individual and team events.

Ammunition All ammunition must be carried by the competitors from the start. Competitors use long rifle rimfire ammunition.

Competitors On November 1 of the year in that a competitor turns 20, they are eligible to compete in the men's or women's classes. Before that they must compete in the junior sections.

Course The network of ski trails that competitors must follow. It has flat areas, downhills, climbs and at least two separate trail loops.

Damage A competitor may change one ski if it's broken or damaged. Broken poles and straps may be changed as often as necessary. Skis may be swapped among team members.

Disqualification Occurs when a competitor takes part in a competition for which they are not eligible, for failing a drug test or evading doping control, for receiving prohibited assistance and using nonregulation equipment.

Dress May be strengthened and protected on both elbows and shoulders. Padded material may be used.

Equipment Competitors may have one pair of marked skis, two ski poles and one marked rifle.

Finish A biathlete finishes when he breaks the electric eye beam at the finish line or, for manual timing, when one or both feet cross the line. In team competitions, a team finishes when the last member of the team crosses the line.

Finish area Begins 11yd before the finish line and ends at least 38yd after the finish line at the finish control point.

Handover zone At the end of a straight section of a trail, marked at the beginning and end with red lines. It is 33yd long and 6.5yd-9yd wide.

Individual competition Events take place over 12 miles for men, 9 miles for junior men and women, and 6 miles for junior women. Competitors start at one-minute intervals, and must complete a specified number of bouts between certain distances on the course.

Jury Responsible for arranging medical examinations, imposing penalties and ensuring that competitions are carried out according to the rules.

Lost or misfired rounds These may be replaced if a competitor is carrying spare rounds. They are also available from the range official.

Organization Competitions are run by the organizing committee, competition committee, jury and officials.

Penalties Serious offenses such as taking shortcuts, using means of propulsion other than skis or poles or changing the trigger pressure of the rifle are penalized by disqualification. Time penalties of one minute or two minutes are issued for other offenses.

Penalty course For relay and sprint races, a 164yd oval loop is laid out on even ground near the shooting range. Competitors who have penalties must run around this oval the requisite number of times before crossing the finish line.

Penalty loop 164yd long by 5.5yd wide. Set up by the shooting range for sprint, relay and team competitions.

Procedure A competition has four main components: the start, skiing, shooting and the finish. Biathletes or teams are randomly assigned start numbers before the competition.

Procedure at firing range The competitor should load the rifle with five rounds to be fired in the competitor's own time. The first and third shots are taken in the prone position and the second and fourth standing.

Procedure on course Competitors follow a flagged track using no other means of propulsion than skis and poles with no pacemaker. If a competitor is passed, he must give way, and anyone who observes an accident should report it at a control point.

Range The shooting range is located in the central area of the stadium. The range must be level.

Relay Each team comprises four members in the men's events and three in the women's events. Every team member has to ski 6 miles with two bouts of shooting.

Reserve rifle If a rifle is damaged and cannot be repaired, the reserve rifle – that is kept on a designated rack on the range – may be used.

Rifles These may be automatic or semi-automatic. Loading and unloading must be done by the competitor. The rifle must weigh at least 7.7lb.

Safety Biathletes must be behind the shooting line when the range is open for shooting; load and unload rifles with the barrel pointing toward the target and make sure no live ammunition is left in the chamber after each shooting; aim and fire only at the targets; and have their rifles checked at the finish.

Scoring The running time from start to finish, including shooting, plus penalty minutes.

Shooting lanes Each lane measures between 2.7yd and 3.3yd wide.

Shooting mat One in each lane of 1.7yd square and 0.4in-0.8in thick.

Shooting ramp Should be at least 12in above the ground, and covered with groomed, solid, level snow.

Shot penalty Incurred because a competitor missed a target. The penalty is one minute added to the finish time in individual competition and a 164yd penalty loop in all other competitions.

Skis At least as tall as the competitor, minus 1.5in There is no maximum length. Skis must be at least 1.2in wide at the tip and between 1.7in and 1.9in at the ski waist and weigh at least 1.6lb

Ski poles Competitors use two ski poles of fixed, equal length, no longer than the competitor's body. There is no weight limit for the poles.

Sprint competition Men and junior men race over 7.5 miles, women and junior women over 6 miles. Competitors start at one-minute intervals individually or in groups. Competitors fire over 55yd at the same targets as in individual races.

Targets Set up in straight, level lines parallel to the shooting ramp. The center of the target is in the middle of the width of the shooting lane, usually of metal or paper. A target has a white face and black scoring plates. For the prone competition, the competitor aims at a target 1.7in in diameter, and 4.5in in diameter in the standing-shoot competition.

Track Parallel grooves along a trail that fit the skis.

Types of competition There are four: individual, sprint, relay and team.

Weapons All nonautomatic weapons with a caliber up to 0.2 may be used, but magnifying optical sights are not allowed. The minimum trigger pressure is 1.1lb. There must be no round in the rifle during the course.

Wind flags Set up at the side of every third shooting lane.

Ski Jumping

Ski jumping is a Nordic discipline that requires the competitor to use a combination of strength, courage and grace. Each ski jumper takes two jumps from a specially built hill. They are judged on style, technique and the distance reached.

Airfoil position The position a jumper takes while in flight. The skis are kept still and parallel while pointing slightly up, with the body leaning forward with straight legs and hands pressed to the body to balance the upward pressure of the skis.

Camber The arc in the ski that ensures that the skier's weight is spread along the whole of the ski and not just the middle of it.

Canting A method of adjusting your boots so that you remain flat on your skis.

Chattering The noise made by skis when traveling at fast speeds over hard snow.

Corn snow Granular snow that quickly turns to slush in warmer weather.

Critical point A calculated point on the outrun where the slope begins to flatten and no longer coincides with the trajectory of the airborne skier.

Crud The slang term for snow that is firm on the surface and soft underneath. Usually due to warmer weather conditions.

Distances Jumps are measured to the nearest 1.6ft Distances of 180yd, reached first in 1967, are now common.

Edge change To transfer the pressure from the edge of one ski to another.

Edges The metal strips running along each side of the ski. Their function is not only to protect the skis but to aid in gripping the snow when pressure is placed on them.

Edging Means to tilt onto the metal edge of the skis.

Egg position Occurs when the ski jumper crouches down and places his head lower than his back, with his elbows held close to his body to lessen the wind resistance.

Falls A fall on the inrun loses 20 points, and a fall anywhere else results in a deduction of up to 12 points.

Fall line The most direct line of descent down a slope.

FIS The Fédération Internationale de Ski, that is the world governing body for ski events.

Inrun The place where the skier starts his run and then speeds up to the moment of takeoff from the table. The length is determined by the length of a trial jump.

Jumping hill An artificially engineered site for carrying out ski jumping competitions. Consists of an inrun, a table, an outrun and a finish.

Judges' tower Placed to the side of the jump and high enough for the judges to get a clear view of the competitors.

K point Marks the critical point on the slope that indicates to the competitor the maximum safe landing distance.

Lip The top point of the slope from where the ski jumper takes off.

Nordic combination Event devised to test the ability of skiers in both jumping and cross-country racing, over a 9.3 miles course.

Officials There are five judges for

international competitions and three for any other events. All judges make an independent assessment of the jumps.

Outrun The actual landing slope of a ski jump. The slope angle and curvature are mathematically calculated and based on the theoretical maximum jump length for that hill.

P point Marks out the norm point, which is the ski jumper's expected landing point. It is indicated by a board and a 13yd blue line on either side of the landing slope on the snow.

Plate binding A ski safety binding in that a plate firmly attached to the boot is fixed to the ski by means of one or more safety devices.

Powder Name given to light, dry snow.

Safety strap The small strap that binds the skis to the skier to prevent them coming loose.

Satz Another word for takeoff.

Scaffold Name for the tower where a jump skier begins his downhilll run.

Side-cut Describes the waisted shape of a ski.

Ski flying A type of ski jumping where competitors are judged on the distance achieved rather than style.

Skis These are narrow and light, with a toe fastening that allows for greater freedom of movement for the heels.

Snow cement A compound used to hardern the snow surface.

Telemark Describes a turn. The outside ski is moved forward until the boot is next to the tip of the inside ski. The skier lowers himself down, bending his inside knee low as the outside ski steers the turn. Used to cushion the landing after a jump.

TP point The table point marks out the end of the ski jumper's expected landing point and the beginning of the critical point. It is indicated by a board, and green lines on the snow on either side of the landing slope.

Tracking Describes the skis' ability to maintain line and direction.

V-style position Performed by flying in the air with the ski tails together and the tips apart so that they form a V-shape. Gains extra distance for the skier.

Waist The narrowing of the center of the ski to provide straight running control. Also forces an edged ski to track in a wide-radius circle.

AIRFOIL POSITION: The ski jumper keeps his skis parallel, with his back and hips slightly curved

Snowboarding

Snowboarding is a fun and demanding sport that includes free riding and racing while standing on a single board that is shorter and wider than a ski. In freestyle events, snowboarders perform spectacular stunts that involve taking to the air. The racing event is a timed discipline, with competitors racing around gates or poles.

Air Another word for a jump.

Big air Competition in which riders are judged on the height and difficulty of the air, the control of the move and the precision of the landing.

Binding An attachment that secures the boot to the board.

Bleeper A transmitter that gives out a high-pitched signal. It is used by snowboarders who go off-trail, and rescue workers who are looking for riders lost or buried in an avalanche.

Boarder-X Competition course that includes obstacles such as jumps, gaps and a spine.

Boning To straighten one leg during a trick and hold the position while in the air.

Boots Soft boots are the most popular for performing stunts, while hard boots are used for racing. Both should provide good ankle support and usually have high-back bindings.

Bumps Raised areas in the snow.

Camber The arc in the board.

Chicken salad The name given to an air maneuver. The rider puts their front hand between their feet and legs on the heel edge.

Chutes Natural gullies that snowboarders ride through.

Carve A high-speed turn where the board stays on an edge.

Cliff drops The snowboarder launches off the face of a cliff to become airborne.

Contact point The point where the board is in contact with the snow.

Dendex The plastic material from that dry slopes are made.

Dual slalom Where two riders compete head to head on a slalom course.

Edge The side of the board that comes into contact with the snow.

Extreme A sport that involves skill and danger. Includes cliff jumps in the most challenging terrain.

Fall line The direction in which gravity pulls you when descending a slope.

Fakie Means to ride backward or with the leading leg following.

FIS The Fédération Internationale de Ski, that is the world governing body for snowboarding and skiing.

Flex To contract or tighten.

Free riding Snowboarding style that allows the snowboarder free rein in their use of style.

Freestyle Describes when a snowboarder takes air and rides the pipe.

Gap A table top with a gap in the

INDIE: An air stunt where the boarder places his back hand between his feet on the heel edge

middle that the snowboarders jump over.

Giant slalom A long, timed race in that the markers are farther apart than on a slalom.

Goofy A snowboarder who rides the board with their right foot forward.

Grab Arm and leg variations on a move.

Half-pipe A half-pipe shaped channel that is carved out of the snow. Usually measures 33yd by 164yd.

Heel edge The edge of the board on your heel-side.

Heelside The side of the board behind your heels.

Helmets Worn for safety reasons.

Hit Either approaching a jump, or another word for a jump.

Indie The name for an air maneuver in which the rider puts his back hand between his feet on the heel-edge.

ISF The International Snowboard Federation, that arranges a major competition annually.

Kicker The name given to a steep jump.

Method Air maneuver in which the rider places his front hand between his feet from behind, on the heeledge.

Mute An air maneuver in which the rider's front hand grabs between the feet on the toeedge.

Nose The name given to the front end of a snowboard.

Ollieing To launch into the air without using a jump.

P-tex Material used for fixing holes in your board.

Park An area used by snowboarders to perform jumps and kicks.

Pipe A half- or quarter-pipe shape that is carved out of the snow.

Pulling tricks To perform stunts or special moves on a snowboard.

Quarter-pipe A quarter-pipe shaped channel that is carved out of the snow.

Racing Means to snowboard against the clock.

Regular The name given to a snowboarder who rides the board with their left foot forward.

Roast beef An air maneuver where the rider's back hand grabs between his feet and through his legs on the heeledge.

Run-out The flat area at the bottom of a slope. Must be long enough to stop the rider from hitting anything. Used for landing from a cliff jump.

Sidecut The shape cut into the sides of the board.

Side sliding Means to slide down the fall line on one edge of the board.

Slalom A timed race through a set of markers or gates.

Slope style A competition event in that boarders combine jumps and quarter-pipes.

Spine A ridge or rail on that the snowboarder can perform tricks.

Stale fish Air maneuver in which the rider takes his back hand from behind to grab between his feet on the heel-edge.

Stance angle The angle at which you set your bindings.

Stance width The distance between the bindings on the board.

Switch To perform a trick backward.

Table top A raised area of snow over which riders can jump and perform tricks.

Tail The back end of a snowboard.

Terrain The type of land over which you ride.

Toe edge The edge of the board on the toe side.

Toeside The side of the board in front of the toes.

Traversing To cross the hill by edging sideways with the body in the direction that the skier wants to travel.

Waist Describes the narrowest part of the board. The smaller the waist, the faster the turn.

Speed Skating

Speed skating is an invigorating sport to watch and participate in. Two competitors race against each other in a counterclockwise direction around an ice track, the winner being the competitor who achieves the fastest time around the track.

Age classes 11 years and younger, midget; 13 and younger, juvenile; 15 and younger, junior; 18 and younger, intermediate; 19 and older, senior; 35 and older, master; 50 and older, grand master.

Boots Usually made of leather and composite materials, with steel blades of 12–18in.

Change in track In Olympic-style racing, the skater who starts on the inner track changes to the outer track at the crossing straight, and the person on the outside crosses on to the inside track. The skater coming from the inside must not touch the other skater.

Charging A foul that occurs when a skater tries to pass on the inside but makes contact with the other skater.

Crossing line The whole length of the straight from the end of the curve.

Disqualifications Skaters may be disqualified for interfering with another skater; intentionally moving or skating inside markers; ridiculing other skaters; delaying the start of an event; causing danger; unsportsmanlike conduct or not giving honest effort. A skater who is disqualified may not take any further part in the competition.

Dress The skater who starts in the inner lane wears a white armband, the skater in the outside lane, a red one.

Drifting A foul called when a skater drifts out of his lane or changes lanes and interferes with another skater. In sprint races, skaters may not leave their lanes.

Elimination system In individual races when a maximum of eight skaters compete. After four laps, the skater in last position is eliminated and another in each of the two successive laps, until only the winner remains.

Equipment Skaters wear safety helmets, shin guards, neck guards, gloves and skates.

Fall-down mark 11yd beyond the starting line.

Falls If a skater falls in the first 11yd of a race, the starter may recall the race. If the fall was not caused by interference and does not impede other skaters, it will not be recalled.

Interference This is called if a skater, in passing another competitor, is at fault for obstructing or colliding with the other skater.

Lanes Decided either by a draw or by the skater with the lower total of points skating in the inner lane.

Lapping In races of 1640yd or less, a skater who is lapped must drop out unless he is in a position for that a prize is offered. In longer races, a skater is not considered lapped unless on the last lap of the race.

Long-track course A 437yd oval.

Marathons Contested over 26 miles.

Officials In major competitions, they include a chief referee, assistant referees, clerks, starters, finish judges, timers, scorers and a lap counter.

Olympic style Otherwise known as metric style. Two skaters compete together in separate lanes and race against the clock. The distances are in meters;

500m, 1000m, 1500m and 5000m, plus 10,000m for men only.

Pack style Up to six skaters compete at once, not confined to lanes, using race strategies. Distances vary depending on age category.

Passing rules In long-track races, a skater with inside or pole position must be passed on the right-hand side unless there is enough space on the left for the skater to pass. In short-track races, skaters may pass on either side.

Points In pack-style racing, skaters are awarded five points for first, three points for second, two points for third and one point for fourth place. In Olympic-style racing, the winner is determined by the fastest time, and the points are the sum of the equivalent time for 500m, calculated to the third decimal point. The champion is the skater with the fewest points.

Procedures Skaters may compete in short track, long track, relays and marathons.

Pursuit races A type of short-track speed skating. Each race is held between two skaters and lasts a maximum of 10 laps. The winner is the skater who overtakes the other one or finishes in the quickest time.

Pushing A foul in which a skater uses their hands, arms, elbows, shoulders or hips in contacting another skater, causing the skater to fall or lose balance.

Relays Teams of four skaters compete over varying distances. Each member must take part in the race. A skater finishing a portion must touch the team member who is taking over.

Restarts A race may be restarted after a false start, if a starter is interfered with or if a skater or obstacle – apart from a broken skate – prevents a skater from finishing the race.

Short track Individual and relay events where the first skater to cross the finish line wins. In international competition, the distances for men and women are in meters: 500m, 1000m, 1500m and 3000m.

Short-track course A 121yd oval. Safety padding covers the walls around the ends of the rink.

Skates Long-track skates have light, low-cut boots with thin blades that are only slightly curved on the bottom. Short-track skates have sturdy, high-cut boots with thicker adjustable blades that have more curvature on the bottom to negotiate the sharper turns.

Skater's path Considered to be 0.5m outside the survey line.

Speed skating Skaters compete in short-track and long-track events, racing in either packs of four to six or against one other. Points are awarded in relation to the skater's time in each event. The overall winner is the skater with the lowest number of points.

Starting a race At the command, "Go to the start", skaters stand motionless at the pre-start line. At the command, "Ready", skaters assume their start position at the line and remain motionless. After a one-second pause, the starter fires a shot to start the race. Competitors race counterclockwise.

Substitutes In relay races, substitutes may be allowed if a skater is injured during a race or contest.

Survey lines Snowlines or blocks set on the ice to define track lanes.

Teams In the Olympics, each country may enter a maximum of 12 male competitors and eight female competitors.

Ties If two skaters tie, the points for that place and the next are added together and then divided equally between the two skaters.

Track An international speed-skating track is a closed, two-lane circuit 364yds or 437yd long. There must be two curved ends, each of 180 degrees.

Figure Skating

Figure skating is split into four different types: singles for men and women, pairs skating and ice dancing. Competitors are marked on technical merit and artistic impression.

Accountant The official who collates the judges' marks and deals with the placing of competitors.

Arabesque A sustained edge that is not necessarily curved, with the free foot extended to form a line or upward curve with the body.

Artistic impression All competitors are judged on their deportment, flow of movement, harmonious composition, conformity to the music and use of the rink. The highest score possible is six points.

Axel jump A free skating jump where the skater rotates one and a half times in the air. In pairs the woman is turned one and a half times above the head of the man.

Backward pumping Describes the skater pushing with the outside foot while gliding on the outside edge of the inside foot.

Barrier The low wooden or plastic wall marking the edge of the ice surface that surrounds the rink.

Blade The metal runner on the boot on that the skater glides over the ice.

Boot The leather part of the skate that reaches up to the ankle and laces up.

Bye Allows a skater to compete in a higher level of competition without having to qualify at a lower level.

Camel spin A one-foot spin performed with the body in a continuous line with the free leg extended behind so that both are parallel to the ice.

Carriage The term used to describe the posture and poise of a skater.

Centering To keep the spin over one point on the ice without traveling from that spot.

Change-foot spin A spin where a change of foot is needed.

Check Stopping the rotation of a spin or jump by extending the arms and free leg.

Clean An unmarked skating surface, or a program with no errors.

Closed position Also known as the waltz. The partners face each other with one skating backward and one skating forward.

Compulsory dance The first part out of three in an ice dancing competition. Two compulsory dances must be selected out of a possible 21, with every competitor performing the same routine to the same music.

Compulsory figures Include steps, turns and edges performed on specific points of the ice.

Crash and burn When a competitor makes a number of mistakes in a program after a fall.

Crossovers Describes moving from the outside edge of one skate to the inside edge of the other skate by crossing the free leg over and in front of the skating foot, then placing it on the ice while retracting the original skating foot and then replacing it ahead of the new skating foot.

Death spiral A pairs movement in which the woman is swung around by the man, with her head almost on the ice. He stays in an upright position. This maneuver is performed at high speeds.

Disciplines In the Olympic Games,

there are four disciplines, singles for men and women, pairs skating and ice dancing.

Double jump Describes a jump with two complete midair rotations.

Edge The sharp side of the blade that comes into contact with the ice.

Elements Parts of a program, that include jumps, spins, footwork and lifts.

Free Describes the skate, leg or foot not being skated on.

Free dance The third and final phase of an ice dancing competition, making up half of the final score. It lasts four minutes, and competitors are allowed to choose their own music and routine.

Free skate Also known as the long program. The second and last phases of singles and pairs competitions are worth two-thirds of the final score. For men and pairs, the phase lasts four and a half minutes, and for ladies' singles the phase lasts four minutes.

Flip jump A toe jump in which the skater leaps from a back outside edge while turning in midair to land on the back outside edge of the other foot.

Flying spin A spin that starts with a jump.

Half-turn A turn through 180 degrees.

Helicopter A pairs lift in that the man skates backward and the woman skates forward. Once in the air, she is held parallel to the ice with her back arced and her legs held in a V shape so which as the man turns, she looks like the blades of a helicopter.

Hollow The blade of the figure skate with its concave groove between the two edges.

Ice dancing A figure-skating phase in which the couple dance without lifts and turns. It is made up of three phases: two compulsory dances, an original dance and a free dance.

Inside edge The edge of the blade that corresponds to the inside of that particular foot.

ISU The International Skating Union, based in Switzerland. It governs the rules and events of figure skating.

Judges At all major competitions there is a panel of nine judges for each discipline.

Jump Describes the skater taking off from the ice and rotating in midair before landing to continue skating in either direction.

Lateral twist jump Used in pairs skating where the woman is tossed and spun in the air while parallel to the ice.

Layback spin A one-foot spin with the body bent backward so that the trunk is parallel to the ice.

Lift Occurs in pairs where the man lifts the woman into the air above his head.

Lobe Part of a circular figure.

Long free program A free skating program that forms the last and major part of the singles free-skating program.

Long program See "Free Skate".

Loop jump A jump with a midair rotation of 360 degrees.

FREE SKATING: Part of the program where the skater can choose his or her own routine

Lutz jump A toe jump in that the skater makes a clockwise turn from a backside edge.

Marks Competitors are awarded points for each performance based on a scale of six points.

Mirror skating Describes a couple skating who mirror each movement exactly.

Mohawk A turn made by moving from the skating foot to the free foot.

Non-flying spin Describes a spin that starts without a jump.

Open position Also known as the fox-trot. The couple skates slightly away from each other.

Ordinal The term used to describe a skater's rank position within a group of other skaters.

Original dance The second of three phases in an ice dancing competition. It lasts for two minutes, and competitors must perform an original choreographed program to music selected by the ISU.

Outside position Also known as the tango. Two partners stand hip to hip with the man to the woman's right. They face in opposing directions.

Pairs Describes the competition with a man and a woman teaming up. They perform lifts and jumps separately and together.

Parallel spin Another name for a sit spin.

Pirouette Name given to the spins in ice dancing. Skaters must not make more than three rotations.

Pivot Describes when a skater turns around the toe pick of one skate while the other traces a circle on the ice.

Pop Describes cutting short the number of preplanned rotations of a jump by landing early.

Presentation mark Also known as the artistic mark. Judges award points based on the choreography and quality of the presentation of that choreography.

Program Made up of numerous movements and routines, including music, choreography, and timing of spins and jumps.

Pull through Occurs when the man pulls his partner through his position to the opposing side in a fast and rapid movement.

Quad A jump that has four revolutions.

Quality edges Skating that is quiet.

Relative strength The strength that is relative to your body weight, needed to perform jumps on the ice.

Repeated element Means to try an element already performed in a program. Not allowed to be used in a short program.

Reversed kilian Dance maneuver in which the woman stands on the left side of the man.

Reverse lasso A pairs lift in which the woman begins the lift while facing backward.

Reversed tango position The man stands to the woman's left. Also known as the reverse outside position.

Rink The maximum size should be 65.6yd in length by 32.8yd in width. The minimum size should be 61.2yd in length by 28.4yd in width. There should always be a music system available.

Rocker The curve from heel to toe on the blade. Also known as the rock of the blade.

Run-through Another term for practising a routine.

Russian split A jump that begins in a sitting position with the legs spread wide and the knees straight with the toes pointed, and the hands holding the ankles. The skater should always be facing forward with the chin held high.

Salchow jump A jump in which the skater takes off from a backward inside edge and turns in midair to land on the outside edge of the other foot.

School figures Another term for compulsory figures.

Shadow skating A pairs partnership that dances in unison without actually coming into physical contact.

Short program The first part of singles and pairs competition. Worth one-third of the final score, and has eight elements that must be performed.

Sit spin A spin performed on one foot. The skater starts from a standing position before sinking down into a sitting position with the free leg extending forward.

Skate guards Used to cover the blade of the skate when they are not in use. Made of wood, rubber or plastic.

Skates The high boots worn by skaters. The blade at the bottom of the boot is made of steel and measures about 0.1in wide.

Solo lift Occurs when the woman holds one position while in the air.

Solo spin Occurs when a couple performs a spin side by side in unison.

Spiral A glide on one leg in either direction with the skater extending the free leg behind them.

Split twist lift Used in pairs dancing. The woman's legs are split during her spin in the air.

Spread eagle A two-footed glide with the skater's heels turned inward together and the toes pointing out.

Star lift A pairs lift. The man holds his partner hand-to-hand with one arm and hand-to-hip with the other. The woman holds a scissors position while parallel to the ice.

Stroking Describes gliding strides over the ice with alternate feet propelling the skater.

Sweet spot The place on the blade of the skate where you balance when spinning.

Swizzle A two-footed movement that takes you backward.

Technical program Another name for the short program.

Technique mark The first of the marks that are awarded in compulsory dance.

Three A one-footed figure that looks like the figure three because of the tracing of the turn at the extremity of each circle.

Throw jump Performed as a pairs movement where one partner jumps and the other partner helps on the take-off to aid in gaining height.

Toe box The area of the skate where the toes go.

Toe pick The serrated points positioned at the front of the blade.

Trace Describes marking out the outline of the figures on the ice with the blade of the skate.

Tricks Term used to describe jumps and spins performed.

Triple In relation to jumps, this term means three complete turns made in midair.

T-stop Occurs by placing the free foot at a right angle behind the skating foot so that it scrapes along the ice bringing the skater to a stop.

Two-footed landing Occurs when the skater lands on his landing foot while the free foot brushes the ice slightly as it comes down.

Upright spin Occurs when the skater spins with the skating leg straight and the free leg crossed in front.

Utilization Referring to the rink, where competitors spread out their spins and jumps across the surface of the rink and crisscross as they perform.

Whaxel Occurs during an axel where the skater swings the free leg forward too soon and loses balance as a result.

Wrapped jump A jump that has not been finished because the skater's free leg is wrapped around the skater's landing leg, indicating that the final revolution hasn't occurred to complete the maneuver.

Ice Hockey

Ice hockey is a fast contact sport played between two teams with no more than six players from each team on the playing surface at one time. The object is to put the puck into the opponent's goal as many times as possible during the three 20-minute periods of play.

Alternate captain Is identified by the letter A on their sweater. Each team needs up to two alternate captains who will take over the captain's responsibilities if he is off the ice.

Assist Credit given to a player after passing the puck to the scorer of the goal. A maximum of two assists can be awarded per goal.

Back check Occurs when a player skates back to their own goal area to help the defense.

Back checking Describes the action of forwards who try to regain possession of the puck while skating toward their own goal.

Backhand shot A shot taken with the back of the stick and a reverse shooting motion.

Bench penalty Occurs when a team commits an infraction that causes them to remove one player from the playing surface for two minutes. Any member of the offending team, as designated by the captain, may serve the penalty by taking a place in the penalty box.

Blind pass Describes a pass that is made without the player observing where the puck is going to.

Blue lines The playing surface shall be divided into three equal parts with blue lines measuring 12in in width. The two blue lines on the ice surface designate the attacking and defending zones of the two teams.

Boarding Describes the illegal act of checking an opponent into the boards in an aggressive or violent manner, over and above a normal checking action, where the opponent has no chance of protecting himself.

Boards Are the boundaries that enclose the rink.

Breakaway Describes the action of an offensive player, who has no defensive player between himself and the opposing goalkeeper, moving the puck at a rapid pace for a scoring opportunity.

Breakout Describes the act of a team moving the puck out of the defending zone toward the opponent's goal.

Breakout pass Is a pass to a team member who is accelerating for a breakaway.

Cage Another term for the goal, or the wire face protector sometimes worn by players and goalies.

Center Describes the middle player of the three attacking forwards.

Center face off circle The area at the center of the playing surface in the middle of the center red line where the opening face off takes place, as well as face offs after any goals being awarded, or errors on the part of the officials.

Check When a player makes physical contact with an opposing player to break up a play.

Clipping Describes the action of a player deliberately falling into or checking an opponent who is in possession of the puck by making contact below the knee. This action results in a penalty being assessed to the offending player.

Covering When a defending player

marks an opponent resulting in the opponent not being able to participate in the play. If carried out to the extreme, the defending player may incur an interference penalty.

Crease The playing area directly in front of the goal laid out with a semi circle measuring 5.9ft in radius and 2in in width. This area is often painted light blue in color to denote an area where the goalkeeper cannot be interfered with during the course of the game.

Criss cross attack Describes the action of two wingers who swap sides of the rink during an attack.

Cross-checking Means to hold the stick off the ice with both hands to check an opponent. Incurs a penalty.

Crossover Describes a skating technique where the player alternates one foot to cross over the other; this action usually occurs when the skater is turning while skating.

Dead Describes the puck when it is either hit over the boards or becomes lodged in the side netting of the goal. Also when the puck is out of play due to a goal being scored or when the whistle is blown.

Defensive zone Describes the area of the playing surface inside the blue line where the team's goal is located.

Defenseman A player whose main focus is defense, playing between his goaltender and his forwards. Each team typically has two defensemen on the ice when it is at full strength.

Deke Is a fake by the puck carrier to wrong-foot an opponent.

Dig Describes an attempt to win possession of the puck in the corners of the rink using the stick.

Directing the puck Means to move the puck along the ice with the stick and change the direction of the puck.

Draw Describes the act of getting the puck to a team member at a face off.

Drop pass Means to leave the puck behind for a team member to pick up.

Dump When a player shoots a puck from the neutral zone into the opposing team's defensive zone, either to allow time for substitutions or in the hopes of having one of his teammates gain possession of the puck deep in the zone.

End zones The two zones at each end of the ice behind the goal.

Face off Used to start or restart play. The referee will drop the puck between two opposing players who will both try to gain possession.

Flip pass Occurs when the puck is lifted over an opponent or his stick during a pass.

Fore checking The act of checking or pressuring the opposing team while the opposing team are in possession of the puck in their defensive zone.

Forehand shot Describes the action of shooting the puck with a forward motion, i.e. shooting the puck on the left side if you are a left-handed shooter and vice versa.

Forward Team's three players other than goaltender and defensemen with the main aim to creat offensive chances.

Freezing the puck To deliberately hold the puck against the boards and cause a stoppage of play.

Game misconduct penalty When this penalty is assessed against a player, he is removed from the playing surface for the duration of the game.

Garbage goal A goal scored from a scramble in front of the net.

Goal Is worth one point. In order for a goal to be valid, the puck must pass over the goal line.

Goal judges There shall be one goal judge positioned directly behind each goal off the playing surface. Their job is to signal a goal when the puck completely crosses the goal line.

Goaltender Also known as the goalie. This is the player who guards the goal.

The goaltender wears a face mask and extra padding, and he is allowed to use a larger stick than the other skaters and a catching glove on one hand.

Gross misconduct penalty When this penalty is assessed against a player, he is removed from the playing surface for the remainder of the game. He cannot play in any further game until the league officials rule on a possible suspension.

Hard pass A pass made with a great deal of pace and force.

Heel of the stick Is the part of the stick between the straight part of the shaft and the flat part of the bottom of the blade.

High sticking The act of carrying the stick above the shoulders and making contact with an opponent. This act will result in a penalty being assessed against the offending player.

Hip checking To use your hip to knock an opposing player from their stride.

Hooking Using the blade of the stick to pull or tug an opponent by his body or stick.

Icing the puck Occurs when a player shoots the puck from his own half of the ice into the opposing end zone and it is then touched by a defending player other than the goalkeeper. Once the defending player touches the puck, play is halted and a face off occurs in the half of the ice from which the puck was shot.

Interference To impede an opponent who is not in possession of the puck.

IIHF The International Ice Hockey Federation is the world governing body for the sport.

Left defenseman Describes the person playing on the left-hand side of defense.

Left wing Is the forward player positioned on the left side.

Lie of the stick The angle between the blade of the stick and the shaft

Light the lamp Slang term for scoring a goal, referring to the red light that goes on behind the goal when a team scores.

Linesman Two of the three on-ice officials whose job is to signal and call offsides and icings, complete all faceoffs other than those at the start of periods and after goals are awarded, and to assist the referee with officiating duties.

Major penalty A serious infraction that results in the offender being ruled off the ice surface to the penalty box for a period of five minutes. This penalty often results in a game misconduct penalty also being assessed in most situations, especially those infractions resulting in injury to the opponent.

Match penalty A serious infraction that results in the offender being ruled off the ice surface for the remainder of the game. A substitute shall be allowed to take his place on the playing surface after serving a five-minute penalty in the penalty box.

Minor penalty A penalty assessed for minor infractions that involves a player being removed from the playing surface and serving a two-minute penalty in penalty box.

Misconduct penalty Is a penalty that incurs a 10-minute banishment to the penalty box.

Neutral zone The third area of ice located in the middle of the playing surface between the two blue lines.

NHL The National Hockey League, based in North America, considered to be the elite league in the world.

Offensive zone The area of the rink where the opposing team's goal is.

Off-the-board pass A pass made to a team member that bounces off the boards.

Offside A player is deemed offside if he precedes the puck into the attacking zone. This is decided by the position of the player's skates.

One-timer A shot that is taken directly off a pass or a loose puck in one fluid motion without stopping to gain control of the puck. One-timers are usually slap shots, and can be very difficult to stop.

Pass out A pass from an attacking player who is positioned behind the opposing goal to a team member who is in front of the goal.

Penalty box The small bench area each team has for players sent off the ice due to penalties. The penalty boxes are on the opposite side of the ice from the regular bench areas. Also known as the "sin bin".

Penalty box assistant The off-ice official who determines and controls the players returning to the playing surface from the penalty bench upon the completion of penalties.

Penalty killing Describes defensive play by a team that has fewer players on the rink than the opposing team because of penalties incurred.

Penalty shot Awarded to a team because of an infringement committed on one of their players during a breakaway opportunity. It involves a free skate and shot at goal with only the goaltender to defend on the play.

Point Is the position that an attacking defender takes up on the opposition's blue line.

Poke check Occurs by using a sudden thrust or jab with the stick to move the puck away from the player in possession of the puck.

Possession of the puck Describes any player who is touching the puck.

Power play This occurs when a team has the advantage of more players on the ice than the opposition, as a result of penalties being assessed. During this timed advantage, the full-strength team will attempt to control the puck in the opposition's zone in order to create goal-scoring opportunities. A power play ends when the penalty expires or the penalized team allows a goal.

Puck Is made of black vulcanized rubber and measures 1in thickness with a diameter of 3in.

Pulling the goalie A phase describing the removal of the goalkeeper from the playing surface and substituting an attacking player in his place.

Push pass Occurs by moving the puck up the ice with a shove rather than a full swing of the stick.

Rebound Occurs when the puck bounces off the boards or the goalkeeper's equipment.

Red line A central line 12in in width, red in color, that divides the ice into two halves. The center face off spot is located halfway along the red line.

Referee The chief on-ice official whose job is to assess penalties and award goals during the game. He must also ensure fair play within the rules of the game, and his decisions are final.

Right defenseman The player who plays on the right side of the defense.

Right wing Is the forward player who plays on the right side.

Rink The iced playing area. Measures between 61.2yd-66.7yd in length and 28.4-32.8yd in width.

Roughing An infraction that incurs either a minor or major penalty for actions considered over and above normal checking.

Rush Describes a combined attack by some or all players of the team in possession of the puck.

Scorer Keeps a record of all goals, scorers and players who have assists awarded and all players who played.

Scratch The term for a player who has been scratched from his team's lineup prior to the game due to injury or a coach's decision. That player may not dress for or participate in that game.

Screen A term describing the act of players positioning themselves between the puck and the goalkeeper, so as to obstruct the goalkeeper's view of the puck and play.

Shut out Describes a game in which a goalkeeper has not allowed a goal.

Short-handed Describes a team that has fewer players on the ice surface than the opposition because of penalties incurred.

Sin bin The slang term for the penalty bench.

Skates All skates must be fitted with a safety heel or heel guard to conform to IIHF standards. The use of speed skates, fancy skates or any skate so designed that it may cause injury is not allowed.

Slap shot Describes a player swinging his stick back and then bringing it forward to strike the puck with maximum force toward the goal.

Slashing The action of swinging the stick at an opponent. Whether or not contact is made, this action is deemed illegal and a minor or major penalty will be assessed based on the degree of the infraction.

Slot The imaginary area on the ice in front of the goal.

GOALTENDER: In charge of defending the goal area. they must be agile and wear extra padding

Snap shot A quick shot made with the snap of the wrist.

Spearing The act of stabbing an opponent with the point of the stick blade whether or not the stick is being carried with one or both hands. This action will result in a penalty being assessed.

Spot pass Describes a pass where the puck is sent to a predesignated area of the rink rather than to a team member.

Stick Made of either wood or aluminium. The maximum length must be 60in from the heel to the end of the shaft with the blade measuring not more than 12.6in. The goalkeeper's stick is slightly larger.

Stick handling Describes the action of controlling the puck with the stick.

Substitute goalkeeper A player positioned on the team bench who is fully dressed, equipped, and ready to play.

Team A team shall not have more than six players on the ice at one time while the play is in progress. The six players are designated as follows: goalkeeper, right defense, left defense, right wing, center and left wing. Under IIHF rules, a team may dress 20 players and two goalkeepers for each game, but any league can modify this.

Telegraphing A term that describes the act of letting your opponent know your actions prior to the action taking place due to your body movements.

Tripping A minor or major penalty will be imposed on any player who places his stick, knee, foot, arm or elbow in such a manner that it causes his opponent to trip or fall.

Wrist shot Performed by sweeping the stick along the ice with the shot being made with a quick snap of the wrist at the last moment before contact is made.

Bandy

Bandy is very similar to ice hockey, but with some basic differences. Bandy is played on a large ice rink, and 11 players from each side may be on the ice. There is no play behind the goals, and the players use a curved stick to hit the ball. Matches are decided on goals scored.

Attacker A player who tries to score as many goals as possible for their side, and will normally play in the opponent's half of the rink.

Ball Made of colored plastic, it should bounce between 6in and 12in when dropped on to the ice from a height of 5ft. It weighs 2oz-2.2oz.

Ball baskets These are placed behind the end line. The goalkeeper is allowed to pick a ball out from this basket to restart play after the ball has gone out.

Corner stroke If a defender plays the ball over his own goal line, a corner stroke is awarded to the attacking team. They will play the ball in from within 3.3ft of the nearest corner angle and cannot touch the ball again until it has been touched by another player.

Crossbar A long pole connecting the two goal-posts. It is 115ft long.

Defender An outfield player who tries to stop the attacking side from scoring a goal. They will play just in front of the goalkeeper.

Direct throw The goalkeeper is permitted to clear the ball downfield after a goal throw has been awarded.

Dress Players must wear skates that should not have sharp points or projections. They must also wear helmets, shin pads, and exterior mouthguards or approved face masks.

Duration The game consists of two halves of 45 minutes each, with a 10-minute interval at halftime. If the scores are level at the end of the match, extra time is played.

Expulsion A player can be thrown out of a match if they have been found guilty of severe or continuous infringements. They can be expelled from the rink for five or 10 minutes or from the entire game.

Extra time Played if the scores are even at the end of the match. Two 15-minute halves will start, and will be repeated until the one team scores.

Face off When an accidental stoppage has taken place, play restarts at the point at that the ball ended up when play stopped. Two players face each other with their backs to the goal line and their sticks parallel on either side of the ball.

Free stroke Awarded against an offender for any kind of infringement caused outside the penalty area. It takes place from where the incident occurred unless it was in the penalty area. The player who takes the free stroke is not allowed to touch the ball again until it is played by another player. The opponents must stand at least 5.5yd from where the stroke is played.

Goal The area that the goalkeeper defends. The goal has a crossbar and two goalposts, and if the ball goes past the goalkeeper and over the goal line, a goal is awarded.

Goalkeeper The player in the side who defends the goal and tries to stop the attacking side from scoring a goal. They are not allowed to use a stick, and can only be challenged when they have the ball or are challenging an opponent.

Goal line The line that marks the end

of the playing surface. If a defender runs the ball over this line, then the opposing team takes a corner stroke. If the attacking team plays the ball over the goal line, then the goalkeeper starts play again with a goal throw.

Goalpost There are two goalposts in each goal that support the crossbar. They measure 3.25ft in length, and the ball must cross between the two posts and under the crossbar for a goal.

Goal referee A goal referee stands at each end of the field. They judge incidents on the goal line and signal when a goal has been scored.

Goal throw Awarded against an attacker if they play the ball over their opponent's goal line. The goalkeeper takes a ball out of the ball basket and restarts play with a direct throw.

Halftime A 10-minute interval that comes at the end of the first half. Players will also change ends for the start of the second half.

Ice rink The rink is rectangular and is 65.6yd-120yd long and 49yd-71yd wide. It is surrounded by a movable border and it stops at least 3.3ft from each corner.

Infringement A player stops an opponent from reaching the ball. The referee will award a foul to the opposing side.

Match secretary An official who assists the referee with timekeeping and is responsible for penalizing players.

Offside A player can be caught offside if the ball has been played by one of his teammates while he is in front of the ball, unless there are at least two opponents nearer to the goal than he is.

Penalty Awarded against a defender in the penalty area if they have committed dangerous or violent play against an opponent. The player who takes the penalty must hit the ball forward from the penalty spot toward the goal.

Scoring A goal is scored when the ball crosses between the two goalposts and under the crossbar. The whole ball must cross over the line. A goal cannot be scored directly from a stroke off, corner stroke, goal throw, stroke in, face off, or a direct throw from the goalkeeper.

Start The teams toss a coin to determine who takes the stroke off and choice of ends.

Stick The stick is made of wood and has a maximum length of 4.7in and a maximum width of 2.4in.

Stoppage This refers to any time lost during the game due to a player being injured or any other circumstance. The referee will add this time on at the end of the half.

Stroke in Awarded to the opposition when the ball is placed over the touchline. The ball is placed on the ice within 3.3ft of where it crossed the line.

Stroke off Taken from the center of the ice to begin each half. It also restarts play after a goal has been scored. Players remain in their own half and have to stand at least 5.5yd away from the ball until the ball is passed. The player stroking off plays the ball into their opponents' half.

Substitutes Players who do not start the game but can replace a participating player during the course of the match. They can be used at any time but the players have to leave the rink before the substitutes can go on. Each team is allowed to have three substitutes (four in international matches).

Tackling Players can physically challenge an opponent who has the ball or is challenging for it.

Teams Each team has 14 players, of whom 11 can be on the ice.

Touchline Runs up the side of the pitch and measures 120yd in length. When the ball crosses over this line, play stops and the opposing team is awarded a stroke in.

Curling

Curling is played with four players, who deliver round stones across the ice to a marked scoring area called the house.

. . . .

Biting Occurs when a stone touches the outside circle.

Broom Used by each curler to sweep the ice ahead of the moving stone.

Burnt Occurs when a stone is touched accidentally.

Check To lay a stone down at an angle near another stone.

Counter Any stone that is either within or touching the house.

Crampit A narrow piece of metal that the curler stands on to deliver their stone. Placed on the outside of the ice.

Double take-out Describes a strike that takes out two opposition stones.

Draw The controlled line that the stone moves along as a result of the turn given to the handle at the moment of delivery. Also means a stone that has just enough weight to reach the house.

End The delivery of all 16 stones to one end of the rink.

Every inch The skip's order to his sweepers to sweep hard all the way.

Fill the port To place a stone in the port so that opposing players cannot play a stone through it to get to the tee.

Freeze To draw right up to another stone without actually moving it.

Game of points Form of curling where the curlers score for themselves. The thrower may sweep his own stone.

Guard A stone placed in front of the shot with the purpose of protecting it.

Heavy Describes a stone that has been played with too much weight and takes it past the required mark.

House The circles placed at either end of the rink. They are either cut into the ice or painted on the ice.

In-hand The stone's curl to the right at the end of its draw.

In-turn or out-turn The twist a curler gives the handle of the stone on delivery to gain a draw.

Keen ice Fast ice.

Kiggle-caggle The rocking movement of the stone when it has not been thrown squarely on to the ice.

Out-hand The stone curls to the left at the end of its draw.

Peels Occurs when both rinks have the same number of shots.

Port The space between two stones that another stone could pass through.

Pot lid A central part of the circle where the tees meet.

Promote To hit another stone so that it moves forward. Also called raising.

Runner A fast-moving stone.

Shot A winning stone inside the house and nearer the tee than any other.

Stone The smoothly curved granite circular curling stone. Including the handle and bolt, it must not weigh more than 44lb. It can have a maximum circumference of 36in and a minimum height of 4.5in.

Take out To remove an opposing stone from the house.

Tee The center of the circles.

Through the house Describes a stone that moves on past the tee.

Toucher A stone just touching the outer circle and therefore a counter.

Well-laid A delivery of the stone that follows the skip's instructions perfectly.

Wick A stone that hits another stone and rebounds off at an angle.

Wick and roll A stone that rolls after wicking.

Wide Stone outside the skip's broom.

11 Activity & Adventure Sports

The common feature of many of these sports is a sense of action and adventure, and there are obvious dangers attached to sports such as ballooning, mountaineering, hang-gliding and parachuting. Others, such as sand-yachting and skateboarding, are less dangerous, but are characterised as all-action sports.

Safety Measures

Belay Is a safety measure that anchors the climbers in case of a fall occurring.

Belt Used in weightlifting competitions to support the lifters back and avoid major injury.

Box *See* protector.

Chalk Used in gymnastic events by competitors in order to gain a better grip on equipment, such as the bars and rings.

Control stations Are used in a number of winter sports. They are situated at critical points of the course and are connected by telephone and radio to the main control building. They ensure that the course is clear before each heat and that all safety regulations are adhered to.

Crampon A metal frame with steel spikes which is fitted on to the shoes by straps to aid the climber when climbing on ice and snow.

Do A leather covering worn over the chest by participants in kendo as they compete with large bamboo sticks called "shinai".

Doctor At all major sporting events, a doctor will be present to deal with any major injuries caused to a player during a competition.

Fire resistant clothing Worn by competitors of motor sports. Must cover arms, legs and torso as a crash often results in the car going up in flames.

Gumshield Plastic shield that fits into the mouth and protects the teeth. Mainly used in boxing and karate events.

Helmet Players wear a helmet to protect their head from the ball and from their fellow competitors when being tackled to the ground. The best example of this can be seen in American football. Also worn by competitors in most adventure, activity sports where height or speed are involved.

Lifeguards Officials in swimming events whose job is to keep an eye on the competitors during the course of the race and help them if they get into any difficulties.

Mat Padding placed on the floor at most martial arts events to help prevent competitors from being too badly hurt when flung onto the floor.

Padding Sportsman wear these to protect any part of their body that is vulnerable to being hit or knocked. Especially true of most goalkeepers.

Parachute Used in all air sports. Must be worn by the pilot in case an emergency landing is necessary. Made of nylon, the parachute once opened slows the descent of the pilot.

Protector Another word for jockstrap. Protects the groin area from injury.

Studs Worn by players at the bottom of their boots to help them in wet conditions, especially when they have to play on a muddy pitch.

Water patrol Consists of a boat and team of trained lifesavers who are at hand for any water sports performed on open waters.

Cycling

Cycle racing is divided into two main events: track and road racing. They include national and international competitions, both indoor and outdoor. Indoor events include track races and stationary races held on sets of rollers.

Australian pursuit A race in that the riders start at differing equidistant points around the track. The object is to catch the rider in front and therefore eliminate him from the race. The winner is the first of the remaining riders to cross the line.

Bidon French term for the water bottle that the riders carry on their cycles.

Bit-and-bit The action of the riders who share the effort of riding at the front of a group while the other cyclists shelter behind.

Block Description of the sprockets and freewheel on the back hub of a road-racing cycle that is fitted with Derailleur gears. Also the deliberate obstruction of another cyclist.

Blow up To be overcome with exhaustion on a tiring leg of a race.

Bonk The slang term for exhaustion resulting from over-exertion and a lack of blood sugar.

Bonk bag See "musette."

Box Occurs when a cyclist rides just behind and to the outside of another rider, causing them to swing wide if they wish to pass.

Break To get clear of the other riders in a road or track race.

Bunch The main group of riders in a race.

Cadence The number of times the pedals revolve in a minute.

Category The race in that a cyclist is entered into according to their age and level of experience.

Chain gang A training exercise where a line of cyclists exchange the lead, as in bit-and-bit.

Chain set The chain, chain wheels, and rear cogs or sprockets.

Circuit races Road races where the riders have to cover a certain distance or number of laps. They are held on a road closed to normal traffic, an airfield or a motor-racing track.

Classics A group of one-day races held in Europe from one town to another.

Close passing When a rider passes another cyclist while being as close as possible to them. Not a safe practice.

Control points See "pits."

Course des primes A race where primes (awards) are given at certain points.

Cowboy A cyclist who rides erratically.

Criterium A road race in that the streets are closed and the cyclists ride through the roads that link villages.

Cycles Any kind of cycle is allowed for road racing, as long as it has not been streamlined and does not exceed specific dimensions. For track racing, freewheel gears, brakes and quick-release wheels are not allowed.

Cycleway A specially-built cycle route.

Cyclo-cross Raced in winter over cross-country courses that vary in length, the maximum being 24km. If a track is used, then each lap should be at least 3km. Competitors either cycle or run carrying their bikes depending on the terrain, that can include woodland, paths and roads, walls, stiles and streams.

Demi-fond French term for motor-paced racing. Means middle distance.

Derailleur A gear-changing mechanism that allows the chain on the bike to be moved onto sprockets of differing sizes that are fitted to the rear hub of the cycle. It is operated by levers on the handlebars or down-tube.

Devil-take-the-hindmost A track event in that the last rider in the field to pass the finish line is eliminated every so many laps, until only two riders remain to ride in the final sprint.

Dismounting Once a rider has dismounted from his cycle, he is allowed to finish the course by carrying, dragging or wheeling his cycle.

Domestiques Members of a road-racing team whose job is to support the leader, even to the extent of handing him their cycle if his is damaged.

Dress Competitors must be covered from the neck to the knees. They must wear a racing number on their backs and a crash helmet for safety reasons.

Drop See" break."

Echelon A diagonal line of riders positioned across a road to shelter from a crosswind.

Free-wheel A sprocket that drives the rear wheel, but that also can run free without the pedals being turned.

General classification The overall ranking of riders in a stage race based on the total time taken to cover the stages completed.

Handicap A race in that lesser riders are given the advantage of either a time allowance or a number of meters' head start. Not longer than 1000m.

Hill climbs Events where the riders aim to be the fastest up a hill. The course measures approximately 5km.

Homeward The journey from the half way turn to the finish during time trials.

Honk To ride off the saddle, standing on the pedals to gain more power.

Human pacing Allowed only in track events. Each competitor is permitted to have one pacer. They must wear normal racing dress and crash helmets. Men are allowed to pace women.

Individual pursuit A track race between two competitors who start off at opposing ends of the track and have to try to catch each other. The winner is either the one to catch the opposing cyclist or the one with the fastest time.

Italian pursuit A team pursuit race in that each team drops a rider at the completion of every lap until only one rider per team is left to race in the final lap. The winner is the rider with the fastest time.

Jump A sudden sprint in an attempt to break away from the main part of the field.

Kermesse A form of circuit road racing.

King of the mountains Title given to a road-racing cyclist who attains the best times in a one-day or stage race held over hill and mountain courses.

Lanterne rouge French term for a red lantern. This is a booby prize awarded to the last person in a stage race.

Limit man The rider with the greatest advantage in a handicap race.

CRITERIUM: A road race where the streets are closed and the cyclists race between villages

Line-out A string of riders behind the leader, whose pace stops them from bunching together.

Madison A track race where two team members compete to ride the greatest number of laps in an allotted time. The riders take turns racing so that they are given an opportunity to rest.

Maillot jaune The yellow jersey worn by the leader of the Tour de France and other major competitions.

Massed-start racing Another term for road racing.

Minute man The cyclist starting in a time trial either a minute ahead or behind another rider.

Motorcycles Used in motor pacing, they must have engine capacities between 500cc and 1000cc. Each motor-bike must carry a roller placed at the back of the rear wheel to stop the other rider from moving too close to the pacer.

Motor paced A track race where the cyclists are paced by motorcyclists who shelter them from the wind and take them along in their slipstream.

Mountain classification The award-ing of points on certain mountain sec-tions of a road race or tour according to the difficulty of the gradient.

Musette A cotton bag containing food and drink, which a rider picks up as he passes through a feeding station.

Omnium A track event in that the rider takes part in a number of races such as sprint, motor paced, etc.

Pacing To set a speed for a cyclist as well as giving them protection from the wind in order to make better progress.

Pack To stop racing.

Peloton The French term, meaning crocodile, for the main bunch of riders in a road race.

Pits Set up along certain points on long events for repairs and to feed the cyclists.

Points classification A feature of stage races in that the points are awarded to competitors according to their finishing position at each stage, without timing being a factor.

Point to point A track race where riders accumulate points at certain intervals in relation to their position. The winner is the rider to gain the most points, even if they are not the first rider to finish.

Prime A prize or bonus given to the rider who is the first to pass a certain point during a race.

Pursuit See "Australian pursuit."

Recumbent A bike on that the rider pedals in a horizontal position.

Repechage A heat added to a race that has the sole purpose of allowing losers from the qualifying rounds another chance to reach the next stage of the competition.

Road racing Held on normal roads that are used by other traffic.

Roller race A stationary race where the rider uses a cycle mounted on three rollers, that revolve to record the dis-tance covered over a set time.

Safety line Also called the sprinters' line. Marked distinctively in red, the line is placed 90cm from the inside of the cycle track.

Sag wagon A vehicle used in road events to pick up riders who have dropped out of the race.

Scratch races Track races where all competitors start on equal terms.

Scratch winner The rider who races the fastest time in a timed trial.

Selection from behind The tech-nique of a rider who sets such a severe pace that the other riders behind him have no choice but to drop back. Used instead of trying to break from the field at a later stage of the race.

Sidewalls The sides of a tire.

Sit in To stay in the bunch so that you

do not have to set the pace of the race.

Six-day race An indoor race where two-man teams race over a six-day period. Events include sprints, madisons, time trials and elimination races.

Sprint Occurs on a knock out basis. A track race where riders race differing circuits with the final 200m being timed.

Sprinters' line See "safety line."

Stack up When a rider falls off his bike in a spectacular manner, often followed by other competitors.

Stage race Describes a long-distance race where the distance is separated into stages and ridden over a number of days. The winner is the cyclist who covers the entire distance in the fastest time.

Station Used in pursuit races for the riders to start from.

Stayer The name given to a motor-pace rider.

Stoker The name given to the rider who sits behind on a tandem bicycle and provides extra power.

Tandem A bicycle designed for two people to ride. The rider in front steers the cycle while both riders pedal the bike.

Team pursuit A track event with teams of four riders. Each team member rides one lap before slotting in at the back. The race is 4000m long.

Tester The name given to a time trialist.

Time trial A road race set over a specified distance with the riders being timed. Also known as a race against the watch.

Toe clip A metal frame that is attached to the pedal of a cycle and fitted over the foot with a strap to prevent the foot from slipping off while pedaling at high speeds.

Toe-in The amount at that the brake blocks are set at an angle to stop them from squealing when the brakes are applied.

Tour de France Cycling's most famous event, an international competition held once a year that covers 3,400km over 24 one-day stages in various locations, several of them mountainous.

Track racing Racing that takes place on specially made tracks. They are mostly oval in shape with high banking at the corners to allow competitors to maintain their speed around bends. Surfaced with wood, asphalt or concrete, they can be indoor or outdoor. Competitors ride in a counter clockwise direction.

Tube set The collection of tubes that makes up a frame.

Turn The point of the race where the rider finishes the outward half of the race and begins the homeward part. Occurs in a time trial.

UCI The Union Cycliste Internationale, that is the world governing body of cycling.

Unknown distance A track race where competitors do not know the final distance over that they will race until the bell rings for the final lap.

Up the banking The position near the top of the corner banking where the sprinter is able to develop an attack.

Wheelbase The distance between the centers of the front and rear wheels on a cycle.

Whip The name of the official whose job is to ensure that all the riders are positioned at their starting places on time.

Work To help set the pace of the race.

Mountain Biking

Mountain bike racing is a challenging sport that uses high tech machines to race over varying courses such as cross-country and dual races.

Aluminium Frame metal commonly used for lightweight race bikes.

ATB Generic term for mountain bike, short for All Terrain Bike.

Berm An artificially created bank that enables a corner to be taken at an exaggerated angle and therefore at higher speeds.

Bike mark Process whereby at the start of a race, similar numbered stickers are placed on both wheels and the frame. These are then checked at the end of the race to ensure the racer has completed the course on the same equipment as he started on.

Body armor Protective equipment worn by downhill racers that protects vulnerable areas of the body such as the knees, elbows, spine, face, chest and thighs.

BCF The British Cycling Federatio, the national governing body for cycle sport in Great Britain.

Bunny hop An advantage technique, that involves a rider lifting both wheels off the ground by crouching and then springing up with their bike; enables a rider to clear obstacles such as holes in the ground and fallen branches.

Carbo-loading A nutritional process where riders increase their intake of carbohydrates before a race to increase energy levels and endurance.

Carbon Space-age frame material. Very strong and, most important, light. Also very expensive.

Clipless pedals System whereby riders click securely on to the pedal with an attachment on the sole of the shoe, known as a cleat.

Cross-country A racing discipline. Events usually consist of a number of laps on a marked course, that will encompass all types of terrain such as technical descents, steep climbs, single track and river crossings. Depending on the course, laps may vary in length. Racers are graded according to ability, with the less able and experienced racing over fewer laps than the experts.

Disc brake Braking system where the braking surface is a metal disc placed between two hydraulically operated brake pads rather than brake pads forced on to the rim of the wheel.

Doubles Section of a downhill or dual course where two jumps are placed close together, in other words, a double Jump. Riders will either clear them in one extended jump or ride through them one at a time.

Downhill A racing discipline riders compete one at a time over a marked course, with the rider with the quickest time being deemed the winner. The course will often consist of almost 100 percent descending, with between 500 and 2500 ft of vertical drop between the start and finish.

Drop-off Obstacle where the trail drops vertically. It may only be a few inches or considerably more. Riding drop-offs requires considerable skill, often needing the rider to raise the front wheel of the bike while letting the rear wheel touch down first to ensure a smooth landing. Drop-offs differ from jumps in that the riders gain no height in negotiating them, but literally drop off to the lower level.

Dual racing New format of racing where two riders race head to head on a short predominantly downhill course made up of various obstacles with the first across the line being deemed the winner. A series of knock out heats lead to a head to head final between the fastest riders.

Feathering Advanced technique of applying brakes, that slows the rider down rather than bringing the rider to a complete stop. Enables a good rider to maintain the maximum speed through difficult terrain.

Feed station Part of the course where racers can take on additional food and water during a cross-country race.

Full face helmet Due to the high speed and technical nature of downhill racing, riders require additional protection for the head. They use full-face helmets that protect the face, teeth and jaw, with an integral guard across the lower face.

Full-suspension All downhill bikes now have suspension at front and rear. This enables higher speeds to be maintained over rough terrain without the penalty of the extra weight involved having much effect.

Gas Bomb Device that rapidly inflates an innertube - carried by cross-country racers to help with quick repairs after a puncture.

Get air Literally to fly in the air, take off from a jump. To get big air is to fly high into the air.

Granny gear Also known as Granny ring, the lowest gear on mountain bikes, that is used on long steep climbs.

Hardtail Bike with front suspension only.

Knobbly Tire with a heavy broken tread pattern, enabling it to grip in slippery and muddy circumstances. A term borrowed from off-road cycling.

Pump Used to inflate an innertube.

Semi-slick Combination tire with heavy tread at the edges but smooth center-section. Favored by cross-country racers in dry conditions where they offer less rolling resistance and therefore more speed.

Singletrack Section of a cross country course wide enough for one rider to pass. Requires considerable skill to ride at speed and therefore a favorite of racers and course designers alike.

Snake bite Flat tire, caused when the innertube is trapped between something hard like a stone and the rim of the wheel. Often results in a double hole in the innertube, as though bitten by the fangs of a snake, hence the name.

Suspension fork Innovation where the front fork is sprung like a motorcycle so as to soak up trail bumps.

T-bone Action usually seen in dual racing where one racer deliberately or accidentally rides into the side of his opponent (the impact has the two bikes making a T-shape, hence T-bone), often resulting in knocking them off their cycles.

Triples Section of a dual or downhill course where there is a series of three jumps placed closely together. Riders can either choose to jump them or ride them – requires a similar technique to doubles.

UCI The Union Cycliste Internationalo, the world governing body of cycling.

V-brake The ultimate traditional brake system (i.e. brake blocks rubbing on the rims.)

World Cup Season long UCI competition that takes the best riders all over the world.

Worlds World championships, that take place every year.

Mountaineering

Mountaineering is an outdoor sport where competitors use their skill to climb difficult routes up a mountain.

Abseiling A way of making a descent down a mountain by sliding down a rope that is fixed to a natural or artificial protrusion.

A cheval A method of climbing a ridge or steep edge. The climber places one foot on either side and grips the crest to hop up.

Artificial climbing The use of man-made instruments such as bolts and pitons to assist in climbing very difficult rock.

Belay An important safety measure that anchors the climbers in case a fall occurs.

Bergschrund A crevasse that separates the upper slopes of a glacier from the upper snows of the mountain.

Bottoming Occurs when a piton reaches the back of a crack before the blade is fully secured.

Bridging A method of climbing by placing one foot and hand on one wall and placing the other foot and hand on the other wall.

Chalk Used by climbers to prevent their hands from slipping on rocks. Usually carried around the waist.

Chimney A vertical and narrow opening in the rock that is wide enough for a man to climb up.

Chockstone Can be used as an anchor point for a belay or runner. The stone is jammed firmly into a crack or chimney.

Climb The route taken.

Col A dip in a ridge between two peaks. Also known as a saddle.

Cornice A bank of snow that is formed by the prevailing wind and hangs over the edge of a ridge.

Couloir A furrow or gully caused by erosion on a mountain face. Can be rock, ice or snow.

Crack A narrow opening in the rock face used for holds.

Crag The name given to a steep rock-face.

Crampon A metal frame with steel spikes that is fitted onto the shoes by straps to aid the climber when climbing on ice and snow.

Crevasse A crack or cleft in the surface of a glacier.

Cirque A valley.

Dead man A snow anchor that is embedded in the snow.

Duvet A down-filled jacket.

Etrier A movable stirrup or step that can be attached to a piton or a sky hook so that the climber can stand on it.

Fixed ropes Permanent ropes placed on a popular mountain climb.

Free climb A climb performed without any artificial aids, but the climber may be protected against falls by a rope.

Front-pointing An ice-climbing technique where the climber uses two ice-axes and the front prongs of his crampons into the ice to achieve a four-point contact.

Gangway An inclined ledge on a rock face.

Gardening To remove vegetation from a rock climb.

Glissading Controlled sliding down a snow slope using an ice axe as a brake.

Grading A way of assessing the difficulty of a climb.

Hammer axe A short ice axe with a hammer head instead of a blade and a specially curved pick for front-pointing.

Hand traverse A method of climbing when there aren't any footholds. The climber crosses the rock face sideways with most of his weight on his hands.

High altitude Generally applied to climbs over 6,000m.

Hold A crack in the rock where a climber can place their hands or feet during a climb.

Jumar A clamp that is attached to a rope and is free moving, but if downward pressure is applied then it automatically locks.

FREE CLIMB: A difficult climb up the face of a rock, performed without any artificial aids

Karabiner An oval or D-shaped spring-loaded clip used for attaching to such aids as ropes, slings, screws or pitons.

Layback A climbing method used on corner cracks. Both feet are positioned against the outer edge, while the hand grips the nearer edge and the hands and feet are moved alternately along the crack.

Mantelshelf A climbing method where the climber places the palms of the hands on the hold and pulls up his body until one foot can be placed on the

same hold. The climber then stands upright.

Mixed climbing Form of climbing that encompasses rock, ice and snow climbing.

On sight Term that describes a climb that the leader has not inspected before.

Outcrop climbs Small climbs on rock faces that are no more than one pitch long.

Overhang A rock face that extends out beyond a vertical plane.

Pass An alternative name for col or saddle.

Peel The slang term for a fall.

Pillar A tall, narrow column of rock that extends from a mountain.

Pitch The distance that a climber has to travel from one belay to the next.

Piton A metal spike hammered into either ice or rock cracks. Also known as pegs.

Rib Describes a ridge or steep edge.

Ridge The point where two opposing faces of a mountain meet.

Roof The underside of an overhang.

Run-out The length of rope between the leader and the second man on a climb.

Scramble A rough climb up rocks, but not as difficult as any graded climbs. Usually does not require artificial aids such as ropes.

Scree Describes the fragments of rock that have fallen from a crag to the slopes below.

Stance A place where a climber is able to stop at the top of a pitch in order to secure a belay.

Traverse To move sideways across a mountain face, or to climb a mountain by one route and come down by another.

Verglas A thin coating of ice over the rocks that adds to the difficulty of the climb.

Ballooning

Ballooning competitions are based on precision navigation of the balloon using the available winds. The balloon is controlled by regulating the temperature of the air, that makes it either ascend or descend.

Auxiliary equipment Can include air-to-ground radio, aircraft radio, compass, maps, helmets, inflation fan and spare fuel cylinders.

Balloons Average size is 1,841 cubic meters. The actual balloon, or envelope as it is known, is made of rip-stop nylon while the basket is made from woven willow cane.

Bullet A metal peg that is attached to the top of the rip line.

Burn Means to turn the on/off control and allow the main burner to work at full power.

Burner Describes the unit consisting of the coiled stainless steel tubing that feeds the propane fuel to the jets.

Car lines Stainless steel wires that run around and underneath the basket and emerge at the top, extending up and attached to the underside of the burner offload ring.

Ceiling The height above ground or water of the base of the lowest layer of cloud.

Center of gravity The point at that a balloon will balance exactly.

Copybook landing Describes a perfect landing, without tipping the basket over and with the minimum of vertical speed.

Course The intended direction of flight.

Crew A small balloon may carry only the pilot while a large balloon may carry up to 12.

Crew chief The senior ground crew member who is responsible for the inflation and launching of the balloon.

Crown The name given to the top of the balloon.

Crown line A strong line attached to the top or crown of the balloon that is used to hold the canopy down during inflation.

Doghouse landing A very fast landing that results in the balloon basket turning upside down.

Drift Means to deviate from the intended track.

Drop line Measures 30-45m in length. Used by the pilot whenever he needs assistance in landing.

Dump To open the dump valve in order to lose hot air and thus height.

Dump line The line made of stainless steel wire attached to the dump valve or window and running down to the basket.

Dump valve A fabric window that can be opened by means of the dump line to allow sufficient hot air to escape for the balloon to make a descent.

False lift Occurs when the balloon lifts off and starts to climb and then begins to descend again. Normally due to incorrect weighting off or being assisted off the ground by unskilled helpers.

Fuel Balloons use liquid propane to power them along.

Good landing Means a landing that you can walk away from.

Handling line Describes a thin rope that measures approximately 61m in length.

Hands off Method used to see if the balloon is ready for takeoff. The helpers start by standing around the balloon

BALLOONS: Come in a variety of shapes and sizes. All competitions are based on precision navigation

holding the basket. They will then raise their hands vertically and if the balloon begins to rise, the command "hands on" will be given. When the pilot is ready for take-off, he will signal the helpers by saying "hands off and stand back."

Heading The direction in that a balloon is traveling.

Heavy Describes the balloon when it is not hot enough to stay in the air and begins to descend.

Knot One nautical mile per hour. Is the standard unit of speed measurement.

Light Describes the balloon when it is ready to leave the ground or is ascending.

Load ring The metal surround that holds the burner unit suspended by the rigging lines beneath the mouth of the balloon.

Mayday The international distress call.

Mouth The bottom open part of the balloon.

Meteorology The art of understanding how the weather works, needing a knowledge of cloud types, fog types, temperature, humidity and the forma-

tion of frontal systems.

Navigation The art of map reading, cross-country flying and an understanding of the effects of wind on track and ground speed.

Pilot light A small pipe and jet that enables a constant flame to be available for re igniting the main burners.

Required track A line drawn on a map joining the point of departure and the destination.

Rigging lines Stainless steel wires running from the load tapes to the burner ring.

Rip Means to open the rip panel in order to deflate the balloon.

Rip line Attached to the top of the rip panel and runs down to the basket.

Rip panel A large triangular section of the balloon canopy that is laced or fixed in place with Velcro. Pulled open in order to deflate the balloon.

Skirt Fire resistant material that is hung around the mouth of the balloon.

Tie-off thread Describes the breaking thread that is used to secure the rip.

Parachuting

Sport parachuting is held over a drop zone where competitors must land. Classes of competition include team jumps, free-fall jumps, accuracy jumps, style jumps and canopy contact jumps.

AOD Is an automatic opening device. Most types use the changes in barometric pressure to trigger the mechanism that opens the pack.

Apex The hole at the top of the canopy.

Attack point In accuracy jumping, an imaginary point over that the jumper should be positioned.

Back loop A backward somersault during a free fall.

Barrel roll A 360 degree left or right movement around a horizontal axis during a free fall.

Bridle line A nylon cord that connects the pilot chute to the sleeve.

Bungees The slang term for the elastic opening bands that run across the back of the pack.

Canopy The name given to the nylon part of the parachute that fills with air when opened in order to slow down the speed of the parachuter's fall.

Capewell release Describes the method of connecting or disconnecting the main part of the parachute to the harness. There are two different types for men and women.

CIP The Commission Internationale de Parachutisme, the body in charge of international parachuting.

Connector links There are four in total and they connect the rigging lines to the four risers.

DC The dead center of the target used for accuracy jumps.

Deep Describes the parachutist being upwind of the opening point required for landing in the drop zone.

Delta position A free-fall position where the sky diver has the legs straight and 30 degrees apart with the arms held back at the same position as the legs.

Drogue Another term for the pilot chute.

Drop zone The area on the ground where the parachuters may be safely dropped.

Elastics Another term for the pack-opening bands.

Forward loop Term used to describe a forward somersault performed during a free fall.

Free fall Describes a descent to a certain altitude without having opened the parachute.

Frog position A version of the stable free fall position. The parachutist falls with his back only slightly arched and his arms bent at right angles from the elbows with the hands pointing forward in line with the head and the legs bent at the knees.

Full cross The ground signal that lets the sky divers know that conditions are safe for parachuting.

Gore The wedge-shaped piece of canopy that is positioned between the two rigging lines.

Ground signals Made with colored panels including red, yellow, orange and white, and used to make the full cross and the letters T, I and L. These symbols are used to advise the jumpmaster on the conditions for parachuting.

Group jump Describes an accuracy group jump where four divers leave the aircraft almost at the same time.

High Describes the last jumper to open their chute during group jumping.

I The ground signal that tells the Jumpmaster that all parachuting is temporarily suspended, for whatever reason.

Jump and opening altitude The minimum jump level above the ground for free falls is 700m for an individual and 800m for a team. The parachute must be open at 400m for all jumps.

Jumpmaster The person in charge of all the jumps from the aircraft.

L The ground signal that all parachuting has been suspended and that the aircraft must land.

Lift Describes the number of parachutists jumping from an aircraft during a flight.

Lo-Po Describes a low-porosity canopy that allows less air to pass through.

Low Describes the first parachutist to open his or her parachute in a group jump.

Mouth lock A flap of fabric that is placed on the bottom of the sleeve. Its function is to prevent any suction from dragging the canopy from the sleeve before the rigging lines are clear.

Pack Container where the pilot chute, rigging lines and sleeve are kept until it is time for the parachute to be opened.

Piggyback rig A method where the reserve parachute is mounted above the main parachute in the pack.

Pilot chute Describes the small chute that opens immediately on the pack being opened. Its function is to pull out the rigging and sleeve from the pack.

Reserve chute A smaller chute worn as a safety measurement in case the main chute fails to work.

Rigging lines The nylon lines that join the canopy to the harness by means of the connector links and risers. Also known as suspension lines.

Rip cord A stainless steel cable that the parachutist pulls in order to open the parachute.

Risers The straps that run from the harness to the connector links.

Short Describes being downwind during freefall of the opening point required for landing in the dead zone.

Skydiving Means to free fall.

Sleeve The long wind sock-like container held in the pack where the canopy for the chute and the rigging lines are held.

Spotting Describes selecting the correct moment to jump from the aircraft in order to land in the target area.

Stable position The basic exit position used by jumpers once they have left the aircraft and are on their way down. Also known as the full spread stable position.

Static line A length of webbing used to open a pack without a rip cord.

Stick The slang term used for a lift.

Streamer The slang term used for the wind drift indicator.

T The ground signal that jumping conditions are safe only for experienced parachutists.

Target A cross, colored either white, red, yellow or orange, that is placed in the dropping zone.

Terminal velocity Describes the maximum speed at that a sky diver travels during free fall.

Toggle The steering line attached to the rear riser on either the left or right.

Tracking Means to cover ground in a horizontal direction during a free fall.

Turn A 360-degree movement in either direction around a vertical axis. Also known as a spiral.

WDI The Wind Drift Indicator. It is a weighted rod that has a strip of colored paper attached to it.

Wind sock Indicates the wind direction at ground level.

Paragliding

`Paragliding is an accessible sport as long as you have the nerve for heights. The paraglider is placed into a harness, that is a swinging seat with a bar placed across the body and attached to a canopy.

....

Accuracy Competitive aspect of tow-launched paragliding involving extremely accurate spot landings.

AFNOR (The Association Franchise de Normilisation) Widely recognized airworthiness tests for paragliders.

Aerodynamics The study of air in motion.

AGL Above ground level.

Airspeed Speed of a glider through the air, not necessarily its ground speed.

All-up weight Total airborne weight of the pilot, harness, equipment and canopy.

Alpine launch A take off technique for light winds.

Altimeter Electronic or mechanical instrument to measure an aircraft's altitude.

AMSL Above mean sea level.

ASI Airspeed indicator.

Best glide speed Airspeed at that the maximum glide is achieved.

Big ears A rapid-descent technique.

B-line stall A rapid-descent technique.

Blue thermal Rising bubble of air with no attendant cloud.

Brakes Primary controls used to steer or alter speed.

Building the wall Means to prepare the canopy before flight can take place.

Canopy The fabric wing of the glider. Also a term for the complete paraglider.

Control lines Connected to the trailing edge of the canopy and manipulated by the pilot so as to control and maneuver the paraglider.

Convert Trade excess airspeed for height.

Cravat A wing tip deflated and trapped in the suspension lines.

Cross-bracing Method of harness construction that provides stability.

Cross-port vents The holes that connect the canopy cells to allow pressure equalization.

Cumulus Small, fluffy clouds that often form at the top of a thermal.

Deep stall Stalled state in that a paraglider has no forward airspeed but a very high descent rate. Also called a parachutal stall.

Deflation Occurs when the paraglider wing is presented to the airflow at too low an angle of attack. Also known as a tuck or collapse.

Dual Describes two people flying on one glider.

Fichet A small peg used to mark the first point of ground contact in accuracy competitions.

Flare Action taken to slow or stop a paraglider to effect a landing.

Glide angle/ratio Ratio of height lost to horizontal distance traveled by a glider in still air.

Gust A sudden increase in wind speed.

Hang glider Weighs approximately 32kg. It is made of an aluminium airframe that is covered with a Dacron sailcloth and braced with stainless-steel flying wires.

Harness Consists of a swing seat with a bar going across the pilot's body to strap him in.

ISA International standard atmosphere.

Keeper Metal ring attached to a paraglider's rear riser to retain brake lines.

Landing When coming in to land, the pilot must pull the steering toggles down to slow the descent of the canopy before making a soft stand-up landing.

STEERING: The pilot steers by using toggles, that are placed in front of him at all times

Lift Upward aerodynamic force acting perpendicularly to the direction of motion, created by the wing moving through the air.

Lines Thin cords of the suspension system connecting risers to the canopy.

Mallon Small steel link connecting the paraglider to risers and often used to connect risers to the harness.

Max glide Best possible glide ratio of a particular glider and pilot. Also another term for best glide speed.

Minimum sink A glider's lowest possible rate of descent.

Polar curve Graphical representation of a glider's performance.

Pump Use of the paraglider's controls to reinflate a collapsed part of canopy.

Rigging The suspension system. Steel wires support the structure.

Risers The webbing connecting the harness to all the suspension lines.

Roll Angular movement of the paraglider about its longitudinal axis, either increasing or decreasing bank.

Rotor Potentially dangerous turbulence downwind of a ground feature or mountain.

SIGMET Warning of severe weather issued by meteorological offices, "significant meteorology".

Sink rate The rate of descent of a paraglider measured in still air.

Speed bar Base bar with bends that allows the pilot to shift his weight farther forward.

Speed system Increasing a paraglider's top speed by altering the relationship of risers, controlled by a foot stirrup.

Stall Loss of lift due to increasing the angle of attack to the point where airflow separation occurs. Normally the result of flying too slowly.

Stirrup Part of the speed system in that the pilot uses the stirrup to control the risers.

STOL Short take off and landing.

Suspension lines The lines connecting the canopy to the risers. They start at the leading edge and move toward the rear or trailing edge.

Thermal Rising bubble or column of air heated by earlier contact with the surface, in that a glider can gain height.

Toggle Another name for paraglider control handles. They are placed in front of the pilot so that he is able to steer the hang glider toward the correct direction. Also used when landing to slow down the descent.

Trim speed Speed at that a paraglider flies without any input to the pitch control.

Trim tubs Used for adjusting the relationship of risers to alter a paraglider's trim speed. Also called trimmers.

Wave Standing waves generated in an airflow that can give remarkable height gains but also heavy sink.

Yaw Angular movement of an aircraft about its vertical axis.

Hang gliding

Hang glider pilots remain airborne for long periods of time, executing turns and other aerobatics. Pilots use thermals or ridge lift to remain in the air, and are judged on distance and speed. Pilots use their legs to launch and land the aircraft.

Airfoil Longitudinal cross section of a wing, shaped to produce lift efficiently. Also used to describe streamlined uprights.

Adiabatic Change in temperature of a mass of air caused by changes in pressure without any gain or loss of heat from its surroundings.

Aerodynamics The study of air in motion.

SOARING: The means by that the hang gliding pilot stays in the air during areas of lift

A-frame Triangular frame used to control a hang glider; part of its structure. Also called a control frame.

AGL Above ground level.

Airspeed The speed of a hang glider through the air, that is not necessarily its ground speed.

Altimeter Electronic or mechanical instrument that measures an aircraft's altitude.

Altitude The vertical distance above mean sea level.

AMSL Above mean sea level.

Angle of attack The angle at that the airflow meets the chord line of a wing.

Angle of incidence Rigged angle of the wing or parts of the wing relative to a datum point.

ASI Airspeed indicator.

Aspect ratio The ratio of wingspan to the width (chord) of the wing.

Back up A hang glider's secondary hang loop. Usually slightly longer than the main hang loop. The term is also used for a reserve parachute.

Base bar The horizontal part of the hang glider A-frame. Also known as the control bar.

Batten Profiled aluminium or composite shafts in a hang glider wing that maintain its section.

Best glide speed Airspeed at that the maximum glide is achieved.

Blue thermal Rising bubble of air with no attendant cloud.

Chord The width of the wing measured from the leading edge to the trailing edge.

Chord line The imaginary straight line between the leading and trailing edges of a wing.

Clip in weight The total suspended weight of the hang glider pilot, harness and equipment.

Crosstubes Pair of large-diameter tubes of a hang glider airframe holding the leading edges out and the sail in tension. Also known as cross booms.

Dihedral Upward angling of a wing

viewed from the front or back. Promotes roll stability.

Drag Aerodynamic force resisting the forward motion of a body.

Dual Describes two people flying in one glider.

Fichet A small peg used to mark the first point of ground contact in accuracy competitions.

Glide ratio Ratio of height lost to horizontal distance traveled by a glider in still air.

Ground effect Enhanced glide performance achieved by a wing being flown near the ground.

Groundspeed The speed of the glider over the ground. Varies according to wind strength and direction.

Harness The sling in that the pilot is situated while flying the glider. May also be a swing seat with a lap strap.

Hang loop Loop of webbing that connects the pilot's harness to the glider.

Keel Longitudinal member of the hang glider structure.

Kingpost The upper tubular support for the rigging wires.

Leading edge Forward edge of the wing.

Lift Upward aerodynamic force acting perpendicularly to the direction of motion, created by the wing moving through the air.

Luff lines The wires or cords between the kingpost and the trailing edge of the sail, holding reflex into sail.

Minimum sink A glider's lowest possible rate of descent. Also the airspeed at that this occurs.

Mylar Stiff plastic inserted in the leading edge of the sail to maintain its shape.

Polar curve A graphical representation of the glider's performance.

Reflex A narrow upward curve of the airfoil along a section of the wing parallel to the keel. This provides the hang-glider with some stability in pitch and makes it want to pull out of a dive.

Rigging wires Wires that brace the hang glider and that hold the airframe rigid.

Rogallo General name given to the original delta-shaped hang gliders that were based on the designs of Francis Rogallo for a space re entry vehicle parachute.

Rotor A turbulent area of wind found behind the edge of a sharp cliff that curls over into the sheltered area and blows in the opposite direction to the main wind.

Soaring The ability to keep the glider airborne in areas of lift. The pilot may have to tack forward and backward when close to the brow of the hill because there is little wind and a narrow lift band.

Span The total width of the glider from wingtip to wingtip.

Speed bar Base bar with bends to allow the pilot to shift his weight farther forward.

Spiral dive Used for losing height. This maneuver increases the loading on the glider.

Thermal Formed when the lower parts of the atmosphere are warmer than the upper parts. This is normally caused by the sun warming the ground. It results in a rising bubble of warm air in that the glider can circle to gain height.

Trailing edge The rearmost part of the wing.

Uprights The two more-vertical components of the A-frame.

Variable billow A system of increasing sail tension to increase performance.

Washout A twist in the wing that reduces the angle of incidence toward the wingtips. Essential for pitch stability.

Yaw Sideways movement in that the glider is not flying through the air in the direction it is pointing.

Gliding

Gliding describes flying in an aircraft without the assistance of engines (it is perfectly possible to glide in aircraft with engines that are not being used). Gliders are towed into the air by a winch or other aircraft, and gain height by seeking out thermals. In competition, pilots are judged on altitude, distance or speed.

Absolute altitude The record category for heights achieved.

Aero-tow A launching technique where a light aircraft is used to tow a glider into the air on the end of a rope. At an altitude of approximately 500m, the glider pilot releases the rope.

Ailerons Placed on the outer trailing edges of a glider's wings, the control surfaces are used to control the glider's lateral balance and angle of bank.

Air brakes Used by a pilot to control his rate of descent when landing. They are usually placed either above or below the wings and, when extended, they dump lift from the wings and increase the rate of descent.

Angle of attack The angle of the wing in relation to the aiflow over it. To obtain lift, the wing of the glider has to meet the airflow at an angle that causes the air to flow efficiently over it.

Auto-tow A technique used to launch a glider by towing it into the wind behind a car, similar to the principle of flying a kite.

Artificial horizon An instrument that gives the attitude of a glider without the pilot having to check the natural horizon.

Aspect ratio The relationship between the length of the wingspan and the chord on the glider.

Attitude Describes a glider's position in relation to the ground. Also describes the pilot's view of the horizon in relation to the nose of his glider.

B badge Awarded to a pilot who has made three solo flights and can take off, land and turn in both directions.

Bronze badge Awarded to a pilot who has achieved two soaring flights with a duration of 30 minutes and has passed examinations in navigation, airmanship, meteorology, principles of flight and air law.

Bungee launch Launching a glider by catapulting it from a hilltop with a rubber rope stretched out in a V-shape, with five or six people on either side of the V.

C badge Awarded to a pilot who has completed his first soaring flight.

Calculator A circular slide rule that is used to work out the height needed to glide a certain distance, or the distance of glide needed from a certain height.

Chord The width of the wing from front to back.

Climb rate The speed in meters per second at that a glider ascends.

Converging When two aircraft are converging at the same altitude, the aircraft that has the other on its right shall give way.

Diamonds The three highest attainable badges. Awarded for a flight of 500km, a triangular course flight of 300km and gaining a height of 5000m.

DI Daily inspection that should be carried out before the first take off on every flying day, after every outlanding and when a glider has been left unattended in a public place.

Distance to a declared goal The record category for a distance flight to a point determined before take off.

Distance to a turn point and back The record category for an out-and-return distance or speed flight.

Elevator A control surface placed on the trailing edge of the tailplane to control pitching.

Gain of height As well as being a record category, it also describes the height to that the glider has climbed after release from the tow.

Gold badge Awarded to a pilot who has made a flight of five hours, flown for 300km and to a height of 3,000m.

Induced drag Caused by the wing in producing the necessary lift to fly. This phenomenon is worse at low speeds.

IGC The Internationai Gliding Commission, that is the world governing body for gliding.

Lift The upward force from the wing, that acts at right-angles to the relative airflow.

MacCready ring The circular scale on some variometers that gives a pilot the best speed at that to fly between thermals.

Outlanding A landing that occurs elsewhere than at an airfield.

Parachute All glider pilots should wear a parachute when in the air. Worn on the back, they are slender in shape as there is not much spare room in the cockpit of most gliders.

Pitch The upward and downward movement of a glider's nose.

Pure distance The category for a distance flight. Measured as a circular course between the starting and landing points.

Profile drag The drag of the structure, wheels, etc, as the aircraft moves through the air. This increases as the airspeed increases.

Rudder The control surface on the trailing edge of the tailfin to control yaw.

Sailplane Term for a specialized glider that is designed to glide as far as possible. It is normally of very slim design, and has very high aspect-ratio wings (very long in relation to the distance between the leading and trailing edges.

Silver badge Awarded to a pilot who has made a flight for five hours, flown 50km across country and made a gain of height of 1000m.

Slope lift To soar on upcurrents that are produced by the wind blowing against and over the face of hills and mountains.

Standard class Competition class where the wingspan of the gliders must be at a maximum of 15m.

Thermals Rising bubbles of air that are normally produced from the sun's heating of the ground. Large concrete areas and cornfields are well known for producing good thermals.

Trim The balance of a glider fore and aft. A control surface called a trim tab is attached to the elevator to adjust the trim precisely.

Tug Colloquial name for the aircraft that makes an aero-tow launch.

Turn and slip indicator Similar to an artificial horizon, in that it shows the pilot in which direction he is flying.

Variometer Displays to the pilot the climb and sink rates of his glider while in the air.

Wave lift To soar on the upcurrents that have been forced over the top of hills and mountains, and then flow down and rebound into waves.

Winch-launch A technique of launching a glider by towing it with a cable wound around an engine-driven drum. Winch launches are very steep, and the glider gains height very quickly, but the eventual height depends on the length of cable and the skill of the pilot.

Skateboarding

Skateboarding is a fun and exciting sport for both spectators and competitors. It is mainly an individual sport made up of slalom courses, downhill sprints and trick performing.

Backsiding A turn on the board that is made in the direction in that the rider's back is facing.

Barrel jumping Moving from one skateboard to another while jumping over an obstacle course such as small barrels or cones.

Blank The flat deck of a skateboard.

Blue-tile fever The "high" a skateboarder feels when reaching the blue tiles around the edge of swimming pools.

Body cranking To move the arms and shoulders backward and forward to gain momentum.

Bongo A head injury resulting from an accident while performing on the skateboard.

Bunny hop The skater crouches down on the board and grabs both ends of it to lift it off the ground and perform small jumps.

Carving Making a wide turn without the wheels sliding sideways.

Catamaran A maneuver in that two skaters on two separate boards sit sideways and facing each other, and hold the two ends of their own boards while placing their feet on their partner's boards.

Christie Riding on the board while in a crouched position with one leg out straight to the side.

Coffin A maneuver in that the skater lies with his back on the board, with his arms crossed across the chest, as a body is laid in a coffin.

Coned The name given to wheels on a skateboard that have worn down to a taper as a result of overtightening of the trucks.

Curbie Riding up and down curbs.

Cushion The small rubber ring placed on the board to absorb vibrations and aid steering.

Daffy The skater rides two boards simultaneously, with the front foot on the front board performing a nose wheelie and the back foot placed on the back board performing a tail wheelie.

Double decker Performing on two boards with one positioned on top of the other.

Downweighting The action of the skateboarder sinking down on to the deck of the board to apply body weight.

Drop-in Dropping into a bowl or pool from a high point on the lip.

Eating it Falling off the board.

Endover While moving forward at all times, the skater takes the board through several 180-degree pivots alternately at the nose and tail wheels.

Flex memory The degree to that a board returns to its original shape after bending, and the time it takes to do it.

Frontsiding A turn on the board made in the direction in that the skateboarder's chest is pointing.

Goofy A skateboarder who rides with his right foot forward.

Gorilla grip Describes gripping each end of the board with bare toes and jumping into the air.

Gremlin A bad skateboarder.

Grip tape An adhesive tape that is applied to the deck of the board to give the skater a firm foothold.

Hamburger A scrape or cut received while on a moving board.

Hanging ten To ride the board with

the toes over the front edge.

Helicopter A 360-degree spin in the air while on the board.

High jumping Performed by jumping over a high bar, while the skateboard moves under it so that the skateboarder can land back on the board.

Hot dogging To perform freestyle riding that incorporates tricks.

Kick-tail The raised end of a deck on the board.

Kick turn To turn the board's direction by lifting the front wheels with the feet and pivoting on the back of the board until the turn is complete.

Lip The curved edge at the top of a bowl, bank or tool on that various maneuvers can be performed.

Natural A skateboarder who rides with their left foot forward.

Nose wheelie Riding on the front wheels while the back end of the board is off the ground.

Pavement pizza Scars incurred by falling off the board while in motion, also known as road rash.

Pirouette Performed by jumping off the board into a 360-degree turn before landing back on the board.

Power slide Used to change direction by leaning sharply into a turn, touching the ground with either one or both hands, and spinning the board around with the feet so that the back wheels slide sideways across the surface.

Pumping Moving to the left and right of the board and unweighting it so that the board increases its speed.

Radical The name given to difficult, exciting skateboarding.

Riser pad Made of rubber, wood or plastic and placed between the truck and the underside of the deck.

Rocker A one-piece deck used for bowl riding. It is curved up at either end so that the center of gravity is as close to the ground as possible.

Seven-twenty Two 360-degree turns performed on the back wheels of the board.

Shoot the duck Performed by crouching on the board with one leg extended out to the front and both arms stretched out to either side.

Skateboard Made up of a deck with two sets of two wheels. Bowl riders use a board with a kick tail. Slalom riders uses a flat board and downhill riders use a flat stiff board.

Slalom Describes riding the board through cones or similar objects.

Slide stop To come to a stop by sliding the tail of the board sideways at an angle to the forward movement.

Space walk Performed by riding with the nose of the board to the ground and waving from side to side.

Speed wobble To ride too fast and lose control of the board.

Stoked To get a buzz out of skateboarding.

Tail saver Also known as a skid plate. Placed on the tail of the board to stop the tail from being damaged during dragging.

Tail wheelie Riding with the feet placed over the back wheels to make the nose lift off the ground.

Three-sixty A 360-degree turn performed on the back wheels of the board.

Tic-tacking Performing alternate front and back kicks to gain momentum if riding along a flat surface or uphill.

Unweighting To jump up off the board to release the bodyweight from it.

Walking the dog A continuous series of 180-degree turns. One foot remains attached to the deck of the board, acting as a pivot, while the other foot lifts the other end.

Wedeling Quick, rhythmic turns.

Wipe out The slang term for a fall from the board.

In-line skating

In-line skating is an exciting sport that includes speed skating, skate-to-ski and extreme/street skating. The latter is a great spectator event.

A-frame A wide stance used to start turning movements. It aids the skater in maintaining balance and a low center of gravity.

Allen key A tool used to unscrew the bolts that hold the wheels and the brake in place.

Bearing Describes a case that holds seven ball bearings that are shielded and pre packed in grease. This reduces friction and allows the wheels to spin smoothly.

Brake The rubber stop normally found on the right skate. It is either round or square in shape.

Center edge The flat part of the wheel.

Center of gravity The distribution of weight that keeps the skater evenly balanced.

Corresponding edges The feet are held 15cm apart with the left ankle turned in and the right ankle turned out. Used when making a turn.

Crossover A turning technique that is used by skaters when traveling at great speeds. The name comes from the first step of this turn where the outside skate crosses over the other skate.

Diameter The size of the skate wheels, measured in millimeters.

Durometer Term used to describe the hardness of a skate wheel. Ranges from 74A-93A. The higher the number, the harder the wheel.

Edges The side and center of the skate wheels. They are used for stopping and turning.

Extreme skating Tricks and stunts performed, such as jumping off ramps or grinding on rails.

Frame The part of the skate underneath the boot that holds the wheel in place.

Freestyle General term for dance movements.

Grind Occurs when a skater slides along a rail. The rail slots in between the wheels. Special street-style skates are required for this maneuver.

Grind plate A metal frame that fits onto the skate frame to protect the frame from damage and aid the sliding action when grinding.

Helmet The most important part of a skater's protective gear. It is made with an inner shock-absorption layer and an outer protective shell.

Heel stop The braking foot is held in front with the brake beside the front wheel of the back skate. The toe of the braking skate is lifted until the brake is resting on the ground. The back knee is bent to give the skater more control of the brake.

In-line racing The 10km race is the most popular. The competitors skate at top speeds with the winner having finished first.

Inside edges Standing with the feet wider than the shoulders, the skater automatically leans on the inside edges. Used mainly for moving forward.

Inside skate The skate that is closest to a turn.

Momentum The force with that you move forward.

Outside edge The feet are held together with the ankles leaning outward and balancing on the outside edges.

Outside skate The skate that is outside or away from a turn.

Pads Protective safety equipment made of plastic and foam to protect the elbow and knee joints in a fall.

Parallel turn An advanced method of turning using corresponding wheel edges. The feet are placed in a scissor stance with most of the body weight put onto the front skate. The skater then leans his body into the turn while positioned on corresponding edges. The upper body and head are twisted while the lower body is kept in the scissored position until the turn is completed.

Power slide A means of stopping when traveling backward. The body weight of the skater is centerd over the front leg while the back leg is slowly raised with the toes turning out. The back foot is then repositioned onto the ground in a sliding position on the inside edge. The upper body faces the same direction as the front skate.

Power strap An extra buckle used to tighten the skate.

Quad skate Describes the original, four-wheeled skate.

Ramp A wooden or metal structure used to jump off.

Ready position The skater stands in a relaxed position with the arms at the sides, the legs shoulder-width apart and the skates on their center edges.

Rockering Lowering the middle skate wheels to create a curved wheel line. This allows a skater to make quicker turns.

Rotation Wheels should be rotated to improve their performance and make them last longer.

Scissor stance Used to glide, stop and turn. With the feet about 15cm apart, the skates are shuffled with one skate in front of the other until the back wheel of the front skate is beside the front wheel of the back skate.

Skates Have a hard outer shell and soft inner shell. They are tightened with either laces or buckles. The right skate usually has a heel brake.

Skate to ski Similar to skiing, and used by skiers to practice in the summer months.

Slalom Competition in that skaters move in and out of evenly-spaced markers in a line.

Spacer Made of plastic or metal, and placed in the center of the wheel to prevent the bearings from making contact with each other.

Speed skating Speed skaters use a very low skating position with their knees bent to almost 90 degrees. Their arms either swing from side to side in big arcs or are kept behind their backs.

Spin stop A means of stopping without using the heel brake. The feet are positioned in a scissor stance before the skater lifts one leg and pivots around on the skating foot. The other skate is then placed on the ground with the heels together and legs bent. Both skates will now be traveling into the spin. Once the spin is completed, the skater will come to a stop. The arms should be held out for balance throughout the maneuver.

Stance The correct way to stand on inline skates.

Street skating See "Extreme skating."

Swizzling Skating technique in that the skates are moved in and out while never actually leaving the ground.

T-stop Used to brake. The skater places his non-lead leg at the back of the leading leg to form a T-shape. Both knees are bent as the skater puts pressure on the back skate to drag along and stop.

V-frame The skater stands with his feet together and the toes turned out. The wheels are rolled onto their inside edge.

Roller skating

Roller skating is very similar to ice skating, except that it is not performed on ice. Skaters perform individually or in pairs for events such as figure skating and dancing. Although the sport holds national and international competitions, it is not yet recognized by the Olympic Games.

Arabesque Performed by using a form of spiral and skating with the body bent forward from the waist with the free leg stretched out behind and lifted up.

Bracket A one-foot turn made in a reverse rotation of the curve with the edges changing.

Character The type of edge skated on either inside or outside.

Chasse Performed by bringing the free foot onto the floor beside the skating foot, before lifting the skating foot and then replacing it while extending the free foot to its former position.

Choctaw A two-foot turn moving from one foot to the other using a different character. There are five forms: open, closed, crossed, uncrossed and swing.

Circle eights Figure eights performed through two circles on either foot.

Compulsory program Made up of compulsory movements in free skating and pairs skating.

Counter A one-foot turn that is made in the reverse rotation of the curve and then continued in natural rotation. The second circle performed is made in a reverse direction to the first curve. The character of the edges remains the same.

Continuous axis An imaginary line running around the rink.

Crossed chasse Performed by placing the free foot on the rink behind the skating foot, and then raising the original skating foot ahead and to the side of the other foot so that it again becomes the skating foot.

Cross over Technique used for going around corners. The skater moves on the outside edge of the inside leg, bringing the free foot over and in front of the skating foot before transferring to the inside edge of that skate and then bringing the original skating foot back alongside to continue stroking on the outside edge.

Curve Also called an edge. The arc described by a skater.

Curve eight A figure eight where the first circle is skated on the outside edge of the right foot and the second circle is skated on the outside edge of the left foot.

Edges Used to describe the way a skater curves. When body weight is put onto the side of the roller skate, the wheels turn to that side. There are inside and outside edges for moving forward and backward.

FIRS The Fédération Internationale de Roller Skating, that is the sport's governing body.

Footplate The part of the skate that is attached to the boot.

Free foot Describes the foot that is not being skated on, and also refers to any part of the body on that side. Also known as the unemployed side.

Free skating A skating program that involves jumps, steps and spins performed in rhythmic movements to music.

Inside edge Describes the side of the skate that corresponds to the inside edge of the foot.

Kilian hold A dance hold in that the two partners face the same direction with the woman's left shoulder resting on the man's right shoulder.

Midline An imaginary line that bisects the length of the rink.

Mohawk Two-footed turn that moves from one foot to the other on edges of the same character. There are five types: closed, open, crossed, uncrossed and swing.

Natural rotation To move in the same direction as that of the curve being traced.

Outside edge The side of the skate that corresponds to the outside of the foot.

Progressive A maneuver in that the free foot is brought ahead of the skating foot and placed on the rink so that it becomes the skating foot, while the other foot trails behind to become the free foot. This is then repeated.

Reverse rotation To move in the opposing direction to that of the curve being traced.

Rink The area where roller skating is practiced and performed.

Rocker A one-foot turn made with the natural rotation of the curve, but then continued in reverse rotation. The skater then moves into a second circle traveling in a reverse direction to the first curve. The character of the edges stays the same.

Roller derby Two teams of five that race around an oval track and win points by lapping the opponents.

Roller skates There are three types of skates and all of them have two sets of wheels. The rink skate is worn over normal shoes and held on by two leather straps. The free skating skate and the competition skate screw on to a specially constructed boot.

School figures Compulsory figures.

Spin A series of fast-moving turns on one or both feet.

Spiral Describes an edge skated on one foot at a constant speed and held for at least one circle.

Spread eagle A position in that the raised heel of the free foot is placed alongside the heel of the skating foot. Also a free skating maneuver in that the skater glides sideways on both feet with the heels turned in toward each other and the toes pointing away from each other.

Strokes Made by the skater gliding on both feet. Pushing the side of the foot in a T position propels the skater forward.

T position The feet make a T position by placing the heel of one foot at a right angle to the middle of the other foot.

Teapot Performed by the skater bending the skating leg and moving into a crouching position to then bend forward from the hips while keeping the free leg pointed out to the front.

Toe stop Placed at the front of the skate, it's made of rubber and used for braking.

Three jump Performed when the skater takes off from the outside edge, turning in mid air to land on the inside edge of the same foot.

Three turn The skater skates in a figure of three by performing a one-foot turn to change the character of the edges while following the natural rotation of the curve.

Tracing The path that the skating foot takes on the surface.

Tracing foot Describes the foot that is skating or tracing a figure. Also known as the employed foot.

Transverse axis An imaginary line that bisects the midline of the rink.

Turns Movements a skater uses to change from a forward direction to a backward one without stopping and vice versa. The skater can use either one or both feet.

Roller Hockey

Roller hockey involves two teams of five players each. The game is played professionally on a rink, and either a ball or a puck is used. The winning team is the one that scores the most goals.

Back-handed shot Used as a passing or scoring shot. Performed by placing the puck on the reverse of the scooping side of the blade while keeping the blade parallel to the feet. The player then shoots in the direction of their strong hand while following through with their body weight and shifting from the weaker to the stronger foot.

Ball hockey Played with a hard ball made of rubber.

Body checking An illegal move in roller hockey.

Box strategy Occurs when the players (except the goalkeeper) move into a box-like pattern in response to the opposing team's attack. All the players move as one.

Butterfly Used by a goalkeeper to stop a low-aimed shot. The goalkeeper drops to his knees with his shins facing outward and the stick between his legs. This enables him to shift quickly in either direction.

Circles There are five circles on the rink altogether, a center circle and four face-off circles. Each circle measures 3m in diameter with a dot measuring 0.14m–0.19m in diameter in the center.

Control zone The same width as the distance between a player's shoulders. This is the area in that a player controls the puck and ball while moving.

Crease The goalkeeper's area, that no other player is allowed to enter. If they do so, the referee will stop play. It measures 3.6m from the mouth of the goal and 3.6m from either side of the center of the goal.

Diamond strategy The same as the box, except that this strategy is rotated on its side.

Dress A face mask and guard are essential, as are shin, wrist, knee and elbow pads. A goalkeeper should also wear chest and arm pads, a catching glove and a jockstrap (if male).

Duration The game is divided into two 22-minute halves, with a three-minute interval in between.

Expulsion A player can be sent off for up to five minutes' playing time or for the rest of the game. He may be replaced by a substitute. If a second offense is committed, the player will be sent off for the rest of the game.

Face off Used to start the game and after each stoppage. The referee drops the puck between two opposing players in the center circle for the start, and in any face off circle afterward, nearest to where the stoppage occurred. Both players must have their backs to their own goal areas with their blades touching the floor, nine inches from the ball.

Faking To make false movements so that the opposing team members do not know what move you are going to make next.

Fouls Players are punished for playing the ball illegally, charging unfairly, deliberately obstructing, fighting, tripping, kicking, holding an opposing player, tackling unfairly or using their stick against another player.

Goal area Measures 465cm between the goal posts and 310cm from the surface of the rink to the top of the net.

God's country An offensive strategy in that the team's shooting area is defined by a trapezoid. The posts of the defender's goal are used as the upper corners of the trapezoid. Imaginary lines extend out from these posts.

IISA The International In-Line Skating Association, that is the governing body of the sport.

Indirect free hit Awarded to the opposing team of the last striker of the ball when the ball goes out of play. All other players must be at least nine feet away, and the player taking the hit is not allowed to touch the ball again until it has been touched by another player. Goals are not allowed to be scored from a free hit.

Offside There are no offside penalties, so a player may receive a pass from a team member in any point of the rink.

Penalty shot A direct shot from the penalty spot, awarded for serious infringements of the rules within the penalty area. All players other than the defending goalkeeper and the player taking the shot must be behind the center line. No player is allowed to move until the puck/ball has been hit.

Puck Weighs 85g, and is made of hard rubber.

Rink Measures 44–61m in length and 20–30m in width. The rink is divided by a center line. It must be surrounded by an 8in-high barrier.

Skates Hockey in-line skates are made to be extra rugged. The boots must be bolted to the skates. The material on the boots is stronger than normal skates and they have no back brake. The cir-cumference of the wheels must be at least one and a quarter inches in diameter.

Slap shot The player's weaker hand should be on the end of the shaft, with the stronger hand held two-thirds of the way down to the blade end. The stick is then lifted back behind and above, before swinging at the puck in one fluid motion.

Snap shot Similar to a slap shot, except that the stick is brought back to only mid-thigh level. The stick motion is kept parallel to the ground for as long as possible before being lifted.

Sticks Can be made of wood, plastic, aluminium, graphite or a combination of materials. The blade is curved but flat on both sides. The stick must not exceed 1.14m in length or have a diameter of more than 5cm. The maximum weight allowed is 510g.

Substitutes Up to nine substitutes are allowed on the bench. Players may be substituted during a game, but the goalkeeper is allowed to be replaced only during stoppage time. A player who has been shown a red card may not be substituted.

Teams Made up of five players each, including a goalkeeper, a left winger, a right winger, a left defender and a right defender.

Wrist shot Performed by holding the stick with the weak hand on the end of the shaft and the strong hand one-third of the way down from the top of the stick. The stick is then swung close to the ground to propel the puck forward.

Tug-of-War

Tug-of-war is a traditional sport that dates back many centuries. There are two types of competition: the points tournament and the knockout competition. Two teams of eight players compete in pulling a rope's white marking over the marks on the ground.

Anchor man's grip To pass the rope under one armpit, diagonally across the back and over the opposite shoulder from rear to front. The remaining rope should pass in a backward and outward direction and let the slack run free.

Arena The site on that tug-of-war is held. It should be flat, measuring a minimum of approximately 55m by 11m. Ideally it is oval in shape and surrounded by a firmly erected barrier.

Boots The boots of a competitor must not be "faked" in any way, and the sole, heel and side of the heel should be perfectly flush.

Borrowing A maximum of two men can be borrowed for a specific weight competition, but no club is allowed to borrow any man for any competition at catchweight where eight pulling members have been present.

Caution If an infringement has been made during the pull, the judge naming the team calls "First caution," and points a finger. If two cautions have been committed the judge shouts, "Final caution," and points with two fingers in the direction of the offender.

Dress Teams need to be dressed properly for all competitions. They have to wear appropriate shirts, shorts, stockings and approved footwear.

Dropping a man If a team loses a man through injury, the decision to "drop a man" from the opposing team is left to the discretion of that team's coach. The "dropped man" can rejoin the team for the next round.

Footholds Making indents in the ground before the command "Take the strain," is given is not allowed.

Grip The rope has to be taut from the very start of the contest, and every pulling member has to hold the rope with both bare hands. Therefore, the palms of both hands face up and the rope passes between the body and the upper part of the arm. The feet must be extended forward of the knees, and team members need to be in a pulling position at all times.

Ground markings One line is marked on the ground diagonally to the rope.

Infringement Awarded against a team if they deliberately do something that is not within the rules of the game. This can be anything from deliberately sitting on the ground to passing the rope through the hands.

Puller's grip The palms of both hands should be facing up and the rope should pass between the body and the upper part of the arm. Each pulling member should hold the rope in this way from the start.

Rest Six-minute rests are allowed between each round of a competition and between separate competitions.

Rope markings There are five markings on the rope altogether. The center-line of the rope is red, with two white markings on either side placed 4m apart, and two blue markings placed 1m away from the white markings. The first puller in each team grips the rope 30cm of the outer blue markings.

GRIP: Each team member has to hold the rope with both bare hands and keep feet forward of the knees

Side judge An official who stands in a position alongside the competing team on the opposite side of the rope to the judge. They are not allowed to make any remarks to the coach or any members of the team unless told to do so by the judge.

Start When the judge receives the signal from the two coaches that everybody is in position, he calls out "Pick up the rope," and the competitors extend their arms forward and horizontally. The judge will then shout "Take the strain," and raise both hands above his head as the team members put sufficient strain on to the rope. The judge will finally expose the palms of his hand with the added word "Steady," and then after a slight pause shout the word "Start."

Substitutes Substitutes are not allowed once the team has pulled in a competition. A man injured in a previous competition may be substituted in a catchweight team at the discretion of the chief judge.

Team numbers At the start of each competition, teams consist of eight pulling members. A competition starts for a particular team when it is in position to pull under the direct supervision of the judge. No substitutes are allowed once the team has pulled in the competition.

Trainer An individual who takes control of the team and advises them on how best to win the contest. Only one trainer is allowed with each team. During the pulling, the trainers must take up a position well clear of both teams, and are not allowed to say anything to them during the actual pulling.

Types of competition There are two types of competition: knockout, and the points tournament.

Weigh-in Takes place at the start of a contest to determine the combined weight of a team. Each team member steps on a set of scales to be weighed, and then all the competitors' weights are added together to give a combined total for the team.

Winners The winning team is the one that wins a pull. This occurs when one of the white markings on the rope has been pulled over the mark on the ground. This is signaled by the judge, who blows a whistle and points in the direction of the winning team.

Weightlifting

Competitors aim to lift a weighted bar above the head and hold it under control until signaled by the referee to replace it on the platform. Weightlifting is split into two separate lifts – the snatch, and the clean and jerk. Competitors get a maximum of three attempts at each lift.

Bandages Competitors are allowed to wear a protective bandage on their wrists, knees, hands, fingers and thumbs. A lifter alternatively can wear leather wrist straps or elastic knee caps to give them extra protection and support.

Barbell The apparatus used by a competitor that is lifted into the air with both hands. It is made of a steel rod with evenly distributed metal discs or rubber weights attached to both ends by collars. Each end of the bar has a revolving sleeve so that the bar can be turned during a lift.

Bench press One of the lifts in power lifting. A competitor lays on his back on the bench. The barbell is pressed up from his chest by an even extension of the arms.

Body weight The weight at that a lifter weighs in before a competition is about to begin. There are eight bod yweight categories for men and seven for women under IWF rules, ranging from 52kg to over 105kg.

Categories Each lifter is entered in a body weight class. Each lifter may enter one category only.

Collar A locking device that is employed to keep the weighted discs on the end of the bar.

Competitors The participants taking part in the men's or women's competition. In a major international competition, countries can enter a team of eight athletes for men spread over the different categories. For a women's major championship, they can enter seven lifters. They can compete in only one weight division.

Dead lift One of the lifts in power lifting. A competitor grips the bar with both hands before raising it until they are standing erect with the bar touching their thighs.

Deep knees bend Another name for the squat in power lifting.

Discs Each disc is marked with a separate weight, and they are loaded on the barbell with the largest inside and the smallest outside. The discs are locked on to the bar with a collar. They weigh between 0.25kg and 25kg, and all have separate colors to distinguish them from each other.

Dress The competitor is expected to wear a one-piece costume. They are allowed to wear a short-sleeved, collarless T-shirt underneath their costume. Trunks can be worn over the costume, with the maximum width of the belt being 120mm at its widest point. A weightlifter's boot cannot have a sole projecting from the shoe by more than 5mm at any point, and the maximum height of the shoe measured from the top of the sole must be 130mm.

Dumbbell Apparatus that can be lifted with one hand. It is made of a short steel rod that has disc weights attached to both ends by collars.

Duration Once a competitor has been called, they have one minute in that to make the attempt. An audible warning signal is made after 30 seconds. If the lifter fails to lift the barbell within the time period, the attempt is declared a "no lift" by the referees.

Hook grip A competitor is allowed to hook the fingers around the bar. They cover the last joint of their thumb with the fingers of the same hand at the moment of gripping the bar.

IWF International Weightlifting Federation. Founded in 1920, it provides the official set of rules for the sport.

Jury Officials who make sure that the technical rules are applied throughout the entire competition. They can also correct refereeing mistakes.

Lifting In a competition, weights are lifted using the snatch clean and jerk. Competitors are allowed three attempts in each kind of lift. If they succeed they may progress to a heavier weight for the next lift.

Lifting order Each competitor receives a number indicating the order in that they go for the weigh-in and the order of lifting. The same number is kept by the competitor throughout the competition.

Locked arms Full extension of the arms with the barbell placed above the head.

No lift In either the snatch or the jerk, the lift is deemed invalid if it fails to meet with the approval of the referees because of an infringement of the rules for that particular lift. This could be anything from the bar reaching the knees in an unfinished movement to the arms of the competitor being bent or extended during the recovery.

Platform The area from that all competition lifts are made. The platform is normally made of wood and measures 4m square. A lifter has one minute in that to come to the platform to make their lift. If, during the lift, a competitor touches the floor beyond the platform or leaves it, they are disqualified.

Power set There are three kinds of lifts that depend more on sheer strength than actual skill and speed. These are the bench press, the dead lift and the squat.

CLEAN: The barbell is placed horizontally in front of the lifter's legs

VALID LIFT: The weightlifter must fully extend his arms with the barbell positioned above the head

Press A lifter extends his arm in an even manner.

Red light Signaled by the referee to show that the lift has failed.

Referees Three officials whose job is to ensure that the equipment and the lifts conform to the IWF rules. Each referee judges the lift independently and signals their verdict on the light signals. One of the referees takes up the position of chief referee, who gives the signal to lifters to lower the bar at the end of the lift. The chief referee sits directly in front of and not less than 6m from the lifter.

Scoring The snatch and jerk places are won by the competitor who lifts the highest weights in each category. The competitor who lifts the heaviest combined weight in the snatch and jerk is declared the overall competition winner.

Signals The referees signify their opinion of a lift at major events by means of a light signal. Each referee has their own light panel on the signals indicator.

The clean The barbell is placed horizontally in front of the lifter's legs. The lifter then grips the bar palms down, and in a continuous movement lifts the barbell from the platform to the shoulders without making any contact with their body. They are allowed to split or bend their legs while doing this. Once the lift has been completed the lifter must stand erect with their feet on a line parallel with the bar.

The jerk An explosive movement in that the competitor lifts the bar from his or her shoulders to an arms-extended position above the head. They bend their legs and drive their arms out ver-tically in order to get the bar above the head. The lifter is allowed another recovery before becoming motionless. The referee will signal for the bar to be replaced, under control, to the platform.

The recovery The lifter is allowed as much time as required after the jerk to return their feet to the same line.

Tie At the end of a contest, the scores are even and the competitor who reached the result earlier in the course of the competition is deemed the winner. In the event of a tie in the classification of teams, the team having the largest number of first places is the winner.

Timekeeper An official who makes sure that the lifters make their attempts within the time permitted.

Two-hand snatch The barbell is placed before the lifter's legs. The lifter picks up the bar and pulls it in a single movement from the ground to the full extent of both arms above his head while bending his legs.

Weigh-in The bodyweight of the lifters is determined at the weigh-in. For international competitions lifters are weighed two hours before the start of the tournament. The weigh-in takes place in front of three appointed referees, one official from the lifter's team and the competition secretary. If the lifter is too heavy, they have one hour from the start of the weigh-in to reduce their weight to the correct limit.

Weights Only disc barbells are allowed to be used in competition. The barbell and collars together weigh 25kg.

White light Signaled by the referees to indicate that a legitimate lift has taken place.

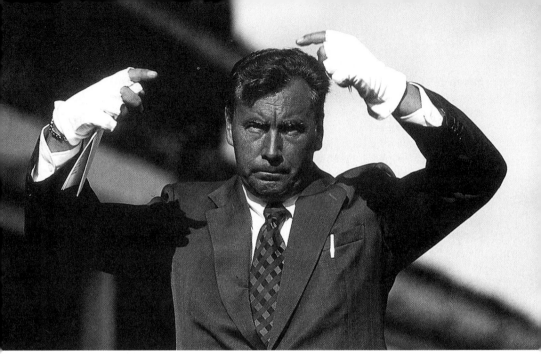

12 Animal Sports

A wide range of sports involve animals – from straightforward racing, with horses, dogs or birds, to complex and highly disciplined equestrian events such as dressage and eventing. Many of these sports involve partnerships between humans and animals, whilst angling is the only one which involves the animal as a "target".

Betting

Accumulator A bet involving four or more selections in different events. The return from the first selection runs into the second and so on.

Ante-post Term applied to betting before the day of the race.

Co-favorite Three or more horses, dogs, etc. that are favorites with the same odds.

Ear 'ole Slang for odds of 8 to 4.

Enquiry Held by the stewards concerning an incident in a race.

Going The state of the ground, e.g. firm, soft, good.

Handicap A race in which horses carry differing weights designed to give them all the same opportunity.

Jolly Slang term used for the starting price favorites.

Monkey Slang term for £500.

Penalty The extra weight a horse is set to carry for winning the previous race.

Pony Slang term for £25.00.

Punters Slang expression for members of the betting fraternity.

Quinella A form of betting in which punters select the horses they think will finish first or second.

Starting price The odds for a horse or greyhound declared at the start of a race.

Tic-Tac Man An on-course bookmaker's assistant.

Tote Stands for Totaliser, which is the state run betting organization.

Trifecta A form of betting in which punters select the horses they think will finish first, second and third.

Weigh-in Jockeys must weigh-in after a race to ensure that they have completed the course carrying the correct weight. It signifies that the result is official and that the bets can then be paid out.

Fishing

Fishing, or angling, is a very serious and competitive sport, demanding concentration of both body and mind and varying from catching small trout in a stream to catching sharks in the open sea. Fish are divided into three types: coarse, game and sea fish; fishermen use different tactics and equipment to catch them.

....

Action (rod) The way in which a rod behaves when casting.

AFTM (American Fishing Tackle Manufactor) scale The rating of a rod, based on the actual weight of the line. The lower the number, the lighter the line, and the more effective the cast.

Alevin The name given to young trout and particularly young salmon.

Angler Slang term for a fisherman.

Anti-reverse lever When released, it allows you to back wind, if the fish is large enough to power across into the main current.

Artery forceps When locked, a really good grip is maintained on the hook, that can be gently eased out.

Artificial flies Used for fly fishing, and can be made from silk, fur, feathers or other man-made materials.

Attractor A fly that does not imitate any form of life but arouses a fish's aggression.

Backing line A long length of line connecting the fly line to the reel. Used when a fish makes a long run.

Baggot Term used for a salmon that has returned to the river and remains there for some time.

Bait Used to tempt fish to bite. Bread, cheese and lunch meats are used for coarse fish, and natural baits such as shellfish, ragworm and lugworm for sea fish. Game fishing often involves the use of artificial flies.

Bend Bottom part of the hook that bends around.

Bird's nest Describes a line that has got into a tangle.

Bites Vary a great deal. From continuous tweaks and rattles to a full-blooded lunging of the rod.

Bloodworm Natural bait that is present in almost any enclosed water where waterfowl are found or cows drink.

Boat fishing Fishing from a boat at sea. In certain circumstances, the boat will be anchored; in others it will be drifting.

Bob fly The top dropper or tool placed on the main line that enables the angler to fish with two or three lines at the same time.

Bodied waggler Has a cork-type material added to the lower part of the quill in order to allow more weight to be used.

Boron rods Fishing rods named after the material from which they are made. (Boron is a form of carbon fiber.) They have improved dramatically since their first generation, and with the new engineering leave nothing to be desired.

Bread A cheap, easy and highly effective type of bait used. Especially good for bottom-feeding fish like carp.

Bread crust Can be used for floating on the surface, weed bed or just off the bottom.

Bread paste Made by mixing the center of the loaf with water. Can be flavored or colored. Two good additives are cheese and custard powder.

Brown trout Has distinctive brown, green and dark-red spots along the upper half of its body, and is an extremely powerful fighter. It is found in unpolluted rivers, and is being introduced to ponds, lakes and gravel pits.

Bubble float A device usually used in conjunction with monofilament line to provide weight to cast a fly with coarse tackle. It may be filled with water.

Carbon fiber rods Considered to be better value for money than glass rods, as the handling and design attributes have been improved in recent years. The best rod for beginners to use.

Casters An excellent bait that some anglers consider to be the most important, as it will catch any type of fish. Ideal as loose bait, and is often mixed with ground bait.

Centerpin reel A reel that revolves round a central axis.

Check A ratchet or drag that may be used to increase or relax the tension on a reel to provide resistance to a running fish.

Chub Fish with large mouths and thick leathery lips. They are very good fighters, and will swim for the nearest weed once hooked.

Close-faced reel A more recent development that is now well established. The line is enclosed inside the reel housing and released through a gap at the front of the reel by finger pressure on a button. Easier to handle when using a running line.

Clothing In most cases, the most suitable clothing is a waterproof jacket, stout shoes or rubber boots, and warm undergarments. Several layers are better than one, thick one as they can be removed gradually. Hats are useful in the summer to protect you from the sun.

Coarse fish Any fish that lives in fresh water and is not a member of the salmon family.

Common carp One of the most intelligent fish that become harder to catch as they get older and bigger.

Counting Counting the float down can help; the count starts as the float enters the water and continues until the strike is made at the next bite.

Country code Showing concern for the environment and wildlife. Hooks and line should be disposed of in a suitable place.

Dapping Method allowing the fly to blow in front of you and skid along the surface as the line is taken by the wind.

Double grinner A very strong knot for joining a line to eyed hooks or swivels.

Double haul An advanced casting technique to gain extra distance. Performed by using the left hand in synchronization with the rod to increase the speed of the line.

Double loops A knot that is easy to tie and has many uses.

Double taper profile A line normally 30 yards in length with the fineness of the tips at each end gradually thickening out to a maximum diameter at the exact midpoint, 15 yards from either end. Considered to be the best for short, accurate and neat casting purposes.

Drag An effect created by varying current speeds or snags that affect the line in such a way that it pulls the dry fly across the current instead of allowing it to float down naturally at the same speed as the current.

Drift fishing Fishing from a boat that is allowed to drift with the wind.

Drilled bullet Type of leger that is ideal if the bed is sandy.

Drogue An underwater parachute-type device attached to a boat to slow the drift or hold it in a certain position.

Dropper An additional fly on the leader.

Dry fly Can be tied with wings in many ways. The hackle always extends a full circle around the hook shank unless it is tied in parachute style. The body is dressed with light material.

Ephemerid One of a group of real water-bred upwing flies that are short-lived.

Eye Otherwise known as the spade. The top part of the hook to that the line is joined.

False casting Process of lengthening the line in the air until enough is aerialized to make the final cast.

Fast recovery reel A reel geared to revolve the drum at a higher ratio per turn of the handle.

Fiberglass rods Very light, easy to handle and carefully engineered to fulfil specific functions.

Figure-eighting A method of bunching the line in the palm of the hand when retrieving. An excellent way of maintaining constant movement of the fly.

Free-lining A deadly way of catching chub, especially in the shallows. Mold a large lump of cheese paste around the hook, and it will often be grabbed violently so that the rod is nearly pulled from your hands.

Flash The reflecting of light by a fly due to the inclusion of tinsel in the dressing.

Floatants Products used to induce a fly, leader or a fly line to float high on water.

Fly fishing Artificial fly tied to a hook in a way that it imitates an item of natural food and tricks the fish into taking it.

Fly line The weighted line used in fly-fishing.

Fly reel A simple centerpin reel. Holds the line and tends not to be used for any other purpose.

Fly rods Made from reinforced hollow fiberglass and hollow boron reinforced.

Forward taper line Developed for long casting purposes, and carries the bulk necessary to action the rod com-

pressed into about 10 yards at one end of the line, before rapidly tapering down to a fine diameter that shoots very easily through the rod rings when the cast is made.

Gaff An instrument consisting of a metal hook attached to a stout pole used for landing heavy fish.

Game fish In freshwater fish, a term used for members of the salmon family.

Gills Set behind the head of the fish between the eye and the pectoral fin. Used to take in oxygen from the water.

Glides The most predictable of all kinds of river swim. Glides come in all shapes and sizes depending on the dimension of the river in question.

Greased line A method used in low water conditions to fish for salmon. The term was used for silk lines that were greased to make them float.

Grip Can be single handed or double handed.

Gudgeon Small fish commonly found on gravelly river beds.

Gozzer A very soft, white maggot that is the larvae of bluebottle but smaller in size, with a jet black body.

Groundbait A mixture to introduce into the swim you are fishing, or into a swim days before you fish it.

Hackle A single feather tied on a fly immediately behind the eye of the hook.

Hand tailing Method of landing a salmon after playing it into shallow water by seizing it by the wrist of the tail.

Hemp seed Very good bait, even as loosefeed or mixed in ground bait.

Hooking The best penetration can be achieved with the sharpest hooks, so always ensure that hooks are as sharp as possible.

Hook There are five types of hook: short shank, medium shank, long shank, up-eyed and barbless.

Hook removal Grip the fish firmly but

gently behind the gill covers. If the hook is slightly embedded near the front of the mouth, it is possible to use your fimgertips or disgorger to remove it.

Hook size Hooks are designated by size. Dry flies and nymphs can be tied on a hook as small as a No22 or as large as a long-shank 10. Lures and salmon flies normally range from a size-10 long shank (that is small) to a size-20 long shank, that is very big.

Imitator A fly that represents a form of food that a fish may be feeding on.

Keepnets Used to keep fish in when caught before being returned to the water.

Keepsacks Used to retain large fish once caught; they will lie quietly.

Lateral line The row of very sensitive cells that runs down both sides of the fish from the gill cover to the tail.

Leger tactics In a flowing river, a swim can be explored just as effectively with a leger as with a float. The type of leger that will allow a bait to trundle along a river bed depends a great deal on the nature of the bottom.

Licenses In England and Wales, a valid rod license is needed to fish anywhere. These can be bought from post offices, and last between a day and a year.

Lie In running water, fish take up a position in the current known as a lie. From here, a fish will feed, content to let the current carry its food to it.

Loop to loop A knot used for joining the main line to hook length.

Lunch meat Good for chub and barbel. Should not be opened and left on the bank side.

Lure Generally larger than wet or dry flies. Heavily dressed to create the impression of bulk. Usually fished on sinking lines.

Maggot The most convenient and widely used form of bait. The main one used is larvae of the low fly, but pinkies and squatts are used as feed. Maggots should be stored in a cool, dry place to keep them at their best.

Marrowspoon Used to extract the stomach contents of a caught fish in order to determine its main diet.

Nymph Anglers' term for the stage in the life cycle of some eater-bred insects, after the egg and before the winged stage.

Open-faced reel The more established type in which the line is exposed and released by the lifting of a sprung bale arm.

Parts of the hook Include the eye, shank, bend, barb and point.

Perch Boldly colored fish that is present throughout Britain in rivers, lakes, canals and ponds.

Pinkies Otherwise known as runners. The larvae of greenfly that lay their eggs in a big cluster. They are bred in the same way as maggots.

Playing a fish "Fighting" the fish after hooking it so that it may be landed.

Point The tip of the hook that is used to catch the fish.

Polarized sunglasses Should be considered a necessity when fly fishing a,s if one is careless, especially in a difficult wind, it is easy to catch oneself with the hook. Light reflections from lakes can be very trying, and have been known to give anglers blinding headaches.

Pole code Look out and up for electricity cables. Do not pull directly toward you to free snagged tackle. Assemble pole sections safely clear of the water's edge. Make sure you fish in a safe and stable position.

Pollution monitor 1A–Excellent. 1B–Good. 2–Fair. 3–Polluted. 4–Grossly polluted.

Potato Tinned potatoes are a good bait to start with.

Pre-baiting Describes when groundbait is introduced to a swim days before you fish it.

Priest A small club with that trout can be quickly and humanely dispatched after capture. May be as simple as a short stick, about 6in long and weighted at one end.

Profile The actual shape of the line and the way it varies in thickness. Created by a systematic overlay of plastic on a core of woven man-made fiber.

Rainbow trout Colorful, spotted fish found commonly in reservoirs, lakes and ponds.

Rapids Many anglers think of rapids as turbulent, foam-crested waters rushing over large boulders. This can be ideal for big chub and dace.

Redworm A very lively worm that is good for catching perch.

Reel clutch Must be adjusted prior to fishing so that it yields line when the pressure on it is just below the line's breaking strain.

Reels There are two types of reels in most common use for coarse fishing – the fixed spool and the closed face spool.

Retaining and returning fish Fish should be retained in a large knotless keepnet. Larger fish are best retained in keepnets where they will lie quietly. When returning a fish gently, gather up the net until the area occupied by the fish is in the water, then release the net.

Retrieving Fishing the fly back toward you by recovering the line.

Rod length Most people use rods of between 8.8-9.5ft, although it is better to handle several rod lengths before deciding that length to use.

Scissors Needed to cut leaders from spools, and flies often have to be cut from leaders.

Sea fish There are over 350 species including haddock, pollack and cod.

Seed baits Will tempt fish, and most are prepared for the hook in a similar way.

Shank The long part of the hook placed between the barb and the eye. Short or medium shanks are used for dry flies and wet flies. Lures and salmon flies are tied on either medium- or long-shank hooks to accommodate the extra dressing usually used to provide bulk and shape.

Shooting head Variation on the forward taper. Amounts to little more than the bulk section of a forward taper, that is spliced to heavy nylon monofilament backing.

Single taper line Tapers only one way and much more quickly after the center tapers are off.

Sinker A weight at the end of the fishing line to hold the line still and low in the water.

Sliding float Generally made from peacock quill with a balsa body at the lower end of the float.

Spey cast The method used to cast the farthest possible distance without the line actually extending behind the rod.

Split cane rods Hand-made from sections of selected cane, and after a lengthy process the rod ends up as six triangular strips of cane glued together.

Spooning The object is to find out what your fish is feeding on. You can then select a fly to imitate that food in an attempt to catch more fish.

Spring balance Used for checking a fish's weight at the waterside.

Squatts May be called feeders, and are the larvae of the cheesefly that is smaller than the house fly.

Stick float Extremely sensitive, and is best when river conditions are perfect. Should always be fished with top and bottom rubbers.

Straight balsa slider Uses the same principle as the bodied slider except that it is used on deep flowing rivers.

Straight waggler Simple float consisting of a piece of peacock quill with a cane insert at the bottom of the float.

Swan shot link leger Better than a drilled bullet on gravelly sections. Holds the bottom easier with less weight.

Sweet corn Used as bait. Its greatest attraction is availability and convenience in its ready-to-use state.

Swimfeeder fishing Quite a sophisticated technique for what is potentially an easy method of fishing. Once the swimfeeder is attached to the line, the rod springs up as a fish bites, dislodging the swimfeeder. The fish quite often hook themselves.

Taper A tapered fly line or leader.

Tares Very effective bait when used with hemp.

Tippet The thin end of the leader, often knotted into it. Also called the point.

Tools The basic tools required for fly tying are a vice, hooks, bobbin holder, hackle pliers, scissors and dubbing needle.

Treble hook A hook that has three bends and barbs brazed together to give all-around hooking capacity.

Trolling Trailing the line behind a moving boat.

Trotting a float The bait and the float are allowed to travel down a section of the river at the pace of the current.

Types of knots Double loop, loop to loop, three-turn loop, spade end, clinch knot, blood knot, turle knot, half blood knot, needle knot and double grinner.

Wading Entering the water to gain distance or to overcome bankside obstacles.

Wagglers Come in either straight or bodied versions.

Wet fly The wings are tied back over the hook shank and the throat hackle does not extend all around the shank. The body is dressed to sink and is usually ribbed with tinsel.

Whips Shorter than long poles. There are two distinct actions to whips: sloppy ones, that are usually telescopic; or tip-actioned ones, that tend to be either the take-apart type or hybrids of the two.

Wire-stemmed stick float A slight variance on the normal stick float, with the cane stem being replaced by wire rod. It is very sensitive and is more stable than the standard stick float.

Worms Used as bait for fishing

Pigeon Racing

Pigeon racing is a traditional sport that involves the pigeon fancier being a breeder, dietician, manager, trainer, coach and competitor. The birds are released from a predetermined point and race back to their own lofts. The bird with the fastest speed is declared the winner after all clocks and rings have been checked and verified.

Amalgamations Federations join amalgamations for long-distance and international races.

Average speed Over the course of a season, the average race speed is between 35 and 40 mph.

Breeding A vital part of pigeon racing; the fancier must study a bird's pedigree, performance, conformation, type and eyes.

Clubs Each fancier joins a pigeon club. There are approximately 3,000 in the UK.

Cocks The name given to male pigeons.

Conveyer The driver of the road transporter who has sole responsibility for the birds from the moment he collects them from their clubs until the moment he releases them.

Diet Usually corn, mixed with maple peas, maize, wheat and tares. Breeders must be very careful to ensure a balanced diet for their birds – not only for health and fitness reasons, but also weight.

Enemies Falcons and sparrow hawks are the main enemies of racing pigeons, because they take them in flight.

Fancier The name given to a pigeon racer/breeder.

FCI The Fédération Colombophile Internationale, that is the international advisory body of the sport with a delegate from each member country on the committee.

Federations All clubs join a federation to enlarge the racing numbers.

Hens The name given to female pigeons.

Identity ring Each bird must have a ring placed on one of its legs, that carries an individual serial number that can be traced to its owner.

Incubation period 19 days after the egg is laid.

Liberation point A predetermined point from which the conveyor releases the pigeons to race.

Loft Made of wood or brick, a loft's average size measures 12ft by 6.8ft. Good ventilation and dryness are essential to the bird's comfort.

Molting All birds shed their feathers annually.

Natural system Describes where a breeding pair is allowed to follow a normal nesting pattern with only the hatching of the young being controlled. This system allows both sexes to be trained and raced.

Old birds Describes any bird that is born before January 1 in the year of the race.

Paramyxovirus A disease that can affect pigeons and even be fatal. All racing pigeons must be inoculated annually against it.

Pigeon clock Used to record a pigeon's racing time. Can record the distance raced to the nearest yard. They are always tamperproof.

Race distance The sprint distance is 60-100 miles, middle distance is 100-250 miles and long-distance races 250-600 miles. The latter races usually take off from Spain and France.

Race pannier Another name for the transporter crate.

Race sheet Each owner must record the racing pigeon's ring number, color, sex, sidestakes and rubber race ring number.

Road transporter Used to transport the pigeons to a prearranged spot. It can carry up to 6,000 pigeons at a time. It has an instant-release mechanism that allows for simultaneous liberation.

Rubber band When racing, each pigeon wears a secretly numbered band that is removed and placed in a tamper-proof clock when the pigeon returns to its loft.

Season Normally runs from April to July for the older birds (over two years old) and from July to September for the younger birds.

Squeakers The name used to describe baby pigeons.

Training toss All birds must train before a race. They perform training flights throughout the year.

Velocity The term used to describe the pigeon that records the greatest number of yards per minute.

Widowhood The system where only the cocks are raced. They are mainly kept separated from the hens so that when they return to the loft, they will enter the trap very quickly because they know their hens are waiting for them.

Wing stamp Each pigeon should have its owner's name and address stamped on its wings in case it gets lost.

PIGEON RACING: The birds are released simultaneously with the winning bird being the one who reaches its home loft first

Greyhound Racing

Greyhound racing is usually contested between six or eight dogs over distances between 230yd and 1208yd. The dogs are held in traps before being released to chase a mechanical hare around the track.

Age In the United States, the dog's age is counted from the first day of whelping.

Clearing trial Any greyhound that has been disqualified from a race for fighting must run at least three clearing trials before being permitted to race again officially.

Color The standard colorings of greyhounds are black, blue, brindle (a brown color with streaks of another color mixed in such as black or white), fawn, red, tickled (light or dark specks) and white.

Distance The minimum distance for any race is 230yd and the maximum is 1208yd.

Fighting Fighting during a race leads to disqualification. Repeated fighting leads to permanent exclusion.

Graded race A race in which the greyhounds are selected by the racing manager from those in the charge of any professional or greyhound trainer.

Green light Shown at the end of a race to display the fact that the finish order is final.

Handicap race A race in which each greyhound is allotted a handicap – either a scratch handicap or a distance-in-meters handicap. All traps will open simultaneously.

Hurdles A race in which the greyhounds must run over at least four flights of hurdles or at least three flights of hurdles in a race of 437yd or less.

Identification All registered dogs receive identity books or cards, that detail physical characteristics that distinguish them as individuals, the name of its current trainer, all inoculations received, races, trials, withdrawals, disqualifications for fighting, and all details of a bitch coming into season, whelping a litter or being spayed.

Intertrack race A race between two or more teams of greyhounds with each team representing a licensed racecourse.

Kenneling procedure Greyhounds are identified and weighed. They are then checked by the veterinarian before being locked up for security reasons.

Lure Used to get the greyhounds out of the traps and around the track. It is normally an artificial hare that is powered by electronic motors and controlled by a licensed lure controller. It must be 12yd ahead of the starting trap when the greyhounds are released.

Match A race between two greyhounds that have different licensed trainers and that belong to different owners.

Middle runner Describes a greyhound that, in the opinion of the racing manager, is best suited to starting on the inside of wide runners and on the outside of unseeded runners.

Minimum age The youngest age at that a greyhound is permitted to race is 15 months.

Muzzles Compulsory for all dogs when racing. They are made of steel wire.

Name All names of the dogs must be registered, as must any change of name that occurs. This is recorded in the stud book.

No-race Declared if there is a mechani-

GREYHOUNDS: Must wear a muzzle made of steel wire and a racing jacket that displays each individual trap number

cal fault with the lure equipment or starting traps, the lure is not kept at a reasonable distance from the leading greyhound, no dog completes the course within a reasonable time or there is any outside interference with the race.

Officials Include the racing manager or secretary, stewards, judges, paddock judge, clerk of the scales, starter, lure operator, security officer, veterinarian and racecourse trainer.

Paddock admission The following people are allowed in the paddock area: racecourse officials, stewards, trainers and kennel hands, owners and holders of temporary appointments.

Private sweepstake A race between three or more greyhounds that have different trainers and different owners.

Prizes A disqualified greyhound will have to return any prizes already received. If the race ends in a draw, the prize will be split equally.

Produce race An open race where the greyhounds are of defined origin, usually members of a litter originally entered as such for the race.

Puppy A greyhound shall be termed a puppy for a period of 24 months from and including the month of whelping.

Race card Provides information on the racecourse, meeting and officials. Also details of each race and each dog.

Racing jackets Each greyhound must wear an approved racing jacket that has the trap number on either side. Jackets are colored according to trap number.

Red light Shown at the end of a race to indicate that a "no race" has been declared.

Registration All dogs racing on officially approved courses must be regis-

tered with the national governing body.

Rerun Occurs within a minimum time lapse of a "no race" being declared.

Running out A greyhound that runs out of the defined course is regarded as not having completed the course, even if the dog returns and crosses the line.

Substitute race Included in the program, but raced only to replace a void race that is not being rerun.

Sweepstakes Describes a race where the prize money comes from the entry fees or subscriptions of the greyhound owners.

Tiebreaker When this occurs, the prize money shall be shared between the two greyhound owners.

Timing Recorded by photo or ray-timing apparatus. It is measured from the time that the trap door reaches 45 degrees to the perpendicular until the winning greyhound's nose crosses the finish line.

Traps Numbered 1–8 from the inside trap out, they are metal cages that hold the dogs until the starting signal is given, at that the trap doors fly up and release them.

Walkover Describes a greyhound that is the only one not to have been disqualified from a race. The greyhound is walked past the local steward's box and then deemed the winner.

WGRF The World Greyhound Racing Federation, the international governing body of the sport. It was founded by Britain, Ireland, Spain, Australia and the United States.

Wide runner A greyhound that, in the opinion of the race manager, is best suited to starting outside runners not so classified across the course.

Sled Dog Racing

Sled dog racing involves a race between harnessed dog teams that are controlled by drivers. The number of dogs per team depends on the race distance and the terrain, that can often be covered in snow. The winning team is the one to finish the course in the fastest time.

Brushbrow Placed at the front of the sled to keep the dogs at a distance from the sled.

Competitors One "musher" per team. Drivers often have a dog handler to assist them.

Dog handler Used to assist the driver in looking after the dogs.

Harnessing All of the dogs except the lead dogs must be harnessed with neck lines. Lead dogs are harnessed without neck lines.

Holding area All teams must be placed here one hour before the first scheduled run.

Iditarod The famous annual race throught Alaska.

Intervals All sleds start at intervals, usually every two minutes.

Markers Red indicates turns on the course, and green markers that are placed beyond an intersection or around a turn indicate a straight ahead.

Mush The command given to the dogs to go.

Musher The name given to the driver of the sled dog team.

Muzzles Prohibited from being used.

Numbers Starting position numbers must be worn each day. All numbers must be returned at the end of each heat.

Officials Include the chief judge, judges and a course manager.

Out of bounds If a team deviates from the race trail, it can return to the point at that it left and continue from there.

Outside assistance Allowed only in order to stop an unmanageable team.

Right of way A team coming within 6m of the team ahead has right of way.

Sled Should be big enough to accommodate an injured or exhausted dog. The driver stands at the back. The sled is constructed with the brake on the right-hand side and the brushbrow and snubline placed at the front.

Sled bag Made of canvas or similar material, and should be big enough to fit a dog into. It is used to keep a dog warm if it is injured.

Snubline A small notch at the front of the sled, used for hitching the main rein that connects all the dogs to the sled.

Starting order The order is drawn before the start of the race. The starting order for the following days is determined by the elapsed time, with the fastest team leaving first.

Timing Dogs are timed from when the sled's brushbrow crosses the starting line until the first dog reaches the finish line.

Whip Each driver carries a whip, but they are only allowed to use it for snapping unless the dogs become unmanageable.

Horse Racing

Horse racing has two main categories: flat racing and racing over jumps. Both events have many variations, with differing entrance qualifications, distances and prizes.

Acceptances Those horses that are still entered for a race after a specified date.

Added money The money that is added to the prize money made up from the entrance fees.

Age In the Northern Hemisphere, a horse's age is calculated from January 1 of the year of foaling; in the Southern Hemisphere, in countries such as Australia and South Africa, from August 1, and in South America, from the preceding July.

Aids The way in which the rider communicates with his horse by using the hands, legs, body and voice. Artificial aids include a whip, spurs and martingales.

Apprentice A young boy who will serve his apprenticeship under a trainer for a certain period of time. He will learn to ride and look after horses and, if good enough, he will take part in races.

Auction plate Describes a race for horses that are bought at public auction. They may be handicapped according to their purchase price.

Bearing Describes the horse's carriage and balance.

BHB The British Horseracing Board, that is the governing authority for the sport.

Blinders Attached to the bridle or hood, they are stiffened shields used to block a horse's sideways vision so that they will concentrate on the race at hand.

Blind obstacle One in which the horse cannot see the landing side when taking off.

Brood mare A mare that is used at stud for breeding purposes.

Bumpers Describes National Hunt jumps in flat races.

Cadence The quality of the horse's pace, displaying rhythm, energy and springy steps.

Camera patrol Responsible for filming the crucial points of the race in order to aid the stewards and help determine objections.

Cast a plate Means that a horse's shoe has become loose or fallen off.

Chalk jockey Describes an inexperienced or unknown jockey. They get their name from the fact that bookmakers chalk their names on a board, whereas established jockeys have their names painted on.

Change of hand A change of direction; also known as a change of rein.

Change of lead A change of the horse's leading leg when cantering or galloping.

Claiming race Occurs where a runner may be claimed by a buyer for its entered price.

Classics The most important races in the calendar for a country.

Clerk of the course The official who is responsible for the running of a course and all the meetings held there.

Clerk of the scales The official who is in charge of the weighing in and out of all the jockeys in a race.

Colt Describes an entire (see entry) male racehorse of 4 years of age and under.

Conformation Describes the physical structure of the horse.

Contact The amount of feel on the reins linking the rider's hands to the bit.

Coupled entry Two or more horses in a race owned by the same person. Applies in France for vetting purposes.

Dam The name given to a brood mare that has produced foals.

Dead heat If a tie occurs, then both horses are deemed joint winners, with the prize money for the first two places being shared equally between them.

Distance A winning margin of 22yd or more.

Disunited Describes a horse that is cantering with a diagonal pair of legs leading instead of the near or offside pair.

Dress The jockey must wear a helmet or skull cap, a shirt in the owner's colors, trousers, boots and spurs.

Engagement Describes the action where the horse's hind legs are brought farther underneath the body.

Entire A male horse that has not been gelded.

Extension Occurs when the horse lengthens its stride during a walk, trot or canter. Extension should occur in both hind and fore legs.

Field The name given to the runners in a race.

Filly Describes a female racehorse of 4 years of age or under.

Flexion The rounding of the horse's neck in response to the aids.

Flexion, lateral The suppleness and muscular development of the horse that allows it to bend on a circle throughout the length of his spine.

Foal Describes a horse that is younger than a year in age.

Gait The pattern of a horse's stride.

Gelding Describes a horse that has been castrated.

Going The name given to the ground conditions of the course. It will be hard, firm, good, soft, yielding or heavy.

Ground line The projecting base of a jump used by the horse to judge its take-off point.

Half-halt Occurs when the rider braces his back to act as a warning to the horse before a change of pace, balance or direction.

Handicap A race in which the weight a horse carries is adjusted so that all the entries have an equal chance.

Handicapper The official in charge of arranging the weights for handicap races.

Horse A male racehorse of 5 or more years of age.

In-hand When the horse is led from the ground rather than ridden.

Jockeys All jockeys must be licensed. They can operate independently or be retained by an owner.

Jumps The obstacles in hurdle and steeplechase races.

Leaning on the bit Occurs when the horse seems to lean against the rider's hand for support in order to balance himself.

Leathers The straps that connect the stirrups to the saddle. They are set to a length that suits each jockey's riding style.

Length Measure used to determine distances between horses, that equals the length of a horse.

Maiden A horse that has never won a race.

Mare A female racehorse that is 5 years of age or more.

Match A race between two horses that has been arranged between the two owners.

Nags (The) Colloquial term for horse racing.

Napping Any kind of resistance from the horse, i.e. rearing or bucking.

Near side The left side of the horse.

Novice race Held for horses that have not won a race of the type concerned at the start of the current season.

Numnah Soft material that is shaped like a saddle. Placed under the saddle to absorb sweat and make it more comfortable for the horse.

Nursery A handicap race for 2-year-olds.

Odds The proportion of return offered by bookmakers or the Tote on a bet.

Offside The right side of the horse.

One-sidedness A horse that works more efficiently in one direction than the other, as his muscles are more developed on one side than the other.

On the aids A horse that is responsive to its rider's commands and will do whatever is asked of it.

On the bit A horse that needs restraining by its jockey while riding easily.

Open races Races in which every horse carries the same weight.

Optimum takeoff zone The ideal place from which a horse must take off in order to clear a jump successfully. Varies according to the height of the jump and the type of jump.

Over-bent Occurs when the nose of the horse comes behind the vertical, normally with an exaggerated bend of the neck, with the head close to the chest.

Over-facing When the horse arrives at a jump that is too large or difficult to jump.

Over-reaching When the toe of the horse's hind foot strikes the heel of the forefoot.

Paddock The area in which all the horses congregate before the start of a race.

Pipe-opener Term used to describe a short, sharp gallop where the horse's lungs are cleared and its circulatory system stimulated. Performed before the horse begins fast or extended work.

Plate A race where the prize money is of a definite amount. Also the description of a horse's shoe.

Position to Flex or bend the horse to the left or right before asking for lateral movement.

Presentation The way in which a rider puts his horse at a jump.

Running downhill A horse that is taking quick, hurried strides with too much weight on its forehand.

Running out A form of refusal where the horse veers to the side of a jump and fails to clear the obstacle.

Schoolmaster The name given to an experienced, well trained horse.

Scratch To withdraw a horse from a race.

Selling race When a horse wins a race and is then offered up for auction.

Silks The name given to the blouse and cap worn during a race by the jockeys. Each jockey wears the colors of the owner of his horse. Harness racing drivers wear jackets.

Sire A stallion that has fathered foals.

Slip the reins Used by the rider to allow a horse to use his head and neck to recover after an awkward landing or stumble. The rider allows the reins to slide out through the fingers to their maximum length.

Spread A jump that is wide as well as high.

Stallion A male horse that is kept at stud for breeding purposes.

Stalls The starting boxes.

Starter's orders Once the flag is raised, the field is then under starter's orders. Under normal circumstances, no horse is then allowed to be withdrawn from the race.

Starting price The final odds offered by the leading bookmakers before the start of the race.

Stewards The officials who control the running of a race meeting.

Sweepstake A race where all or most of the prize money comprises entry fees, subscriptions, forfeits from owners and any added money.

Thoroughbred A racehorse that has had its pedigree entered into the General Stub Book.

FLAT: Describes a race in that there are no jumps or hurdles for the horses and riders to overcome

Tote The Horserace Totalisator Board, which, while promoting a pool betting facility, also makes money that is used for the benefit of horse racing.

Track The path followed by the horse's fore and hind legs.

Tracking up Occurs when the horse's feet overlap the imprints of its forefeet.

Trotted up A race in which a horse has won with ease.

Walkover A race in which there is only one horse left in the race, and it is a formality for the rider to pass the judge's box to be declared the winner.

Weighing-out Every jockey has to be weighed before the start of a race with his silks on and carrying his saddle, breastplate, martingale, number cloth, blinkers and any lead make-up weight.

Weight-for-age Races where a scale of weight allowances operates according to a horse's age, the distance and the time of year.

Yearling A horse that is between 1 and 2 years of age.

Show Jumping

Show jumping is an equestrian event that tests the horse's jumping ability and the rider's skill over a set course of differing obstacles. The winner is the competitor with the fastest time, the lowest number of faults or the highest number of points.

Arena The area where show jumping is contested.

Bank A permanent obstacle on the course that the horse must climb over. It tests the horse's balance and judgement.

Bareme Means a scale or table, and refers to the rules used for judging under international rules.

Barrage See "Jump-off".

Bell The signal used to start a round.

Brush and rails An upright obstacle made of brush surmounted by one or more poles.

Clear round Completing a round without committing any faults.

Collecting ring The area near the main arena where the competitors make their entrance.

Combination jumps Two (double), three (treble) or more obstacles placed within 13yd of each other, that result in the horse having to take a number of restricted strides between each element.

Course The maximum length of the course measured in meters is the number of obstacles multiplied by 60.

Deviation When a competitor fails to follow the set course by going around the wrong side of the flag, taking an obstacle out of the correct order, missing one or jumping an obstacle that is not part of the course.

Disobedience Incurs faults for a refusal, running out or resistance, a rectified deviation, circling, passing an obstacle or approaching it sideways.

Falls A rider is deemed to have fallen when he is separated from his horse and has to remount. A horse is deemed to have fallen when its shoulders and quarters have touched the ground or obstacle and ground.

Fault A penalty point received for knocking down an element of an obstacle, failing to clear the water jump cleanly, for a fall or for disobedience.

FEI The Fédération Equestre Internationale, that is the sport's governing body.

Grand Prix A major individual competition that is held at international level.

High jump Using only one obstacle, that increases in height after it has been successfully cleared.

Hog's back A spread obstacle that is made up of three parallel poles.

Impulsion Describes the horse's power that is controlled by the rider when approaching an obstacle or jump.

Interrupted time Occurs when an obstacle has been knocked down and needs to be rebuilt. The clock is stopped.

Jumping derby A competition held over a long course that has natural obstacles.

Jump-off Used as a deciding round after a competition when a tiebreaker has occurred.

Multiple obstacles Two, three or four obstacles that are taken in successive jumps. Includes banks, slopes and ramps, with or without fences. The distance between any two parts should be 8yd-13yd.

Nations Cup A team competition that is held at international level. At least three riders per team must take part. Also known as the Prix des Nations.

Officials Include judges, course designers, timekeeper, arena and collecting ring stewards, veterinary commission, and an appeal committee.

Overface The need to make a horse jump higher or farther than it is capable of doing.

Oxer A brush or hedge fence with a pole placed on the takeoff side.

Parallel bars A spread jump that consists of poles on separate supports placed parallel to each other.

Plan of the course Shows the general layout of the course – the start and finish posts, the position of the obstacles with their type and numbers and any compulsory passages or turning points, the length of the course, the correct track to be followed, the marking system to be used, the time allowed and the time limit (if applicable), the obstacles to be used in any jump-off and the length of the course and time allowed for the jump-off.

President's Cup The trophy awarded yearly to the country that gained the most points that year in the Nations Cup competition.

Puissance A competition held to test a horse's jumping ability over a decreasing number of obstacles, the height of that is increased as the competition goes on. Consists of between four and six obstacles with straight fences measuring a minimum of 4.5ft high.

Recording time Time is recorded in seconds, tenths of seconds and hundredths of seconds.

Refusal When a horse stops in front of an obstacle and will not jump over it. If after three attempts the horse still refuses to jump, the horse and rider are eliminated from the competition.

Resistance When a horse refuses to move forward. Rider and horse will be eliminated if the horse resists for longer than a minute, fails to pass the starting line within one minute of the starting signal or takes more than a minute to jump an obstacle (except in a fall).

Saddlery There are no restrictions on saddles or bridles, but hoods and blinkers are not allowed. Whips longer than 30in or weighted at one end are also forbidden.

Six bar A competition with six obstacles placed in a straight line with two or three strides in between each one.

Speed competitions Determined by the rider who clears the jumps and course in the fastest time.

Spread An obstacle that is made up of elements in different planes so that the horse has to jump both height and width. Includes triple bars, double-oxer and hog's back.

Straight obstacle One where the elements are placed vertically one above the other in the same plane – in other words, gates, walls, posts and rails.

Table A Used to determine the result of a round by giving penalty points for faults committed on an established scale, with the emphasis being on jumping rather than speed.

Test Another name for a puissance competition.

Time limit Twice the time allowed for a round or competition. Any horse that fails to complete in the allotted time is eliminated.

Touch class Any touch of an obstacle incurs a fault in this class.

Triple bar A spread obstacle that comprises three poles that are placed on separate supports in order from front to back.

Upright An obstacle with the elements placed one above the other in the same vertical plane.

Water jump A small pole or brush fence that is immediately followed by a water ditch measuring 4.5-5.5yd wide.

Dressage

Dressage tests the horse's physique and ability, and the horse and rider's understanding of each other. They perform a series of paces, halts, changes of direction, movements and figures.

Aids The signals used by the rider to give instructions to the horse.

Arena For international competition, the arena must measure 66yd by 22yd. It is covered in sand and must be perfectly level.

Balance The equal distribution of the weight of the horse and rider, enabling the horse to perform at its best.

Cadence The rhythmical movements of the horse's stride.

Canter A three-time pace that makes up the one-step. The hooves touch the ground in the following succession: left hind leg; left diagonal and right foreleg followed by a time of suspension. There are three canter paces: medium, collected and extended.

Capriole An haute école maneuver in which the horse kicks out with its hind legs while jumping with all four legs off the ground.

Collected canter A slow, controlled canter in which the pace is more elevated than at the medium canter, with the hind legs being placed as far as possible under the horse.

Collected trot Performed with short, elevated steps, with the horse showing much forward and upward impulsion as well as gaiety in its steps.

Collected walk A slow walk performed with a shorter and more elevated stride than the medium walk. The hind feet touch the ground behind the footprints of the forefeet.

Collection A controlled mixture of elevation and forward movement producing cadence and rhythm in every stride.

Contact The way in which the rider holds the reins to ensure constant contact between the bit and his hand.

Counter-canter The horse, while making a circle, leads on the leg opposite the direction of the canter.

Courbette An haute école movement in which the horse jumps forward several times on its hind legs with its forelegs off the ground.

Demi-pirouette A 180-degree turn with the forehand of the horse making a small circle around the hind quarters.

Diagonals When the fore and hind legs are diagonally opposite. The right diagonal consists of the left hind and the right fore with the left diagonal of the right hind and the left fore.

Disunited A canter when the steps change to an incorrect sequence.

Dress Military uniform may be worn, otherwise a dark coat with white breeches, top hat, hunting stock and spurs should be worn.

Extended canter A fast controlled canter. The steps are longer but not quicker than at a medium canter.

Extended trot A fast controlled trot with the steps being longer but not quicker than at a medium trot.

Extended walk A fast controlled walk with the steps longer but not quicker than at a medium walk.

FEI The Fédération Equestre Internationale (International Equestrian Federation), that is the governing body of the sport.

Forehand The parts of the horse that are in front of the rider.

Forward movement The urge of the horse to move forward freely as it develops impulsion from its hind quarters, yet still remaining under the complete control of the rider.

Free walk Allows the horse to walk forward with freedom of its neck and head and its tail moving side to side.

Half-halt An exercise used to improve the horse's balance and attention before changing to another pace.

Halt Describes the horse standing stock still with its spine straight and its weight evenly balanced over all four legs.

Hand Describes the method by which a horse is measured. Human hands are placed one after the other along the horse's body to gauge its size.

Haute école Means high school, and is the style of riding practiced at the famous Spanish riding school of Vienna.

Impulsion The driving action of a horse's hind quarters.

Lateral work Where the horse moves forward and sideways with the horse at an angle.

Levade An haute école movement where the horse holds a raised position on its hind legs.

Medium canter A pace between collected and extended walk.

Medium trot A pace between collected and extended trot.

Medium walk A pace between collected and extended trot.

Nappy Used to describe a horse that will not go forward in response to aids.

Passage A slow trot with lots of elevation and defined period of suspension.

Piaffe A marking time on the spot with an elevated trot.

Rein back Describes a backward walk with the legs diagonally paired, raised and set down all at the same time.

Renvers A suppling exercise in which the hind quarters stay on the outer track with the horse moving forward at an angle, that sees its forelegs on the inner track and its body bent to the direction of travel.

Saddlery Competitors must use an English hunting-type of saddle and a double bridle.

Shoulder-in A suppling exercise on two tracks. The horse's inner feet step in front of the outer feet as it travels at an angle with its body bent to the inside, away from the direction of travel.

Size All horses must measure more than 14.2 hands.

Straight Occurs when the horse moves with its hind legs following in the same track as the forelegs.

Submission Description of the horse's obedience, balance and general demeanour throughout a test.

Test The display of required movements by horse and rider within the time allowed.

Track The line in that a horse moves, either straight or on two tracks. Tracks are designated inner and outer in relation to the center of the arena.

Tracking-up Occurs when the hind feet come to the ground at the same spot as the front feet.

Travers A suppling exercise on two tracks. The horse moves at an angle with its forelegs on the outer track and the hind legs on the inner track, with the outer legs stepping in front of the inside legs.

Trot A double-time pace with the legs moving on alternate diagonals separated by a period of suspension.

Two tracks An exercise performed by the horse moving at an angle with its front and back legs on the inner and outer tracks, the forehand always slightly in advance of the hind quarters.

Volte Describes a small circle performed by the horse.

Walk Four steps to one stride, each one following the other in regular sequence.

Eventing

Eventing takes place over three days and is made up of three main categories, dressage, show jumping and endurance. Competitors must use the same horse throughout.

Cavalletti A series of low rails that are used to teach a horse to jump obstacles.

CCI Concours Complet International, that is a three-day event that is open to competitors from other nations other than the hosting country.

CCIO Concours Complet International Officiel, which is a major three-day event such as the Olympic Games. Each country is allowed to enter one team only.

CCN Concours Complet National, which is an event held for nationals of the hosting country only.

Chef d'equipe Describes the manager of a national team.

Combined training The British name for eventing.

Deep going Soft, wet ground into which a horse's hooves sink.

Deviation Occurs when a rider fails to follow the correct route.

Dress All competitors must wear a hard hat for safety reasons. For the dressage and jumping events, either military or hunt dress is worn. For the endurance event, a polo-neck jumper or shirt may be worn.

Dressage This part of the event aims to test the harmonious development of the horse's physique as well as the degree of understanding between the horse and rider.

Drop fence Describes an obstacle where the ground on the landing side is lower than on the takeoff side.

Endurance Tests the jumping ability of the horse over cross-country terrain and the rider's knowledge of pace and riding across country. Consists of four phases, roads and tracks, steeplechase, roads and tracks, and cross country.

English-type saddle Used in the dressage stage of the event. It is a shallow seated spring or tree saddle.

Fence An obstacle that the horse and rider must clear. Used in the steeplechase, cross-country and show jumping courses.

Flags Used on the cross-country course to mark the jumps. Riders must keep the red flag to their right and the white flag to their left.

Get under Occurs when a horse misses its stride and takes off too close to an obstacle.

Good going Ground that is firm with elasticity that allows the horse to move easily without sinking.

Hard going Bone dry ground that jars a horse.

Helsinki step-fence Obstacle used in cross-country. Made up of two or three steps cut into sloping ground going downhill.

Horse trials Another name for eventing.

In and out Describes a cross-country obstacle made up of two elements that are spaced closely together allowing the horse to only make a few strides.

Island Fence A cross-country obstacle isolated from the field boundary.

Jumping Tests whether the horse can continue in service after the endurance event as well as its obedience, fitness and attitude to fences.

Military Name used by European countries for eventing.

Napping Describes a horse's unwillingness to go past a certain point.

Outside assistance If given to a rider in order to gain, an advantage will be penalized by exclusion.

Override To tire a horse out and force it beyond its capabilities.

Palisade A cross-country obstacle that has a top rail across a row of vertical spars.

Parallel bars A cross-country obstacle that is also known as double rails.

Peck Means to stumble on landing.

Pedestrian crossing A cross-country obstacle that is similar to the parallel bars but has staggered gaps in the rails.

Penalties Punishable by either points or time being taken away from an offending rider.

Post and rails A cross-country obstacle made up of one or more horizontal bars that are attached to the top sides of vertical posts.

Refusal See "Run out".

Ride A road or lane that takes competitors through the woods. Used as part of the roads and tracks phase of a three-day event.

Roads and tracks Riders compete on roads and tracks where they are allowed to move at their own pace and may even walk the horse through, providing they are mounted when they pass the finishing post.

Run off To deviate from the correct course.

Run out Means to miss an obstacle by moving to either side.

Spooky The name given to a nervous horse.

Stand back To take off some distance in front of an obstacle.

Summer holding Describes the condition of the ground when the weather has dried out the surface but has left the subsurface sticky. Makes galloping difficult for the horse.

Teams For national teams in international events, teams consist of three or four members.

Three-day event One day is allocated to each event, dressage, endurance and show jumping.

Time limit Riders must finish a course within a certain time frame if they are to avoid elimination.

Trakener A cross-country obstacle built into a ditch and made up of a knife-rest construction that has a rail attached to the cross-pieces.

Wall Used in the cross-country event. Made of either brick, concrete blocks, railway sleepers or stones.

Weight cloth Describes a cloth that is placed underneath the saddle, with pockets to hold lead weights. The maximum weight to be carried is 165lb,. only during the endurance event.

Winter holding Ground conditions where the going is wet but at the same time easier to cope with than summer holding.

CROSS COUNTRY: The terrain can be rough, with the horse enduring all kinds of conditions

Harness Racing

Harness racing is performed with a rider in a two-wheeled carriage called a sulky. The horses are trained to either trot or pace, with separate races held for the two disciplines.

Age A horse's age is calculated from January 1 of the year they were foaled, unless they were foaled in November or December, where their age is calculated from the following January 1.

Bars The fleshy area between the front and back teeth on either side of a horse's mouth.

Bit A mouthpiece made of either metal, rubber or vulcanite. Is placed in the horse's mouth and kept in position by the bridle to aid the rider's control.

Breast harness Secures the horse to the sulky. Consists of a breast collar, traces, saddle and girth plus a bridle with long driving reins. Classified races are held between selected horses regardless of the money they have won.

Claiming races Describes races where all starters may be purchased in conformity of the rules.

Conditioned races Races where the horses have to be of a specific age or sex or have had a certain amount of success over a given time.

Coupled entry A race where two or more horses who are entered are owned or trained by the same person, management or stables.

Dash Is a race decided by a single heat.

Dress Each driver must wear their own distinctive colors. A protective helmet with a chin strap is compulsory.

Extension The lengthening of a horse's stride at any pace. Does not mean an increase in speed.

Forehand The front part of a horse encompassing the head, neck, shoulders and forelegs.

Fetlock Lowest joint on a horse's leg.

Futurity A race in which competing horses are nominated before being foaled.

Gait The pace at which a horse moves. Either a walk, trot, canter or gallop.

Gaiting strap Used to stop the horse swinging the rear and moving sideways on its gait. Is tied on the inside shafts of the sulky.

Handicap races Races in which performance, sex or distance allowance is made.

Head pole A cue used to keep the horse's head straight. Is tied alongside the head and neck. Must not protrude more than 10in beyond the horse's nose.

Heats Usually between one to three per race.

Hobbles Leather straps that encircle the front and hind legs on the same side to aid the horse in maintaining its gait. Once worn, a horse must wear them throughout a race.

Hock The joint in the center part of a horse's hind legs. Responsible for most of the horse's forward force.

Horn The hard, insensitive, outer covering of the hoof.

Impulsion A strong but controlled forward movement in a horse.

Matinee A race with no entrance fee.

Nearside The left-hand side of a horse.

Officials Include a program director, a presiding judge, a paddock judge, a starter, patrol judge, finish wire judge, timers and a clerk of the course.

Offside The right-hand side of a horse.

Overnight events Races where entries close not more than three days before the race.

Pacers The name given to horses who run with a swaying, lateral gait. The front right and hind legs are swung forward together followed by the left front and hind legs.

Pacer's shoes Flat or half-round shoes are worn on the front hoofs while combination shoes, half-round inside and half swedges outside, are worn on the hind hoofs. Shoes normally weigh 5oz each.

Paddock The area where the horses are kept until they are ready to race. All horses must be in the paddock at least one hour before competing and then are allowed to leave only to warm up before the race.

Points Names given to the different parts of a horse. Also used to describe the mane, tail and lower legs.

Post positions These are starting positions that are determined by lot for a dash or first heat. Post positions for later heats are determined by the winner of the previous heat, who takes the inside position with the rest of the competitors placed according to how they did in the previous heat. In the case of a dead heat, a lot is used to decide.

Recall Will occur under the following conditions: if a horse scores ahead of the gate, there is interference, a competitor's equipment is broken, a horse falls before the starting command is given or if a horse refuses to come to the gate before the gate reaches the pole ⅛ mile before the starting gate.

Recall signal Sounded by the starter and signaled to the drivers by flashing lights.

Shadow roll A sheepskin-covered noseband used so that a horse can see straight ahead but cannot see the ground in front.

Shy The reaction of a horse when they jump to the side after having been frightened.

Stake A race where entries close the year before the race and all fees are added to the purse.

Starting gate Must have arms that are perpendicular to the rail and a screen positioned in front of each horse.

Starting point Must be at least 200ft from the first turn and is marked on the inside rail.

Sulky Name given to the light, two-wheeled vehicle guided by the driver.

Track Oval in shape and varies in length between 0.5 to one mile in total length.

Tiered starts Maximum of two tiers of horses, permitted 8ft per horse, is allowed to start in any race. If a horse is moved from a tier, then the horse on the outside moves in to fill the empty place.

Timing Either an electronic device or three official timers. Times must be announced publicly or posted.

Toe weights Clipped to each hoof, they weigh 2–4oz and are used to extend a horse's stride.

Trotters The name given to the horses who run with a high-stepping diagonal gait. The right front and left hind legs are brought forward in unison followed by the left front and right hind legs.

Trotter's shoes Level shoes are worn on the front feet and swedge shoes on the back feet. The swedge shoes are creased and provide traction when the horse's hind foot hits the ground. Shoes normally weigh 8oz each.

Two in three Describes a race where a horse must win two heats to win the race.

Whips Must be no longer than 4.6ft. Excessive use of the whip is forbidden, as is whipping under the arch of the silky.

Wire The finish line.

Withers The point at the bottom of a horse's neck from that their height is measured.

Carriage Driving

Horse Driving Trials encompass three main events, Dressage, marathon and cone driving. There are classes for singles, pairs, tandems and teams.

Age All horses and ponies entered for competition must be over 4 years of age.

Blind The marathon course is driven blind, with each competitor being given a map and course marker.

Carriages Competitors may use the same vehicle for all three events, but usually have a second one for the marathon events because this places more stress on the vehicle. There are two main types of carriage, vintage and modern, although there are carriages built on traditional lines with modern components such as metal spoked wheels and disc brakes.

Cob Horse that is characterized by its smallness and strong stocky build.

Colt A male, ungelded horse up to the age of 4 years.

Cone event This competition tests the fitness and suppleness of the horses as well as the skills of the driver. The object is to pass through the cones without touching any of them. This is the third phase of a Horse Driving Trial.

Cones Each cone has a ball balanced on the top. If touched, the ball will fall and incur the driver penalty points.

Dress Whips and gloves are compulsory. A helmet is obligatory in National Horse Driving Trials for the marathon event. For dressage, traditional dress is required. For men, a dark suit and a bowler hat is worn. For women, a smart suit is appropriate.

Dressage Consists of a set sequence of movements that are judged against a standard of absolute perfection. The freedom and regularity of the paces, harmony, impulsion, suppleness, lightness and correct positioning of the horses/ponies are all taken into account when being judged. The horses/ponies in teams, pairs and tandem are judged as a collective unit and not individually. This is the first phase of a Horse Driving Trial.

Dressage arena Measures 109yd by 44yd, set in letters with the center being marked out with a cross in sawdust.

Driver Also called whip. Traditionally sits at the right of the carriage.

Filly Describes a female horse that is no more than four years of age.

Flags Are used to display the direction of travel at each lettered gate on the obstacle course for the marathon. White on the left and red on the right.

Foal A horse of either sex up to the age of 1 year old.

Gelding A castrated male horse.

Gray Describes any horse that is colored from pure white to dark gray.

Groom Rides with the driver. Their job is to help with an emergency such as a broken trace or caught rein. In the marathon events, the groom helps the driver stay on the correct course and remind him of the planned route through the obstacle course. They also help balance the carriage by shifting their weight in tight turns or uneven ground. Also responsible for keeping an eye on the time during an event.

Halts At the end of sections B and D in the Marathon end are two compulsory 10-minute halts with veterinary checks for the horses/ponies.

Horses/ponies There are no restrictions on the breed used during any of the events.

Knockdown Occurs during the obstacle course when a pole or piece of wood is dislodged. Will incur penalty points.

Leader The name given to the front horse in a tandem. A leader is not kept in shafts and moves with the minimum of control.

Marathon A cross-country event that is divided into three or five sections. This competition tests the fitness and stamina of the horses/ponies with the judgement of pace and horsemanship of the driver. The second phase of a Horse Driving Trial.

Marathon elimination Competitors will be disqualified for failure to correct an error of course, failure to pass through a gate or exceeding the time limit of five minutes.

Marathon penalties Incurred for breaks of pace, for failure to complete each section in the time allotted, for putting down a whip at any time, driver or groom dismounting, turning over a vehicle, correcting an error of course or knocking down a dislodgeable element.

Mare A female horse over 4-years old.

Memory Drivers must memorize the dressage course that they will take.

Modern harness Made from webbing that can be a mixture of leather and webbing parts or man-made materials.

Modern horse driving trials Came into existence in 1968 when Britain's Prince Philip initiated the formulation of the rules.

Obstacles Usually about eight on the course. Can be either natural or built features such as water, trees and steep banks.

Obstacle path Drivers may take any path through an obstacle as long as they drive through each lettered gate in the correct alphabetical sequence.

Outside assistance During the dressage and cone events, the groom is not allowed to indicate the course to the driver. This is deemed as outside assistance and will lead to disqualification.

Pair event Involves two horses or ponies driven side by side pulling a four wheeled carriage.

Presentation All equipment is inspected for safety and to ensure it fits correctly.

Private driving A show class that can either be formal or casual. Takes place either in the ring or on the road.

Scurry events A different type of cone event. Competitors run against the clock. Usually small ponies are used.

Sections The marathon is divided into five sections: Section A, 16 miles, where any pace can be used. Section B, 0.6 miles, where any walk can be used. Section C, 2.5miles, with a fast trot. Section D, 0.6 miles, with a walk and Section E, 6 miles, with any pace including obstacles.

Single event Involves either one horse or one pony pulling either a four-wheeled or two-wheeled carriage.

Tandem event Involves two horses or ponies driven one in front of the other while pulling a carriage.

Team event Involves four horses or ponies driven in pairs, one in front of the other.

Traditional leather harness Can be black and brown in color and can have brass or white metal fittings. Have either full collars or breast harnesses.

Transition Describes the act of changing pace. A walk to a trot and a trot to a canter are known as upward transitions. A canter to a trot and a trot to a walk are known as downward transitions.

Wheeler The name given to the horse who pulls the carriage in a tandem.

Whip Name given to the driver. Also the equipment used by the driver to spur the horse/ponies on.

Yearling A colt or filly that is between 1 and 2 years of age.

Polo

Polo is played by two teams of four players mounted on horseback. Players control their ponies with their left hand because the stick can be held only in the right hand. Each team aims to score as many goals as possible by striking the ball with their sticks to score between the opponents' goalposts.

....

Approach shot A long-distance shot aimed toward the goal, but the ball is intended to stop before it reaches the goal line. A striker or teammate will then attempt a second shot with much greater accuracy.

Arena polo A three-a-side game that is played on a ground within a covered or open-air walled area using a soft, leather-covered ball. The playing area is much smaller than that used for standard polo. Sometimes known as indoor polo.

Back The No. 4 player in the side who plays a defensive role and marks the opposing strikers.

Backhander A stroke taken by a player that strikes the ball in a backwards direction.

Boards Barriers that run along the sideline of the playing area to keep the ball in play.

Brace Term given to a player in the standing-in-the-stirrups position when playing a shot.

Change of ends After a goal is scored, the two teams change ends. If no goals have been scored, they change ends at halftime.

Chukka The colloquial Indian name given for a period of play. The duration of a match is 42 minutes, divided into six periods of seven minutes each with specified intervals between each period.

Circular windup A method sometimes employed to play the offside-stroke. A player swings through one and a half revolutions on their right-hand side before making contact with the ball.

Crossing Occurs when a player rides across or enters another player's right of way. An infringement is called if there is a risk of a collision or danger to any of the players involved.

Cut Stroke that is made at an angle away from the horse's line of advance.

Disengage stroke A player feints at the ball in an attempt to draw his opponent into an early hook. If they prove successful, they will withdraw their stick and beat off his opponent before playing his shot.

Drive A backhand or forehand shot which is made in a line parallel to the horse's line of advance.

Forehander A player strikes the ball in a forward direction.

Free hit In the event of an infringement having been caused, a player is allowed to have an unimpeded hit at the ball. This is awarded to the non-offending side.

Handicap Players are rated according to their playing ability and their value to the team. The higher the handicap, the better the player. They range from minus 2 to plus 10. A team handicap is the aggregate of all the players in the side.

High goal polo The team handicap of each team in a tournament is 17 or more.

Hit-in When an attacking player hits

the ball over the goal line, the defending side restarts play by taking a hit-in from where the ball crossed the line.

Hooking A player uses a stick to deflect or beat away an opponent's stick. They will try to prevent him from making his stroke.

HPA Hurlingham Polo Association. Formed in 1925, its main rules have formed the basis of this game in most countries of the world.

Mallet American name for the polo stick.

Near-side Left-hand side of a horse.

Normal grip Grip in which a player wraps their thumb around the handle to rest against the index finger. It can be used for off-side forehand shots and near-side backhand shots.

Off-side Right-hand side of a horse.

Penalty A punishment is incurred if a team infringes any of the rules. This can take the form of a penalty goal, a free hit, a hit-in or a retirement of a player in the event of an injury to an opponent who has been fouled.

Penalty goal Awarded by the umpire if they feel that someone on the defending side has committed a foul when a goal would have been scored.

Polo pit Place in which a learner sits on a wooden horse while practicing hitting a ball.

Pony power A team is evenly mounted throughout a match or will be better mounted in some chukkas than in others.

Pull Stroke taken at an angle that crosses the pony's line of advance.

Referee An official who stands off the field to adjudicate in the event of the umpires disagreeing.

Reverse grip A grip that a rider uses with the thumb pointing down the handle of the stick. This shot is used for near-side forehand shots and off-side backhand shots.

Ride-off Term given to a rider who pushes or bumps against an opponent and his pony in an effort to move him from the line of play or stop them receiving the ball. This can be done only if they are riding in the same direction as their opponent.

Right of way A player is entitled to move in a forward direction without checking his pace because of another player.

Safety zones Areas that are set aside beyond the goal lines and sidelines so that players can cross the boundary line at top speed and at any angle without fear of injuring themselves or the pony.

Stroke Method used to hit the ball. There are four basic strokes: the off-side forehander, off-side backhander, near-side forehander and near-side backhander. All of these strokes have the drive, cut and pull.

Throw-in The umpire bowls the ball underhand and hard between the two teams, which both line up facing the umpire. This takes place at the start of the match to put the ball into play, after a goal has been scored or when the ball crosses the sideline.

Topping A rider hits the ball too high up as a result of forcing the hand ahead of the stick, instead of letting the stick bring the hand along.

Wooden horse Used to practice players' strokes.

Umpires Two mounted officials who control the game from the field of play. Each official takes responsibility for half of the field.

Under-the-neck shots A complicated stroke in which the stick is swung under the pony's neck in order to strike the ball at right angles to the line of advance.

USPA The United States Polo Association.

Index